Kung Fu Cult Masters

Kung Fu Cult Masters

Leon Hunt

WALLFLOWER PRESS

LONDON AND NEW YORK

12-4-2003
WW
+ 22.95

WALLFLOWER PRESS
4th Floor, 26 Shacklewell Lane, London E8 2EZ
www.wallflowerpress.co.uk

Cover image: Japanese poster for *Once Upon a Time in China 2*

A catalogue for this book is available from the British Library

ISBN 1-903364-63-9

Design by Loaf Design

Printed in Great Britain by Antony Rowe, Chippenham, Wiltshire

Contents

List of Illustrations   vii
Acknowledgements   ix

Introduction: Once Upon a Time in China   1

1   Wicked Shapes/Wicked Lies: Performance and 'Authenticity' in Hong Kong Martial Arts Films   21

2   Burning Paradise: The Myth of the Shaolin Temple   48

3   Exit the Dragon, Enter the 'Shadow': *Game of Death*, *The Clones of Bruce Lee* and Other Posthumous Adventures   76

4   Fat Dragons and Drunken Masters: Kung Fu Comedy   99

5   The Lady is the Boss? Hidden Dragons and 'Deadly China Dolls'   117

6   Last Hero in China? Jet Li and the 'New Wave' Kung Fu Film   140

7   Transnational Dragons and 'Asian Weapons': Kung Fu and the Hong Kong Diaspora   157

8   'I Know Kung Fu!': Martial Arts in the Age of Digital Reproduction   184

Postscript: Kung Fu Reloaded and Updated   201

Notes   203
Filmography   211
Bibliography   216
Index   224

List of Illustrations

1   *Secret Rivals*   38

2   *Once Upon a Time in China 2*   44

3   *Heroes Two*   56

4   *Five Shaolin Masters*   59

5   *The 36th Chamber of Shaolin*   62

6   *Legend of Bruce Lee*   82

7   *Drunken Master*   101

8   *Prodigal Son*   110

9   *Knockabout*   115

10   *My Young Auntie*   125

11   *Hapkido*   127

12   *Swordsman II*   133

13   *Crouching Tiger, Hidden Dragon*   137

14   *Black Mask*   150

15   *Fist of Legend*   153

16   *Fist of Legend*   155

17   *Enter the Dragon*   164

18   *Battlecreek Brawl*   171

Acknowledgements

The following people read draft chapters of *Kung Fu Cult Masters* and I am grateful for their comments, suggestions and encouragement: Geoff King, Tanya Krzywinska and Julian Stringer. Tony Williams' Reader's Report was very helpful in refining the manuscript. Toby Russell was extremely generous in providing stills and was an invaluable supplier of hard-to-find videos. Thanks also to Yoram Allon at Wallflower Press for supporting the project, and to John Aplin of the Department of Performing Arts at Brunel University for his help in obtaining funding. Master Tsu ensured that I know at least something about real (and not just movie) martial arts, even though he thinks all kung fu films are "rubbish". Finally, I would like to thank the students on the 'Hong Kong Cinema' module at Brunel University.

Note: The transliteration of Chinese words and names is a minefield, especially if (like me) you speak neither Cantonese or Mandarin. This minefield is further marked by the tension between consistency and a homogenisation that erases cultural differences. I have followed the practice of using the increasingly dominant *pinyin* system for Chinese film titles when known. However, it is widely recognised that *pinyin* is designed for the Mandarin dialect rather than Cantonese, and so I have sometimes used other conventions for names. Sometimes the different versions of a name tell a story; the Cantonese Lau Kar-leung is often billed as Liu Chia-liang (Liu Jialiang in *pinyin*) because of the Shaw Brothers studio's Mandarin orientation. In many cases, I have used the northern/southern distinction in deciding on names (thus Lau Kar-leung rather than Liu Jialiang, Wong Fei-hung rather than Huang Feihong). In others, I have used the name that a performer or film-maker is best known by in English; Ti Lung rather than Di Long, for example.

Introduction
Once Upon a Time in China

There's a part of me that feels that unless you make a martial arts film then you are not a real film-maker.

      – Ang Lee (quoted in Morrison and Wells 2001: 64)

"Ah, but this man knows Chinese kung fu"
"Kung ... fu ...?"

      – *Way of the Dragon/Meng Long Guo Jiang* (1972)

In 1963, Bruce Lee published *Chinese Gung Fu: The Philosophical Art of Self Defence* in the United States. Although born in San Francisco (in 1940), Lee spent his childhood and (by all accounts, turbulent) teens in Hong Kong, not claiming full US citizenship until 1959. Except to martial arts cognoscenti (and not many of those), 'gung fu' (or 'kung fu') was virtually unknown outside South-East Asia and diasporic Chinese communities. Prior to the 1970s, North Americans and Europeans were more familiar with Japanese and Okinawan martial arts like Karate, Judo and Ju-Jitsu. The phrase 'kung fu' identified regional as much as national difference – it is a Cantonese expression meaning accomplishment with effort (the Mandarin *wu shu* is closer to 'martial art'). Ten years later, 'kung fu' had permanently entered the transnational imaginary – it was the name of a television show, a genre, a pedagogic industry, the subject of comics, magazines and other merchandising. On 20 July 1973, Bruce Lee died, but was already well on his way to being a 'Legend' – "part man, part myth, part magic", as the trailer for his final film, *Enter the Dragon* (1973) put it. *Enter the Dragon* was the commercial high-point of a global 'kung fu' craze, but Lee's transition to global superstar had first required another journey, back to Hong Kong, where three local productions made him the biggest star in Asia. The place of Chinese martial arts in a "borderless world" (Yau 2001) has been marked by a series of journeys: the apocryphal journey of Buddhist monk Bodhidharma from India to China; Shaolin Boxing's transmission from temple to populace, from Southern China to

Hong Kong; the transnational careers of Jackie Chan, Jet Li and Michelle Yeoh. Chinese martial arts have also travelled across different media and technologies: Beijing and Cantonese Opera; serialised novels and comics; film and television; computer, arcade and console games. These journeys often seem to cast Hong Kong in a familiar entrepôt role, a "doorway, a point in between" (Abbas 1997: 4); more specifically, between China and 'somewhere else'. As if to reinforce this impression, this is not simply a book about Hong Kong cinema; the kung fu film has important connections with China, Taiwan, Japan and the US, amongst others. Nevertheless, the Hong Kong martial arts film is undoubtedly my starting point and connective link. There are important martial arts film traditions elsewhere, most notably in Japan, but they have not sustained the same transglobal presence. While the Hong Kong film industry now seems to be in decline, its influence and its talent pool has never been more visible.

This book, then, is a study of the transcultural impact of 'kung fu', from the early 1970s to the crossover of Hong Kong stars, directors and choreographers into Hollywood and other cinemas, and its mediation by developing aesthetics and technologies. At one level, the kung fu film can be seen as what Steven Shaviro (1993) and Linda Williams (1995) call a 'body genre' (although neither include it as one) alongside pornography, horror and the 'weepie', films that offer a "display of sensations that are on the edge of respectable" (Williams 1995: 140). Kung fu is a genre *of* bodies; extraordinary, expressive, spectacular, sometimes even grotesque bodies. Like Williams' chosen genres, this ecstatic excess extends to the aural dimension; Bruce Lee's panoply of shrieks and roars, rhythmically orchestrated thuds and swishes, the reverberative (orgasmic?) aftershocks that follow definitive strikes (and excessive responses) in Sammo Hung's fight scenes. Martial arts films remind us that there are culturally specific and historically located 'body genres'; witness, for example, the debates surrounding Bruce Lee's muscular body or the shifts marked by the slapstick performance of Jackie Chan and Sammo Hung. Kung fu is, moreover, a genre that acts *on* the spectator's body, a body characterised by its "capacity for being affected" (Shaviro 1993: 59). Williams' discussion of "the body of the spectator ... caught up in an almost involuntary mimicry of the emotion or sensation of the body on the screen" (1995: 143) anticipates the work of David Bordwell (1997; 2000a) on Hong Kong action's 'Motion Emotion' and Aaron Anderson (1998; 2002) on North American and Asian martial arts films. But the "physical jolt" Williams talks about (1995: 140) is taken much further by the martial arts film's technological mediation. This is evident not only in Hong Kong cinema's aesthetic evolution – its mastery of montage techniques – but the way the 'jolt' both anticipates and later responds to the body-shock of computer and console games.

As a genre, the kung fu film has always been a cultural hybrid. It is well known that the 'new style' martial arts films of the late 1960s drew heavily from the Japanese Samurai film, even sending film-makers to Japan to learn their techniques (Sek 1980: 31; Zhang 1999: 17),[1] while director Zhang Che attributed his slow motion violence to the influence of Sam Peckinpah and Arthur Penn (Zhang 1999: 18). In his recent book on Hong Kong cinema, David Bordwell argues provocatively that some pleasures are 'universal': "in our multicultural milieu, there are more commonalities than differences in human cultures: universal physical, social, and psychological predispositions and the facial expressions of many emotions will be quickly understood in a film" (2000a: xi). One might suggest that some of these universalities say more about the inequalities between 'core' and 'peripheral' cultures, and the imperatives for the aesthetics of the latter to resemble the former in order to find international acceptance.

In 1966, Hong Kong cinema set itself the aim of breaking the Western market within five years (Rayns 1974: 138), achieving the goal with the Shaw Brothers film *King Boxer/ Tianxia Diyi Quan* in 1972. Between 1971 and 1973, approximately three hundred kung fu films were made for the international market, some of them never released in Hong Kong itself (Leung and Chan 1997: 145). Aimed at a heterogenous audience, both 'local' and 'global', Esther Yau suggests that post-1970s Hong Kong movies "appear extroverted, laced with multiple cultural references and engaged with expressive possibilities rather than the deep values of culture" (2001: 6). Moreover, while kung fu's corporeal exhilaration seems to act on a 'universal' body, moving it to ecstasy through Bordwell's 'Motion Emotion', the genre sometimes seems ambivalent about its non-Chinese audience. As Stephen Teo (1997; 2001) has emphasised, there is an insistent strain of nationalism in the Hong Kong martial arts film, observable in a range of films from *Fist of Fury/Jingwu Mun* (1972) to *Once Upon a Time in China/Huang Feihong* (1991). Watching kung fu films as a white, Western fan (like myself) may involve a degree of identification with Bruce Lee or Jet Li, but it may also lead, at some point, to finding one's counterpart in the *gwailo* ('white devil'), either associated with imperialist oppression or the American karate experts that Bruce Lee was fond of humiliating. I may not want to (and, simply, don't) identify with Chuck Norris in *Way of the Dragon* – hairy back, not as cool or glamorous as Bruce – and yet part of me knows that the Lee/Norris coliseum fight embodies a patriotic structure of feeling that is supposed to at least partly exclude me. However, it is my left-liberal 'postcolonial' self that recognises this exclusion; significantly, as a teenage Bruce Lee fan, I didn't feel remotely excluded by his films.[2] In any case, the kung fu film offers a third way in, allowing the 'outsider' to feel like an 'insider'; that of the cult aficionado, the hardcore fan who knows the difference between Mantis and Crane, Shaolin and *wu dang*, 'northern leg' and 'southern fist'. This esoteric cult capital, often nostalgic for 'old' martial arts films with 'authentic' techniques, is sometimes transformed into new (urban) mythologies such as The Wu Tang Clan's kung fu-inspired hip-hop or *The Matrix*'s cyber-mysticism. This 'third way' is partly facilitated by the pedagogic, initiatory narrative structures of many martial arts films. These films don't just tell stories about learning and transmission; they are, themselves, a form of learning, an ongoing 'education' of the audience. Lau Kar-leung's kung fu films teach us about the traditions and application of Southern Shaolin styles. Bruce Lee explains his 'no style' Jeet Kune Do in the television series *Longstreet* (1972) and the incomplete *Game of Death/Siwang Youxi* (1972/1978). In Jet Li's sci-fi movie *The One* (2001), the 'good' and 'bad' Jets practice the internal martial arts *bagua* and *xingyi* respectively, the 'circularity' of the former and the straight-line attack of the latter used to express the characters of the antagonists. *The One* may be less 'authentic' than earlier martial arts films, but it suggests that the genre has not lost its interest in 'teaching' a heterogenous audience.

Martial Arts Films: Definitions and Developments

In *The Martial Arts Films*, Marilyn Mintz defines such a film as one in which "competence as a martial arts performer determines role and behaviour in the plot" (1978: 11). At that time, it was probably still possible to delimit the genre in this way; the Chinese kung fu film and Chinese and Japanese swordplay films marked out a fictional world as distinct as the western. When the Hong Kong International Film Festival (HKIFF) surveyed the genre(s), it adhered to a more common division of the territory – *A Study of the Hong Kong Martial Arts Film* (Lau 1980a) focuses on what we might think of as kung fu films (largely empty-handed combat), while *A Study of the Hong Kong Swordplay Film 1945–1980* (Lau 1981/1996) examines its more prolific counterpart. All three books (at least in their initial imprints) were written before films like *Project A/A Jihua* (1983), *Winners and Sinners/Qimou Miaoji Wu Fuxing* (1983) and *Police Story/Jingcha Gushi* (1985) revolutionised Hong Kong action by locating martial arts in a predominantly urban space and mixing it with broad comedy, dangerous stunts and other kinds of action such as gunplay. Craig Reid has called these later films *wu da pian*, fight films using martial arts (1994: 21), while Siu-leung Li identifies them as "a sub-genre that remotely feeds on yet delocalizes and transnationalizes 'kung fu'" (2001: 517). But in other ways modern-day action films are more visibly 'local' than 'proper' kung fu, more likely to be set in Hong Kong than the 'China' of classic martial arts films. The hybridity of 1980s Hong Kong cinema is even more pronounced in *jiangshi dianying* (cadaver movies) like *Encounters of* the Spooky Kind/Gui Da Gui (1980) and Mr Vampire/Jiangshi Xiansheng (1985) or Tsui Hark/Ching Siu-tung's *Chinese Ghost Story/Qiannu Youhun* series (1987, 1990, 1991), which also throw in ghosts, hopping corpses, and even (in the latter series) Cantopop.

Jackie Chan's perennially popular *Police Story* is clearly not a martial arts film according to Mintz's definition (nor, it seems, Li's) – his character Ka-kui's "competence as a martial arts performer" does not "determine role and behaviour in the plot". He fights with fists and feet only when he loses his gun, does not appear to be an 'expert' and does not follow any recognisable martial arts style; like *Project A* and *Winners and Sinners*, the fights follow a kickboxing-enhanced streetfighting style. However, Chan's "competence" as a martial arts performer is clearly another matter. The precision, kinetic power and hyperbolic stunts are heavily indebted to skills acquired first through Chinese Opera and then years of work in martial arts films as stuntman and star. Stardom is an important dimension of generic definition, too, especially in a field which hinges on performative skill. Jackie Chan no longer describes himself as a kung fu star and one might argue that his resistance to generic labelling has aided his survival in an industry with a notoriously short attention span. However, in Western cult circles, Chan is still consumed, at least partly, as a martial arts star, thus his presence in video documentaries like *Cinema of Vengeance: Martial Arts and the Movies* (1993) and the BBC's *I Love Kung Fu* (2001). Chan's own *Jackie Chan: My Stunts* (1999) fetishizes his dangerous stunts, an inititiative for distinguishing himself from other action stars, but also places great emphasis on his contribution to fight choreography, which is explicitly located within the Hong Kong martial arts tradition.

If stars are important to definitions of the martial arts film, so too is Hong Kong cinema's studio system. The kung fu film's 1970s 'Golden Age' can partly be attributed to the competition between Shaw Brothers, Golden Harvest, and, to a lesser extent, Ng See-yuen's independent Seasonal Films. Shaws and Golden Harvest had units specialising in martial arts films and evolved distinctive cycles and sub-genres. At Shaws, director Zhang Che worked with writer Ni Kuang, choreographers Lau Kar-leung/Liu Jialiang (later, a director in his own right) and Tang Xia, and an evolving roster of contracted stars; David Chiang/Jiang Dawei, Ti Lung/Di Long, Chen Guantai, Fu Sheng and the 'Venoms' team. The Shaolin Temple cycle is one of Shaw Brothers' most distinguished contributions to the genre. Golden Harvest, founded by former Shaws employee Raymond Chow, put themselves on the map by signing Bruce Lee, the comedian Michael Hui and, later, Jackie Chan. Shaws were vertically integrated, their stars bound to inflexible contracts, while the less centralised Golden Harvest offered short-term contracts and the opportunity for its bigger talents to set up autonomous production companies (for example, Lee's Concorde and Chan's Golden Way). Moreover, film-makers like Lee, Chan and Sammo Hung enjoyed greater autonomy than their Shaw Brothers counterparts, with the added bonus of more generous budgets and production schedules; Sammo Hung spent over a year on *Prodigal Son/Baijia Zai* (1981), while Chan's obsessive perfectionism is legendary. Both companies employed directors who were not choreographers or martial arts performers – Zhang Che at Shaws, Lo Wei and Huang Feng at Golden Harvest – but increasingly their house styles were epitomised by their respective director-choreographers, Lau Kar-leung and Sammo Hung. The relationship between Hung and Lau was, by all accounts, intensely competitive, but with exceptionally creative results. Lau specialised in the Southern Chinese legacy of Guangdong heroes and the *Hung Gar* fighting style. Hung made two films about southern *Wing Chun*, but was otherwise more eclectic; he brought Korean talent and kicking techniques into Chinese martial arts films. Each borrowed from the other. Hung seems to have followed Lau's lead in exploring Master/Pupil relations, albeit more irreverently, while Lau borrowed his rival's more dynamic stylistic innovations, adding speed and heightened impact to the authentic techniques he showcased. Soon, there was a third tiger on the mountain; Yuen Wo-ping, the top choreographer at the upstart Seasonal Films. Seasonal's production values were threadbare, but their eye for physical talent was unerring. They signed the Korean 'superkicker' Huang Jang-li as their most formidable heavy, and made a star of the struggling Jackie Chan, who subsequently jumped to Golden Harvest where he built his own film-making unit. Yuen Wo-ping, too, would later work at Golden Harvest, whose kung fu comedies had higher production values than Seasonal and were both more modern and more 'local' than Shaws' studio-bound dynastic 'China'. Hung, Chan and Yuen were to be major figures in the modernisation of Hong Kong genre cinema, while Shaws ceased production in the mid-1980s. During the 1990s revival, Golden Harvest were in the forefront again with the *Once Upon a Time in China* series.

The different branches of Chinese martial arts cinema find their origin in the *wu xia pian* or 'martial chivalry film'. As *wu xia* director Zhang Che explains, the name itself points to the two component parts of the genre – "the martial arts (*wu xia*) pictures use the notion of martial arts (*wu*) to express the content of chivalry (*xia*)" (1999: 19). Most historians see the *wu xia pian* as having two distinct branches, those demaracated by the HKIFF's two volumes, the swordplay film and the kung fu film (or *gung fu pian*).[3] Stephen Teo suggests that *wu xia* has become synonymous with the swordplay film, which originated in silent Shanghai cinema; swordplay usually draws on a "northern style which audiences believed was more ancient and historical than the southern style" (1997: 98). Swordplay films tend to be set further back in time than their empty-handed counterparts, detailing the chivalrous exploits of 'Knight-Errants' and 'Lady Knights' in ancient dynasties.[4] *Wu xia pian* encompasses a *fantastique* tradition, often featuring flying swords, 'Palm Power'

(Taoist inscriptions allowing lightning bolts to be fired from hands), and 'weightless' flight.[5] The kung fu film, by contrast, opts for more recent and comparatively realistic settings, favouring those that feature foreign aggressors, such as the Qing Dynasty (1644–1911) and the early Chinese Republic. If swordplay is predominantly northern, then kung fu frequently celebrates the south, especially the Shaolin heroes of Guangdong Province.

If the *wu xia*/swordplay film can be seen as a Shanghai émigré, then the kung fu film originates in Hong Kong, in the black-and-white exploits of mythical southern heroes like Fong Sai-yuk/Fang Shiyu and Wong Fei-hung/Huang Feihong and a tradition of charismatic stars; Kwan Tak-hing, Wang Yu, Bruce Lee, Fu Sheng, Jackie Chan and Jet Li. Of the two sub-genres, kung fu is both the more local and the more global. On the one hand, it is Hong Kong cinema's indisputable creation; "with the term itself in the local dialect, the genre was named as the territory's own" (Chu, Foerster and Sek 1994: 24). Yet at the same time, it has travelled more easily into Western popular culture than the swordplay film. With some notable exceptions – the Cannes Film Festival success of *A Touch of Zen/Xia Nu* (1971) and the more substantial impact of *Crouching Tiger, Hidden Dragon/Wo Hu Zang Long* (2000) – the *wu xia pian* seems to have been judged by distributors as too esoteric for non-Asian audiences. Some swordplay films were exported *as* kung fu films, like *Golden Swallow/Jin Yanzi* (1969), which joined the kung fu 'flood' as *Girl With the Thunderbolt Fist*. *Crouching Tiger* puts more work into explaining the codes of *jianghu*[6] (the 'World of Vagrants' in which martial arts heroes operate) than its earlier local/regional equivalents would have done. Even so, many Western critics compared it with Bruce Lee and Jackie Chan rather than King Hu. The kung fu film, on the other hand, could be sold as a 'Cinema of Vengeance', both exotic and familiar; "films which have many of the characteristics of the Cowboys and Indians stories and offer plenty of thrills and excitement" (*Cinema/TV Today*, 28 July 1973: 11). As kung fu films became more specialised from the mid-1970s, they were careful to explain their historical underpinnings and the workings of specific martial arts styles; Shaw Brothers' Shaolin cycle constitutes a populist history lesson on the latter part of the Qing Dynasty, the Southern Shaolin Temple and the evolution of its fighting styles. Kung fu offers 'history' sliding into myth, if you want, or lots of scores being violently settled if you don't.

Li sees the different temporalities of kung fu and swordplay as indicative of the former's ambivalent mediation of modernity:

> Hand-to-hand fighting signals an in-between, heterogenous, overlapping temporal space in which on the one hand, swords, weapons of the pre-industrial age, were already outdated and largely ineffectual, and, on the other hand, firearms, the most

efficient killing instruments in the age of modern science and technology, had to be employed sparingly only. (2001: 519)

However, technology impacts on both genres at the level of spectacle. Some swordplay films verge on science fiction (the Flying Sword as *Star Wars* lightsaber) or James Bond gadgetry in their iconography, while post-1990s kung fu films locate a futuristic spectacle in a historical 'past'.

If *wu xia pian* originates in Shanghai, when does the Hong Kong kung fu film begin? Strictly speaking, *Fong Sai-yuk's Battle in the Boxing Ring* (1938), a remake of a Shanghai silent from 1928, is the first, and initiated a series of films featuring the precocious Cantonese hero. Fong is an important figure in the genre, memorably incarnated by Fu Sheng in the 1970s and Jet Li in the 1990s, but another Cantonese black-and-white series devoted to another southern hero has overshadowed Fong in film histories as "the 'martial patriarch' of Hong Kong *wu xia pian*" (Sek 1980: 29). Wong Fei-hung (1847–1924) was a martial artist, teacher and doctor in Guangdong in the period straddling the late Qing Dynasty and early Chinese Republic. Li (2001: 530) characterises Wong as a marginal figure in martial arts histories, and certainly few 'facts' are known about him for such a recent historical figure. But newspaper serials and a long-running film series (1949–70) of over seventy films, reclaimed him as a local hero within Cantonese popular culture. Master Wong was played by paternalistic Kwan Tak-hing in 74 of the 76 films, a 13-episode television series (TVB 1976) and three further films for Golden Harvest in the 1970s. Kwan's Wong embodied Confucian virtue and patriarchal authority. The actor allegedly modelled his performance on speeches given by Sun Yat-sen (Hong Kong Film Archive 1999: 37), the revolutionary who founded the Chinese Nationalist Party after the overthrow of China's last Dynasty, the Qing, in 1911. According to Sek Kei, the series depicted "authentic Chinese martial arts" for the first time, but he suggests that it was "not until the 1960s and 1970s that martial arts came to be used as a powerful form of cinematic performance" (1980: 28). By that time, Cantonese cinema was fighting a losing battle with its glossier Mandarin counterpart. Up until the late 1970s, Hong Kong cinema produced films in two dialects; Mandarin, the language of northern China, and Cantonese, the language of southern China and the dominant dialect in Hong Kong itself. Shaw Brothers, the largest studio in the territory prior to the emergence (in 1970) of Golden Harvest, made films exclusively in Mandarin, which accounted for the largest export market in South-East Asia; thus, what Bordwell calls "the peculiar fact that each year Hong Kong made dozens of films in a tongue spoken by less than 5 percent of its population" (2000a: 65). In the mid-to-late 1960s, 'new style' *wu xia pian* dominated the local box office with their enhanced spectacular production values; colour and widescreen, and editing and cinematography influenced by Japanese and Hollywood cinema. In 1966, the year that Hong Kong set its sights on the West, King Hu's *Come Drink with Me/Da Zui Xia* (1966) and Zhang Che's *The Magnificent Trio/Biancheng Sanxia* (1966) epitomised this 'new wave'; the following year Zhang's *The One-Armed Swordsman/Dubi Dao* (1967) and Hu's *Dragon Gate Inn/Long Men Kezhan* (1967) broke South-East Asian box office records. King Hu and Zhang Che epitomised antithetical but equally influential approaches; Hu's films were stylised and montage-based, his fight scenes abstract, poetic and airborne, while Zhang's used progressively longer takes, worshipped the male body, and adopted a more 'authentic' approach to action and violence.

By the early 1970s, swordplay was rubbing shoulders with Mandarin-language kung fu films. *The Chinese Boxer/Longhu Dou* (1970) is often seen as the first modern kung fu film, although that generic label had to wait until the impact of Bruce Lee. *Southern Screen*, for example, described *Chinese Boxer* as "an action-packed drama ... Swords and other weapons are not employed – it's always fist-to-fist confrontation" (quoted in Foster 2000: 13). When Wang Yu's teacher explains the difference between Chinese Boxing and Japanese Karate, one gets the distinct impression of the initiation of a cycle. Star Wang Yu, a "handsome he-man" and "flashy rip-roaring type" according to *Southern Screen*, cut a very different figure from the stern Kwan Tak-hing. Shaws' top male swordplay star, Wang, had a penchant for losing limbs (*One-Armed Swordsman*, *One-Armed Boxer/Dubi Quanwang*, [1971]) or bringing about his own blood-spattered demise (*Golden Swallow*), but was not averse to leaving trails of corpses along the way. This graphic quality didn't exactly hurt the films' international appeal. *King Boxer* was virtually a remake; both films' heroes learn the 'Iron Palm' technique in order to defeat irredeemably dastardly Japanese fighters. From Wang Yu to Bruce Lee, the *wu* perhaps became more important than the *xia*. This is not to say that Lee did not embody 'chivalry'; the end song in *Fist of Fury* defines his sacrifice in precisely those terms. But Lee embodied a physical authenticity that Wang simply couldn't match. Scornful of what he saw as fanciful Mandarin fight films, Lee grounded his action in crisp, rapid techniques, multiple kicks, 'realistic' exchanges and a fluid grace that the genre had never seen before.

Martial arts expanded Hong Kong cinema's market, which grew from twenty to eighty countries (Leung and Chan 1997: 145), but it was the trans-Pacific figure of Bruce Lee who seemed to build a bigger if, as it turned out, precarious bridge between East and West. Kung fu's global appeal seemed to die with Lee, although he arguably paved the way for Western martial arts stars like Chuck Norris, Stephen Seagal, Jean-Claude Van Damme and Mark Dacascos. Norris and Van Damme, in particular, mark what David Desser calls "the rise of white male martial arts stars who, in a sense, co-opt the Asian martial arts for the American action hero" (2000: 39). The white warrior is often explicitly connected to "an Asian context: Vietnam and the Vietnam War" (39) and Norris and Van Damme, who both played villains in Hong Kong, seem to embody a colonial 'reclaiming' of Asia. Several Norris films are set in Vietnam, while Van Damme 'conquers' other parts of South-East Asia in *Bloodsport* (1987) and *Kickboxer* (1989).

After Lee's death, it was more common to find 'real' martial artists starring in films in both Hong Kong and Hollywood. The trailer for Golden Harvest's *The Magnificent Butcher/Lin Shirong* (1980), about Wong Fei-hung's pupil Lam Sai-wing, insists that "only Sammo Hung can bring Butcher Wing to life, can be as good as Butcher Wing, can demonstrate Butcher Wing's prowess – a real man, a real fighter", and sings the praises of "Golden Harvest's Macho corps". Shaw Brothers' stars were recruited primarily for their looks and were taught martial arts as and when they needed it, but the nature of that teaching was significant. Lau Kar-leung, working mainly as Zhang Che's fighting instructor, was virtually running a martial arts school within the Shaws enclave, training actors to deliver the techniques they would need in the Shaolin Temple cycle that began in 1974. If Lee marked a shift "from an emphasis on directors to an emphasis on stars with authentic martial abilities" (Sek 1980: 33), then Lau marked out a new role for the *Longhu* ('Dragon-Tiger Master', a Cantonese Opera term for martial arts choreographers). Fighting instructors would now "often not only arrange fight scenes, but also plan the shots; they virtually take over the role of director and in some instances, become considerably more important than the director himself" (34). Lau made the transition to director in 1975; Sammo Hung and Yuen Wo-ping followed suit in 1977 and 1978, respectively. Hung and Yuen, along with Jackie Chan, confirmed a growing shift towards comedy. All three came from Opera backgrounds, and their films combine northern acrobatic routines with an irreverent approach to fighting styles. The cynicism and 'inauthentic' techniques of the kung fu comedies paved the way for the hybrid action of modern-day films.

If Mandarin period films dominated Hong Kong cinema in the 1970s, Cantonese popular culture thrived on television, but began to resurface in successful film comedies like *House of 72 Tenants/Qishi'er Jia Fangke* (1973) and *Games Gamblers Play/Guima Shuangxing* (1974).[7] By the end of the decade, a 'new wave' of film-makers, trained in television and Western film schools, emerged. This was indicative of a more significant shift. Ackbar Abbas points to the emergence of the new wave in 1979 and the signing of the Sino-British Joint Declaration in 1984 returning Hong Kong to Chinese sovereignty in 1997 as two events enabling the territory to see itself "with new eyes": "the new Hong Kong cinema ... has found Hong Kong itself as a subject" (1997: 23). In some ways, this new 'Hong Kong consciousness' marginalised the China-centred kung fu film; period escapism was everything the 'new wave' opposed, while genre films offered a slick, highly evolved urban aesthetic with little apparent interest in the Shaolin Temple or the Qing Dynasty. Nevertheless, one of the 'new wave' directors, Tsui Hark, has retained an ongoing interest in the *wu xia pian* and kung fu film. Tsui's first feature, *The Butterfly Murders/Die Bian* (1979), combined swordplay with elements of mystery and horror, and he revived kung fu and swordplay in the early 1990s with two successful franchises, the *Swordsman/Xiao'ao Jianghu* trilogy and six *Once Upon a Time in China/Huang Feihong* films. Both were visibly made under the shadow of the 1989 Tiananmen Square massacre and the approaching 1997 deadline, but they also represented a new aesthetic approach to the period martial arts films; MTV-style cutting, special effects, glamorous stars and 'Western' production values. *Once Upon a Time in China* re-invented Wong Fei-hung both by casting Jet Li in the role, a younger and more reflective Wong than Kwan Tak-hing, and by locating the character against a backdrop of China/Hong Kong's colonial history and encounter with Western modernity. The cycle lasted two to three years at the box office, but long enough to catch Hollywood's eye. Jet Li, Tsui Hark and choreographer Yuen Wo-ping would all be working on English-language films by the end of the decade.

"But still...": Asiaphilia, Camp and Cults

> The story is flimsy and clichéd. Outrageous dubbing, often making the film unintentionally humorous, removes any possibility of evaluating acting. Production values, at their highest, equal those of your average B-movie ... Violence exaggerated to the point of absurdity, but entertaining absurdity.
> – Review of *King Boxer* (US title: *Five Fingers of Death*) (Warner 1974: 37).

In *King Boxer*, virtuous country boy Chi Hao (Lo Lieh) finds himself embroiled in a conflict with a rival martial arts school and the Japanese heavies employed to intimidate our heroes. Chi's training gets off to a shaky start, but his humility and tenacity pay off. He learns the Iron Palm technique, which involves plunging his hands into an iron cauldron to deaden the nerves; even having his hands smashed with bamboo sticks by the villains doesn't deter him. He defeats a literally hard-headed Chinese mercenary, winning his loyalty in the process, wins a martial arts tournament, and single-handedly avenges his murdered teacher. The violence is often extreme; eyes are gouged out, heads are removed, and, in one scene, Chi Hao's fingers penetrate someone's abdomen. As Chi Hao channels his *qi* into his fingers, his hands literally glow red, accompanied on the soundtrack, by snatches from the theme from *A Man Called Ironside*. The dubbing of the English version can render scenes comic for even the most sympathetic viewers. Over time, fans started to notice how often the words "But still..." turned up in kung fu movies to allow the English voices to catch up with Mandarin lip movements (Hammond and Wilkins 1996: 204). "The movie was totally dumb. We loved it!" enthused one writer, symptomatically (Wolfman 1974: 51), but Bordwell suggests that the genre increasingly invited such a response – "Endless zoom shots and slow motion ... shamelessly recycled film scores ... Like Italian peplum and Mexican masked-wrestler movies, kung-fu screamed kitsch" (2000a: 207). But wasn't that way back then? Wasn't that a response to the 'old' Mandarin Hong Kong cinema, with its trampolines, reverse footage and people being punched through walls, in the days when exported Asian films were dubbed, not subtitled? Not entirely. For bad dubbing, read badly translated subtitles; favourite examples are posted on websites and distributed by email (Bordwell 2001a: 91). I cannot pretend to be immune to such lowbrow pleasures. The dubbed version of Sammo Hung's *Prodigal Son* sounds as though it was recorded by the casts of various 1970s British sitcoms. But Julian Stringer reminds us that there are some issues of cultural power surrounding the 'camp' gaze at Hong Kong cinema, which is, after all, a "largely white gaze at a Chinese 'Other'" (1996/97: 55).

Programmes like the nostalgic *I Love Kung Fu* confirm that it is possible to both 'love' something and condescend to it, especially if it constitutes a cultural Other. *King Boxer* was a major success in the West – on 16 May 1973, it was number 3 at the US box office during its seventh week in the chart (Desser 2000: 20) – but box office figures do not tell us much about *how* a film was received and the conditions under which its success was permissible. More subtly, many 'appreciative' accounts of Hong Kong cinema celebrate its 'mindlessness', "a cinema of incessant action, eye-popping effects, and cartoon-like violence" (Dannen and Long 1997: 5). Of course, the camp gaze is an extreme version of the power relationship inherent in the Western consumption of kung fu. But that power relationship has a firm basis in what Desser calls the 'Encounter with Asia' (2000: 27), an encounter marked by conquest and appropriation. The Western interest in Asian martial arts parallelled the United States' shifting relations with South-East Asia. American servicemen 'brought back' Judo and Karate from the post-war occupation of Japan, later incorporating it into training for the Korean War. The 'kung fu craze' of the 1970s overlapped with both the Vietnam War and President Nixon's visit to China.

Broadly speaking, there are two ways of looking at the West's 'Asian romance': "a controlled setting in which to be exposed to and (perhaps) examine certain notions of linguistic, racial and cultural difference" (Fore 1997b: 240) or "a flirtation with the exotic rather than an attempt at any genuine intercultural understanding" (Marchetti 1993: 1). Then again, given kung fu's complex origins (a 'Chinese' subject (re)made in Hong Kong), it is not always clear what such a genuine understanding would be *with*.

Much more than modern-day urban Hong Kong cinema, exported kung fu flirts with an Orientalist imaginary. In Edward Said's definition, Orientalism describes "a Western style for dominating, restructuring, and having authority over the Orient" (1978: 3); the word 'Orient'/'Oriental' "designated Asia or the East, geographically, morally, culturally" (31). The packaging of kung fu movies in the West has played a role in this designation. "Revenge is a basic Chinese passion dating back to Confucian times", claimed National General Pictures' publicity for *The Big Boss/Tang Shan Daxiong* (1971).[8] Globalism, one might suggest, has more subtle ways of handling the Other; it is, Stuart Hall argues, "enormously absorptive of things ... wanting to recognize and absorb those differences within the larger, overarching framework of what is essentially an American conception of the world" (1991: 28). In some ways, this describes Hollywood's handling of Hong Kong all too perfectly, fostering it as an 'Other' (cult) cinema, before absorbing its talent into what has so far (*Crouching Tiger* apart) been an oppressively 'American' cinema. Thus Orientalism gives way to the "deceptively benign" Asiaphilia, Darrell Hamamoto's term for the "fetishization of all things Asian in popular culture" (2000: 11):

> [Asiaphilia] naturalizes and justifies the systematic appropriation of cultural property and expressive forms created by Yellow people. The classic colonial system of unequal exchange was based on the theft of human and material resources from the underdeveloped countries of the periphery and its removal to the imperial core society. The politics of cultural appropriation extends the history of exploitation into the 'post-industrial' information economy. (12)

In an interesting argument, Julian Stringer contrasts the white subcultural fantasy of "wanting to be black" (or, if your name is Quentin Tarantino, announcing that you *are* black) with the lack of a comparable desire for white Hong Kong fanboys "to assimilate, introject, and express their worldview through Chinese style and culture" (1996/97: 58) – "you can *have* the Chinese, but you can *be* black" (60). While the response to black culture is marked by unease, the consumption of Hong Kong cinema "works with confidence to restore textual power to white Western spectators at the very time when economic and social privilege is being lost by white people in Hong Kong" (58). I would broadly agree with Stringer here, but there is one thing that complicates things a little, namely stars. Stars don't entirely work as others – they are objects of desire and/or identification – and, make no mistake, Hong Kong fandom is heavily star-focused. As a teenager, I desperately wanted to be Bruce Lee (albeit within limits – the 'international' Lee of *Enter the Dragon* rather than the 'local' Lee of *Way of the Dragon*). Jackie Chan's and Jet Li's relationship with their global fanbase is marked by a high degree of accessibility, on their websites, through their fanclubs and meetings with fans around the world. In a small but by no means insignificant way, Hong Kong star cults can be seen as contributing to a 'postcolonial' project, "the deconstruction of the centralised, logocentric master narratives of European culture ... dismantling the Centre/Margin binarism of imperial discourse" (Ashcroft, Griffiths and Tiffin 1995: 117).

Kung fu's transnational status is neither 'positive' or 'negative', but a complex negotiation of different interests. Nor is its fan culture monolithic, any more than it can agree about which kung fu star is the 'best'. *Sex and Zen and a Bullet in the Head* aims anti-intellectual jibes at "pointy-headed" film scholarship trying to read too much into films designed purely to entertain (Hammond and Wilkins 1996: 11). Bordwell responded good-naturedly (1997) and was granted approval in *Sex and Zen*'s follow-up: "even some film studies professors have rediscovered their own passion upon exposure to this dynamo cinema, tossing their baked brie in the trash can and becoming infused 'with the delusion that they can vault, grave and unflappable, over the cars parked outside the theatre'" (Hammond 2000: xii). But if *Sex and Zen* resists the 'pointy-headed', it is prepared to modify the shape of its head briefly, as demonstrated by the following caption for a still from Shaw Brothers/Hammer Films co-production *The Legend of the Seven Golden Vampires* (1974):

Semiotical types who study this Hammer-Shaw co-production would tell you that there's a great deal of relative power-structure information contained in the fact that all of the Chinese brothers die, and none of the Englishmen do, while the Englishwoman who loves a Chinese man dies, and the Chinese woman who loves an Englishman doesn't. (Hammond and Wilkins 1996: 214)

Colonialism, global and gender issues are condensed into this astute, if partially disowned ("semiotical types" would say this), reading. As they cross and blur boundaries, maybe kung fu movies do teach more than the difference between Tiger and Crane.

Looking for the 'Local': the (Trans)national and the (Post)colonial

In the 1970s, kung fu movies seem to have been conceptualised as a cinema exported by Hong Kong without actually belonging to it. According to Ackbar Abbas, prior to the emergence of Hong Kong's 'new wave', "stories about Hong Kong culture always turned into stories about somewhere else, as if Hong Kong culture were somehow not a subject" (1997: 25). By implication, this 'somewhere else' is China; Hong Kong is conspicuous by its virtual absence from 'classic' martial arts films. Even modern-day kung fu films tend to deal with Hong Kong Chinese abroad, in Thailand (*The Big Boss, Duel of Fists/Quan Ji*, 1971), Italy (*Way of the Dragon*), or Australia (*The Man From Hong Kong*, 1975). In *Enter the Dragon*, Hong Kong is simply a space to *pass through*, reconfigured by Afro-American Williams (Jim Kelly) as a universalized ghetto. In the main, the 'local' was initially bound up with 'China', with the Chinese diaspora's experience of an abstract nationalism. Roger Garcia finds in kung fu movies a form of "mythic remembrance, an emigrant cinema for an audience seeking not only its identity and links with an often imaginary cultural past, but also its legitimization" (1994: 48).[9] The Shaolin films of Zhang Che and Lau Kar-leung are more regionally specific, seeking to construct a continuity between Hong Kong and the martial arts legacy of southern China. On the other hand, if Bruce Lee's trans-Pacific journeys (and filmic journeys to Thailand and Italy) seem to embody diasporic identity in flux, there have been ongoing attempts to anchor him in Chinese nationalism (most recently, Teo 1997: 110–21). Lau Tai-muk locates Lee's patriotic persona as part of a "seeking for roots", his muscular body "a substitute for the strong but 'vanishing' motherland" (1999: 33). Steve Fore, on the other hand, points to China's ongoing territorial dispute with Japan over the Diaoyu/Senkaku Islands, a group of islands that since the late 1960s has been the sporadic focus of mutual "nationalistic posturing" (2001: 118). *Fist of Fury* is about nothing if not reclaiming space (and, of course, 'face'), set in the Western concession of 1920s Shanghai, under the growing shadow of Japanese imperialism. To complicate matters, given Japan's influence on Hong Kong cinema, it is also a partially colonised aesthetic space. Abbas, moreover, is sceptical about the film's anticolonial posturing, in that it deals with "*memories* of slights and insults suffered in the past ... as if there were no idea who the 'enemy' really was" (1997: 30). Such an impression is reinforced by the famous Shanghai Park sequence, where Chen Zhen (Lee) shatters a sign reading 'No Dogs or Chinese Allowed'. Lee and his antagonists are dressed in something resembling 'period' dress, but the Western onlookers give a very different impression. Their trousers are incongruously flared, and one even has an Art Garfunkel afro. They cannot help but now look a little like *Fist of Fury*'s Western audience, spectators situated outside the film's nationalist dramaturgy, there simply to enjoy the show. The impression is of a film locked in a 'past' it can't quite represent. Its vagueness sbout the 'enemy' is further indicated by it being an Indian who initially bars Lee's way, a colonial subaltern transformed into smirking flunkey. Twenty-two years later, Jet Li's magisterial remake *Fist of Legend/ Jingwu Yingxiong* (1994) makes a more concerted attempt to represent "the unstable shape of coloniality" (Abbas 1997: 29). While it is no more 'successful' in locating the heroic within the colonial, arguably a 'strength' as much as a weakness, it is much more visibly conscious of the issues.

One version of the 'local' returns in the kung fu comedies of the late 1970s. Sammo Hung's *Iron Fisted Monk/Sande Heshang yu Zhuangmi Liu* (1977) was Golden Harvest's first Cantonese-dialect kung fu film. Moreover, Hung used modern Cantonese slang in the dialogue to distinguish the film from Shaw Brothers' Qing Dynasty Shaolin films. The comedies' cynical, quick-witted heroes suggest an urban sensibility within period trappings, the "'virtues' of 'adaptability' and 'using the brain' in capitalist societies" (Lau 1999: 33). But it is the subject of colonialism that most consistently brings the genre back to 'local' concerns, even if it is hard to locate a coherent response. Several writers (for example, Sek 1980: 30) have observed the coincidence of the 'new style', violent *wu xia pian* in the late 1960s with Hong Kong's anti-colonial riots inspired by China's Cultural Revolution in 1967. According to Zhang Che, "the colonial administration was receiving a shock to the system" (1999: 21), pointing to the timely release of *The One-Armed Swordsman* as violence erupted in Kowloon. But what we are usually offered is an abstract connection; it isn't clear how Zhang Che, a right-wing anti-communist, responded to or anticipated anti-colonial sentiments in his films. Kung fu films, Abbas argues, never offer a "direct critique of colonialism, rather ... the ethos of (mainly) male heroism and personal prowess so central to the genre has to define itself in relation to *what is felt to be possible* in a changing colonial situation" (1997: 29). For Siu-leung Li, 'what is felt to be possible' is tied to the martial arts world's encounter with (Western) technological modernity. The genre is about "negotiating the complex and conflicting experience of colonial modernity and postcoloniality" (2001: 516).[10] Moreover, Hong Kong's experience of colonialism is a very specific one. If there is already a debate about when the 'colonial' becomes 'post' – after decolonisation or as a "discourse of oppositionalities which colonialism brings into being" (Ashcroft, Griffiths and Tiffin 1995: 117) – it is further complicated by Hong Kong having "no precolonial past to speak of" (Abbas 1997: 2).[11] Its history and culture has been defined by colonialism, emigration and transnationalisation. Tsui Hark's *Once Upon a Time in China* is the genre's most sustained dialogue with the colonial and the transnational, made in the context of decolonisation and recolonisation by the 'Motherland', wherein it is "no longer possible to appeal with any conviction to some vague notion of Chineseness, as China itself may turn out to be a future colonizer" (Abbas 1997: 31). But while the 1990s Wong Fei-hung cycle depicts the Cantonese hero ('rejuvenated' literally by athletic, charismatic Jet Li) encountering Western modernity, the films themselves embody a new collision of technology and the kung fu star's body.

Cinema, Technology and Kung Fu's 'Disappearing' Body

Look at *Jurassic Park*. Few people know the names of the actors; They remember the dinosaurs and that it was a Spielberg film. Take *Terminator 2*. The director's good; Schwarzenegger is nothing. Anyone could have played his part ... But in Asia, everyone comes to see Jackie Chan in a Jackie Chan film. It doesn't matter what the title is or what the story is about. Only Jackie Chan can do it.
    – Jackie Chan (quoted in Reid 1994: 21)

A history of the body in Hong Kong popular culture is a history of its gradual disappearance. Indeed, no matter how show-offish the muscles from Hong Kong are, they are only a fetish that marks a sublime absence.
    – Kwai-cheung Lo (1999: 120)

The performing body of the kung fu star has been the genre's key transnational commodity and fetish, and maps out some shifting conceptions of the body as spectacle. Kwan Tak-hing's middle-aged body performed moves that were simultaneously 'authentic' (his background in White Crane kung fu) and 'theatrical' (proscenium staging, the lack of 'impact' we associate with later Hong Kong fight scenes). Wang Yu flailed his arms in a no-style-in-particular, his karate background further complicating his films' anti-Japanese narratives and aesthetic debt to Japan. Bruce Lee embodied a similar schizophrenia, his trans-cultural no-style Jeet Kune Do mobilised *for* 'China' without being purely 'Chinese'. Fu Sheng was the first graduate of the Shaw Brothers' Performing Arts training programme, Lau Kar-leung's favourite pupil and tragic 'lost son'. Jackie Chan incorporated his background in Opera and stuntwork to develop a hybrid, urban action cinema. Jet Li's Mainland *wu shu* was more visibly mediated by technology and special effects. The Kung Fu Cult Master can thus be seen as occupying a precarious space in between 'authenticity' and 'disappearance'. The body-centred 'authenticity' debate, examined in more detail in the next chapter, encompasses film-makers like Jackie Chan, fans and critics investing in the nationalist authenticity of Bruce Lee, and Western fanboys who can point to the superiority of hands-on Hong Kong stars to pampered, stunt-doubled Hollywood stars. But what is the position of the 'authentic' in a space defined as a 'culture of Disappearance' (Abbas 1997), a disappearance not only linked to the literal evacuation of a culture by the 1997 re-unification, but the way Hong Kong 'disappears' in discourse, reduced to a series of clichés, a chimerical, hybrid culture shaped by seemingly abstract forces? For Kwai-cheung Lo, the kung fu star from Lee to Chan marks an absence of Hong Kong subjectivity, a 'Hole Punched Out By Bruce Lee's Body' (1999: 109). This disappearance is seemingly intensified by technological mediation, particularly special effects. But does this mean that kung fu loses its "physical dimension", with performers "simply support props for the intensive effects work" (119), or is it more the case that new technologies are being valorized through the retention of bodily spectacle? Such questions are made more urgent by the crossover success of Hong Kong stars in the age of *The Matrix*. Did Jackie Chan and Jet Li achieve global 'presence' just as the body disappeared under the onslaught of the digital? What will it mean when, as currently promised, Bruce Lee is 'resurrected' by CGI for a new feature-length film?

While these developments arguably have more pressing implications for the cultural flux and disorientation of Hong Kong, they cannot be separated from larger global developments. In the age of *The Matrix*, computer games, the CGI 'realism' of *Final Fantasy: The Spirits Within* (2001), and the disorientating perception for many that the events of 11 September 2001 had been foreshadowed by the spectacle of Hollywood special effects, the mediatisation of the 'real' poses some pressing, sometimes disturbing, questions. *Final Fantasy* raised again the question of whether actors will one day be replaced by digital performers, Jackie Chan has an animated and computer-game counterpart, Jet Li fights 'himself' in *The One*. Given that Chan and Li seem to be the 'last' martial arts stars, the Kung Fu Cult Master's imminent disappearance, or, alternatively, mobilisation in 'authenticating' new technologies, is an important issue to consider. Hence, the present volume's extension of its star system to include console game 'performers' from *Tekken* and *Dead or Alive*.

Writing about Hong Kong cinema has blossomed in recent years, most noticably since 1997. Its critics and historians include Chinese writers based in Hong Kong (the HKIFF critics) and elsewhere; some non-Chinese commentators are based in Hong Kong (Ackbar Abbas, Roger Garcia), some can speak one or more Chinese dialect (Tony Rayns), others speak no Chinese (David Bordwell). This breadth of perspective has contributed to the richness of Hong Kong film criticism, but it is always important, I feel, to clarify where one is speaking *from*. I am a British academic and (no less importantly) fan who speaks no

Chinese and has only ever visited Hong Kong as a tourist; the kind of tourist who returns loaded with video cassettes and posters, who feels excited when he recognises locations (even Chungking Mansions!) from Hong Kong films. Stepping back, I know that there is more than a trace of the 'Asiaphile' about this tourist gaze, of Hong Kong as movie theme park, yet it also speaks of Hong Kong's impact on the transnational imagination. Ding-Tzann Lii identifies two broad relations between the 'colonial self' and the 'Other': *incorporation*, where the 'Other' is transformed by imperialism, and *yielding*, a "synthesis which transcends both the self and the Other" (1998: 134). Hong Kong fans like myself, while unavoidably implicated in the core/periphery matrix of globalism and cultural imperialism, have, to a greater of lesser degree, been *yielding* for some time. For people of my generation, it began with Bruce Lee, whose image dominated my bedroom walls as a teenager. As I slide, not entirely gracefully, into my forties, I take no small pleasure in succumbing similarly to Jet Li. The transnational exploits of the Kung Fu Cult Masters ensure that while I can never be an 'insider', I never entirely feel like an 'outsider' either. This is not to say that there will not be blind spots, nuances missed, partialities all too obvious, some readings based on badly dubbed English-language prints, an experience of the genre inextricably linked to its fluctuating exportability. But hopefully as someone who *yielded* to the kung fu imaginary long ago and has an interest in how others outside Asia yielded too, I can bring some fresh insights to a subject that remains comparatively marginalised in canonical Film Studies.

Chapter one of this study examines the debates and discourses surrounding 'authenticity', a term that sometimes refers to the martial arts themselves, to the 'invisibility' of cinematic representation (wide framing, unobtrusive editing) or to the body itself as guarantee of the real (athletic virtuosity, physical risk). Technology's mediation of the real is revisited in chapter eight in the light of digital develoments, which often seek to synthesise the real or 're-mediate' the authentic. In particular, I shall examine the aesthetic and technological dialogue between martial arts console, computer and arcade games (*Tekken*, *Street Fighter*), and 'digital' developments in fight choreography (*The Matrix*, *Romeo Must Die*). Does digital technology allow *anyone* to echo Keanu Reeves' exclamation from *The Matrix*, "I know kung fu!"? Chapters two to six offer more specific case studies; the enduring mythology of the Shaolin Temple and its onscreen mediation; the post-Bruce Lee industries that sought to 'clone' him (through stars like Bruce Li) and 'claim' him, either as Chinese national hero or American immigrant made good; the kung fu comedies of Sammo Hung, Jackie Chan and Yuen Wo-ping; female martial arts stars like Angela Mao Ying, Hui Ying-hung, and Brigitte Lin, often exoticised in the West as 'Deadly China Dolls'; Jet Li's re-invention of the kung fu hero as postcolonial, revisionist and 'digital'. Chapter seven looks at the Hong Kong/Hollywood 'romance', taking in the 1970s 'kung fu craze', but also examining the recent Hollywood vehicles for Jackie Chan and Jet Li. Hollywood's history of absorbing and incorporating 'foreign' talent might make one cautious rather than optimistic about the fate of Hong Kong stars in the West. But in the last couple of years, Chinese martial arts have moved into a much more culturally heterogenous (rather than simply 'American') space; the historical fantasy of *Brotherhood of the Wolf/Le Pacte des Loups* (2001), Jet Li's demolition of Paris in *Kiss of the Dragon/ Le Baiser Mortel du Dragon* (2001) and, above all, the prestigious pan-Asian *Crouching Tiger, Hidden Dragon* and *Hero/Ying Xiong* (2002). If the martial arts film often seems to be a genre living on borrowed time, the success of *Crouching Tiger* suggests that it has yet to lose its grip on the transnational imagination.

Chapter One

Wicked Shapes/Wicked Lies
Performance and 'Authenticity' in Hong Kong Martial Arts Films

In *Once Upon a Time in China 3/Huang Feihong III zhi San: Shiwang Zheng Ba* (1993), Wong Fei-hung (Jet Li) has the latest in a series of 'future shock' encounters with technology. As usual, this comes courtesy of his Westernised love interest, 13th Aunt (Rosamund Kwan). Cameras have already been the source of some conflict in Parts 1 and 2, but the arrival of the first movie camera in Guangdong is too much for even a Confucian patriarch to resist and soon he is coaxed in front of it to throw some shapes. "We can teach others kung fu by movie in future", suggests his student Leung Foon with uncanny foresight. But this attempt to marry the Lumière Brothers to Shaw Brothers is not an unqualified success. When the film is screened, it transpires that Foon's undercranking has inadvertently rendered Wong's forms at *Keystone Cops* speed. As Wong's father, Wong Kei-ying/Huang Qiying, wonders at his son's phenomenal speed and (more importantly) whether it is genuine, he anticipates the musings of many a kung fu cultist to come. This is a characteristically witty piece of revisionism, synthesising the Cantonese legend and the 1990s action superstar in order to retrospectively create the first kung fu film. But Master Wong's excursion into movie-making also suggests that martial arts legends had a complex relationship with cinematic technology from the start.

Wong Fei-hung's film-within-a-film points to four issues that are central to the Hong Kong martial arts film and to this chapter – Documentary ('recording' styles and great practitioners), Performance (Jet Li's beautiful *wu shu* forms), Technology and 'Authenticity'. Debates about 'authenticity' have recurred both in Chinese critiques of kung fu films and in English-speaking subcultures surrounding Hong Kong cinema, although with different emphases. This has been intensified by the increasing visibility of technology and special effects in fight choreography and its implications for a genre with a particular investment in the 'real'. In chapter eight, I shall look more specifically at the impact of digital technology on martial arts films and games, but for now will focus principally on more traditional forms of enhancement, such as editing, undercranking[1] and wirework. Hong Kong cinema has largely been theorised in terms of the hybrid, the transnational, the postmodern and the postcolonial; none of these are authenticity-friendly concepts. What interests me about the 'authenticity' debate is the way it addresses questions of how technology mediates stardom and performance; also that it is a popular debate about the aesthetics of the performing body which has yet to be fully interrogated by academics. Nevertheless, we must beware of conflating different takes on authenticity. In Asian critical debates, authenticity is often linked to questions of identity. Commenting on the 'supernaturalism' of silent Shanghai *wu xia pian*, which eschewed 'real' martial arts in favour of *fantastique* effects, Sek Kei discerns a loss of faith in Chinese culture, in contrast to the regional authenticity of the post-war Hong Kong Wong Fei-hung series (1980: 27). Bruce Lee's trans-Pacific identity raises other issues. For Chiao Hsiung-ping, his avoidance of special effects and fondness for long shot/long take shooting testifies to his cross-cultural credentials, a triumph of Western 'realism' over 'Oriental fantasies' (1981: 33), while for Ackbar Abbas it provides the key to an "authentic and heroic Chinese identity" (1997: 29). While readings focused on Hong Kong's 1997 reunification with China can be simplistic and overdetermined, it seems significant that 'authenticity' has diminished as Hong Kong has embraced a more hybridised, postcolonial identity, both 'Chinese' and not. Ramie Tateishi suggests that the visual and generic pastiche of Jackie Chan's choreography "could reflect the idea of a disappearing subject of Hong Kong film" (1998: 83). At the same time, however, Chan is a stern critic of the FX-based 'new wave' martial arts films pioneered by Tsui Hark:

> I don't like the *wu xia pian*, the flying, the exaggerated kung fu skills. It's not real. You can make anyone fly like Superman or Batman, but only special people can do my style of fighting. (Quoted in Reid 1994: 21)[2]

The 'authenticity' of Western fandom is, as one might expect, less sensitive to issues of cultural identity, but ostensibly has a similar investment in "special people" doing what mere mortals cannot. For them, like Chan, this is partly a matter of product differentiation, of a geographically specific spectacle; Hong Kong cinema's performing body versus Hollywood's technological sophistication. In Western cinema, the musical is the body-genre that comes closest to manifesting a comparable degree of pro-filmic skill. But Linda Williams has likened the musical, with its narrative/number tensions, to pornography, another 'low' genre with an investment in authenticity; like the kung fu film, porn expresses "the desire to see and know more of the human body" (1990: 36), 'documenting' the body *in extremis*. Williams parallels the evolution of porn with the invention of photography and early cinema, both of them embodying "the frenzy of the visible" (36). The *Once Upon a Time in China* films are highly self-reflexive about the impact of photography (still and moving) on the world of the martial artist, and the scene from Part 3 discussed earlier points to the "positivist quest for the truth of visible phenomena" (Williams 1990: 46). The "frenzy of the visible" is present in the spectacle of Bruce Lee's speed, Jackie Chan's self-endangering stunts, Huang Jang-li's mid-air multi-kicks (like Eadward Muybridge's photographs of a horse in motion, the feet *are* visibly off the ground). The two genres prioritise different regimes of knowledge; porn, as Williams argues, is part of a larger history of surveillance and 'knowledge' in the discourses of sexuality. The kung fu film, on the other hand, partly constitutes an archive of body-knowledge rooted in diasporic cultural identity.

I think it is possible to identify three rough phases in the development of martial arts choreography since kung fu's global impact in the 1970s. In the first, Bruce Lee placed a new emphasis on individual, authentic virtuosity, displacing trampoline-aided stars like Wang Yu and embodying the "stuntman as hero" (Abbas 1997: 29). Lee paved the way for *da-zai* (fighting lad) movies – Chen Guantai, John Liu and Huang Jang-li were trained martial artists first and actors second as opposed to the studio-trained stars of the 1960s. Wang Yu, the first modern martial arts star, had been a swimming champion groomed for hunkdom by Shaw Brothers. Why, asks Tony Rayns rhetorically, cast a swimming champion as a martial arts star? "Because he looked 'natural' with a sword" (1981/96: 156).[3] The second phase arguably saw a shift towards the choreographer as hero. Lau Kar-leung was the first choreographer to turn director, but also the first (post-Lee) to bring recognisable fighting styles back into films; Sammo Hung and Yuen Wo-ping, both from Opera backgrounds, made similar transitions. In the films of Lau, Hung and Yuen, the focus is on a team rather than one individual performer. Each assembled a unit or 'clan' to both choreograph and perform. Lau trained established Shaw Brothers stars, but also showcased brilliant new ones – brother Lau Kar-wing/Liu Jiayung, adopted brother Lau Kar-fai/Liu Jiahui/'Gordon Liu', the acrobatic Xiao Hou and the impossibly graceful Hui Ying-hung, a former dancer. Hung used compatriots from the 'Seven Little Fortunes' unit (Yuen Biao, Yuen Wah) and the gifted Lam Ching-ying, while Yuen worked with his brothers, Yuen Cheung-yan, Yuen Hsin-yi and Yuen Yat-chor and father Yuen Siu-tin. Jackie Chan is the biggest star of the post-Lee era, and a more literal embodiment of the stuntman-as-hero. Yet he too is rooted in the team/unit ethos – he worked extensively with the Sammo Hung team in the 1980s and has his own 'Jackie Chan Stunt Team'. Yvonne Tasker observes how Chan's films orchestrate complex group fights, in which "the camera work is carefully choreographed around the scene, rather than the individual hero, as spectacle" (1997: 331). This is in contrast with Lee, whose films allow no margin for anyone to upstage the star. Not only does Lee dominate the frame, but he sometimes 'wastes' performers like the Korean Hapkido expert Wong In-sik – Wong is one of the genre's most spectacular kickers, but you would never guess it from *Way of the Dragon*, where Lee largely uses him as a punchbag. The third phase was initiated by Producer-Director Tsui Hark and choreographer-director Ching Siu-tung, both figures associated with 'new wave' martial arts films. By the time of the martial arts revival in the early 1990s, two things had changed – the role of technology and the nature of the Hong Kong star system. The focal point of the new star system was not kung fu but Cantopop – glamorous stars with dual singing and acting careers (Andy Lau, Leslie Cheung, Anita Mui, Aaron Kwok). Hong Kong's mastery of technology meant that stuntmen could largely go back to being stuntmen – it was perfectly possible to choreograph non-martial artists like Brigitte Lin and Maggie Cheung through a combination of special effects and doubles. Special effects became much more ubiquitous in 1990s 'new wave' films like *Once Upon a Time in China*, which offered a fast-cut, hi-tech spectacle – the prevalence of wires to make fighters defy gravity led some fans to re-dub the genre 'wire-fu'. Of the new martial arts talent to move into films – many from the Mainland – only Beijing-born *wu shu* champion Jet Li became a major star. Moreover, all of Li's post-1991 films have used wirework to some extent and some of them have stunt-doubled him almost as much as his untrained co-stars.

Martial Arts as Performance

> Why did I use kung fu to make movies – to display the art and to aestheticize fist fighting.
> – Lau Kar-leung (Hong Kong Film Archive 1999: 89)

Chinese martial arts have a longstanding association with traditions of performance – Lion and Dragon dances,[4] street theatre and, above all, Beijing Opera or *jingju* (theatre of the capital). Chinese Opera is even sewn into the mythical-historical fabric of the *wu xia* genre – in Guangdong, in Southern China, Opera performers participated in anti-Manchu activities during the Qing Dynasty and associated with Shaolin rebels like Hung Hei-kwun/Hong Xiguan (Mackerras 1975: 147). Opera lends to the genre its structures of teaching and transmission, its painful and rigorous training methods, combining physical conditioning (leg stretches and lifts, bending backwards from the waist, legs encased in sand-padded cloth-binding) with combat techniques and acrobatic skills (Scott 1983: 122). *Da* (martial skills and acrobatics) was one of the four performance skills of Chinese

Opera, alongside *chang* (singing), *nian* (recitation), and *zuo* (acting) (Riley 1997: 13). *Jingju* bequeathed to Hong Kong cinema several generations of stuntmen, stars and choreographers, a tradition that peaked (and, it seems, ends) with Jackie Chan, Sammo Hung, Yuen Biao, Yuen Wo-ping, 'Corey' Yuen Kwai, Yuen Wah and Lam Ching-ying. These are arguably the most gifted physical performers the genre has ever produced because the range of their skills went beyond the talents of conventionally trained martial artists.

Before the Western 'kung fu craze' of the early 1970s, Asian martial arts had already had an impact on Modernism and Experimental Theatre. For people like Brecht and Eisenstein, seduced by *jingju*'s non-naturalistic performance style, this happened via Opera traditions. But from the 1960s, American actor training programmes were incorporating Japanese and Korean martial arts (Nicholls 1993: 19). In the 1970s, Tai Chi was a popular inspiration for such actorly objectives as focus/concentration, "staying in the moment" (20), and, above all, disciplining a holistic "bodymind" (14). The valuing of the somatic over the intellectual anticipates some of the recent attempts to theorise martial arts action (Bordwell 1997 and 2000a; Anderson 1998 and 2002) – certain aesthetic experiences "can only be apprehended intuitively or kinesthetically" (Nicholls 1993: 27). The high cultural emphasis of theorists like Phillip B. Zarrilli limits them in some ways – their theories might tell us why (for some of us, at least) Bruce Lee, Jackie Chan and Jet Li are so much more compelling than Western actors steeped in the turgid orthodoxies of The Method. Instead, it takes a martial arts aficionado like Marilyn Mintz to observe how Bruce Lee's "expressive demeanour" and whole-body performance derives from his dual experience as both an actor (whose father was an Opera performer) and martial artist (1978: 82).

It has become something of a cliché to compare kung fu films with the Hollywood musical (Kaminsky (1974) is one of the first to make the comparison). Jackie Chan is often likened to Gene Kelly, for his athleticism, his sense of rhythm and love of incorporating inanimate objects into choreography. Action choreography is often likened to dance – according to director King Hu: "I've always taken the action part of my films as dancing rather than fighting ... (emphasizing) rhythm and tempo, instead of making them more 'authentic' or realistic" (Rodriguez 1998: 81). If dance is, as Sandra Kemp suggests, "poeticized" walking (1996: 158), then one might usefully see martial arts choreography as poeticised fighting. But there are limits to the comparison. The tension between narrative and 'number' (performance/fight) does not generate the same diegetic tension in the martial arts film that it does in a musical (see Altman 1981; Feuer 1982) – it is always easier to 'motivate' a fight scene (or, in pornography, a sexual 'number') than people bursting into song. Nevertheless, there are points of convergence, not least in the way each puts "the graceful body at the centre of (their) *mise-en-scène*" (Bordwell 1997: 83). Consequently, both have offered performers and choreographers as auteurs as much as (if not more than) directors. The choreographer-as-star, in particular, is unique to the two genres – Busby Berkely, Stanley Donen, Yuen Wo-ping, Sammo Hung.

Greg Dancer touches on perhaps the most useful point of comparison – the co-existence of what we might call 'plastic' and 'performative' traditions, one founded on artifice, authorial style and technological mastery, the other on pro-filmic virtuosity; the films of King Hu, like Busby Berkely's dance numbers, depend on "precise choreography and visual tricks like unusual camera angles, selective framing and editing" (1998: 45). Hu used trained martial artists and Opera performers as choreographers, stuntmen and supporting players (Han Yingjieh, Sammo Hung), but his leading players (Roy Chiao, Xu Feng) did not come from a martial arts background. According to Hector Rodriguez, Hu "treats the human body as a concrete plastic unit to be combined with other stylistic devices" (1998: 81). Pauline Kael seems to be saying much the same thing about Busby Berkely's choreography: "there's no penetrable internal logic for the variations in Busby Berkely's kaleidoscopic dance numbers. (That's part of their surreal charm; so is his indifference to the dancing – he's only interested in the patterns.)" (1984: 198).

In *A Touch of Zen*, a bamboo forest fight makes much use of the director's trademark oblique editing style. Bordwell characterises Hu's style as an aesthetic founded on the *glimpse*, stressing the qualities of extraordinary techniques, "their abruptness, their speed, their mystery ... by treating these feats as only partly visible" (2000b: 118). Thus montage allows Xu Feng to leap to the top of a huge tree, from which she 'dive-bombs' her opponent like a heat-seeking missile.[5] Later in the film, Buddhist monks 'float' towards their opponents, their feet lightly brushing leaves and bush-tops. The 'plastic' tradition also encompasses traditional *wu xia pian*, with its flying swords and animated effects, and the 'new wave' films of Tsui Hark and Ching Siu-tung. In *Swordsman II/Xiao'ao Jianghu II Dongfai Bubai* (1991), we get the closest one could imagine to Berkely-style choreography. Ling (Jet Li) and his *jianghu* 'brothers' encounter a lone swordsmen who they misrecongnise as a Japanese enemy. The brothers go into their (circular) Sword Formation, and what follows is a montage of swirling blades, flying (wire-aided) bodies, swords spinning and flying seemingly of their own volition, bodies organised into geometric formations. When they cannot overpower the stranger, Ling enters the fray and demonstrates his own superior swordplay. Close-ups show his sword spinning around his hand and across his shoulders (he never seems to hold it). Another montage-based fight follows, with swords used as a mode of transport, bodies leaping and spinning. There is a great deal of physical skill on display, but the style totally overwhelms it – Ching was one of the pioneers of MTV-style Hong Kong action with *A Chinese Ghost Story/Qiannu Youhun* (1987). Most significantly, Ling is played by Jet Li and yet there is not one single shot to 'guarantee' that he is actually performing the characters' moves.

The performance tradition, in the musical, is represented by the full-body framing and invisible editing used to authenticate Fred Astaire or Gene Kelly. In the martial arts film, this tradition includes Bruce Lee and Jackie Chan, and the choreography of Lau Kar-leung and Sammo Hung. In an ecstatic review of Jackie Chan's *Drunken Master 2/Zui Quan 2* (1994), *The Essential Guide to Hong Kong Movies* observed, "it will be interesting to see whether Hong Kong directors will now stop over-using high-wire kung fu and return to pull-no-punches action which requires the skill of the actor rather than the director" (Baker and Russell 1994: 47). What is interesting here is the rejection of a certain type of cinematic authorship, a championing of the 'real' over the 'cinematic'. If scholarly work on Hong Kong Cinema has been predominantly auteurist, kung fu cultism invests primarily in stars, and, to a lesser extent, choreographers (who may also be stars). Star-auteurs like Bruce Lee and Jackie Chan are one thing, but when Jet Li turns up in (English-language) scholarly accounts it is usually as a footnote to the *Once Upon a Time in China* series, a series taken to be authored by director-producer Tsui Hark. But fanzines and websites often give greater emphasis to *Fist of Legend*, his remake of Bruce Lee's *Fist of Fury*. While *Fist of Legend* catches some of the same postcolonial resonances as the Wong Fei-hung series, it also works as a vehicle for displaying Jet Li's martial arts skills. Like *Drunken Master 2*, *Fist of Legend* won approval for downplaying wirework and for deploying a wide range of recognisable martial arts styles:

> Plenty of Jet Li *wu shu, chin na* and a slightly more 'street' style (more boxing, Bruce Lee-inspired shuffle feet). Jet and Chin (Siu-ho) perform *mi tsung-i*, the actual style of the Ching Wu Academy that the film is about. The 'challenge' with [Yasuaki] Kurata is a bit wire-enhanced, as is the finale ... but not much to complain about as this is wall-to-wall action. (Lim 1999)

Li has divided kung fu aficionados precisely on the grounds of authenticity. *Oriental Cinema*'s combative editor Damon Foster, for example, finds Li's Westernised name inadvertently appropriate – "many of his movies consist of *flight* scenes rather than *fight* scenes" (1999: 6). *Fist of Legend* has frequently performed the role of 'authenticating' Jet Li, of offering documentary proof of his abilities – "The fighting scenes are awesome and realistic, 'wire-fu' almost nowhere" (Amazon.com 2000). Even Foster, who devoted an entire issue of *Oriental Cinema* to denigrating Li, capitulated to the film's balletic charms.

In *Hollywood East*, Stefan Hammond recalls the audiences who filled London's Scala cinema for kung fu triple-bills:

> When the combatants squared off in their fighting stances, shouts of 'Shapes! Shapes!' would come from the crowd, expressing appreciation for the geometric patterns of robed bodies. An absurd leap or wire effect would be greeted with 'Lies!' but a well-executed manouevre would draw the accolade '*Wicked* Lies!' (Hammond 2000: 79–80).

The concept of 'Shapes' is an invigorating populist intervention in the poetics of martial arts action. Aaron Anderson (1998) is critical of the way action cinema theory emphasises still, posed bodies over moving ones. Like Bordwell (1997; 2000a), he emphasises the rhythmic, kinesthetic qualities of fight choreography. Bordwell, however, points out that the rhythmic pulse of Hong Kong action requires stasis as well as movement, with "lighting switches between quick, precise gestures and punctuating poses" (1997: 86). The "pause/burst/pause" pattern (84) suggests that 'Shapes' can be still as well as moving. At the climax of *The Buddhist Fist/Fozhang Luohan Quan* (1980) – a 'Shapes' movie if ever there was one – the two antagonists pit the Buddhist Palm against the Buddhist Fist. While moves like 'Return to Buddha' and 'Becoming a Buddha' hinge on crisp, graceful movement, some of the scene's highlights involve fighters freezing in stylised stances like 'Buddha in Repose'.

Hammond's anecdote has other implications, namely that 'Wicked Shapes' and 'Wicked Lies' are not polar opposites; rather, they co-exist in a more ambivalent relationship and authenticity is valued rather more reflexively than first appears. Even the most 'authentic' kung fu films, *Buddhist Fist* included, deploy some trickery for some of their effects. Kung fu films have most in common with musicals and westerns, but science fiction has been the generic pioneer in blurring the real and the virtual. Sci-fi and kung fu hinge in different ways on what Brooks Landon (1992) calls 'the aesthetics of ambivalence', an ambivalence predicated on the paradox of cinematic trickery (accepting the 'fake' as 'real') and a seemingly impossible investment in both documentary realism and fantasy. For a genre about physical skill – as opposed to one that is actually *about* technology – there is of course much more at stake. 'Authenticity' is a slippery term, because martial arts excellence does not always translate into exciting cinematic performance. Nevertheless, Bruce Thomas sees Bruce Lee as someone who was both impressive onscreen and 'real' at the same time – "to see Bruce Lee on film is to see a human body brought to a level of supreme ability through a combination of almost supernatural talent and a lifetime of hard work" (1994: 258).

Cheng Yu, on the other hand, notes "a certain paradox in Lee's approach to film" – the disavowal of special effects promised "greater realism", while Lee's invincibility suggested the opposite. In the broader, non-filmic, martial arts world, Lee's "supernatural talent" is by no means uncontested (see Miller 2000: 161–72). The authenticity of a performance – a performance mediated by technology – is a different debate. With this in mind, I want here to outline three types of authenticity that can be discerned in popular debates about kung fu films, which I shall call *archival, cinematic* and *corporeal*.

Archival Authenticity: Wong Fei-hung, Lau Kar-leung and *A Meditation on Violence*

Since director Zhang Che introduced the technique of the Hongs in the great epic *Heroes Two* ... kung fu films have entered a new era. Detailed kung fu practice and complex manouevres. All based on historical fact, these are authentic martial arts.
 – Trailer for *Invincible Shaolin/Shaolin yu Wudang* (1980)

I learned the Hung fist, and that was bequeathed to my family by Wong Fei-hung. The founder was [Lu Acai]. He taught Wong Ke[i]-ying and Wong Ke[i]-ying taught it to his son Wong Fei-hung who in turn passed it on to Lam Sai-wing. Lam had many disciples and one of them was my father Lau Cham. Lau Cham taught it to Lau Kar-leung.
 – Lau Kar-leung (quoted in Hong Kong Film Archive 1999: 70)

Archival authenticity refers to the authenticity of the actual martial arts featured in kung fu films. Chinese martial arts films have showcased, with varying degrees of accuracy, a range of 'real' styles. The following have been particularly prevalent:

1. Southern and Northern Shaolin styles and their derivatives — The differences between northern and southern Chinese kung fu are popularly encapsulated in the phrase 'Northern leg, Southern fist'. The north was flat and open, thus the emphasis on high and flying kicks (supposedly to remove opponents from their horses) and wide stances. The south was marshy, more crowded and (in the case of Guangdong) built up, thus the emphasis on solid stances and fighting styles adapted to enclosed spaces (see Reid and Croucher 1995: 70–3; Chow and Spangler 1982: 36–43). Lau Kar-leung's films focus particularly on Southern Animal styles (Snake, Crane, Tiger, Leopard, and Dragon)

and the Shaolin derived *Hung Gar/Hong Quan*, which also deploys the *wuxing* or Five Elements Fist (Wood, Metal, Water, Fire and Earth). *Hung Gar* is associated with the Southern Shaolin rebel Hung Hei-kwun, who combined the close quarter Tiger style taught to him by the monk Zhi Shan with the White Crane fist practiced by his wife Fang Wing Chun (Chow and Spangler 1982: 60–1). *Executioners from Shaolin/Hong Xiguan* (1976) is one of many films to deal with *Hung Gar*'s development. Popular northern styles featured in films include Eagle Claw and Praying Mantis, the latter recognisable by the hands taking the shape of a Mantis claw.

2. *Wing Chun/Yong Chun* — A southern style originated by a Buddhist nun, Ng Mui/Wu Mei, founded on direct, close-contact fighting, "a combination of straight and intercepting lines and deflecting arcs" (Chow and Spangler 1982: 59). Bruce Lee learned *Wing Chun* from Grandmaster Yip Man, although he adopted a flashier style of fighting for his films. Nevertheless, it can be seen (briefly) in the trapping hands and straight punches he uses against Bob Wall in *Enter the Dragon* and Chuck Norris in *Way of the Dragon*. *Wing Chun* is famous for its one-inch punch, which we see Qi Guanjun/Chi Kwan-chun learning by striking a large bell in *Shaolin Martial Arts/Hong Quan yu Yong Chun* (1974). Sammo Hung's *Warriors Two/Zan Xiansheng yu Zhaoqian Hua* (1978) and *Prodigal Son* are both about one of *Wing Chun*'s legendary masters, Leung Tzan, while *Wing Chun/ Yong Chun* (1994) focuses on Ng Mui's pupil, Yim Wing Chun, after whom the style was named. Given its no-frills utilitarian style – kicks are low – *Wing Chun* is usually mixed with other styles on screen.

3. Korean martial arts — Since the early 1970s, the phrase 'Northern Leg, Southern Fist' might be more accurately represented as 'Korean Leg, Chinese Fist'. Films like *Hapkido/He Qi Dao* (1972) and *When Taekwondo Strikes/Taiquan Zhen Jiu Zhou* (1973) varied the anti-Japanese theme of many kung fu films by having Chinese martial artists team up with Korean ones. Korean martial arts emphasise high, elaborate kicking techniques – they are more spectacular than even northern Chinese kicks. Wong In-sik, Chi Hon-tsoi, Huang Jang-li, and Casanova Wong were all Korean martial artists trained in either Taekwondo or Hapkido – along with Chinese Taekwondoists John Liu and Tang Tao-liang, they constitute what many fans call the 'Superkickers'.

4. *Zui Quan* or Drunken Boxing — According to David Chow and Richard Spangler, Drunken Fist derives from the same originator, Kau See, as the similarly deranged-looking Monkey style (*Houquan*) (1982: 69). Both look deceptively out-of-control, but can suddenly be unexpectedly graceful and lethal. Monkey style hops, squats, rolls, somersaults, scratches and claws;[6] Drunken Fist staggers, threatens to lose balance, mimics holding and drinking from a cup. *Zui Quan* was part of Wong Fei-hung's repertoire, while it is one

of the many styles displayed in *Shaolin Challenges Ninja/Zhonghua Zhangfu* (1978). But it really came into its own with the rise of kung fu comedy, particularly as performed by Jackie Chan in *Drunken Master/Zui Quan* (1978).

5. *Wu shu* — Traditionally the more accurate Mandarin name for Chinese martial arts, *wu shu* became the name of the specific art practiced in the People's Republic after Mao Zedong's victory over the Nationalists. It was established as a national sport as part of Mao's program of national health. Combat-based martial arts were out of favour – *wu shu* is designed for performance and mixes traditional martial arts with gymnastics and techniques from *jingju*. Many do not regard it as a 'real' martial art, but symptomatic of the Chinese phrase "flowery fists and embroidery kicks" (Wong 1996/2001: 4); aesthetically pleasing, but useless for fighting. Nevertheless, it pretty much replaced *jingju* in providing Hong Kong cinema with action performers and stuntmen. Its most famous practitioner is Jet Li, but it is also the style performed by Darth Maul (Ray Park) in *Star Wars Episode 1: The Phantom Menace* (1999). The most balletic of martial arts, *wu shu* is characterised by "strong, swift and extended leaps and turns" (Li and Du 1998: 26) – wide sweeps, extended stances, and its trademark mid-air spinning kicks. In *Shaolin Temple/Siu Lam Si* (1982), a training sequence allows Jet Li to perform the kind of empty-hand and weapons forms that won him gold medals in the early 1970s.

Measuring the accuracy of these styles requires the possession of a certain amount of cult capital. Ron Lim's 'Martial Artist's Guide to Hong Kong Films' (1999) rates movies purely on the basis of the accuracy and execution of their kung fu – in *Warriors Two*, we learn, "no one ... does *wing chun* properly or well" (Lim 1999), even though its trailer assures us that "It's authentic! It's clearly shown!" But this kind of authenticity has its limits – Shaw Brothers films show "pure Southern Chinese styles" but their fight scenes are "Slow, slow, slow" (Ibid.), clearly in need of a bit of inauthentic flash.

Fan investments aside, archival authenticity can be seen as a documentary tradition of sorts, one which has most specifically sought to root Hong Kong culture in Southern China. The old Wong Fei-hung films have been seen as an archive of Cantonese martial arts (and other forms of Cantonese culture), 'recording' fist forms that might otherwise disappear (Yu 1980: 82) and stressing "documentary authenticity" (Rodriguez 1997: 10). 'Real' onscreen kung fu is generally thought to begin with *The True Story of Wong Fei-hung: Whiplash Snuffs the Candle Flame/Huang Feihong Zhuan: Bianfeng Mie Zhu* (1949). But a non-Chinese film predates it by one year in 'documenting' authentic Chinese martial arts, Maya Deren's *A Meditation on Violence* (1948), "based on traditional movements of the *wu dang* Shaolin schools of Chinese boxing". Again, the dance connection seems significant – Deren had made other films focused on stylised movement. The *wu dang* and

Shaolin styles are usually taken to epitomise, respectively, the 'soft' and 'hard' Chinese arts. 'Soft' styles like Tai Chi/*taiji*, *xingyi* and *bagua zhang* are rooted in Taoism and use relaxed, yielding, and flowing movements to turn an opponents' strength against itself. Buddhist-derived 'Hard' styles, on the other hand, meet force with force (see Reid and Croucher 1995: 60). It is generally recognised that the distinction is not rigidly polarised – *xingyi* is a 'hard' application of 'soft' power, while the Shaolin Snake style combines supple flowing movements with sudden attacks. In *A Meditation on Violence*, the performer Chao Li-chi performs Shaolin animal forms, Tai Chi and a Sword form, mostly in front of a plain backdrop. Some of Deren's techniques anticipate the rhetoric of the kung fu film – a Snake-style fingertip blow into the camera, slow motion and freeze-frames during jumps and spins. The music underlines the Hard/Soft distinction – flute for Tai Chi, drums for the Shaolin *hung gar* form. With hindsight, *A Meditation on Violence* now looks like a title sequence from a 1970s Shaw Brothers film, especially those devoted to "the performance, explanation and practice of specific martial techniques" (Sek 1980: 34).

Three Styles of Hung School's Kung Fu (A Demonstration Film of the Chinese Kung Fu) (1974) is a short documentary which preceded the original release of *Heroes Two/Fang Shiyu yu Hong Xiguan* (1974), the first of Shaw Brothers' prolific Shaolin cycle. The cycle marked a shift from what some have called 'swingy arm fighting' – the flailing arms and unextended kicks that characterise films like *The Chinese Boxer* and *The Killer/Da Sha Shou* (1971). *Three Styles of Hung School's Kung Fu* features three Shaw Brothers stars, Chen Guantai, Fu Sheng and Qi Guanjun, demonstrating, respectively, the Tiger killing technique, the Tiger-Crane Form and the Ten Forms (*sup ying*) which combine the Five Animals and the Five Elements. The "abstract, purist presentation of martial skills and styles" (Rayns 1984b: 52) almost seems to pick up where *A Meditation on Violence* left off, and also sets the style for title sequences in subsequent Shaws films. During the first segment, the Chinese character for part of the form (resembling the romanised letter 'I') is inscribed on the floor because the footwork effectively spells it out (emphasised in overhead shots); close-ups depict detailed fist forms or footwork. But if Deren's interest is anthropological, *Three Styles* explicitly locates Shaolin kung fu historically (the spread of martial arts to Southern China), politically (anti-Manchu resistance), and mythically (the heroes Hung Hei-kwun, Fong Sai-yuk and Wu Wei-kin/Hu Huiqian).

When Lau Kar-leung made the transition from choreographer to director, the concrete details of mainly Southern martial arts became an integral part of his films. Not only are Lau's films about the learning and mastering of particular styles, but they are centrally concerned, in Tony Rayns' words, with "the survival of a particular tradition" (1984b: 51) insofar as "the dominant South China martial arts tradition *speaks through* [Lau]" via a "chain of master-disciple relationships" (52). *Challenge of the Masters/Lu Acai yu Huang Feihong* (1976) and *The Martial Club/Wu Guan* (1981) project Lau's patrilineal *shifu*, Wong Fei-hung (Lau Kar-fai), back into the role of pupil. Rejected by his father as a pupil, he is adopted by his father's teacher, Lu Acai (Chen Guantai). The title sequence is a paradigmatic *Hung Gar* training form, again accompanied by onscreen calligraphy − "Giving and taking are equal forces in destiny." A more detailed (diegetic) training sequence shows the mastery of Tiger-Crane and pole technique, but Lu also transmits the Confucian code associated with the mature Wong − "Forgive man and forbear". The film's emotional climax is Wong's fight with the northern bandit Zhen Erhu, played by Lau himself in a nod to the bit parts he played in the earlier Wong Fei-hung series. Zhen has killed Wong's friend, and Fei-hong is presented with an opportunity for revenge when he breaks his enemy's leg − instead he helps him and appears, in Lu Acai's words, to "win his heart".

Rayns is critical of *The Martial Club* for not further developing the Master/Pupil theme (1984b: 53). Certainly the tone is lighter, and yet Lau's choreography had evolved spectacularly. The film climaxes with one of the most persuasive Northern/Southern battles as Wong (Lau Kar-fai again) takes on the northern *Jingwu* master, Shan (Wang Lung-wei), an object lesson in cultural/regional variations and their relationship with space and environment. Zhi Shan's Tiger form, from which Hung Hei-kwun derived his own *Hung Gar* style, was designed for close-quarter fighting − stances were 14 inches wide and the entire form could be performed within four square feet (Chow and Spangler 1982: 60). Wong and Shan fight in a typically narrow Guangdong alleyway − such alleyways were directly linked to the refinement of Southern boxing. As the fight progresses, the alleyway grows narrower − six feet wide, then four, then three. Wong shifts from Animal styles to Ng Mui's Iron Wire Fist, while Shan adapts his northern legwork, his leg fully extended against the wall. Finally, the space is so enclosed that they can only try to weaken each other's stances. While there is no clear 'winner' − Shan is not a villain as such and only wants to test the young southerner − the sequence shows that Wong's style is designed *for* such spaces while Shan has to adapt and extend his style to keep up.

Rayns is right about one aspect of *The Martial Club* − Lau's need to foreground "spectacle for its own sake" (1984b: 53) in order to keep up with the more eclectic, Opera-derived choreography of Chan, Hung and Yuen Wo-ping. *Eight Diagram Pole Fighter/Wulang Bagua Gun* (1983) is, at one level, a stubbornly old-fashioned kung fu film − nominally focused on an identifiable style (the 'soft' *bagua*), concerned with matters of revenge and Buddhist ethics. Kung fu films were out of fashion; Jackie Chan's *Project A* and Tsui Hark's *Zu: Warriors of the Magic Mountain/Xin Shu Shan Jianxia* were released the same year – the first redefined action-comedy, the second brought digital technology into the *wu xia pian*. The death of Fu Sheng midway through production casts a further elegiac pall over *Eight Diagram Pole Fighter*. And yet the film shows that Lau could match, if not surpass, any of his rivals. When the Fifth Yang son (Lau Kar-fei) engages a senior monk (Kao Fei) in a pole duel, they make spectacular use of huge candle-holders and floor cushions, batting them back and forth as they flail and parry. At the climax, their strikes and parries 'arrange' the candle-holder and cushions into a hexagram resembling the 'Eight Trigrams' of the *I-Ching* (see Reid and Croucher 1995: 97–8)[7] – they fight within the circle until Fifth Yang draws a second circle, using chalk on the end of his pole, which becomes the Taoist yin/yang symbol. As a finale, Fifth Yang must rescue his sister (Hui Ying-hung) from Mongol invaders. Lau has already shown himself to be as adept in deploying inanimate objects as Jackie Chan, but the scene also anticipates the ladder and table fights of the later *Once Upon a Time in China* films. Fifth Yang fights on top of a pyramid of coffins, sometimes with his sister strapped to his back – he hops from lid to lid, does the splits across two coffins to duck his opponents' attacks. The Mongols are armed with poles with whip-like ends, which snake around wrists and weapons – as Fifth Yang's leg is fastened, he fights with it fully extended. The two Yangs are rescued by the Buddhist monks, wielding poles and a mechanical, wooden wolf used to teach 'defanging' techniques. In an unforgettably excruciating sequence, they both fight and preserve their Buddhist pacifism by 'defanging' the Mongols.

Lau's commitment to authentic techniques was almost unique. Sammo Hung's *Warriors Two* makes for an interesting comparison. The opening narration suggests a similar concern with documentary accuracy:

> There are many kung fu schools in Southern China. The most famous are Hung, Kui, Chu, Lee and Mo. There is also the school of *Wing Chun*. It was developed by a Shaolin nun, who named it after her student, Yim Wing Chun. Yim passed it to her husband, Leung Bok-chao. Leung taught Wong Wah-bo. And Wong taught Leung Tzan...

The film uses a number of *Wing Chun* techniques – 'sticking hands', in which two practitioners touch hands and try to anticipate and neutralise the others' movements (Chow and Spangler 1982: 59), its three empty-hand forms (*siu lim tao*/a little thought, *tzum kiu*/searching for the opponent's opening, and *biu gee*/shooting fingers), weapons (butterfly sword, six-and-a-half-point staff) and the form's distinctive wooden training dummy. In the role of Leung Tzan, Leung Kar-yan's upper-body fighting style certainly looks authentic and Sammo Hung's Fei Chun uses sticking hands against an opponent in a bamboo forest. But kung fu comedy was indicative of the irreverence, hybridity and impatience with tradition of the 'new' Hong Kong cinema. Hung never lets *Wing Chun* orthodoxy get in the way of his performers' talents – Casanova Wong's Taekwondo kicking, his own flips and somersaults. Wong looks awkward when forced to do *Wing Chun*, magnificent when liberated to send out multi-kicks. When villainous Master Mo (Fong Hark-on) adopts Praying Mantis style, cinematic trickery virtually allows him to *become* a Mantis, to mimic its gait as well as its claw-like attacks. Archival authenticity survives only in fragments. In *Iron Monkey/Shaonian Huang Feihong zhi Tie Houzi* (1993), Donnie Yen's Wong Kei-ying is Southern Chinese from the waist up (*Hung Gar* raised finger salute, Tiger and Snake), but his kicks look very Korean.

Cinematic Authenticity: Bruce Lee, the 'Superkickers' and the 'Venoms'

Cinematic authenticity identifies a desire for transparent mediation, championing long takes and wide framing as a guarantee of the 'real'. For many 'old school' fans, 1970s kung fu is the 'real thing' because of the (comparative) lack of technological intervention: the techniques employed by the Hong Kong cinema of the 1970s "allowed the truly talented artists to shine on screen without artifice. Long extended takes in the fight scenes meant that the camera acted as a reporter, recording reality not altering it" (Davidson 1997: 2).

This may read like naive, lowbrow Bazinian realism, but the idea of kung fu movies 'documenting' their star's ability is not confined to fan culture. Tony Rayns calls *The 36th Chamber of Shaolin/Shaolin Sanshiliu Fang* (1978) "a fictional documentary on the resilience and skill of its lead actor (Lau Kar-fai) ... shot in such a way that the actors' real-life capabilities are tested to the utmost" (1984b: 52). Even those who acknowledge that technology cannot help but alter 'reality' may retain some faith in its documentary facility. Donnie Yen, interviewed on the *Iron Monkey* DVD, suggests that kicking is the guarantee of the real:

> I believe kicking really identifies a person's ability ... as opposed to just upper body movement. Because sometimes upper body movement, you can cheat it with ... camera angles and different ways of cutting the film. For the kicking, you can't really cheat.

Interestingly, Yen acknowledges that "exaggeration" is aesthetically desirable. To re-create Wong Kei-ying's 'Shadowless kick', the camera was undercranked at 16 frames per second. But if Yen's speed is 'fake', the precision of his multi-kicks is not, and the camera remains fixed to prove it. The 'Shadowless kick', Yen seems to be suggesting, is a collaboration between technology and "true ability".

To speak of 'long takes' is, in some ways, misleading – no 1970s kung fu film will be mistaken for a Jean Renoir film. Bordwell explains that two stylistic norms have dominated Hong Kong action. The "one-by-one tracking shot" is most like a long take – the hero/heroine moves laterally through his/her opponents, followed by the camera (which helps to conceal the fact that opponents are helpfully waiting their turn) (Bordwell 2000b: 114–15). 'Constructive editing' laid the groundwork for the faster-cut style of post-1980s films – fragments of action are rendered in individual shots, so that the viewer 'constructs' the unified scene out of the details (116). Flying leaps and mid-air exchanges are the classic example – shots of take-offs, low-angle shots of protagonists in mid-air, close-ups of fists or feet striking, good and bad landings are the standard visual rhetoric. In *Fong Sai-yuk/Fang Shiyu* (1993), Jet Li is able to hop on and off his horse, ride side-saddle and fire a multitude of arrows from a single bow (they *all* hit their targets), because each fragment of action gets its own shot. The length of the fragments decreased as Hong Kong cinema got faster, but I am not sure that shot length is the real factor in determining the 'real'. What is important is the *unity* of an action within a shot – the number of moves or techniques, the precision of a continuous combo, a single-take stunt. Tung Wai recalls Lau Kar-leung demanding forty moves a shot in *Executioners From Shaolin* (Hong Kong Film Archive 1999: 75). My examples 'document' three types of ability – the speed of Bruce Lee, the elaborate kicking techniques of John Liu and Huang Jang-li, and the acrobatic skills of Zhang Che's 'Fourth Generation' team, known affectionately by their fans as the 'Venoms' (Guo Zhui, Lu Feng, Jiang Sheng, Luo Mang and Sun Jian).[8]

Bruce Lee was variously referred to as "the fastest fist in the East" and, in Hong Kong, "Three-legged Lee" (Cheng 1984: 23) – tales still circulate of the camera being slowed down in order to record his moves. In other words, his speed had, to a certain extent, to be taken on trust, because its actual representation was impossible. Nevertheless, such apocryphal stories separate him from the undercranking routinely used by Jackie Chan and Jet Li. Interestingly, it took Chan and Li's Hollywood vehicles – where undercranking carries the stigma of cinematic primitivism – to indicate how fast they really were, with (the admittedly younger) Li coming off better. In *The Big Boss* and *Fist of Fury*, Lee's 'realism' rubs up against the conventions of Mandarin *wu xia* – exaggerated, trampoline-aided leaps, opponents punched through walls, two (limply inanimate) Japanese foes swung around and then thrown through the air. *Way of the Dragon* and the incomplete *Game of Death* are more indicative of the no-tricks aesthetic Lee had in mind. *Way of the Dragon*'s most celebrated fight scene is Lee's Coliseum duel with Chuck Norris. Cheng Yu contrasts it with Lo Wei's fight scenes, which, he argues, made greater use of editing and close-ups to "convey the impact of the fight" (1984: 25). The Coliseum fight favours long and medium shots, so that "the style is closer to capturing the *fight-performance* or representing a reportage of a fight from the ring-side" (25). But Lee's shooting style is not quite as "dispassionate" as Cheng makes it sound. He uses slow motion. Like Lo Wei, he uses subjective camera techniques – Lee kicks into the camera and stares 'us' out. He uses constructive editing, so that we get to see kicks delivered in long shot but actually *land* in close-up. Sections of the fight do conform to Cheng's description – a sequence of low kicks used to deflect Norris' attacks, a slow motion 'dance' that consists of a long take showing Lee gliding and prancing, constantly out of his hirsute foe's reach. The preceding fight against Bob Wall and Wong In-Sik uses the shooting style popular at Seasonal studios from the mid-1970s – zoom shots used to conceal cuts, the action predominantly framed in long shot. No scene captures Lee's speed more impressively – at a National Film Theatre screening in 1999, audiences still gasped and applauded. On two occasions, Lee and his opponent initiate kicks simultaneously – his land before the other's have risen above waist-height. The scene averages three to four moves per shot, but their speed and accuracy are breathtaking.

Secret Rivals/Nan Quan Bei Tui (1976), *Invincible Armour/Ying Zhao Tie Bushan* (1977) and *Snuff Bottle Connection/Shen Tui Tie Shan Gong* (1977) are characterised by spectacular Korean kicking techniques, over-use of the zoom lens and *mise-en-scène* so minimal (forest clearings, indistinguishable courtyards) that they might as well be shot against the single-colour backdrops of Shaw Brothers title sequences. *Secret Rivals* locates northern (John Liu) and southern (Wong Tao) Chinese heroes in Korea, where, for reasons that scarcely matter, they find themselves up against white-haired Silver Fox (Huang Jang-li).[9] The Northern Leg/Southern Fist theme amounts to little – all three films are about the poetics of leg flexibility. Liu has approximately two facial expressions, which is one more than Huang, but this never becomes a problem – the foot triumphs over the face and, more importantly, frequently collides with it. For Baker and Russell, the film "set new standards in fight choreography":

Gone were the flailing arm movements of the early 1970s; now in their place were flashy high kicks combined with acrobatics, stylish crisp hand moves and jumping combination kicks. (1994: 118)

Fig. 1 The poetics of leg flexibility: 'Superkickers' Huang Jang-li and John Liu in *Secret Rivals*

Early in *Secret Rivals*, John Liu trains by kicking pots suspended in mid-air, sometimes three per shot (two without lowering his leg). Later, hands tied behind his back, he kicks suspended logs thrown at him by a young boy. Huang's 'real' abilities are revealed more progressively – his early fights use 'constructed' leaps and blows into the camera to convey his power. But when Liu and Wong Tao are attacking him from either side, his multi-kicks fly in both directions – the film averages between five and nine moves per take. In *Invincible Armour*, Liu sends out six kicks in succession, then grasps his toe and holds his leg fully extended (a trademark move). In *Snuff Bottle Connection*, the kicks have risen to seven – his extended leg-hold then traps his opponent's sword arm, and kicks him in the face before lowering his leg. This is Liu's most astonishing performance – at one point, he wields a Western-style sword with his foot, slashes and stabs its owner and (in the same take) extends his leg, removes the sword and slowly lowers it. When Ken Lo performs similar feats in *Drunken Master 2*, his kicks and balance are wire-aided. But while Liu and Huang's 'real' abilities are caught by 'descriptive' camera framing, the films have no qualms about doubling them for acrobatic feats such as Liu's handstand kicks in *Invincible Armour*.

Crippled Avengers/Can Que (1978) uses longer takes than the 'Superkicker' films – some shots contain between ten and fifteen (complex) manouevres. The Venoms thrive on spectacular team work. Guo Zhui and Jiang Sheng are an impressive double-act with a steel ring – we see Guo catch the ring in mid-somersault, or dive through it in mid-air as it is thrown at him. During their climactic fight with steel-armed Lu Feng, Jiang Sheng dives through the ring in the middle of a lengthy take as Guo uses it as a weapon against Lu. The narrative underscores the spectacle in intriguing ways – it is a cycle of cruelty and mutilation, with the disabled bonding into a more than able-bodied unit. Nobleman Chen Guantai is traumatised by the mutilation of his wife and son (Lu Feng) – the latter survives minus his arms, but gains metallic ones. Father and son take revenge through indiscriminate cruelty – they blind one man (Guo Zhui), sever another's legs (Sun Jian), turn another into a deaf-mute (Luo Mang) and tighten a metal-band around Jiang Sheng's head until he is reduced to a cackling idiot. The *wu xia* genre has a history of disabled heroes, from Jin Yong's novel *The Mythical Crane Hero* to Wang Yu's one-armed swordsmen and boxers. But the spectacle of *Crippled Avengers* serves only to stress how able-bodied the Venoms are – Sun Jian's mechanical legs are impressively flexible, reflecting the actor's Taekwondo expertise. John Liu and Huang Jang-li were 'real' martial artists, the Venoms came mostly from Opera backgrounds – there are no doubles here. Zhang's framing is 'theatrical' in the best sense, as though challenging the Venoms to fill the screen with flips, kicks and somersaults. When the villains surrounding Guo Zhui bang cymbals to counteract his heightened hearing, an overhead shot shows his spinning a pole across his shoulders and then his whole body on the floor in a stylised effort to keep them at bay.

Corporeal Authenticity: Jackie Chan and Sammo Hung

Corporeal authenticity is measured by stuntwork and physical risk as much as fighting ability. By the 1980s, 'pure' kung fu had largely gone out of fashion and Hong Kong action was embracing an increasingly montage-based aesthetic (see Bordwell 1997; 2000a). What is left, therefore, is the body itself and what its owner is prepared to subject it to, a logic incarnated most publicly by Jackie Chan doing all (or, more accurately, most) of his own stunts – "we show only what we can do, what my stuntmen can do" (Logan 1995: 57). A recent ad for the DVD of *Battlecreek Brawl* (1980) underlines Chan's persona as champion of the 'real' – "No wires. Just talent". Chan's films use a much faster editing style than Bruce Lee's – they belong to a more cine-literate phase in Hong Kong cinema – and use other forms of enhancement (undercranking, subtle wirework), but his use of action replays and outtakes re-invent the documentary and inscribe his 'presence' as self-endangerment (Jackie bleeding, Jackie unconscious, Jackie on fire). According to Ramie Tateishi, Chan's stunts ensure "that the screen is always presenting the authentic subject" (1998: 83).

Chan is not alone in this high impact/high risk aesthetic – it is difficult to separate his innovations from those of Sammo Hung, celebrated for his "realistic-seeming fights" and "use of close contact, aggressive and rapid hits and blocks" (Dancer 1998: 49). In *Eastern Condors/Dongfang Tuying* (1986), Yuen Biao somersaults off a table, grabs his opponent on the way down and then throws him – the stunt depends on both performers' athleticism. The Jackie Chan Stunt Team and the Sammo Hung unit are masters of what the language of Professional Wrestling calls "selling" – stylised, exaggerated responses to blows which "sell" their power to the audience. Stuntmen hit in Sammo Hung's films perform mid-air corkscrew spins before slamming to the ground. When Yuen Biao kicks Billy Chow in *Dragons Forever/Feilong Mengjiang* (1988), Chow somersaults backwards before landing neck-and-shoulders first on some steps. Wrestling makes for a useful point of comparison in the way that it mobilises a discourse of authenticity to compensate for its inauthenticity as competitive sport. Wrestling is simultaneously 'fake' and often dangerously 'real', authenticity resurrected through risk; gruelling 'Hell in a Cell' matches, tables, ladders and chair matches, bloodshed, high leaps and falls. The back cover of Mick Foley's autobiography, *Mankind: Have a Nice Day!* (2000), seemingly depicts him as the Jackie Chan of North American wrestling, featuring a diagram of his many injuries (all of them in 'staged' matches). Foley lost most of his ear in Germany, has broken jaws, wrists, ribs, dislocated and separated shoulders and lost copious amounts of blood. In a notorious 'Hell in a Cell' match in 1998, The Undertaker threw Foley both *off* and *through* the fifteen-foot cage – video footage shows one of his teeth stuck to his beard.

'Contact' is central to Sammo Hung's fan reputation. If constructive editing can help to "sell" action, close-ups of blows landing are tough to fake, especially in slow motion which tends to expose 'pulled' punches. A close-up in *Pedicab Driver/Qunlong Xifeng* (1990) shows Sammo's face visibly change shape as Billy Chow's foot connects with his chin. In *Dragons Forever*, Jackie Chan's duel with kickboxing champion Benny 'The Jet' Urquidez – like their earlier set-to in *Wheels on Meals/Kuaican Che* (1984) – is seen by some fans as the 1980s equivalent of Lee and Norris squaring off in *Way of the Dragon*. But if the Coliseum duel foregrounds speed, technical precision and tactical ingenuity, Chan and Urquidez foreground *impact*. Urquidez wears a baggy suit to conceal his padding, but Chan makes a point of stripping to a tight white vest. If Lee sheds clothes to display his magnificent torso, Chan (who is admittedly pretty well cut, too) does so to show he can take the blows. Both Chan and Hung – and their respective stunt teams – excel in bad landings, and environment is paramount in this world of pain. *Dragons Forever* climaxes in an industrial plant and makes memorable 'that's-gotta-hurt!' use of balconies, pipes and gas cylinders. Wherever possible, villains kicked off platforms or ledges make a point of hitting something on the way down – one collides with a window, shattering it, then continues his fall (in the same shot), severing a pipe which spews steam into the air. *Police Story* finds even more mileage in a shopping mall. When Chan kicks Fong Hark-on, he propels him into a backward somersault onto a moving escalator. In *Dragons Forever*, one stuntman goes through a glass table face first, but *Police Story* sets the record for bodies colliding with glass – not for nothing did the stunt team call the films *Glass Story* (Chan and Yang 1998: 324). Chan picks up one unfortunate heavy, wraps his legs around his waist and slams him into a glass cabinet; another cabinet is smashed by a corkscrew-spinning body; Chan's head cracks another pane as he recoils from a punch; he drives a motorbike through several layers of glass with someone's body on the front. The fighting style is gritty – there are no stances or 'Shapes' – so that kinetic grace shifts to the recipients of violence. In any case, as in *Project A*, Chan began to document the physical risks and injuries underpinning his 'new' approach to action. In *Drunken Master 2*, we have already seen him crawl over hot coals as he fights Ken Lo – the end-credits reveal that there was at least one other take of this dangerous scene.

Corporeal authenticity has been central to the Western marketing of Jackie Chan – "No Fear. No Stuntman. No Equal", in the words of publicity for *Rumble in the Bronx/Hongfan Qu* (1995). Chan was sold as the antithesis of pampered, stunt-doubled Hollywood stars. Dave Kehr discerns (rightly, I think) a dark undertone to some of Jackie's later films, in which he becomes "the impresario of his own agony":

> (His stunts) look more like tests of endurance than displays of skill. It's as if, in sensing the diminishing agility and slowed reactions of middle age coming on, Chan had decided that what he had to offer was the spectacle of his own suffering. The end-credit shots of Jackie being hustled off in ambulances are the final proof that he's willing to do anything to keep his audience's attention and preserve the loyalty of his fans. (2000: 118–19)

According to *Jackie Chan: My Stunts*, "For most of his life, Jackie Chan has been risking death for a living" – inevitably, Jackie and Sammo's World of Pain has its cost. Corporeal authenticity must work hardest to prove itself – when Jackie is visibly doubled for a twisting mid-air kick in *Dragons Forever*, it is more potentially damaging than it would be for any other star. But the greatest cost is, of course, to the body itself. If Chan's films foreground the vulnerability of human flesh – he is not the invincible Lee – his stunts, as Kehr implies, operate entirely in denial of it.

'Presencing' the Kung Fu Star: Authenticity and 'Aura'

In the celebrated climactic fight between Wong Fei-hung/Jet Li and 'Iron Robe Yim' in *Once Upon a Time in China*, the protagonists balance on and propel themselves from ladders, or shatter the ladders with kicks as they fly through the air. Suspended cargo flats fly as though of their own volition – at one point, Wong drops into the splits to avoid one. According to Ackbar Abbas, spectacle had shifted from performance to the mastery of technology and film language (1997: 32) – Yuen Wo-ping's wirework, Tsui Hark's mastery of montage, camera speed and framing. This is apparently the opposite of Rick Baker and Toby Russell's ideal, which "requires the skill of the actor rather than the director". Anecdotal evidence supports Abbas' point. Jet Li broke his ankle during filming and contributed only close-ups and some upper-body combat – he was doubled by Xiong Xin-xin. Performance *is* central to the scene – it takes skill to fight on wires and Xiong's leg-trapping skills are formidable. But certainly kung fu stardom is no longer the centre of 'authenticity'. When Abbas argues that "there are no more authentic stars/heroes of the order of Bruce Lee" (1997: 31), he seems to be suggesting that their 'aura' has been erased by technology.

In 'The Work of Art in the Age of Mechanical Reproduction' (1935/1979), Walter Benjamin connects 'aura' to 'presence', 'authenticity' and the 'fabric of tradition', each of them always eluding technical reproducibility. 'Aura' is "that which withers in the age of mechanical reproduction", because technology removes an object (or, in this case, a performance) from the "domain of tradition":

> The essence of a thing is the essence of all that is transmissible from its beginning, ranging from its substantive duration to its testimony to the history which it has experienced. (1979: 852)

In this respect, kung fu stars – and stars in general (as Benjamin explicitly argues) – were always in trouble. When the actor is on stage, "aura is tied to his presence", whereas the technological mediation of film takes performance out of the actor's hands – because of the plasticity of editing and different camera set-ups, "it is composed of many separate performances" (859). David Thomson seems to be making a similar distinction in his comparison of Fred Astaire with Rudolf Nureyev. Nureyev on film, he argues, "is less than in the flesh, because he is himself stimulated by an actual audience and a real leap" (1980: 19). But cinema gives Astaire (implicitly a 'lesser' dancer) an aura not available to Nureyev – he is "a great filmed dancer", because cinema's constructed nature facilitates perfectionism and flawless grace (19). *Once Upon a Time in China 3*'s film-within-a-film can be seen as a comment both on the 'legend' Wong Fei-hung and the star Jet Li, both of them losing their 'aura' to the camera. The 'realism' of the black-and-white Kwan Tak-hing series gives way to the hi-tech mediation of Tsui Hark's franchise. Similarly, Jet Li had a reputation as a live performer before he made films, and some have suggested that Hong Kong cinema's 'Jet Li' has substituted cinematic artifice for his real skills. But there are ways of re-synthesising 'presence', and one can see all three types of authenticity as strategies for achieving this. Corporeal authenticity re-synthesizes the "fabric of tradition", but has no qualms about using some 'tricks' to do so – even Lau Kar-leung uses enhanced leaps and constructive editing. Cinematic and corporeal authenticity work hardest to convey 'presence', the first concealing (rather than removing) mediation, the second sometimes foregrounding mediation (editing, Chan's multi-takes) to guarantee the self-endangering star body. *Jackie Chan: My Stunts* is ostensibly about Jackie revealing his tricks – hidden wires, padded shoes, the importance of camera set-ups in 'selling' action – just as it is simultaneously a documentary about his 'presence'. But there is more to kung fu stardom than authentic ability, which is why Bruce Lee, Jackie Chan and Jet Li are more famous than John Liu or the Venoms. Stardom raises its own set of issues around performance, and Chinese performance traditions have made their own special contribution to film stardom.

In *Hong Kong Action Cinema* Bey Logan recalls the scene in *Enter the Dragon* where Lee, standing stock still but surrounded by movement, fixes his piercing gaze on (the offscreen) Han – "if that shot doesn't raise the hairs on the back of your neck, then you've probably bought the wrong book", he suggests (1995: 23). Lee's 'aura' is often defined in terms of charisma, and charisma is evidently guaranteed by stasis as much as movement – "Many later martial arts heroes failed because the camera finds them uninteresting when they are *not* jumping or kicking or punching" (23). Lee's 'presence' is attention-getting and sexually magnetic – the curled lip, smouldering stare or mocking smirk, his trademark gestures (thumbing the nose, his cocky 'bring it on' hand gesture to opponents). Jet Li's 'aura' is quieter, but no less compelling – in *Once Upon a Time in China*'s ladder fight, he dominates a fight scene in which he actually took little combative part. The camera gives as much as it takes away – Li positively *glows* in close-up. Chinese martial arts, health and performance traditions all embrace the concept of *qi*, a term which carries multiple meanings, including air, spirit, energy and breath. Jo Riley explains that in *jingju*, it also means 'presence' – *faqi* is to radiate presence (1997: 206). A performing body is "a body which is *presenced*. The poses manifest or radiate presence by virtue of the articulation of the body" (179). Or, as Scala fans put it, "Shapes! Shapes!" In *jingju*, the key presencing moment is the *liangxiang* (radiant, glowing appearance) pose – the term suggests an opening of the body to let light shine, "the moment of expressing presence" (212). *Liangxiang* is a transitional moment in which the performer catches her/his breath, expelling the old and taking in the new – "the expression of *qi* (force) which captivates the spectator's gaze happens at (the) same point at which *qi* is returned or gathered" (212). Despite his *jingju* background, Jackie Chan displays *liangxiang* less than Bruce Lee or Jet Li – his choreography uses what Craig Reid calls Perpetual Motion technique – "the maintenance of continuous body motion throughout the entire fight sequence to give the impression of nonstop action" (1993–4: 34–5). Bruce and Jet, however, are magnificent posers – Lee's fifty-yard stare, Li's combination of intensity and calm. In *Once Upon a Time in China 2/Huang Feihong II zhi Nan'er Dang Ziqiang* (1992), one *liangxiang* moment raises the hairs on *my* neck as Wong/Jet Li is fighting the White Lotus cult. He uses some intricate footwork to avoid being trapped by a length of cloth, then leaps into mid-air splits, kicking two cult members simultaneously (with a bit of help from the editing). He spins and lands, dropping into a cross-legged sitting position then rises and freezes in a stylised 'Shape' – standing on one leg, the other knee raised to the chest, arms outstretched, a mocking half-smile on his face. At that moment, Jet Li couldn't be more *present*.

Fig. 2 'Presencing' the kung fu star: Jet Li's *liangxiang* (radiant appearance) in *Once Upon a Time in China 2*

Enhancing the Real: Wirework and Stunt Doubles

If we are considering the 'authentic' and the 'real', we need to consider what 'special effects' are too, a familiar enough question in relation to horror and science fiction, but the martial arts film has not been traditionally thought of as an FX genre. Michael Stern has argued that in some ways 'Special Effects' is a misleading term with its inbuilt implication that 'everything else' is not a cinematic effect of some sort (1990: 67). Nevertheless, degrees of *visibility* seem to be important in defining the 'special'. He reminds us that *Planet of the Apes* (1968) won an Academy Award for its ape make-up while *2001: A Space Odyssey* (1968) was not even nominated (66) – were its apes too 'real'/transparent to be 'special'? A similar paradox surrounds the use of wirework in Hong Kong action. 'New wave' wirework shows us things we know to be 'untrue' – fights on top of ladders (*Once Upon a Time in China*), the shoulders of a crowd (*Fong Sai Yuk*), vertical poles (*Iron Monkey*) or the breathtaking tree-top fight in a vast forest in *Crouching Tiger, Hidden Dragon*. But wires also feature in Jackie Chan's more 'realistic' fights, enhancing moves which at least seem possible – "When I use a wire, it's a small technique. If I don't tell you, you don't even know" (*Jackie Chan: My Stunts*). Hong Kong-based stuntman Jude Poyer explains a sequence in *Thunderbolt/Pili Huo* (1995) in which Chan delivers some flying kicks:

> The three kicks are basic ones and wouldn't pose a problem for any Hong Kong stuntman, but a wire is being used to make the technique appear more powerful. If the stuntman performing a jumping kick doesn't have to expend energy to gain height, he can deliver the kicks with more power and more dramatic impact. (2000: 217)

One might argue that this is much more of a 'Wicked Lie' than Jet Li's gravity-defying no-shadow kick, but, significantly, that is not an argument that is ever offered.

Greg Dancer detects a mixed fan response to wirework in Jet Li's films – disappointment that his fights are not 'real' mixed with excitement over the ingenuity of the wirework itself (1998: 47). Wirework is a reminder that not every aspect of performance can be credited to the performer alone (or at all), but there is a pleasure to be had, he suggests, in 'taking apart' such a performance, in this case wire-spotting (48). I must confess to some identification with these wire-spotters, although my own obsession is with stunt doubles – I am a fan as well as an academic and so entitled to be a little bit obsessive. Doubles are more potentially damaging to the martial artist's 'aura' than special effects could ever be because an aura mediated by technology needs to somehow reassure us of the unity of the star presence. There is a now-you-see-him-now-you-don't quality to some Jet Li fight scenes and plenty of evidence of his grace and speed, but just as much that his double can do pretty much everything he can and maybe one or two things he cannot. This sets me off on my own search for wicked shapes and wicked lies (DVD has made me much worse, another way in which technology impacts on the genre). In *Dr Wai in 'The Scripture with No Words'/Maoxian Wang* (1996), Jet's 'King of Adventure' confronts a team of ninjas led by Billy Chow. He casually links the sections of a chain-whip and goes into action. In the next shot, his double performs a 360-degree spin followed by another (wire-aided) spin. Cut to Jet performing more 'grounded' spins and turns. Three slow motion shots show him leaping and striking opponents with the chain-whip. A 'constructed' montage shows Jet and Billy Chow leaping at each other – the double takes over on impact. Chow and Jet's double trade high kicks, feet blocking feet. Jet takes over, delivering foot-sweeps and spin kicks. Chow kicks the double (framed from behind), who ducks two more kicks. Another wire-stunt allows Jet to fly horizontally, kicking Chow repeatedly – the latter 'revolves' in his shirt like a cartoon character. Finally, the ninjas are sliced-and-diced when Jet attaches the chain-whip to a grille, wielding it like a lethal cheese grate. A follow-up fight with two Sumos use further wires (but little doubling) and allows Jet to throw some beautiful Chen-style Tai Chi 'Shapes'. Part of me wants my kung fu idols to be authentic, especially when they are as charismatic and glamorous as Jet Li. I get enormous pleasure from confirming that a particularly impressive move was actually performed by him. And yet another part of me knows that the authentic kung fu star belongs to history, or perhaps to myth, that martial arts films simply do not need their stars to be trained martial artists anymore, and that the kung fu cult master was always partly the magnificent creation of technology and choreography.

There are some more substantial problems arising from the 'authenticity' debate, and I shall mention two in closing this chapter. I acknowledged earlier that an investment in the authentic flies in the face of some cultural and historical particularities about Hong Kong. 1970s retro buffs, in a sense, want to keep Hong Kong cinema 'pure', pro-filmic, China-oriented, and, by implication, 'primitive', authenticated by the degree-zero visual style of films like *Secret Rivals*, whereas, as Abbas has suggested, the embrace of technology speaks to Hong Kong's transnational, postcolonial identity (1997: 32). Additionally, it is clear that the discourse is narrowly masculine – obsessed with mastery (as the genre is), seeing physical prowess as a sign of value, and technology as implicitly feminising. When Nick Davidson mocks Jet Li for his use of wires and doubles, the reference to his "camp *Wu Shu* pose" (1997: 28) speaks volumes. 'Inauthenticity', moreover, has created a space for female martial arts stars like Xu Feng, Zheng Pei-pei, Josephine Siao and

Brigitte Lin, or, more recently, Zhang Ziyi. "Everybody knows that I am a martial arts star who hardly knows the martial arts", says swordplay queen Xu Feng (quoted in Hong Kong Film Archive 1999: 57), in what sounds encouragingly like an inverted boast. For all this, the debate is central to understandings of the genre, not least its transnational cult following, and sometimes all it takes is a chain-whip and some Tai Chi 'Shapes' to keep this pleasurable myth in circulation.

Chapter Two

Burning Paradise
The Myth of the Shaolin Temple

It seems disaster must come – at best, only postponed. Shaolin kung fu, to survive, must now be taught to more young men. We must expand, get more pupils, so that knowledge will spread.
  – *Shaolin Temple/Shaolin Si* (1976)

The Shaolin Temple has become synonymous with 'kung fu' and the kung fu film, from David Carradine's Kwai Chang Caine to Shaw Brothers' prolific Shaolin cycle, from films actually shot at the Henan Temple to the Temple's new role as tourist site with its monks performing as part of a world-touring franchise. This chapter looks at some of the components of this myth, its foregrounding of the 'heroic' male body and of processes of learning, and its reinvention across different cultures and historical contexts. The word 'Shaolin' has been attached to films about the temple, to films about Shaolin-derived fighting styles, and to films about anti-Qing rebels who deployed Shaolin fighting arts. Sometimes its presence in a title signifies none of the above but can be attached, indiscriminately, to English-language prints of kung fu films as a guarantee of shape-throwing mayhem. More recently, *Shaolin* was the title of a PlayStation game (THQ 1999). While scholars are largely sceptical of the Chinese saying that "all the martial arts known under heaven began in Shaolin" (Reid and Croucher 1995: 63), for generic purposes they might as well have done. Shaolin is central to the mythopoetic origins of Chinese Boxing – fighting movements derived from nature, lethal abilities mediated by spiritual concerns, patriotic rebellion and underground movements, southern identity and heritage, the dynamics of learning and transmission. The Temple also marks the beginning of the kung fu film's 'family tree', stretching from the senior monk Zhi Shan to the films of Lau Kar-leung. However, while the Temple was a mainstay of *wu xia* novels like *The Ten Tigers of Guangdong* (c.1950s), it did not figure prominently in the cinema prior to 1974. The Shaolin films can be seen as a refinement of the kung fu film's dialogue with colonialism. Shaolin heroes like Hung Hei-kwun constitute a kind of diaspora, cast out of paradise by aliens who pose as 'Chinese' (anti-imperialism inflected by anti-Maoism). Moreover, the predominant southern focus suggests a revival of the genre's interest in the 'local' (manifested earlier in the Wong Fei-hung series). While the Shaw Brothers Shaolin films are located institutionally within Mandarin dialect cinema, culturally they anticipate the Cantonese emphasis of the 'new' Hong Kong cinema that emerged at the end of the 1970s. But the cycle also suggests a dialogue between the 'local' and the 'global', specifically the international interest in kung fu. *Heroes Two*, arguably the most influential kung fu film of the mid-1970s, was predated by the American television series *Kung Fu* (1972–5), which clearly had an impact in Hong Kong. According to Jackie Chan, "Before *Kung Fu*, I'd never heard of Chinese martial arts, of the Shaolin Temple, of Buddhism and warrior monks" (Logan 1998c: 22) – in Hong Kong, David Carradine was known affectionately as *cho man jai* (grasshopper boy).[1]

If Shaolin is not exactly the birthplace of kung fu, it *does* seem to have been a significant site in the transmission of Chan Buddhism from India to China. Unlike Taoism and Confucianism, Buddhism was a 'foreign' influence in China, but it converges with 'Chinese' martial arts in the figure of the Indian monk Bodhidharma (or Da-mo in Chinese). Chinese-Indian interchange had a long history, largely determined by trade, but there had been sufficient philosophical dialogue for a Chinese Buddhist community to be established as early as 65 AD (Reid and Croucher 1995: 29). According to the legend, Bodhidharma traveled from India to China in the 6th century AD. There are some entertaining variations on the details of his visit, but for our purposes, his most important legacy is the exercises he taught the weakened monks who fell asleep while trying to meditate (Chow and Spangler 1982: 11–12). It remains unclear whether Bodhidharma taught fighting techniques as such – his contribution sounds more like *qigong*, the cultivation of inner strength through controlled breathing. But the Indian-Chinese interchange does seem to have extended to fighting techniques – one of the frescoes still intact at the Henan monastery shows Chinese and Indian monks training together. Reid and Croucher credit Bodhidharma with another cultural legacy – *wu de* (martial virtue), "discipline, restraint, humility and respect for human life" (1995: 27). Shaolin kung fu – or, at least, its mythical underpinnings – seems to have been transcultural from the start.

With its abstract investment in heroism and 'knightly' virtue, Manichean moral structures and vague sense of time and place, the *wu xia pian* sometimes seems so determinedly escapist that its meaning threatens to dissolve into air. But the Shaolin-based kung fu film at least nods in the direction of history and cultural myth, inviting comparison with the western or the Arthurian legends. As Ng Ho suggests, both the American western and the Shaolin kung fu film "take historical or quasi-historical figures and subject them to the process of myth-making" (1980b: 69). In the words of *The Man Who Shot Liberty Valance* (1962), the Shaolin films 'print the Legend', but also continually re-write and re-define that Legend. The development of the Shaolin legends is comparable to the evolution of the *wu xia*'s other defining myth, the stories collected together as *The Water Margin/All Men Are Brothers/Shui-hu*. The events of *The Water Margin*, detailing the exploits of a band of chivalrous outlaws, date back to the Northern Sung period (960–1127). The stories developed through the Yuan period (1280–1368), adding characters and incidents, but with no attempt to construct a continuous narrative – the stories existed independently or in cycles (Liu 1967: 109). The first integrated *Water Margin* was written at the end of the Yuan Dynasty, enlarged during the Ming period (in 1614) and subsequently 'edited' to deglamourise the rebels during the Qing Dynasty (110). The Shaolin tales are much more recent – the Qing-era novel *Evergreen* was already trying to portray our heroes in a less than flattering light. But their development is like a compressed version of *The Water Margin*'s evolution – adding characters, isolating individual heroes to relate their exploits in more detail. The Shaolin cycle, like many large mythical narratives, is distinctly non-linear, sometimes moving backwards rather than forwards, frequently offering revisions and embellishments of recurring episodes.

Two distinct temples appear in Shaolin texts. The northern monastery in the Songshan (Central Mountain) range in Henan still stands, in spite of at least two burnings and a long period of disrepair prior to its re-opening in the early 1980s. The Henan Temple figures in the *Kung Fu* television series and is used as an actual location in the Jet Li *Shaolin Temple* films that led indirectly to its new status as heritage site. The Jiulianshan Temple in the southern Fujian province appears to have been burned down more comprehensively (in 1738) leaving no physical trace, but its obliteration only seems to have aided its mythical power. Most of Zhang Che's and Lau Kar-leung's Shaolin films are about the Southern Temple and chronicle the exploits of 'Shaolin Tigers' like Hung Hei-kwun, Fong Sai-yuk, the San-de (Three Virtues) monk and Wu Wei-kin. It is the Jiulianshan Temple that figures in the southern family tree – from Zhi Shan we follow the line to Lu Acai, Wong Kei-ying and Wong Fei-hung.

Ng Ho identifies three central foundations for the 1970s Shaolin film – the period 1723–1911 (the latter part of the Qing Dynasty), the events surrounding the burning of the temple and spread of Shaolin techniques to Southern China, and the exploits of the heroes of Guangdong (1980b: 156). The villains are invariably either Manchu Emperors and their underlings or the *wu dang* martial artists who aided them in the burning of the monastery. The destruction of the Temple(s) is most popularly aligned with the presence there of anti-Qing rebels who are thought to have taken refuge at Shaolin from about 1662. The monastery had long been a refuge for rebels, criminals and other dissidents (Ng 1980: 58), and the word 'Shaolin' often refers to these secular activists more than their nominally Buddhist benefactors. In the kung fu films of the early 1970s, Japan stood in for a range of colonial aggressors – *The Chinese Boxer*, *Fist of Fury* and *Hapkido* (1972) are all too geographically specific about where China's woes emanate from, and all are set in the post-1911, pre-World War Two period. The Qing dynasty (1644–1911), during which Han Chinese were ruled by the northern Manchurians, is characterized by Charles O. Hucker as "by far the least burdensome of any imposed on the Chinese by aliens" (1978: 144). But kung fu films certainly do not see it like that. Hucker identifies an initial "Manchu Chinese honeymoon" (146) that lasted well into the eighteenth century, but the Manchus wore out their welcome more comprehensively in their handling of Western incursions into China – the so-called Opium Wars (1839–42) and concessions like the Treaty of Nanjing that established ports for the English, Dutch, Spanish, French and Portuguese. Zhang Che claims that the Qing Dynasty was a taboo period prior to the early 1970s (1999: 21), not least because of the queue (shaven head with 'pigtail' at the back) imposed on the Hans by the Manchus. *Blood Brothers/Ci Ma* (1972) compromised over the queue by leaving the head unshaved – this became the Qing-era hairstyle of Shaws' 1970s films, often allowing eighteenth-century and 1970s coiffures to co-exist on the same heads. The Manchus tend to be represented as iniquitous tyrants, but in other ways they functioned as more flexible bad guys than the crudely stereotyped 'Jap bastards' of the early 1970s. Both foreign and, in retrospect, 'Chinese', they could still allude to colonialism, but Ng Ho suggests that they can also be seen as Maoist, with Ming Patriots complementing them as pro-republicans (1980b: 59). Perhaps the Qing's appeal as a 'bad' dynasty also lay in it being the last, replaced by the short-lived republic and an optimistic reminder that inhospitable governments do carry a sell-by date. Interestingly, the later Shaolin films made at the actual Henan temple largely steer clear of the Qing Dynasty, favouring the Tang-era story of the "13 cudgel-playing monks" who helped Emperor Tai Zheng against foreign aggressors. The 1980s monks are loyal to 'the Party' and the new Chinese economy, and an effective advertisement for tourism.

The *wu dang* grow in prominence as the sub-genre pays closer attention to the intricacies of martial styles. The story goes that Zhang Sanfeng, a Shaolin graduate of the Song Dynasty, formulated the principles of the 'soft' or 'internal' arts (including Tai Chi) at *wu dang* mountain (Ng 1980b: 61; Chow and Spangler 1982: 23–4). The difference between the 'Hard' (Shaolin) and the 'Soft' (*wu dang*) has been likened to a fight between a mongoose and a snake – the former is tensed, aggressive, attacking in a straight line, the latter deceptively relaxed, moving in curved, circular motions (Reid and Croucher 1995: 60). In the Shaolin myths and the films inspired by them, the Shaolin/*wu dang* rivalry turns distinctly ugly. Several Shaolin masters are supposed to have defected to *wu dang*, the most infamous being Bai Mei, the White Eyebrow Monk, who participated in the burning of the Jiulianshan Temple. In *The Men From the Monastery/Shaolin Zidi* (1974), *wu dang* traitors are nominally identified in the temple, but the film does not elaborate – Bai Mei appears ominously in silhouette, unnamed (at least in the English-language version). The internal arts figure more prominently in *Shaolin Martial Arts/Hong Quan yu Yong Chun* (1974), where they offer perverse contrast to the 'wholesome' masculinity of the Shaolin heroes. The blood-soaked crotches and rears of Zhang Che's heroes pave the way for the ambiguously gendered Bai Mei (Lo Lieh), whose lethal groin becomes a kind of *vagina dentata* in *Executioners from Shaolin* (1976) and *Fist of the White Lotus/Hong Wending Sanpo Bailian Jiao* (1980).

The Men From the Monastery: 'Heroic' Masculinity in Zhang Che's Shaolin Cycle

According to Verina Glaessner, "Shaws films ... are individual films only nominally: they function like serials – the names may change but the characters are recognisable from film to film (as are the costumes and sets)" (1974: 111). In the Shaolin films, even the names do not change much and the same shots of the temple burning turn up in film after film.[2] Seeing *Heroes Two* and *The Men From the Monastery*, one could be forgiven for thinking that one is a sequel to the other, but it would be a challenge to work out which is supposed to come first, given that both films follow Hung Hei-kwun (Chen Guantai) and Fong Sai-yuk (Fu Sheng) after the destruction of the monastery. Rather, they offer different perspectives on the same apocryphal events (Fong Sai-yuk's duel with 'Tiger' Lei, Wu Wei-kin's attack on a textile mill). *Heroes Two* is closely focused on the relationship between Hung and Fong (its Chinese title is the two characters' names), tricked into fighting each other by the Manchus. Wracked with guilt about his role in Hung's capture, Fong sets about a daring rescue. An early, failed attempt has him pause in mid-fight to beg Hung's forgiveness. He is then beaten to the point of coughing up blood by way of masochistic expiation. When the two combine their Tiger and Crane fists, respectively, against the Manchu General, the union suggests a kind of emotional/physical intimacy as much as pragmatic technique. *The Men From the Monastery* is divided into four chapters – one each devoted to Fong Sai-yuk, Wu Wei-kin and Hung Hei-kwun, and a fourth which picks up after the temple's burning (*Heroes Two*'s opening shot) as the Shaolin heroes take on the Manchu troops. Two more Shaolin films were made the same year. *Five Shaolin Masters/Shaolin Wuzu*

(1974) follows the 'Five Ancestors of Shaolin': Cai Dezhong (Ti Lung), Fang Dahong (Meng Fai), Ma Chaoxing (Fu Sheng), Hu Deding (David Chiang) and Li Shikai (Qi Guanjun). Although the Five Ancestors are usually thought to have survived the burning of the Henan temple in the north (Ng 1980b: 59), *Five Shaolin Masters* has them surviving the same inferno as Hung Hei-kwun and Fong Sai-yuk, effectively weaving them into the southern legends. *Shaolin Temple* confirms the impression by having the five train alongside Fong, Hung and Wu, with Ti Lung and David Chiang playing the same roles from the earlier film. *Shaolin Martial Arts* does not deal directly with the temple, but the spread of Shaolin techniques through Southern China. *Disciples of Shaolin/Hongquan Xiaozi* (1975) is further removed from the temple. Its hero, Kuan Feng-yi (Fu Sheng), is a *Hung Gar* Boxer (as the Chinese title spells out). But, as Lau Shing-hon argues, the film has more in common with films like *Boxer from Shantung/Ma Yongzhen* (1971), dealing with "a working-class youth whose martial skills enable him to advance himself in society, but whose fate turns out to be tragic self-destruction" (1980b: 91). All five films were directed by Zhang Che, written by Ni Kuang and choreographed by Lau Kar-leung, sometimes in collaboration with Tang Xia. Between them, Zhang and Lau put the cinematic Shaolin legends in place. After their split, each made their own Shaolin films; Lau's increasingly revisionist, Zhang's increasingly repetitive. *Shaolin Temple* makes some important contributions to the mythology and ties together the initial cycle. Focusing on the training of the southern heroes, it is one of the first films to depict the Luohan Hall, site of the legendary 'Wooden Men', the lethal mechanical figures that students must pass in order to fully graduate. By contrast, *Shaolin Avengers/Fang Shiyu Yu Hu Huiqian* (1976) simply expands the Fong Sai-yuk and Wu Wei-kin episodes from *The Men From the Monastery*. Its only interest lies in some elaborations on Fong Sai-yuk's physical conditioning and vulnerability to anal assault.

If the swordplay films of the 1960s favoured 'Lady Knights', the films of Bruce Lee and Zhang Che have been seen as 're-masculinising' a Chinese cinema dominated by female stars. "There are *heroes* too in history!" bleated one contemporary critic (quoted by Bren 1998: 83), while Zhang wrote passionately about *yang gang* (male attributes) in 'My Views on Cinema' (1999: 21). In Lee's films, his body spoke for him, a *muscular* Chinese body that, as Tasker argues, countered a "history of 'feminizing' Western representations of Chinese men" (1997: 322). If Lee's machismo carried political force on a global scale, Zhang's concerns seem more local (or regional) – get the girls out of the *wu xia pian*, fill the screen with half-naked male pulchritude. Muscular bodies occupy a complex and perhaps unstable position within Hong Kong culture. For one thing, *built* Chinese bodies are a comparatively recent phenomenon, part of what has been seen as the colonial government's attempts to shift local identification away from China – in the 'Mr Hong Kong' contest, "the image of the Hong Kong body was designed to fit the modern Western mode of health, posture and physique" (Lo 1999: 107). In this respect, Bruce Lee's body always complicates the nationalist themes in his films, while Zhang Che's simply fetishize rippling torsos. This spectacle has been linked also to the emergence of a Chinese middle class in Hong Kong who went to "gaze at 'healthy' bodies, and realised their subconscious need for worshipping the muscular beauty" (Lau 1999: 32). If the argument here is that 'healthy' bodies equal wealthy bodies, then the erotic (and narcissistic) dimension of this affluent gaze is rather more than a subtext.

In *Yang + Yin: Gender in Chinese Cinema* (1996), Stanley Kwan points out that the martial arts film was one of the few vehicles in which a gay Chinese man could see male bodies on display, while one website describes Zhang as 'The Master of the Longing Look' ('Black Tauna' 2000). Zhang's homoerotic spectacle has also attracted female fans. Sarah Wheatley (2000) celebrates "noble enemies who didn't know whether to kill each other or kiss each other", played by "a herd of lovelies, all talented and acrobatic". Karen Tarapata, too, rhapsodises over "the most eye-blistering male beauty ever tossed on screen" (2000: 82):

An open vest cinched over a hairless chest. A gold-wrapped topknot or pony-tail. A long gown flicked aside before a fight ... These boys have total animal presence, but they're clean; they don't smell. They have virtually no body hair, just impossibly thick, shiny braids to swing around their necks before they begin the carnage. (82–3)

Some of this runs the risk of conspiring with the West's emasculating representations of Chinese men, as well as a pervasive exoticising of the other – "From the waist up he's exposed iron, from the waist down ... concealed silk" (82). And yet, the lower half of the male torso is *not* all that it seems in these films, figuring both as absence and penetrative target. In *The Men From the Monastery*, Fong Sai-yuk and Wu Wei-kin expire with the crotches of their white trousers soaked crimson. Fong is stabbed from below in mid-leap, because, we are told, his body is invulnerable elsewhere. *Shaolin Avengers* goes into more detail about what we might call Fong's Achilles' Rectum. He is soaked in painful herbal oils, whipped raw by his brother and then given a second agonising soak. His mother Miao Cuihua explains that the rectum is his one vulnerable point, penetrable precisely because the oils work for surfaces, not orifices. In other words, the male body can never be fully armoured or distinguished from penetrable 'feminine' flesh. Fong jokes that he will walk with his hands over his rear from now on (the old homophobic joke finds its true context) and covers it defensively when he almost falls into a pit of spikes.[3] Finally, he is impaled by Bai Mei, the White Eyebrow Priest, a figure who, later films will reveal, conceals mysteries of his own "from the waist down".

Zhang made his name with *wu xia pian* like *The One-Armed Swordsman* and *Golden Swallow*, films which arguably facilitated his interest in "male potency, individualism and fellowship" (Teo 1997: 102) more than the Shaolin films would. Jerry Liu discerns one of Zhang's overriding obsessions as the exaltation of death, "the very essence of transcendence", an "orgasmic fulfillment of the hidden 'self'" (1981/96: 160).[4] In *Have Sword, Will Travel/Baobiao* (1969), David Chiang and Ti Lung are ostensibly rivals for Li Ching. When Ti enters a pagoda filled to the rafters with swordsmen, Li begs Chiang to help him. An extraordinary subjective fantasy sequence projects Chiang's foreknowledge of the inevitable outcome – he sees himself hacked bloodily to pieces and the happy couple riding off into the sunset. Cut to the present – Chiang agrees without hesitation, having imagined the most satisfying death for a lone swordsman. In *New One-Armed Swordsman/ Xin Dubi Dao* (1970), Lei Li (David Chiang) severs his own arm when he is defeated by the villain, leaving it pinned to a tree as a reminder of his retreat from *jianghu*. Chiang's graphic, and literal, trophy of a *dead part of himself* recalls Georges Bataille's comments on sacrificial mutilation as a "rupture of personal homogeneity and the projection *outside the self* of a part of oneself" (1989: 68). For Bataille, this automutilation is often a marker of the entry into adult society. In *New One-Armed Swordsman*, it is the first stage in Chiang's transformation from cocky duelist into someone who will fight *for* something, primarily his love for another male hero, Ti Lung's dashing-but-doomed Feng.

Both Tony Rayns (1984: 51) and Bey Logan (1995: 46) locate the Shaw Brothers Shaolin films within Lau Kar-leung's ouevre as much as, if not more than, Zhang Che's. Lau and Zhang were Southern and Northern Chinese respectively, and the Shaolin films are predominantly southern in focus. *The Three Styles of Hung School's Kung Fu*, the documentary 'preface' to *Heroes Two*, suggests most strongly that Zhang was only nominally 'director' and Lau rather more than 'fighting instructor'. The narration clearly sets out the historical/mythical premises of the series – the temple as centre of resistance, its influence throughout Southern China, and the famous Guangdong heroes.

If there is a third 'author' to the series, then it is Shaw Brothers' star system. As Tarapata's comments suggest, the celebration of male heroism was inextricable from the commodification of male beauty. If Wang Yu was the first 'new style' martial arts star, it was arguably the pairing of David Chiang and Ti Lung that established the studio's two archetypes, often paired as "smouldering masculine couples" (Bordwell 2000a: 250). Ti Lung was muscular, incandescent machismo, while Chiang expressed hesitancy even in his

Fig. 3 Opposites attract: androgynous Fu Sheng as Fong Sai-yuk and macho Chen Guantai as Hung Hei-kwun in *Heroes Two*

swagger, was slighter of build, more sensitive. His endurance of pain was somehow more perverse than the teeth-gritting stoicism of Wang Yu. When he learns he is to be tortured to death in *Blood Brothers*, he grins like a schoolboy who refuses to take his punishment seriously. Ti Lung's successors include Chen Guantai and brawny 'Venom' Luo Mang. In his early roles, Chen Guantai is often cast as uncomplicated beefcake, but the Shaolin films transform him into the south's ultimate 'Father', Hung Hei-kwun, originator of the most paradigmatic Southern Boxing style, *Hung Gar*.[5] He is virtually the sole survivor of *The Men From the Monastery*, and an end title tells us that his fighting style is still practised today. In *Challenge of the Masters*, Chen plays another key 'Father', Lu Acai, teacher of Wong Kei-ying and his son Wong Fei-hung. Interestingly, Shaws increasingly favoured the 'David Chiang' type in heroic roles, a figure who became more androgynous in the form of Fu Sheng, Qi Guanjun, Wong Yue and Jiang Sheng. Fu Sheng was arguably Shaws' ultimate boy-babe, with his floppy black fringe; armed with a fan in *Heroes Two*, his precocious swagger comes over as more than a little coquettish. *Disciples of Shaolin* is the ultimate hymn to Fu's beauty. In one shot, he listens to his beloved gold watch, smiling dreamily, an image later replayed in a montage as Huang (Qi Guanjun) remembers his fallen friend. If Chen Guantai was the perfect Hung Hei-kwun, Fu complemented him as the mercurial Fong Sai-yuk. In *Heroes Two*, they are visually represented as yin and yang – Fu dresses in white, Chen in black; Fu has a pale complexion, Chen is dark-skinned; Fu is comparatively slight, Chen powerfully built. Fong Sai-yuk has a generic history second only to Wong Fei-hung, including a long-running black-and-white series (1938–68) and, more recently, two films starring Jet Li, and a Taiwanese television series. The myth is largely based on the Qing-era novel *Evergreen*, in which it was Fong's mother, Miao Cuihua, who trained him. Miao not only taught him kung fu but conditioned him to near-invulnerability. He was bathed in herbal oils as a baby, swathed in layers of bamboo strips, wooden rods and iron bars; training with iron boots on, aged three; learning stances and fighting forms between the ages of six and seven:

> By the age of fourteen, his versatility extended to all kinds of weaponry. Endowed with exceptional strength, his body was all but invulnerable. Fiery and hot-tempered, he was an unrelenting champion of the oppressed. (Quoted in Ng 1980b: 66)

Fong's story can be played as comedy or tragedy – he had killed 'Tiger' Lei in a duel at the age of 14 (a conflict depicted in *The Men From the Monastery* and *Shaolin Avengers*) and died in his early twenties, possibly during the burning of the temple. The black-and-white films represented his sexual immaturity through the convention of dragging up female players like Shi Yanzi in the role; *Fong Sai Yuk* makes much of Fong as irrepressible 'mother's boy', with Josephine Siao stealing the film as Miao Cuihua. Miao is a sterner figure in *Shaolin Avengers*, who implicitly 'castrates' both sons – Fong's conditioning becomes an intense sadomasochistic ritual, while his brother Fang Xiaoyu (Li Chen-pao) is forced into celibacy. The 1970s Fong, not surprisingly, is the one doomed to die young – in some ways the prodigious Bruce Lee had been a Fong Sai-yuk figure and Fu Sheng, too, died prematurely. The cinematic Fong seems to hover just this side of sexual maturity, a child-man, the prototype for the younger Shaolin heroes. Qi Guanjun lacks Fu Sheng's mischievous charisma, and his bodybuilding background equipped him with a more muscular frame – Zhang Che clearly grew increasingly enraptured with Qi's impressive back. But he is similarly adolescent, with his delicate features and doleful eyes. In *Disciples of Shaolin*, he is miscast as Fu's senior (a role better suited to Chen Guantai), but one effect is that his anger at his friend's unwitting exploitation plays more as hurt rejection as the re-united 'couple' spend less time together. In *Shaolin Martial Arts*, neither seems to know quite what to do with their female love interest. Qi Guanjun goes in for chaste hand-holding, while Fu Sheng keeps his at a safer distance with buckets of water; in one scene, he positively recoils at the sight of her. The Shaolin boy-men are auto-erotic, more interested in their own bodies than anyone else's, as though to counter the risk of feminisation. *Disciples of Shaolin* is a rare exception – Kuan/Fu moves in with one of his boss's courtesans and their relationship is unusually tender. But he still chooses death over staying with her – already mortally wounded, he leaves her with a boyish smile and sets off for a battle he cannot possibly survive.

If Zhang Che's earlier heroes embrace identity-affirming martyrdom, the Shaolin films develop a growing investment in continuity, the survival of a tradition; it is hard to resist seeing this as a dialogue between the series' two 'auteurs'. When we first meet Hung Hei-kwun in *The Men From the Monastery*, he is hiding in a brothel. One of the prostitutes asks him why he fights the Manchus when all Emperors are effectively the same. He responds angrily, but does not exactly *answer* her question (any more than the films pin down why the Qing Dynasty is so intolerable). His real answer lies in his ominous greeting to the Qing soldiers he meets outside – "I kill Manchus", he says with a smile. Of course, "I kill Manchus" is closely related to "I am killed by Manchus", as Fong and Wu demonstrate, but Hung survives (in spite of himself?) because the myth declares that he must. Wu Wei-kin, on the other hand, epitomises the brooding adolescent, using the Shaolin Temple as a kind of Charles Atlas gym to stop having Manchu sand kicked in his face. His episode re-tells the story of Wu's revenge on the union of Cantonese weavers who killed his father. His attack on their textile mill, like Fong's killing of 'Tiger' Lei, is thought to have contributed to the Shaolin/*wu dang* conflict (Ng 1980b: 62).[6] Wu launches three unsuccessful attacks before being rescued by Fong, who recommends the temple to him. Shaolin does, indeed, make a man of Wu and he exacts appropriate retribution. But his real destiny is saved for the film's final episode, mortally wounded but vowing to "kill some more first". The film uses what would became a favourite device in Zhang Che's films – as a hero's death approaches, the image shifts to monochrome, with red filters underlining the bloodier moments. This crude device lifts Wu's martyrdom out of the rest of the film, but Fong goes one better. Writhing in agony, sword handle between his legs, he observes that he "may as well end it" – as he pulls the sword out, a freeze-frame captures his gruesome demise. By de-penetrating himself, he once again affirms his identity before dying.

The temple itself barely figures in these films until *Shaolin Temple* in 1976, and is usually only seen in flames. In *The Men From the Monastery*, it appears as an interior only at the point of Fong and Wu's graduation. In *Five Shaolin Masters*, the eponymous heroes are scattered, but effectively re-constitute the temple, and in doing so, anticipate the focus on learning of what Meaghan Morris calls the "Shaolin pedagogy" films (1998: 10). As the five masters recruit Ming Patriots, each acquires their own personal, seemingly invincible nemesis.

Fig. 4 The Shaw Brothers pin-up factory: Meng Fai, Qi Guanjun, Fu Sheng, David Chiang and Ti Lung pledge allegiance in *Five Shaolin Masters*

Recognising that their own fighting skills are inferior, they conclude that the learning process must continue. Their Masters are dead, but by returning to the charred monastery, they once again undergo its pedagogic birthing process, becoming their own masters and re-*embodying* the temple just as San-de will do with his revisionist '36th Chamber'. All five arrive (as legend dictates) at underground rallying point the Red Flower Pavilion, where the Hung Tong (effectively the first Triads) was formed. But the 'Zhang Che code' dictates that even ancestors can be sacrificed, and two out of the five arrive dead.

Shaolin Temple (1976) temporally precedes the earlier films in the series, and deals with the initiation of secular students into Shaolin, a pragmatic decision to ensure the survival of Shaolin kung fu as Manchu hostility increases. As a narrative where the outcome is known to the point of overfamiliarity, *Shaolin Temple* looks at the functioning of the temple itself; its training techniques, its code of ethics, the tension between Buddhist doctrine and patriotic testosterone, the traitors within who conspire with the Qing government. Students master *Wing Chun*, Tiger-Crane, 'weightless' techniques, Shaolin pole and chain-whip, and, in the film's most memorable sequence, Fong Sai-yuk (Fu Sheng) tackles the Wooden Men as he and Wu Wei-kin (Qi Guanjun) escape to settle (offscreen) scores. Such detailed depictions of the vicissitudes of learning became more prominent as the cycle moved into a second phase.

Learning and the Liminal: The 36th Chamber and Beyond

> When the limen becomes the "liminal" – a phase one moves through in order to get from one fixed social structure to another – it becomes a powerful place of potency and potentiality in culture. Ambiguous and paradoxical, it is a time for teaching and decision, play and experiment. When one remains in the liminal for an extended period of time, profound changes can occur. (Harrison-Pepper 1993: 45)

The kung fu film has on ongoing interest in the process of learning, the transmission (and embodiment) of knowledge, the relationship between masters and their disciples. *Heroes Two* and *The Men From the Monastery* elide the learning process and keep the 'masters' offscreen, but *Five Shaolin Masters, Shaolin Martial Arts* and *Shaolin Temple* weave the learning process more deeply into the narrative structure and initiate the 'Shaolin pedagogy' film. There are essentially four sources of learning in the martial arts film:

1. Nature — Animals (Tiger, Crane, Snake, Dragon, Leopard, Monkey), insects (Praying Mantis) and natural elements (Wood, Earth, Fire, Water, Metal).

2. A book or manual — The book may substitute for an absent master, it may be 'incomplete', damaged or with pages missing; in *Executioners from Shaolin, Tai Chi Master/Taiji Zhang Sanfeng* (1993) and *The Blade/Dao* (1995), the pupil must effectively 'complete' the book himself.

3. Shaolin 'technology' — For example the Wooden (or Bronze) Men depicted in *Shaolin Temple* (1976), *Shaolin Wooden Men/Shaolin Muren Xiang* (1976) and *Eighteen Bronze Men* (1976), and the mechanical wolves in *Eight Diagram Pole Fighter* and similar devices in *36th Chamber of Shaolin*.

4. The 'Master' or *shifu* (master/father) — A relationship founded on discipline and subservience, Tony Rayns characterises the Master/Pupil 'gestalt' as "impersonal sadomasochistic units, devoid of all sexual connotations, with both teacher and student driven by spiritual will" (1984b: 52). Roger Garcia describes the process as a "training/learning/ birth process ... framed in pain", but also a form of "hereditary practice" whereby the pupil is moulded into a "facsimile" of the master in order for history to survive (1980a: 123). Given the operatic background of many kung fu stars, *jingju* is an obvious referent here; Jo Riley explains that another word for master is *laoshi, shi* meaning to imitate (1997: 22). In Chinese Opera, the master's body is the teaching text, reproduced in the student by imitation so that performers embody not only themselves alone but also the chain of history that produced them (39).

As Shaolin-Manchu conflict escalates into fatalities in *Shaolin Martial Arts*, the Manchus bring in two *wu dang* heavies, cobra-eyed Yu Pi (Wang Lung-wei), absorbing blows with his *qi*-empowered stomach, and 'Iron Robe' master Pa Kang (Leung Kar-yan). The bulk of the film details the training of two sets of students to defeat these formidable opponents. Ho (Lau Kar-fai) and Mi (Li Chen-pao) learn the (northern) Rolling Claw and the Eagle Claw technique. When both students are killed, Li Yao (Fu Sheng) and Chen Pao-jung (Qi Guanjun) are sent to learn (southern) Tiger-Crane and *Wing Chun*, respectively, from cantankerous Yuen Siu-tin and taciturn Feng Yi. Both must submit to beatings, painful training methods and capricious authority; Chen earns a grudging nod of approval when he can ring a heavy bell with a one-inch punch. But Li sees the 'good' *shifu* within Yuen's trademark cane-wielding martinet; a point-of-view shot morphs him into the kindly master they left back in Guangdong.

Both Garcia (1980a) and Rayns (1984a) identify the Master as an increasingly problematic figure in Lau Kar-leung's films, but Lau is certainly not alone in depicting heroes with *shifu* trouble. In the formulaic *Shaolin Wooden Men*, Jackie Chan's mute hero, Dummy, joins the temple in order to avenge his father. The slow pace of Shaolin training frustrates Dummy, but he finds two alternative (competing) masters; a Buddhist nun who tries to teach him the 'soft' techniques, and Shaolin renegade Fat Yu (Kam Kong), now imprisoned in a cave by the monks. Dummy is seduced by the 'bad father', who promises to teach him how to defeat the Wooden Men out of spite towards his former Shaolin comrades. But there is a problem in this relationship; Fat Yu is revealed to be the killer of Dummy's father. The pre-Oedipal nature of Dummy's story is underlined by the film's climactic focus on the voice. Dummy releases himself from his self-imposed vow of silence, while Fat Yu's killer technique is called The Lion's Roar. Fat Yu simultaneously embodies Master-Father and Father-Killer, and Dummy cannot bring himself to administer the *coup de grace* during their fight: "Once a teacher, always a teacher", he avows, and kneels in submission. Fat Yu must resolve this conundrum by dispatching himself, but not before telling his pupil how proud he is of him. In doing so, he ensures that the wild 'bad father' from the cave wins after all.

The 'Shaolin technology' films take the training process back to the temple, but it is *The 36th Chamber of Shaolin* that most fully explores the monastery as a site of learning. The film, based on another Shaolin hero, San-de,[7] effectively follows a three-act structure. The first section establishes Manchu oppression in southern China, as Liu Yude (San-de's secular name) witnesses the death of his teacher and father. He escapes to the temple, where the second (and longest) act takes place, detailing his slow and painful transition from novice to master. For the third act, he is cast out of the temple, but able to embody

Fig. 5 Creativity in Shaolin's liminal space: San-de (Lau Kar-fai) in *The 36th Chamber of Shaolin*

it sufficiently to transform Guangdong into what Rayns calls "a factory for the production of a patriotic resistance" (1984b: 52). As he recruits anti-Qing rebels, he trains well-known future Shaolin heroes like Hung Hei-kwun, Lu Acai and the rice-grinder Zhuangmi Liu.

This is not the "quick fix" temple attended by Wu Wei-kin in *The Men From the Monastery*, and exceeds the detail of *Shaolin Temple*. San-de must negotiate floating logs to acquire balance; carry heavy water pails with bladed armbands on to keep his arms straight; strike a gong repeatedly with a heavily weighted pole; develop eye-coordination by focusing on a rocking candle reflector, his face burned by incense burners if he turns his head; headbutt sandbags, while chastised by a metallic hand wielded by a senior monk. These sequences precede the learning of actual fighting techniques, which too are "framed in pain" – students kick *through* burning hoops to shatter suspended pots; poling techniques are policed by revolving metal teeth surrounding the students' arms and chastising any errors. San-de must interact, too, with the temple's ethics; he is both re-formed by monastic seclusion from worldly concerns and finally cast out for trying to re-connect the temple to the outside world. Having mastered the 35 chambers, his hypothetical thirty-sixth would teach the populace of South China. It is here that the monastery can be, as Garcia suggests, both fertile and sterile (1980a: 123). Like Rayns, he characterises Shaolin as a "factory", but also observes its "womb-like" structure – it is San-de, he argues, who is "explorer and fertiliser", making the temple more than a mere "archive, a preserver of tradition" (124). San-de, in turn, gives birth to the Shaolin temple of patriotic myth, the one with strong links to southern identity and those styles (*Hung Gar, Wing Chun*) that later traveled to Hong Kong.

Sally Harrison-Pepper identifies a "single dramatic occasion" in certain martial arts, the examining for a new rank, as one in which "borders are crossed, identity symbols stripped away, and the person becomes most teachable" (1993: 44). The three-act structure of *The 36ᵗʰ Chamber of Shaolin* is not dissimilar to the three phases of certain initiation rituals – Separation (the isolation of the initiate), Margin/*Limen* (the rite itself, which may be painful and/or difficult) and Aggregation (reintegration) (44–5). It is the middle phase that is important here, because it provides access to a *liminal* state. *Limen* means threshold, which, as Harrison-Pepper notes, "is not a space one remains in for long, nor a place one notices in the act of crossing" (45). The "liminal" is a phase rather than a moment, and one that brings about "profound changes".

Entry into the liminal is marked by surrender; "one must submit to the power of the liminal in order to pass through to reincorporation" (45). San-de becomes a kind of non-person, soaked, burned, bruised, a *tabula rasa*, "suspended between two states of being" (45). But the experience of the liminal complicates Master/Pupil transmission because it facilitates something other than the replication of the *shifu*. San-de is the consummate Shaolin graduate because he transforms the ethics of the temple without openly challenging them – he is humbly respectful, but still establishes his thirty-sixth Chamber when he leaves. He has already established his ablity to teach himself, to effectively blur the Master/Pupil division, to remain suspended "*between* established cultural systems" (45). As part of Shaolin's hierarchical promotion, he is challenged to an ongoing duel with a senior monk armed with Butterfly Swords. San-de is defeated when he uses traditional Shaolin weaponry, but creates his own weapon (the three-section cudgel) when a training session reveals the flexibility of shattered bamboo. When San-de achieves 'Reintegration', he is able to *embody* the temple, not because (as in *Five Shaolin Masters*) it no longer exists, but because he can reconnect it to History and/or Myth.

If *The 36th Chamber of Shaolin* is the most persuasive version of the pedagogic narrative, *Eight Diagram Pole Fighter* is a darker reworking – it is precisely about the failure of the process San-de undergoes. Fifth Yang's (Lau Kar-fai) suspension between two systems – the patriotic/familial drive for revenge, Buddhist pacifism – is more of a problem. For one thing, he forcibly inserts himself into the temple, hacking off his hair and burning the ritual *jie ba* into his skull, unable to *submit* to Shaolin liminal space. Trained as a soldier, it is more difficult for him to train as a monk and his relationship *is* more fractious; "I know I'm still violent", he acknowledges. His broken spear, reinvented as a pole, is a constant reminder of divided loyalties. The monks refuse to kill the wolves that threaten the temple; they learn 'defanging' pole techniques, which will be used against the Mongol aggressors in the final scene. When Fifth Yang defeats his (reluctant) Master (Kao Fai) and receives his red sash, he is reminded that "Lord Buddha is against killing ... remember the vow you made to Buddha". But Fifth Yang's final battle is played out amidst piles of coffins – the weight of his dead brothers and father is too strong. He cannot be reincorporated either into his family or the temple. David Bordwell likens his fate to that of Ethan Edwards at the end of *The Searchers* (1956) – he has nowhere to go and disappears, similarly, into the wilderness (2000a: 253).

If the experience of the liminal positions the martial arts neophyte in an *in-between* zone, this crossing of borders can also extend to gender identity. Some of this can be traced back to the influence of Taoism, which hinges both on a set of binary oppositions (yang/yin, light/dark, male/female) and the principle that all things contain these two opposing forces. But Taoism is not free from gender essentialism – 'feminine' yin energy is "gentle and receptive", representing "all things that are expanding and flexible"; 'masculine' yang energy is "hard and strong", representing "all things that were active and contracting or dense and very hard" (Little and Wong 2000: 238). The majority of Shaolin films repress the 'feminine' – *Shaolin Temple* both incorporates and marginalises Shaolin women like Miao Cuihua, Yim Wing Chun and Ng Mui.[8] The feminine-within-the-masculine (and vice versa) returns in the form of the *wu dang* practitioners who represent a position of gender instability. In *Shaolin Martial Arts*, the liminal perversity of the *wu dang* is pitted against the masculine *wholeness* of Zhang Che's idealised Shaolin men. Both of the *wu dang* men are killed via gruesome penetrations – a *Wing Chun* strike removes Yu Pi's intestines, while the Tiger-Crane technique leaves Pa Kang with the trademark blood-soaked crotch. This is the film where groins first become troublesome. 'Iron Robe' expert Pa has mastered the skill of 'the White Eyebrow Priest' – he can retract his testicles, trapping his opponent's limbs with the 'Golden Bell Clasp', which, as Teo explains, "utilises the weakest part of one's body, the groin, as the strongest position to defeat attackers" (1997: 105). Early in the film, a prostitute is offered ten taels if she can seduce the two 'internal' fighters. She slips her hand down Pa's trousers and recoils in horror, to the amusement of the Manchus. He's "hard like iron, even down there", according to the (dubbed English) dialogue, but the scene suggests that "down there" is precisely where he *is not* hard. Leung Kar-yan is a large, muscular actor, so that his character is both 'hard' and emasculated, both walking erection and *vagina dentata*. As we have seen, Fong Sai-yuk's body embodies a similar paradox, simultaneously hyper-masculine and penetrable.

The White Eyebrow Priest Bai Mei, a recurring villain in the original Fong Sai-yuk films, makes his first appearance in the Shaws cycle in *Shaolin Avengers* as Fong's anal invader. But his most memorable incarnation is in *Executioners From Shaolin*, which elaborates on his abilities at some length. He returns in all but name in *Fist of the White Lotus* – he is ostensibly Bai's student, but is played by the same actor (Lo Lieh), has the same skills and poses a conundrum for the same hero, Hung Hei-kwun's son Wending. The Chinese title of *Executioners* is the name of its nominal hero Hung Hei-kwun, but in re-writing the evolution of *Hung Gar*, the film takes the style away from its titular 'father'; Garcia's claim that the film undercuts the "masculinity of the legend" (1980a: 127) is no exaggeration. Hung (Chen Guantai) cannot defeat Bai Mei precisely because he adheres stubbornly to the 'masculine' Tiger Fist, even forbidding his wife Fang Wing Chun (Lily Li) to teach the 'feminine' Crane style to Wending. It is the androgynous son who defeats Bai Mei. Hair tied in twin buns, dressed in pinafores, played by one of Shaws' boy-babes Wong Yue, Wending remains positioned in the space of the liminal throughout the film; between genders, between Tiger and Crane. After his father's death, he inherits his Tiger fist manual and a bronze training dummy filled with ballbearings to represent the flow of *qi*. But the manual is incomplete and Wending is unsure of how to 'read' the dummy – "did I attack too fast or too slow?" He must, as Garcia puts it, "improvise around the gaps ... fill them with his own inventions" (1980a: 128). If anything, Wending is taught by the missing pages of his father's book, the space generated by Hung's absence. At one level, Bai Mei constitutes "a kind of sexual 'black hole'" (Rayns 1984b: 55), "perversity-in-Nature" (Garcia 1980a: 128) – his groin does not just *trap* Hung's foot, it *sucks* it in. Nevertheless, he is (like Hung) located within the Master/Pupil lineage. During the final fight, he demands to know who Wending's 'Master' is, but the point is that he does not have one. Wending mounts Bai Mei's shoulders, clamping his legs firmly in place, a technique that combines his mother's Crane stance, Bai's own 'Golden Bell Clasp' and the way Wending playfully 'rode' his father as a child.

Played over the credits against a scarlet backdrop, *Executioners* opens with the death of the Shaolin patriarch Zhi Shan, his leg broken between Bai Mei's legs, prefiguring the death of Hung Hei-kwun later in the film. Bai Mei is positioned as both 'father' and 'mother'. On the one hand, he is Bad Patriarch to Zhi Shan's Good, the object of Hung's Oedipal quest. On the other, he is equated with Fang Wing Chun, who also poses a threat to Hung's masculinity. On their wedding night, she challenges him to part her legs, made formidably powerful by her Crane stance. Thwarted penetration also marks Hung's assaults on Bai Mei – "Can't you find it?" mocks the White Eyebrow Priest as the Tiger Claw probes his groin. Rayns argues that it is not just Tiger Fist that Wending has not learned, but masculinity itself, so that the dynamic of revenge thrust upon him is less oedipal than "a matter of adding a 'male' persona to an established 'female' persona" (1984b: 55). Wending remains in a constant state of pre-pubescent precocity – relatively unfazed by the Priest's wandering phallus, the lethal 'clasp' becomes another opportunity for play, the moment he mounts his shoulders and transforms him into another obsolescent patriarch.

Fist of the White Lotus is a broader reworking of *Executioners*, less a sequel than a semi-comic remake. This time it is Bai Mei's defeat that plays over the credits, double-teamed by Wending (Lau Kar-fai) and another Shaolin graduate. The White Eyebrow Priest is replaced by the White Lotus Chief, who adds to his repertoire a delayed death touch (*dim mak*) and the ability to float weightlessly out of reach of blows and kicks. This time, Wending must unlearn a 'masculine' approach to fighting and his 'master' is unambiguously female, played by Hui Ying-hung. She teaches him first using paper dummies, which float out of reach of powerful attacks but which she can strike with deceptively 'light' attacks. But his real training parodies those filmic regimes where neophytes learn kung fu through apparently mundane activities – Wending must learn to sew and nurse the baby in preparation for "a special woman's style" based on embroidery. This is the style that defeats the White Lotus Chief – Wending penetrates all of his acupuncture points until he finds the right one. But if the Wending of *Executioners* is positioned between fixed gender identities, his incarnation in *Fist of the White Lotus* is moves between genders rather than occupying the space of the liminal. He can slip in and out of 'femininity', assuming an 'effeminate' voice and posture but also deploying Tiger-Crane attacks. His final attack on the Chief seems to recast them as 'masculine' and 'feminine' respectively, unlike the more ambiguous dénouement of the earlier film. When Wending attacks him in the bath, there is a sexual dimension to the assault as the Chief frantically covers himself with a towel, and victory is decidedly penetrative in nature. *Fist of the White Lotus* is a dazzling spectacle, but this is a less complex film than its predecessor. In any case, both films incorporate the 'feminine' at the expense of their female leads – while women are positioned in *shifu* roles, the real battles are still being fought *over* and *by* male bodies. Meanwhile, it was not only Hong Kong cinema that used the Shaolin world to reshape 'heroic' masculinity.

The Shaolin Temple as Countercultural Prototype: *Kung Fu*

> The romance and virility of James Bond, the mystique of the rock and roll star, the gentle presence of the peace and love generation are all wrapped up in the personality of Kwai Chang Caine.
> – Richard Robinson, *Kung Fu: The Peaceful Way* (1974: 24).

At least two years before Shaw Brothers brought the Men from the Monastery to vivid life, arguably the most famous on-screen Shaolin monk was Kwai Chang Caine, the mixed-race hero wandering the 'Wild West' in the Warner Bros. television series, *Kung Fu*. As David Desser reminds us, Warners were prime movers in the Western popularisation of kung fu; the pilot of *Kung Fu* aired in 1972, the same year that they distributed *King Boxer* in the West (2000: 24). Bruce Lee had been considered for the role of Caine, but, depending on which version one believes, was either "too Chinese" for the role or too "muscular" for this sensitive hero (Pilato 1993: 32). Nevertheless, Lee took the lead in Warners' *Enter the Dragon*, which, in re-inventing Lee for an international market, seemed to have one eye on Caine's mystical persona. Lee was aggressively populist in his Hong Kong films, a super-patriot and martyr in *Fist of Fury*, a fish-out-of-water country boy in *The Big Boss* and *Way of the Dragon*. In *Enter the Dragon*, he was a Shaolin monk, a more noticeably contemplative figure prior to turning into a more familiar lethal whirlwind in the latter half of the film. Lee's dual construction as Shaolin hippie, philosophising about fingers-pointing-to-the-moon, and bone-crunching avenger, reinforces the impression that kung fu was primarily targetted at two broadly conceived Western markets in the early 1970s. Desser argues that dubbed 'chop sockeys' were aimed particularly at young Afro-American men; martial arts films were paired with blaxploitation films in "downtown theatres" (2000: 25). But *Kung Fu* suggested that China had replaced India in the (white, middle-class) counterculture's romance with the East. The British poster magazine *Kung Fu Monthly* was edited by former *Oz* editor Felix Dennis, who also co-wrote a Lee biography (Dennis and Atyeo 1974). Richard Robinson's *Kung Fu: The Peaceful Way* is heavily focused on Carradine, and contemptuous of the Hong Kong exports – "the most impressive thing about these films is that people want to see them" (1974: 55) For Robinson, even Lee falls short of Carradine:

> Personally I'm on the David Carradine side of the fence. I see kung fu as an extension of the 1960s experience that brought the thought of peace and love as a way of life into a lot of people's minds. (58)

But the 'China' of Kwai Chang Caine offered something that the 'India' of the "1960s experience" could not, namely the fantasy of a hippie who could fight back, "a successful flowerchild ... (who) *does* win" (O'Shaughnessy 1974: n.p.) For Robinson, Caine might represent the triumph of coutercultural values infiltrating the mainstream, but there is an interesting shift when he suggests that *Kung Fu* was about "peace, love, the natural way, ecology, a raising of consciousness, higher sense of spiritual values, the search for a nonviolent answer to violent confrontations, and *people who can take care of themselves if and when they get pushed to the wall*" (1974: 28; my emphasis). But there is something else going on here. As his name suggests, Kwai Chang Caine is half-Chinese, half-American, and the pilot makes much of him being the first Shaolin monk with a touch of *gwailo* about him.[9] This casts him partly as the Westerner who penetrates the 'Orient' and brings back its secrets – a colonialist in Grasshopper's clothing.[10] And yet this *is* a significant shift in Hollywood's 'Encounter with Asia', where 'American' heroes acquired martial arts via armed excursions into Japan, Korea and Vietnam. Caine's most immediate predecessor was *Billy Jack* (1971), the half-Native American Vietnam vet who wielded his Hapkido skills in defence of a hippy commune. *Kung Fu* does not skip over its hero's assimilation of/into Chinese combat and philosophy, and one might argue that the Shaolin flashbacks were the show's central lure. Because Caine is a nomadic figure, 'home' remains provisional, suspended. Caine's 'real' (dead) father is American, and he pursues an ongoing quest to find two American brothers. But the programme provides him with two substitute parents, blind Master Po, who dubs the young Caine 'Grasshopper',[11] and the stricter Master Kan, who appears to be the Abbott. The flashbacks seem to have been conceived, at least initially, as self-contained units. Episode writers were asked not to include these scenes, which were then added by writer John Faris (Pilato 1993: 16). Given that they provide philosophical guidance for actions in the here-and-now, they do cast Po and Kan as Caine's parents.

Insofar as this, too, is a Master/Pupil text, it is Po whom Caine avenges, absorbs and reproduces. As Master Po dies, he gives his only possession to 'Grasshopper'; "If I had a son, all I could offer him is contained in this pouch". By the third and final season, the Western setting appears to have been wearing thin and several episodes were set entirely in China. The two-part story 'Besieged' (1975) even touches on the burning of the temple, with Shaolin monks from Fukien taking refuge in the Henan monastery.[12]

Yvonne Tasker argues that Kung Fu's "reticence" about violence has its roots partly in the American genre that the show re-invented – the western. Carradine had played Shane on television (1966–67), another "pacifist hero faced with the need for action" (2001: 122), while the writers' guide used on Kung Fu described Caine as "a classic American figure" (Pilato 1993: 27). A contemporaneous Esquire cover depicted Caine kicking the Lone Ranger, accompanied by the caption "At last! A new American hero!" According to the writers' guide, the Shaolin backdrop added "richness and colour" (Pilato 1993: 27), implicitly an exoticising of a familiar genre. But Tasker argues that in offering a counter-cultural heroic masculinity, the show drew on the Western stereotype of 'feminised' Chinese men – Caine is a "'child-man' ... tough and decisive, but with a disposition that was essentially gentle and contemplative" (2001: 125).

As Jackie Chan's tribute to 'Grasshopper Boy' suggests, Kung Fu had an influential as well as co-optive relationship with its cultural source, and its representation was no more 'inauthentic' than the heroic boy-babes of Shaws' films. Caine's 'Buddhism' might be a philosophical melange – writer Ed Spielman admits that some of the philosophy was Judaic (Pilato 1993: 7) – but he does engage with spiritual issues and the temple is more than a factory for producing Manchu-killers. More importantly, it predated the Shaw Brothers films – one can only speculate on its influence in 're-opening' the cinematic temple. Kung Fu's temple recycled the castle set from Camelot (1967), but its depiction of a functioning Shaolin community anticipates the one in The 36th Chamber of Shaolin. There are no Wooden Men and no 35 chambers, but we do see Caine lifting the urn that burns the Dragon and Tiger into his arms and a fighting philosophy rooted in nature. Fight choreography was not the show's strong point, but it did change choreographers from David Chow to Yuen Kam in an effort to authenticate its Shaolin combat.

In both Kung Fu and the earlier Shaw Brothers films, the Shaolin Temple constitutes a prelapsarian space in contrast with a 'fallen world' of either Manchu oppression or Western violence and racism. In Kung Fu, Shaolin paradise is in perpetual soft focus, bathed in an orange glow. The Shaolin patriots are ejected by the burning of the monastery, but Caine is cast out for killing the Emperor's nephew in a moment of anger when his beloved Master Po is shot. There is little sense of Manchu-Han politics in Kung Fu, no resistance for Caine to join, no political enmity between the Qing government and the temple. Fong Sai-yuk's killing of Tiger Lei and Wu Wei-kin's wiping out of the textile factory do not constitute falls from paradise – these boys are aching to fight and their single-minded martyrdom defines their heroic masculinity. On their terms, killing a prominent Manchu is pretty damn impressive, but Caine's outlook is very different. He leaves China in penance as much as self-preservation, and the pacifist ideals taught by stern Master Kan remain intact:

> Learn more ways to preserve rather than destroy. Avoid rather than check. Check rather than hurt. Hurt rather than maim. Maim rather than kill. For all life is precious and cannot be replaced.

Buddha Enjoys Himself in Hell: The Uncanny Temple of *Burning Paradise*

> I built this Buddha. He obeys only me. When I command him to kill, he kills. I have created the Anti-Buddha!
> – Master Sun, *Burning Paradise/Huoshao Honglian Si* (1993).

The Shaolin heroes have remained a generic mainstay of Hong Kong and Taiwanese television series. But the *wu xia* revival of the early 1990s did not accord a prominent place to the myth of the monastery; perhaps its Manichean outlook and heroic certainties did not lend itself to the complexities of the new political situation, or, at the very least, required a revisionist perspective. If Wong Fei-hung faced up to the big questions facing 'China' in the *Once Upon a Time in China* series, earlier heroes were largely recycled as parody. Jet Li played Fong Sai-yuk (twice), Hung Hei-kwun and *wu dang* founder Zhang Sanfeng (in *Tai Chi Master*), but none of these roles were allowed the stature and seriousness of his incarnation of Wong Fei-hung. *New Legend of Shaolin/Hong Xiguan* (1994) follows Hung Hei-kwun and the young Wending after the burning of the temple, but the film is the antithesis of the 1970s films' myth-making. The father/son relationship is modelled on the Japanese *Lone Wolf and Cub* series, while Shaolin renegade Ma Linger drives around in a cross between an insect carapace and a bizarre eighteenth-century mini-car.

It is the critically neglected *Burning Paradise* that most visibly revisits the earlier Shaolin films. It also recycles another generic institution as counterpoint to the Shaolin Temple – the Red Lotus Monastery, den of evil in two versions of *The Burning of the Red Lotus Monastery*, one made in Shanghai in 1928 and one by Shaw Brothers in 1963. The Red Lotus Monastery becomes a prison camp for Shaolin captives, represented as a literal hell on earth – along the approaching road, corpses hang from gallows, two bloody hands protrude from the sand, and skulls litter the ground. The interior is a mass of lethal traps – spiked floors, dart-projecting thrones, fiery pits and a climactic ballistic Buddha that fires bullets at sutra-chanting monks. As Bey Logan puts it, "each of Dante's levels of hell are combined into one ghastly underground prison, a grim fortress that is every bit as much a character in the film as its human stars" (1998a: 32–3). Shaolin relations are marked by distrust and paranoia. Hung Hei-kwun (Lin Kwan) seems to be conspiring with the Manchus, and when he is revealed as a double agent, he is in turn betrayed by a temple spy.

As in the early Shaws films, the Shaolin temple is seen only in flames in opening shots. Most of the film unfolds in its uncanny counterpart, the Red Lotus temple, which effectively *inverts* Shaolin; its traps operate as a parody of the 36 Chambers and the rigors of Shaolin technology. The Red Lotus Temple evokes two of the figurations of the uncanny outlined by Freud – it is both a 'double' for Shaolin and the *unheimlich*/unhomely place that represents the familiar/repressed in disguise. More specifically, the uncanny place is "the entrance to the former *Heim* (home) of all human beings, to the place where each one of us lived once upon a time and in the beginning" (Freud 1919/1985: 368). Ackbar Abbas suggests that the uncanny is one way of understanding the spatial-temporal paradoxes of Hong Kong – "the unfamiliar arises out of the familiar and is a dimension of it: not another space but a space of otherness" (1997: 41). Shaolin can be seen as 'home' in two ways, both linked to a sense of origin. Firstly, as we have seen, it does take on womb-like representations in the birthing process of *The 36th Chamber of Shaolin* and other pedagogic narratives. Secondly, the 1970s films seem to deploy a diasporic sense of home – Shaolin as the origin of kung fu and other aspects of Chinese culture, of a distinct 'Chinese' identity that survives colonialism, displacement and other hostile contexts. But as certainties about identity fracture, Shaolin home gives way to the "space of otherness".

As in the Gothic, the uncanny place also reflects the psyche of its owner or occupant. The Red Lotus Temple is operated by Master Sun (Wong Kam Kong), a combination of Bai Mei (perverse Shaolin nemesis), Sade (artist-libertine) and Prince Prospero from Poe's *Masque of the Red Death* (decadent roue). Sun's Temple of Profligacy testifies to the solipsistic embodiment of his Sadean logic – Buddhist virtue must be shattered for philosophical reasons rather than political ones. But it also reminds him, as he acknowledges, that he is a prisoner of his own desire and his own decaying body:

I was a great General. I was always loyal to the Emperor. But then one day I discovered my hair was going grey. That's when I realised that all men are born to die ... One might as well experience life to the fullest. And I do enjoy life, even its darkest side ... So to this end I've built the Red Lotus Monastery ... I do whatever I please.

The film incorporates Mainland actor-artist Wong Kam-kong's painting into the fight scenes – he mixes blood with paint, inscribing the characters for "Limitless Power, Limitless Force" before hurling droplets of 'paint' from his brush that burn like acid. The Red Lotus temple itself is configured as Sun's work of art, embracing the *jouissance* of hell – one painting carries the inscription "The Buddha, denizen of paradise, enjoys himself in hell".

Bhaskar Sarkar sees the 1990s 'new wave' of martial arts films as hysterical texts, and their hysteria as "allegories of their context: anxieties over the new economic realities, the effects on social and cultural life, and the emerging political alignments are played out onscreen with hysterical abandonment" (2001: 171). One of their strategies, he suggests, is to respond to incomprehensible political structures with "parodic repetitions of symbolic structures (myths)" (171) – thus the recycling of Wong Fei-hung, Fong Sai-yuk and wandering swords(wo)men. *Burning Paradise* recycles the burning of the temple, the southern legends, and even offers an ambivalent parody of Buddhism, a "symbolic structure" subjected to heretical subversion and nostalgic reverence (the Buddha is ultimately recuperated from Master Sun's desecration).

It is Master Sun, however, who is the hysterical centre of the film, a character too excessive to accommodate the kind of schematic '1997' readings often mapped onto such nihilistic films (he certainly does not represent 'China'). Sun's calligraphic kung fu includes the blood-spattered slogan "Limitless world" – his power lies in being able to shape and redefine the world (morally and physically) within a limited sphere, thus his temple's dual role as Dionysian space and Sun's own prison (he calls it his "tomb"). Sun's temple of excess is also a mirror to Hong Kong's "limitless world" of global capitalism, a world which, too, pushes people into uninhabitable spaces and in which objects and values (Buddha/Anti-Buddha) start to lose their meaning and/or value. Sun even insists on the allegorical nature of his subterranean edifice:

The temple is no different from the world of martial arts. As opponents we'll never stop fighting. The winner will end up as master. The losers will be his slaves.

In making Master Sun the centre of the film, *Burning Paradise* highlights the impotence of the genre's traditional heroism. Hung Hei-kwun and Fong Sai-yuk (Willie Chi) are flatly drawn, trapped by their own mythical function; Zhi Shan is an ineffectual, semi-comic figure. Hung and Fong are played by unknowns who evoke the urban cynicism of Ringo Lam's crime films rather than the heroic chivalry of the martial arts film.

In 1980, Ng Ho suggested that the Shaolin myth might already have exhausted itself, and the revisionism and bleakness of *Burning Paradise* supports this impression. Its low-key

Shaolin heroes are effortlessly upstaged by their more resonant antagonist. But the Shaolin Temple had already, in any case, started to assume a new role in marketing Chinese culture and identity.

"Make the Temple feed the Temple": The Shaolin™ Heritage Industries

> This will be the only show to feature ordained Soldier Monks of the Shaolin Temple and, as such, is the only show authorised by The Venerable Shi Yong Xin, Fangzhang (Abbot) of the Temple and supported by the Henan Provincial People's Government. No other show has had this honour, blessing and approval bestowed upon it.
> – Brochure, *Shaolin Wheel of Life* (2000)

For Ervin Nieves, *Kung Fu*'s philosophical earnestness constitutes a kind of authenticity, "the most appealing representation of the legendary Shaolin monks to date" (1999: 45). By contrast, he discerned a contemporary project to "deconstruct the ascetic reputation of Shaolin Temple monks as Bodhisattva aspirants, in an apparent international effort to reap huge commercial profits" (45). By the early 1980s, the Shaolin cycle of films had largely run their course, but new relations between Hong Kong and China allowed a Hong Kong film company to film at the Henan temple. *Shaolin Temple* (1982), either by accident or design, now looks like a tourist information film as much as a kung fu movie. Either way, its success led to the re-opening of the Henan temple, which was to have a new role in China's modern economy. A promotional booklet, *The Shaolin Temple – The Origin of Chinese Kung Fu*, reinforces the impression; historic artifacts like the One Thousand Buddhas Hall (with its 48 indentations left by the monks' stamping feet) and frescoes depicting temple life could be seen for the first time, a location "rich in cultural relics and historic sites" (1982: 4). The film opens with one of the frescoes, the one depicting the cudgel-bearing monks who "saved the Tang Empire". The *Shaolin Temple* booklet makes no mention of the Qing Dynasty, the southern temple, of the temple as a refuge or training centre for rebellion – the Tang-era story was safely apolitical. Moreover, to Nieves' particular chagrin, some versions of the story reward the patriotic monks by revoking the Buddhist commandments about meat and wine. In this story, religious doctrines are negotiable at the behest of secular ruling powers. Similarly, the re-opened temple is permitted its beliefs so long as it serves the economy, a sort of 'Special Buddhist Region'. Pupils are charged fees, there are Shaolin cultural centres in London and other international cities, the Shaolin Buddhist Gift Department performs profitable blessing ceremonies, the monks produce CD-ROMs to teach kung fu, and perform around the world.[13] Shaolin training is predominantly vocational, with graduates taking jobs in the police, army or as bodyguards. Nieves imagines a "parodic dystopic sequel" to *The 36ᵗʰ Chamber of Shaolin* called *The 37ᵗʰ Chamber of Shaolin* (aka *Chamber of Commerce*) as Shaolin 'monk' Shi Yanming appears in a Hewlett Packard commercial or a Wu Tang Clan video (1999: 47–8).

If the tales of Hung Hei-kwun *et al* have any basis in fact, then the Shaolin Temple has a history of balancing spiritual concerns with pragmatic ones and of admitting secular students with worldly concerns. Nor is it a recent development for Shaolin films to downplay Buddhism – Zhang Che's films largely erase it, Lau Kar-leung's set it in philosophical conflict with other imperatives. And yet recent Shaolin narratives do drain the myths of any resonance beyond the tourist industry. *Shaolin Temple* essentially offers three types of spectacle – panoramic footage of Songshan mountain scenery (often in self-contained musical interludes), 'historic sites' like the Buddha Hall and Pagoda Forest, and the formation routines of the Beijing *wu shu* team, standing in for the more authentic Shaolin styles of the 1970s films. In *Kids from Shaolin/Shaolin Xia Zi* (1984), the Shaolin and *wu dang* play out a bizarre kung fu version of *Seven Brides for Seven Brothers*, with even more musical interludes and scenery fetishism. *Martial Arts of Shaolin/Nan Bei Shaolin* (1986) was directed by Lau Kar-leung, who is not so in awe of the Mainland scenery that he forgets to incorporate it into the action – seeing Jet Li fight on the Great Wall is a cherishable spectacle. There are some skilful deployments of recognisable fighting styles – Hu Jianqiang 'parts' floating bamboo rafts with his powerful *Hung Gar* stance. But the script is a pale shadow of Lau's films at Shaw Brothers, and the Qing-era setting amounts to little.

The stage show *Shaolin Wheel of Life* (2000), featuring "ordained Soldier Monks", effectively reproduces *The Shaolin Temple* "on a stage set that evokes the mysterious World of the East". The narration (its performers never speak) specifies the Tang Dynasty, but blurs the Tang-era cudgel-playing monks with the later monks who aided Qing Emperor Kang Xi (1674) and subsequently incurred the wrath of Emperor Yong Zheng (1736), who ordered the burning of the Songshan monastery (Reid and Croucher 1995: 62; Ng 1980b: 57). When they decline the invitation to be the Emperor's personal guard, he drugs them with poisoned incense and cuts their throats. The 'Five Ancestors' are represented as five children who survive the massacre. The final section of the show reanimates the monks as show-stopping circus performers, Shaolin minstrels displaying the kind of *qigong* feats featured in video documentaries like *Shaolin Art of War* (Eastern Heroes 1998). The similarity with *Shaolin Temple* does not end with the narrative – the kung fu performed draws heavily on PRC-approved *wu shu*, full of balletic spins and turns. The public face of the new temple makes it hard to tell to what degree it sustains any real continuity with its former existence. *Under the Sun: Kung Fu Business* (BBC 1999) focuses on the profit-oriented activities of the temple – some of the kung fu classes shown also look like *wu shu*. But there are hints that Shaolin also exists as a separate entity, independent from but also facilitated by the demands of economic self-sufficiency.

Seemingly exhausted as a cultural myth, Shaolin survives as exotic spectacle, as classes which may or may not transmit ancient secrets to Westerners, and possibly as a smaller cell of religious and martial activity with a genuine link to the temple's history. As a sub-genre, it was already being overtaken by new developments by the late 1970s. Nevertheless, it remains the genre's most sustained and seductive cinematic myth. And while the Shaolin films of the 1970s can be seen as paving the way for more 'local' Hong Kong action films, with their emphasis on Cantonese identity and 'émigré' heroes looking for a new home, they also constitute the last 'authentic' China-centred kung fu cycle. The kung fu comedies that displaced them had little patience with patriotism, traditional Master/Pupil relations and stylistic purity, but began to reflect the cosmopolitan hybridity of the island that produced them. But the peak of the Shaolin cycle ran concurrently with the other substantial, if rather less respectable, sub-genre of the mid-1970s – the films that sought to fill the gap left by Bruce Lee. The 'clones' of the late kung fu 'legend', whose exploits constitute a mythical tapestry in their own right, are the subject of the next chapter.

Chapter Three

Exit the Dragon, Enter the 'Shadow'
Game of Death, The Clones of Bruce Lee and
Other Posthumous Adventures

The condition of being a legend is a certain ghostliness, as fame is no more than
the sum of misunderstandings gathered around a great name.
    – Ackbar Abbas (1997: 46)

Now I begin to realise why Bruce Lee says goodbye to this world at such an early
age – 32 years old! Is Jesus not crucified when he is thirty-three years old? Yet our
merciful Bruce Lee dies one year earlier. From this we can know how great he is.
    – Lee Chung-lung, Bruce Lee fan from Osaku (quoted in Hui 1976: 26)

Not one ... not two ... but three Bruces!
    – Publicity, *The Clones of Bruce Lee/Shen-wei San Meng-lung* (1977)

While Jackie Chan is arguably Hong Kong cinema's most globally successful star, Bruce
Lee remains its undisputed 'Legend'; like Elvis, he is the 'King' of an ambiguously defined
domain. Lee's premature death certainly expedited his elevation to myth, and his name
became the locus of what Tony Rayns describes as an "interlocking network of stories,
dreams and fantasies with entirely different levels of veracity, authenticity and credibility"
(1984: 26). Such tales place him in the company of 'historical' heroes like Wong Fei-hung
and Fong Sai-yuk as much as other Hong Kong action stars. Like the Shaolin movies, the
'Legend' was subject to ongoing, and not necessarily linear, revisions and embellishments.
But the Lee 'Legend' was mass-mediated from the start, and continued to blur the line
between real-life exploits and those of his on-screen characters. In low-budget biopics from
the mid-1970s, there is often a slippage from 'Lee' to *Fist of Fury*'s super-patriot Chen
Zhen or *Way of the Dragon*'s self-sufficient émigré hero Tang Lung. Even our perception
of Lee as a superlative fighter seems based on cinematic evidence as much as anecdotal
hyperbole. Lee the fighter was, as Davis Miller reminds us, comparatively "untested"

(2000: 162). But even Miller's more sober appraisal ("compared to boxers he was not a consummate mover ... he pranced instead of gliding" [162]) relies on movie fights. Lee's defeat of world karate champion Chuck Norris in *Way of the Dragon* somehow seems as 'real' as, say, Mohammed Ali's victory over George Forman.

The Bruce Lee publishing industries extend well beyond his comparatively modest cinematic output – biographies and, more frequently, hagiographies, collections of his essays, interviews and letters, discussions of his 'scientific streetfighting', Jeet Kune Do. As Meaghan Morris observes, such books (and videos) cast Lee as teacher and 'Muse' for aspirant martial artists around the world (1998: 9–10): "What I knew in every molecule of my body was this", attests Davis Miller, "Bruce Lee was who I'd always wanted to be, what I'd always believed I could become" (2000: 6). This is precisely the role 'Lee' plays in *No Retreat, No Surrender* (1986), in which his ghost (Kim Tai-jung) tutors a bullied suburban teenager. For the 16-year-old Miller – four feet ten, 63 pounds, nicknamed 'the foetus' – *Enter the Dragon* is a pedagogic epiphany. Given that Lee died before the film's release, his 'ghost' was already impacting on the consciousness of daydreaming teenage boys. This is not to deny that his image has also endured as "an object, even a fetish" (Teo 1997: 120). Action (or should that be leisure?) figures in Medicom's 'Bruce Lee Fashion Show', designed by Hong Kong artist Eric So, preserve him in the flamboyant 1970s clothes that had the Hong Kong press dub him the 'Worst Dressed Man' in the territory.

Lee completed four star vehicles prior to his death, three Mandarin dialect films in Hong Kong, and the Hong Kong-US co-production *Enter the Dragon*, shot in Hong Kong from an English-language script. These four films are not my real focus in this chapter. There are some excellent studies of Lee,[1] and I do not wish to simply reiterate them. My interest here is, rather, in Lee's transition, subsequent to his death, into myth, 'legend' (fetish, even) and cult worship via lookalikes, biopics, the posthumously completed *Game of Death* (1972/1978) and a further spin-off, *Tower of Death/Siwang Ta* (1979).

Lee's death created a crisis for the genre and a rush to fill what Kwai Cheung Lo calls the "Hole punched out by (his) body" (1999: 110). At least three cycles of 'clone' films can be identified – hagio-pics endowed with an especially permissive dramatic license, unofficial sequels to *Fist of Fury* and ersatz versions of *Game of Death*, and tales of avengers of, and successors to, Lee, such as *Exit the Dragon, Enter the Tiger* (1976). A comic variant points to a self-reflexivity inherent in parts of the cycle. In *Enter the Fat Dragon/Feilong Guojiang* (1978), Sammo Hung's Lee-obsessed Mainland farmboy seeks stuntwork on the set of a Lee-clone movie. Riled by the film's 'star', he teaches him a lesson; he not only outfights him but out*clones* him. The film's best joke is how skilfully the 'Fat Dragon' can mimic Lee's every move and facial expression. 'Lee' has made additional appearances as a ghost in *The Dragon Dies Hard/Chin Se Tai Yang* (1974) and *No Retreat, No Surrender*, calling for revenge or playing teacher from beyond the grave. In *City Hunter/Chengshi Lieren* (1993), he 'teaches' Jackie Chan from a movie screen during a fight in a theatre where *Game of Death* is showing. Ackbar Abbas has written of the 'ghostliness' of the cinematic image (both 'present' and 'absent'), drawing on Paul Virilio's characterization of the star as "a spectre of absorption ... *a ghost that you can interview*" (1997: 46) (or be taught by).[2] In one fan publication, the Lee doubles used in *Game of Death* are described as "shadows" – "Shadows of Bruce Lee continue to come without letting others know their names" (Hui 1978b: 44–5) – as though his clones constitute cinematic afterimages, preternatural traces of his 'presence'. Lee undoubtedly haunted the genre in the years following his death, and not just in the form of what Logan calls the "Leealikes" (1995: 24). Jackie Chan's early career was dogged by Lo Wei's determination to package him as the 'new' Lee, most obviously in *New Fist of Fury/Xin Jingwu Mun* (1976). Chan's subsequent reinvention of himself as the antithesis of Lee (comic underdog, as opposed to macho superman) sometimes sounds like an exorcism of sorts.

There is no clear boundary separating the 'official' from the more exploitative cinematic tributes to Lee – the myth does not lend itself to such neat demarcations. *Game of Death* 'clones' Lee to pad out footage of the star and exploits the rumours surrounding his death. *Dragon: The Bruce Lee Story* (1993), on the other hand, seems to have drawn its inspiration from the 'Bruce Li' films of the 1970s as much as widow Linda Lee Cadwell's credited biography. Taken together, these texts constitute an ongoing dialogue about Lee's cultural significance; even the tackiest, most tawdry rip-offs somehow contribute to this dialogue. *The Clones of Bruce Lee* can be dismissed as worthless dross, a testament to nothing more than "opportunism and deceit" (Rayns 1984: 27), or indulged ironically as "Kung Fu Kamp" (Schveinhardt 1998b: 33). But whatever their intentions, which we should have no illusions about, these films do contribute to the heterogenous myth of 'Bruce Lee', offering variations on apocryphal stories, speculating on the many rumours surrounding his death, posing questions about identity and cultural belonging. According to Stephen Teo, the mirror reflections of Lee in *Way of the Dragon* and *Enter the Dragon* point not to his narcissism, but to "the Chinese masses looking back", the "aspirations of Hong Kong people" (1997: 120). But the cloning of Lee, the endless recycling of footage of his funeral (the corpse as star 'presence'), and the sex and drugs scandals in the Hong Kong press seem to me to also reflect a body in crisis, overwhelmed by the discourses willed onto it – both Chinese and 'Western', omnipotent and all too vulnerably human, unique and 'clonable'.

Cloning the Dragon

The Clones of Bruce Lee is the *ne plus ultra* of what has been called 'Bruceploitation' (Kenny 2001: 79), a film that borders on the eloquent and the self-reflexive, a film that is *almost* 'about' the Bruce Lee rip-off industries. If the film is decidedly fuzzy about the finer details of its nominal subject – it tells us that Lee died of a heart attack – it nevertheless engages, in its trashy way, with Lee the commodity, the way that his image "multiplied endlessly, weirdly split and resplit" (Bordwell 2000a: 53–4). What, after all, could be more apposite than a science fiction plot about using Lee's DNA to manufacture a trio of crimefighting lookalikes? The film opens with Lee's lifeless body wheeled into a hospital. "It's Bruce Lee!" exclaims an intern, prompting the response, "The actor?" as though 'Bruce Lee' were already an unstable field. Mad scientist Professor Lucas (Jon Benn) is enlisted by the FBI to multiply Lee like a Warhol screen print or the reflections from *Enter the Dragon*'s Hall of Mirrors. "Hmm, the Clones of Bruce Lee", muses Lucas with the sort of deranged gleam in his eye that only audiences seem to notice, "What a scientific achievement this will be." Within minutes, he is unveiling Bruce Lee 1 ('Dragon Lee'), Bruce Lee 2 ('Bruce Le') and Bruce Lee 3 ('Bruce Lai'). Their training, like their physical maturation, takes place on fast-forward, and soon Bruce 1 is throwing Mantis shapes to the accompaniment of the *Rocky* theme. When Bruces 2 and 3 go to Thailand on a mission, they meet what appears to be a fourth clone ('Bruce Thai'), although the English dialogue dubs him 'Chuck' (as in Norris?). Bruce 1's mission requires him to pose as a kung fu star in order to deal with a gold smuggler fronting as a film director. When his cover is blown, the villainous director hatches a plot to dispose of Bruce 1 on-camera, simultaneously despatching him and bestowing instant cult appeal – "We can capitalise for years on his death when the picture comes out ... maybe we could tie this kid's death in with someone like Bruce Lee." By the end of the film, diabolical scientists and unscrupulous film-makers seem to have become interchangeable, and the Clones escape Lucas' mind control and team up to defeat him. "You're hurting my arm", he grumbles bathetically as the FBI take him away.

The Clones of Bruce Lee has run out of steam long before its dénouement, and there is a danger in willing the film to be more coherent than one could reasonably expect it to be. Its title and its sensational premise are its *raison d'être*, yet its central conceit cannot help but stutter into periodic poignancy. Ruthless men create new 'Bruce Lees' to serve their own ends, but the Bruces take on a life of their own and ultimately cannot be controlled. If the narrative does not offer sufficient evidence of this, then the extraordinary spectacle of Dragon Lee surely does. While his counterparts need to put on gradient sunglasses to look remotely like the original, Dragon Lee actually looks as though he could conceivably have been cloned from Bruce's DNA (perhaps with David Cronenberg at the helm). He has been described, memorably and not entirely inaccurately, as a "Bizarro Bruce Lee, a mutant caricature of the late star's bone structure and exaggerated facial expressions" (Schveinhardt 1998b: 32–3), a man who can flex *his entire face* (33). The Clone has not just escaped Professor Lucas' control but the bonds of representation that one might expect to constrain a 'shadow' of the original star.

In his discussion of Elvis impersonators, Greil Marcus suggests that 'fakes' have a special licence, a freedom sometimes unavailable to the 'real thing':

> As a fake, the Elvis imitator can do anything ... Everyone knows it isn't real, that it isn't really happening, and so the dispensation, one's distance from one's own desires, is sealed. (1991: 120)

This implicitly liberates the spectator, too. The 'authentic' star can be "thrilling and terrifying", leaving the fan trapped within the unfulfillable desires provoked by the star's 'presence'; "no wonder", Marcus concludes, "so many prefer the Elvis imitator to Elvis, irreducible in his absolute subjectivity" (120). Of course, the Bruce Lee clone and the Elvis impersonator are not quite the same thing, any more than the originals are.[3] Nevertheless, the clones, like Marcus' hypothetical Elvises, fed a desire driven by more than an audience's inability to distinguish the 'real' from the 'fake'. And if Dragon Lee is seen as little more than exotica for the amused consumer of 'Kung Fu Kamp', 'Bruce Li' (Ho Chung-tao) acquired something like a cult following in his own right.

From 1974 to 1977, one could be forgiven for thinking that Professor Lucas' clones were, indeed, roaming the globe as "a legion of grimacing and screeching, pseudo-similar androids" (Miller 2000: 95). *Bruce Lee Against Supermen* (1975), *The Black Dragon Revenges the Death of Bruce Lee* (1975) and *Bruce's Fingers* (1976) are just some of the lurid titles from this period. Some films give the impression of existing as unconfirmed rumours – has anyone actually ever seen the Brazilian *Bruce Lee Against Gay Power* (Tombs 1997: 11; Bordwell 2000a: 50)? Tony Rayns contends that "few Westerners" were aware that Lee only completed four star vehicles (1984: 27), that the rip-offs had been absorbed into the 'Lee' corpus outside of Asia. 'Bruce Li' was the *bête noir* of British poster magazine *Kung Fu Monthly* (1974–84), their chief objection being precisely that 'casual' viewers would mistake the 'Infamous Imitator' for the real thing.[4] But it was not unheard of for Lee and 'Li' films to be paired on double-bills – I can recall seeing *The Dragon Lives/Yang Chun Da Xiong* (1976) with a reissued *Enter the Dragon* in the early

1980s. In 1976, the US distributors of *Goodbye Bruce Lee: His Last Game of Death/ Legend of Bruce Lee/New Game of Death* (1974) were prosecuted by the Pennsylvania Bureau of Consumer Protection for passing it off as a Lee film – a subsequent disclaimer was added to posters clarifying that this was merely a 'tribute' (Gaul 1997: 175). Toby Russell's well-researched Lee documentary *Death By Misadventure* (1995) uses clips from 'Bruce Li' films not only as 'dramatic reconstructions' ("Bruce Lee's life recreated by Bruce Li" claims the video box) but also to stand in for (presumably off-limits) clips from Lee's headlining features. But *Death By Misadventure* also testifies to a significant shift; by 1995, 'Li' had a (small) cult of his own, winning a degree of (possibly nostalgic) affection from old school kung fu fans.[5]

Ho Chung-tao, a gymnast and sports teacher from Taiwan, was signed by Hong Kong-based Alpha Films on the basis of his physical resemblance to Bruce Lee. "Little was known about him except the obvious physical facts", claims a publicity brochure for *Goodbye, Bruce Lee: His Last Game of Death*, admittedly not the most reliable of sources. This 'discovery' is occasionally integrated into the narrative of Ho's films. In *Goodbye, Bruce Lee*, film producers search for a double to complete *Game of Death*; "You were born to be Bruce Lee the second!" Ho is told, and the camera cuts rapidly between his left and right profile as if to convince us. As he sits in a screening room ostensibly to watch the footage shot by Lee, the film effectively starts again, with its pseudo-*Game of Death* taking up the rest of its running time. We never return to the framing narrative, presumably in order to suture Ho into what we are meant to take as the 'real' *Game* footage. *Dynamo/Bu Ze Shou Duan* (1979) comes late in the clone cycle, but is set shortly after Lee's death – the head of a large corporation finds her car delayed by the crowds at his funeral. *Dynamo* is cynical about the exploitative sub-genre it seems to be trying to transcend. "A lot of people are cashing in on his death", someone observes, and taxi driver Li Tien-yi (Ho) is snapped up as someone who "looks and fights like Bruce Lee". This time, the distinction between 'Li' and Lee is more sharply drawn, and another actor plays Bruce in a dream sequence. Li Tien-yi starts to resist his transformation into a commodity, but is told to remember the "slums" he came from and to where he could just as easily "vanish". Being the 'new Bruce Lee' seems here to be connected to the 'get rich quick' culture of Hong Kong's 'economic miracle', but *Dynamo* views it with marked scepticism. *The Chinese Stuntman/Long De Ying Zi* (1980), a fascinating glimpse of Hong Kong action cinema looking at itself, goes further. Lee is now consigned to nostalgic fetish, a poster on a wall, the assertion that "he's still the greatest". Tang Wei (Ho Chung-tao) finds stuntwork in the post-Lee kung fu film; the studios have exhausted all the animal/insect/drunken styles and seek new ones while jaded US distributors breath down their necks. The stunts become more dangerous, the

Fig. 6 The 'Legend' and one of his 'shadows': 'Bruce Li' in *The Legend of Bruce Lee* (aka *Goodbye Bruce Lee: His Last Game of Death*)

producers more venal and Tang falls foul of the self-serving star he is brought in to double. Like *Dynamo* and *Enter the Fat Dragon*, *Chinese Stuntman* both mourns Lee's passing and seeks to escape his shadow. The stuntman-hero is an especially interesting figure given that Jackie Chan and Sammo Hung would be the genre's saviours. The film climaxes with two iconic fights; Tang defeats Dan Inosanto, Lee's opponent in *Game of Death*, and then demolishes a Qing Dynasty film set as he settles his differences with the kung fu star.

In some Asian territories, Ho was renamed 'Li Xialong/Li Siu-lung' (Lee's Chinese name – 'Little Dragon Lee'), with English prints modifying it to 'Lee Roy Lung'. But outside Asia, the 'Bruce Li' name began to stick, even though Ho was later vocal in his denunciation of the name, calling it "a kind of cheating" and asserting that "I want to be myself" (*Cinema of Vengeance*, 1993). Ho is a rather underwhelming performer in his early films, but he improved dramatically in the many that followed. By the time of *The Secret of Bruce Lee/Zhong Yuan Biao Ju* (1976), he was sufficiently skilled to carry off an impressive kicking duel with fearsome bootmaster Huang Jang-li. Ho's onscreen fighting style seemed to develop along the lines of the Korean-derived kicking techniques popular from the mid-1970s; a *Secret Rivals*-style training sequence in *The Secret of Bruce Lee* shows him kicking suspended pots in preparation for his fight with Huang. *Dynamo*, choreographed by the Yuen clan, leaves us with few doubts about the education Ho received in Hong Kong action films. In marked contrast to the Lee-centred *Kung Fu Monthly, Eastern Heroes* enrolled 'Bruce Li' in their illustrious rollcall of 'Kings of Kung Fu' – "On screen, he displays an electrifying excitement which is most engrossing ... [he] deserves more respect for his performances" (Baker and Russell 1995: 121). But it is Nick Davidson who mounts the most sustained defence of Ho in his fanzine *Fists of Fury*. *Dynamo* and the self-directed *The Chinese Stuntman* are read by Davidson as metaphors for Ho/'Li's' predicament; the former is about "image manipulation and compromised integrity", the latter about "grasping producers and the expendability of the individual" (1997b: 36). Like any fanzine zealot worth his/her salt, Davidson is taking no prisoners. Ho's detractors are "trendy smart-alecks" (39), and Davidson insists on his subject's 'superiority' to Jackie Chan and Jet Li. This kind of iconoclastic fervour is characteristic of what Jeffrey Sconce calls 'paracinema', a subcultural sensibility articulated through the valorisation of lowbrow cinematic forms ('trash'), "aggressively attacking the established canon of 'quality' cinema and questioning the legitimacy of reigning aesthetic discourses on movie art" (1995: 374). But the canon being attacked here is not that of 'quality' cinema (which would exclude all kung fu films), but one explicitly located *within* kung fu/Hong Kong cultdom.[6] The paracinematic aesthetic "is particularly rich with 'cultural capital' and thus possesses a level of textual sophistication similar to the cineastes they construct as their nemesis" (375). The kung fu cultist brings considerable 'capital' to a film like *Dynamo*, in this case the in-depth knowledge of Ho's career and the Hong Kong film industry. But what also emerges in Davidson's appreciation is the sense of the star as a liminal figure, both 'Bruce Li' (the 'shadow' as commodity) and 'Ho Chung-tao' (the underrated martial arts performer struggling for an identity of his own).

Apart from the Lee biopics, it is the unofficial 'sequels' that engage most visibly with the 'Legend' of Bruce Lee. But only one film in the Lee canon actually generated sequels (and, later, remakes and revisions). *Fist of Fury* is arguably the key Lee film for those eager to construct nationalist readings of his persona, "his strongest statement for the cause" (Teo 1997: 115). But, significantly, it is also the only one in which his character dies, generating another 'void' to be filled. The original *Fist of Fury* follows the death of real-life martial artist Huo Yuenjia/Fok Yun-gap (1857–1909), founder of the *Jingwu Mun* (Doorway to Excellence in Martial Arts) school, and posits his poisoning by Japanese aggressors in the Western concession of Shanghai.[7] In *Fist of Fury*, Huo exists only as an "absent father" within an "adolescent crisis of identity" (Rayns 1980: 111). His (fictitious) Fifth Disciple Chen Zhen (Lee) must defy the non-aggressive code of his deceased *shifu* to preserve the dignity of his fellow Chinese, taunted by a plaque designating Chinese as 'The Sick Man of Asia'. Chen's response is delivered in singularly tactile form when he defeats an entire karate school. When the Japanese are conclusively implicated in Huo Yuenjia's death, patriotism is wedded to brutal revenge and Chen comes into conflict both with a more protean colonial power and the compromised Chinese police inspector (Lo Wei) who must keep the peace. Chen's sacrificial death amidst a hail of bullets generates a space for avengers and successors. *Fist of Fury 2/Jie Quan Ying Zhao Gong* (1976) is an unexpectedly sober and often effective follow-up; too modest to equal its predecessor's chivalric grandeur, but enlivened by interesting touches. The film opens with Chen Zhen's funeral (as *Fist of Fury* opened with Huo's), conflating Chen with Lee (a photograph from *Way of the Dragon*) and Lee with Huo (the 'master' who dies under suspicious circumstances). Bruce Lee/Chen Zhen/Huo Yuenjia – three deceased 'Masters' – mark out a void in the opening section of the film, the sense that Jingwu Mun have gone back to being the 'Sick Man of Asia'. Tien Feng's senior instructor, retained from the original film, becomes an alcoholic and the Jingwu Mun building itself is taken over by a new wave of Japanese bullies. The film is almost a third of the way in before Chen's brother, Chen Shen (Ho Chung-tao), arrives. Chen initially castigates those Chinese who will not fight back, but becomes less of a loner than his martyred brother. Chiao Hsiung-ping notes how Bruce Lee was "visually ... never on the 'people's side'" (1981: 41); the narrative may insist that he fights *for* a group, but that fight is ultimately undertaken in isolation. Ho

Chung-tao cannot match Lee's charisma or the physical authenticity that lifts *Fist of Fury* out of formulaic xenophobia, but his modest presence places him more securely within a group dynamic, even though he, too, fights alone. Chen Shen must restore Jingwu Mun to its former dignity, not make an individualistic gesture; the subtext of *Fist of Fury 2* is that Chen Zhen's sacrifice has achieved nothing. Lo Wei's pragmatic police inspector from *Fist* has a successor in the sequel, who releases Chen several times after having the inequalities of colonial law (and his implication in them) explained to him. Lo Lieh's villainous Miyamoto, meanwhile, is a more nuanced figure than *Fist of Fury*'s sword-wielding Suzuki. When Chen arrives for their climactic face-off, he is surprised by Miyamoto's skill in Chinese calligraphy and the Japanese swordsman is honourable enough to fight empty-handed. In other words, Miyamoto engagement with China is more explicitly colonial, and he expresses a degree of aesthetic attraction to the culture he seeks to dominate. Chen defeats but does not kill him, leaving Miyamoto to commit seppuku, but not before Chen modifies the 'Sick Man of Asia' speech from the original film:

We're tolerant, patient. But you read it wrong. They're our virtues, not signs of weakness. And now you've learned that.

These lines are echoed in the climax of the loosely 'biographical' *The Secret of Bruce Lee*, as Bruce stands over a defeated opponent; "Chinese aren't cowards ... and what's more, Chinese believe in righteousness, so I'll spare you". *The Secret of Bruce Lee* imagines an unchronicled episode from Lee's time in San Francisco, but also weaves in allusions to *Way of the Dragon* (*gwailo* bullies subdued in a Chinese restaurant) and *Fist of Fury* (rival schools, the effete Chinese quisling played by Wei Ping-au). *Exit the Dragon, Enter the Tiger* also references *Fist of Fury*, with Ho Chung-tao effectively playing Chen Zhen to Bruce Lee's Huo Yuenjia. David (Ho) visits Lee (also played by Ho Chung-tao) on what one presumes to be the set of *Enter the Dragon*; "If something should happen to me", Bruce tells him, "you'll be my successor ... you must always uphold, as I have, the honour of the martial arts". Cut to the Lee funeral footage, and a distraught David. Back in Singapore, David's shrine to Bruce Lee conflates Huo Yuenjia's shrine from *Fist of Fury* with the bedroom wall of a teenager covered with posters. "Why did this happen?" David sobs, "Please, I don't understand ... I worshipped him!" But *Exit the Dragon, Enter the Tiger* also inhabits the world of Bruce Lee the 'fetish' and Bruce Lee the 'scandal'. Posters of the deceased Dragon turn up on virtually every set, and David's nemesis seems to be the press as much as the drug-traffickers who killed Lee. "The stinking liars!" he fumes on hearing the rumour that drugs were linked to Bruce's demise. The plot hinges on a tape of the traffickers talking to Suzy Yung, a Betty Ting-pei figure who blurts out that Bruce was "more than a friend". Suzy was being blackmailed into persuading Bruce to work for them; as a 'world traveller' he is the perfect courier. There is a fascinating trail of references here – gossip, movies, the dangers embedded in transnational mobility. But it was another cycle of films that engaged more explicitly with the 'real' meaning of Bruce Lee.

Dragon Stories

"Bruce Lee, you will be a Chinese hero, you will conquer the Western world."
– *Bruce Lee: The Man, The Myth/Li Xialong Chuanqi* (1976)

If Bruce Lee is the 'King of Kung Fu', where does his 'kingdom' reside? As Tony Rayns suggests, even the two most popular versions of his name tell different stories (1984: 26). 'Bruce Lee' – born in San Francisco during the Sino-Japanese war; Cantonese father, Eurasian mother; claimed US citizenship in 1958; opened his *Jun Fan Gung Fu* Institute in Seattle (1963), Oakland (1964) and Los Angeles (1967); found supporting roles in film and television shows such as *The Green Hornet* (1966), *Marlowe* (1969) and *Longstreet* (1970); posthumous international success with *Enter the Dragon*. 'Li Siu-lung/Li Xialong' – the name used in Cantonese films made in Hong Kong during his youth and resumed for his mature star vehicles; learned *Wing Chun* (probably indirectly) from Grandmaster Yip Man, and practiced it on the streets of Kowloon; became the biggest star in Asia through three films casting him as a local hero, defending diasporic Chinese in Thailand (*The Big Boss*) and Italy (*Way of the Dragon*), or fighting imperialist aggression (*Fist of Fury*).[8] Lee's two funerals also tell different stories. The one in Hong Kong may have been "only symbolic" (Chiao 1981: 31), but its many appearances in exploitation movies have done little to diminish the spectacle of mass grief, the loss of a local hero. It is difficult not to be moved by the streets of Kowloon packed with tearful admirers. The Seattle funeral was a more sober affair, but distinguished by its celebrity cast (James Coburn, Steve McQueen, Kareem Abdul Jabbar, George Lazenby), as though to mark his belated 'acceptance'.

Little wonder, then, that Lee remains a contested figure, a focus for debates about nationalism, the local and the global, 'Chinese', 'Hong Kong' and 'Chinese-American' identity. There are equal dangers in essentialising Lee and in de-territorialising him. Teo is especially resistant to the heterogeneity of Lee; the Little Dragon's nationalism is essential if one is to "appreciate fully his appeal to Chinese audiences" (1997: 110). This is an "abstract" nationalism, "an emotional wish among Chinese people living outside China to identify with China and things Chinese" (111). Lee's Chinese persona is a populist incarnation of Sinicism, "the ideology of One China, one people and one culture" (Tan 2001: 1). More specifically, films like *Fist of Fury* can be seen in terms of what See Kam Tan calls *belligerent* Sinicism; "transhistorical, essentialist and idealized ... unconditionally nationalist and racialist; vehemently anti-Japan(ese)" (6). But Lee's abstract Sinicism is rooted in something altogether more corporeal, namely his body. Lee, Teo insists, is "putting his bravest face (and body) forward in order to show that the Chinese need no longer be weaklings" (1997: 114).[9] Davis Miller, on the other hand, characterises Lee as the first "Western-style athlete in the martial disciplines" (2000: 102), a man who "revolutionized Asian fighting disciplines, made them 'organically' American" (148). It seems to be Lee's 'athleticism' that Westernises Lee here; prior to Lee, Davis claims, most martial artists "were basically incapable of defending themselves" (102). Both Teo and Miller identify important aspects of Lee, but both accounts are, in themselves, problematic. Siu-leung Li argues, more interestingly, that Lee's heterogeneity points to another contested territory, namely Hong Kong, "a place colonized, marginalized, hybridized, and yet privileged by a modernity given rise in the ambivalent interaction with the colonizer and Western culture" (2001: 528). If Kwai-cheung Lo finds "alienation and distance" in Lee's "void" nationalism (1999:110), Li finds the paradoxical subjectivity of 'Hong Kong' in precisely the contradictions embedded in the Lee myth – "a cosmopolitian postcolonial ... a former 'hometown boy' who carries the aura of the empire's modernity" (Li 2001: 528). But these debates are not consigned to critical and theoretical discourse alone – they are also, I would suggest, precisely the issues being addressed in the Bruce Lee biopics.

One might argue that Hollywood's 'acceptance' of Lee came not with *Enter the Dragon* (whose success seemed to surprise Warner Bros.), but Universal's *Dragon: The Bruce Lee Story*, a film whose budget exheeded the combined cost of Lee's star vehicles.[10] To be accepted, in this context, is a double-edged blessing. One might more accurately say that Lee was being 'claimed', as a Hollywood star, as an 'American', as the immigrant made good within a master-narrative of America's 'melting pot'. I have already mentioned *Dragon*'s debt to a less reputable cycle of Lee biographies – at a superficial level, it is a more expensive 'Bruce Li' film – but such a comparison also draws out significant differences in their respective Bruce Lees. I offer here three narrative episodes or tropes for comparison: the fictionalization of Lee's appearance at the 1964 Long Beach International Karate Tournament; apocryphal tales of real fights taking place on film sets; and Lee's use of technology to enhance his physique.

When Bruce Lee appeared at the Long Beach Tournament, he did not actually compete (he scrupulously avoided competitive combat throughout his life) but demonstrated his *Wing Chun* one-inch punch and other techniques. Naturally, it makes better dramatic sense for Lee to actually fight at Long Beach in a feature film; my concern is not with 'accuracy', but with the different narrative emphases this facilitates. In *Dragon*, Bruce (Jason Scott Lee) demonstrates Jeet Kune Do by defeating burly Johnny Sun in less than a minute (prompted by chants of "Prove it!" from the audience). This conjoins a number of narrative lines; Bruce has just fought back from a crippling back injury, he has a score to settle with Johnny (who caused the injury in an earlier encounter), and his performance here will lead directly to the role of Kato in *The Green Hornet*. *The Dragon Lives* offers a particularly memorable variation on this scene. As Bruce enters the ring, the American audience laugh uproariously at the spectacle of a small Chinese man who thinks he can fight a Westerner. His Afro-American opponent towers over him, and tousles his hair condescendingly before the fight. Bruce initially takes a beating, his humiliation exacerbated by the laughter of his audience. When he finally triumphs, the catcalls turn to cheers, but there is a strong sense of two opponents being defeated and an 'othering' of the Westerners who see Chinese as fundamentally weak. In *Dragon*, Bruce is positioned *in between* sceptical Americans (who are 'colour-blind' and respect a man who can back up what he claims) and a *Chinese* opponent; Lee has earlier fought Johnny to defend his right to teach foreigners.

There are many tales in circulation of real fights taking place on the sets of Lee's films. If one extends the dramatic license a little further, it is only a short step to these fights actually being filmed. *The Dragon Lives*, for example, would have us believe that we were watching real fights in *Enter the Dragon*. In *Dragon*, Johnny Sun's brother visits the set of *The Big Boss* to exact revenge. 'Lo Wei' is ecstatic about the fight caught on film until Lee exposes the celluloid to light, prompting the director to bluster that Bruce will "never work again!" But it is *Bruce Lee: The Man, The Myth* that fully capitalises on this conceit, by tying these challenges to the international locations used in *The Big Boss* and *Way of the Dragon*. These fights unify the myth of the immigrant hero proving himself, 'showing face' to foreign aggressors onscreen and off. By contrast, Jason Scott Lee's Bruce explicitly *separates* the two by deliberately exposing the film.

The third trope is Lee's relationship with technology. In *Dragon*, he is wired up to a muscle-stimulating machine as he is visited by producer Robert Wagner (a composite of William Dozier, Fred Weintraub and various other producers Lee worked with). Lee apparently possessed such a contraption, the same one used by the UCLA football team (Thomas 1994: 250). In the 'Bruce Li' films, this kind of technology is connected both to Lee's untimely death and configured as the dark side of his 'Westernisation'. It is easy to laugh at some of these scenes; in *The Dragon Lives*, one contraption consists of a boxing glove on a huge spring. But their significance is more striking when set against

Miller's comments about Western-style athletes. In *Dragon*, Bruce talks, types and listens to American Rock music as he is wired up; the Western ideal of the self-made body, a meeting of technology, intellect and will. In *The Dragon Lives* and *Bruce Lee: The Man, The Myth*, technology 'others' his body; in *The Man, The Myth* his gym resembles both torture chamber and scientific laboratory, lights flashing ominously, the scene bathed in eerie reds and greens. When he passes out during weight training, a white-haired mystic tells him that he will die young and then "live again". *Dragon*, then, owes a lot to the earlier cycle of 'Bruce Li' films, yet at another level, it is not like them at all. I want to explore this further through a comparison with *Bruce Lee: The Man, The Myth*, probably the most widely seen of the 'Bruce Li' films.

Both *Dragon* and *The Man, The Myth* are concerned primarily with the 'Legend' as immigrant. They follow roughly similar time-frames; in each case, the narrative proper begins with Bruce's imminent journey to America, necessitated in part by his streetfighting activities. In *Dragon*, however, Lee Hoi-chuen (Bruce's father) also seeks to protect Bruce from the 'Demon' that claimed his first son soon after birth; "You'll die in Hong Kong", he insists. There is some biographical evidence that the Lees feared losing Bruce to bad spirits; he was first named Sai-fon (Little Phoenix), a girl's name, to misdirect them (Thomas 1994: 4). But this Demon is represented as a presence throughout Lee's life in *Dragon*, a medieval armoured knight that physically assaults him and has to be defeated. The timing of its appearances are suggestive of what the Demon embodies within *Dragon*'s schema. Its first manifestation takes place while Lee is at university, reading Hegel's 'Theory of Synthesis'. The second actually happens on the set of *Enter the Dragon*, the Hall of Mirrors transformed into a phantasmatic space of combat. These are transitional moments in the Westernisation of Lee; one initiates him into European philosophy and an American University education, the second into Hollywood cinema. When one also takes into account the Demon's Orientalist appearance, it is hard to escape the conclusion that it represents Lee's 'Chineseness', that which both 'he' and the film must partially exorcise. *Dragon*'s 'Bruce Lee' is firmly American, and his experience of American racism is defined within an ultimate dream of the immigrant 'making it'. And yet, one or two scenes point to a 'Lee' that the Asian films show little interest in – Bruce Lee as Chinese-American.

In one of *Dragon*'s best scenes, Bruce and Linda (Lauren Holly) go to see *Breakfast at Tiffany's* (1961) at a 'Laff Fest Revival'. On screen, Mickey Rooney is grotesquely made up as Audrey Hepburn's Japanese neighbour, complete with buck teeth, narrowed eyes and challenged linguistic skill; "Miss Gorightly, I plo-test!" he hollers, and the audience (Linda included) laugh.[11] But Bruce is not laughing, as Linda soon notices and she makes a sobering realisation: "Let's get out of here", she says, and they both leave. Meaghan Morris describes the scene as "a parable of change and reciprocity" (1998: 13), "a rhythmically exact little story about people being differently 'moved' ... in the cinema, their wishes and dreams diverging and then, on this occasion, reaching new empathy as the responses of others around them ... inflect and colour their own" (12). But hybrid identity means that challenges come from different directions. The *Breakfast at Tiffany's* scene finds its counterpoint in a well-known episode from Lee's life. Bruce is summoned to a Chinatown Mahjong parlour by parochial Chinese elders who forbid him to teach the *gwailo*. "Bruce", begins their leader before adding the barbed aside, "I know you like to be called 'Bruce'". Bruce is not chastened by this separatism, represented as being as much of a barrier for him as America's 'Yellowphobia', and fights a duel to defend his right to teach non-Chinese.[12] *Bruce Lee: The Man, The Myth* passes over this episode fairly quickly; Bruce's antagonist is a paper tiger with a silk suit and a cigarette holder. *The Secret of Bruce Lee* re-works it to include a reconciliation between Bruce and his challenger. He explains that his motive was not only to "let foreigners experience kung fu" but to "teach them that the Chinese are not cowards and that you can't oppress them ... I believe that I'm doing good for the Chinese here". *Dragon*, on the other hand, primarily articulates a discourse of assimilation, ethnic pride tempered by a de-othering of the 'Orient':

They see something strange, something they don't understand, and they get afraid. You teach them the beauty of that strange thing and they're no longer afraid because it's become part of them.

Interestingly, though, it is in Hong Kong that Bruce's divided loyalties are more thoroughly tested. As he becomes a local hero after the premiere of *The Big Boss*, this division is constructed as being between his 'people' and his (interracial) family. "This place is eating us up", complains Linda, unlike the Linda of *Bruce Lee: The Man, The Myth*, who only says things like, "Here's your tea, honey". As Bruce edits *Way of the Dragon*, Hollywood comes to call, offering him his "ticket back to America". As the scene opens, an establishing shot reveals a Mandarin swordplay film set at 'Pearl of the Orient' (read: Golden Harvest) Studios. Two swordsmen dangle on wires; one of them drops his sword, the other gets slightly tangled, making the 'local' films look naive and provincial. As Wagner's producer promises "a Hollywood feature with all the trimmings", Bruce looks out of the window, and the sound of swords clanging tells us what he is looking at, underlining his growing desire to go 'home'. This invests Bruce's gaze with a cosmopolitan modernity. Reading back from the Westernised *Enter the Dragon*, the film seems to ask rhetorically; isn't he too sophisticated to be so 'local'?

Dragon may de-emphasise the 'local' Lee, but it does not entirely ignore it. "You want their love so bad", says 'Philip Tan' (Raymond Chow in all but name) when Bruce tells him about *Enter the Dragon*, "our love isn't good enough for you". It is both an affecting line, and an indication that the film is not monolithically ethnocentric. In *The Man, The Myth*, Ho Chung-tao's Lee gets "their love" (even if he has to occasionally beat it out of them), but "our love" (that of other Chinese) always comes first. Jogging in Hong Kong, Bruce is stopped by local road workers who have just seen *Fist of Fury*. He does his "Sick Man of Asia" speech, gives one a quick lesson and then deals with the arrogant British joggers who bully the workers. This is the populist patriot of *Fist of Fury*, not the melting-pot mediator of *Dragon*. When he tells one of his friends that he wants to make "big films to reach the whole world", he is told that "you're doing alright ... one step at a time". Even Linda, as much the centre of *Dragon* as Bruce himself, is a shadowy presence, invisible until the *Big Boss* premiere, where she functions as a piece of authenticating *mise-en-scène*.

When Bruce leaves for America in *Dragon*, it is at the behest of his father; his mother is a notable absence. On the boat, a Chinese history teacher tells him about how the *gwailo* treated the railroad workers, but Bruce insists that he is "different". In *The Man, The Myth*, it is his mother who sends him to America, while Yip Man stands in as 'Father'. Bruce is reluctant to go, preferring to stay in Hong Kong, but *Shifu* Yip instils a more serious purpose in his migration: "you can teach kung fu all over the world, you can bring honour to your people".

Bruce Lee: The Man, The Myth manages to touch most of the signposts in Lee's life – Washington University; San Francisco; Long Beach (he fights, naturally); *The Green Hornet*; rejection in Hollywood; back to Hong Kong, and film-making sojourns in Bangkok and Rome; death in Betty Ting-pei's apartment (a relationship conspicuously missing from the Linda-centred *Dragon*).[13] But at the same time, the film is structured as a series of challenges; all of the Asian bio-pics are designed to work as straight kung fu movies as well as telling a story which the audience most likely already knew. He defeats a Japanese karate master (David Chow) simply to prove that kung fu came first, or trounces a Tiger-Claw exponent who unwisely insinuates that Lee can fight "only in the movies".

With its crude machismo and choppy narrative, *Bruce Lee: The Man, The Myth* is clearly an 'Exploitation' movie in contrast to the glossy signifiers of 'quality' that distinguish *Dragon*. But their real differences lie in their preference for this or that part of the myth. *The Man, The Myth* captures something of the 'local' Lee, a figure who was probably always a hybrid of movie myth, conjecture and more reliable biographical information. And if *Dragon* constantly tries to take Lee out of Hong Kong (and vice versa), it takes some small steps in attempting to tackle the 'Chinese-American' Lee, the Lee partly constituted in reaction against Hollywood's 'Yellowphobia'. *Dragon*'s final image sees him on the set of *Enter the Dragon*, saluted by hordes of admiring extras. *The Man, The Myth* is framed by his death; the credits run over scenes of Raymond Chow trying to rouse him in Betty Ting-pei's apartment, the ambulance taking his lifeless body away. The film ends with a collage of speculations, rumours, found footage; Lee attacked by a cleaver-wielding gang, Lee told that he can cheat death by 'borrowing a soul' and living as a recluse until 1983, footage of Lee's Hong Kong and American funerals. The myths and rumours surrounding Lee's death, the possibility that he might not be dead, became particularly entwined with his 'final' film, not least in its title – *Game of Death*.

The Ghost in the Pagoda

Someday, French film critics will discover these pictures and hail them as a unique example of cinema discrepant.
 – Greil Marcus (1989: 245)

Somebody wake me up. Can people really not tell?
 – *Critique of Game of Death* (1991)

No Bruce Lee film has inspired quite the same cult obsessiveness as *Game of Death*. Like the Lee myth itself, *Game of Death* is fragmented, unstable; there is, literally, no definitive version. The footage Lee shot in 1972 was incomplete, and reportedly lacked a complete script, but no consensus exists as to how much he actually filmed. For five years after his death, it remained unseen except as tantalising stills; Lee in his famous yellow and black jumpsuit (with matching nunchakus), Kareem Abdul Jabbar towering above him in the film's climactic fight or taken down by a Lee flying kick. The premise was well-known: a martial artist (Lee) fights his way up a pagoda, each floor occupied by a different martial arts master; a Filipino Escrima expert (Dan Inosanto), a Korean Hapkido fighter (Chi Hon-tsoi/Ji Han-jai), and the master of an 'Unknown' style (Kareem Abdul Jabbar).[14] Lee would triumph because of the flexibility of his fighting style, which in fact could transcend individual 'styles'; dialogue and his intended opening sequence used the symbolism of bamboo, yielding and enduring in its flexibility. This was the essence of Lee's own Jeet Kune Do. These ideas had been hinted at in *Way of the Dragon*'s climactic fight, but *Game of Death* was clearly more ambitious and less formulaic, taking on the reputation of a curtailed 'mature' work. In its unorthodox way, *Game of Death* would have been the first 'scientific' kung fu film, exploring the interaction of different fighting styles in the same way that Lau Kar-leung would later do with more classical forms. I suspect that, in exploring martial arts so solipsistically, *Game of Death* would have problematised some of the more essentialist claims made for Lee. I say this because, as many have noted, Lee's approach to fighting did not seek to be authentically 'Chinese', but de-territorialised, boundary-crossing, absorptive of 'essences' from different styles. His dialogue in the original *Game of Death* (shot silent and left unrecorded) testifies to Lee's flirtation with the American counter-culture – he calls Inosanto "baby", and uses the word "groove" as a euphemism for "fight".

It was arguably the rise of a new home entertainment technology, DVD, that allowed the 1972 *Game of Death* a new life. Lee's 'original' always defied completion without its star, plus one of his co-stars – Chieh Yuan – died soon after Lee of similar causes (a swelling of the brain). DVD has been extensively marketed as a medium that can provide the most exhaustive version of a text; 'Extra features' regularly provide deleted footage, 'Director's cuts', alternative scenes, behind-the-scenes documentaries and other fetishistic lures. Lee's rushes had been discovered by Bey Logan in 1999, and work began on their restoration. While the 'restored' *Game of Death* did enjoy a theatrical release in Japan, the footage has been more widely seen on disc and tape; in the documentary *Bruce Lee: A Warrior's Journey* (2001) and Hong Kong Legends' two-disc *Game of Death*, which even included 'fluffed' outtakes (Lee flying into a rage during a nunchaku sequence). But neither version cohered into a definitive text; each had to make choices from different takes, different interpretations of the dialogue. And yet, it is striking how fully-formed Lee's footage looks; character dynamics seem clearly defined, and Lee's martial arts philosophy is more explicit than it had previously been. "I'm telling you", he chides Dan Inosanto during their fight, "it's difficult to have a rehearsed routine to fit in with a broken rhythm ... Rehearsed routines lack the flexibility to adapt."

The 1978 version of *Game of Death* discarded Lee's premise for an entirely new story about a kung fu star 'Billy Lo', who tangles with a crime syndicate who want to control his career. When Billy resists, he is shot on the set of his latest film, fakes his own death and takes revenge. Lee's original fight scenes were shortened, re-edited and re-framed (to eliminate other actors) to form part of the climax. For the rest of the film, 'Billy' comprised at least three doubles, poorly integrated footage from his earlier films (watch those hairstyles change!) and, inevitably, footage of his funeral to stand in for Billy's.

Asian-American independent film-maker Kip Fulbeck offers a commentary (in subtitled form) on the film's opening scenes in the shrewd and witty *Critique of Game of Death*.

Some of his observations relate to the doubling of Lee, others to his 'Americanisation' – "good white girlfriend (successful Chinese man)".[15] He only gets it wrong on a minor point of fact – 'Bruce Li' did not double Lee in *Game of Death*. Chen Yao-po, a Hong Kong businessman, played Billy in dialogue scenes. Korean Taekwondo expert Kim Tai-jung (aka 'Tang Lung') handled the bulk of the action, but in both *Game of Death* and *Tower of Death*, doubles were, in turn, doubled; Yuen Biao was Kim's acrobatic stunt double, but did substantially more than that in *Tower of Death*. The following description of the 'shadowing' of Lee gives the impression of a composite star:

> The screen-writer then had to find Bruce's shadow ... Some of them looked like Bruce physically, while others were good pugilists. But not one had the two qualities together in one to become a complete Bruce Lee ... Finally, [Golden Harvest] decided to use a number of 'Bruce Lees'. They all had a part which looked like Bruce. And these parts would be synthesized to form a Bruce Lee. (Hui 1978b: 50)

Given that this 'synthesis' effectively fails, however, the effect is rather different. For example, is Kim Tai-jung Bruce Lee's stunt double, or Lee his facial double (given the evidence in *Tower of Death* that Kim cannot carry a close-up)?

Many have commented on the disorienting experience of watching *Game of Death* and *Tower of Death*. "Fake. Real. Fake. You get the idea", offers Fulbeck's *Critique*, while Tony Williams describes *Game of Death* as "the first postmodernist martial arts film in an accidental sense in which the referent has no coherent reality" (quoted in Zhang and Zhiwei 1998: 173). Greil Marcus once conceptualised old Elvis movies as 'innocent' examples of Isidore Isou's 'Manifeste du cinéma discrepant' (1951), a negationist aesthetic committed to the "destruction of the cinema" (1989: 323): "When Elvis strums his acoustic guitar ... an electric solo comes out. When bass and guitar are seen backing him, you hear horns and piano. When he sings, the soundtrack is at least half a verse out of synch" (245).

Isou's main target was image-sound relations, whereas *Game of Death* and *Tower of Death* 'innocently' negate the star presence, blowing it to atoms. Neither film can anchor performance in a coherent 'presence'. In the opening scene of *Tower of Death*, shots of Lee from *Fist of Fury* and *Enter the Dragon* are inserted at intervals into a scene of Kim Tai-jung (playing the 'Lee' character) writing at his desk. Kim has to constantly change outfits throughout the scene to integrate (or, rather, not) Lee in a blue suit, Lee in a white shirt, Lee bare-chested. Both *Game* and *Tower* exist in different versions, with fight scenes missing or added, or appearing in a different order. Sammo Hung, choreographer of the new footage for the 1978 *Game of Death*, shot a fight between Kim Tai-jung (doubled by Yuen Biao) and Casanova Wong in a greenhouse. The scene appears in the Asian version of *Game of Death* (in place of another fight using the 'shadows'), but also in the English-language version of *Tower of Death*, like a mobile attraction that could randomly slot into a kung fu narrative. The international version of *Tower of Death* even uses footage from *The Kid/Xilu Xiang* (1950) and *Thunderstorm/Leiyu* (1957) as flashbacks to the 'Lee' character's childhood.

Game of Death was sold as Lee's 'return', by implication from the grave, yet it now seems to me to be about his disappearance. His three fights are extraordinary, amongst the best he put on film, but 'he' now seems to be the least interesting aspect of the 1978 version, and I would rather watch the longer version of his fights as a self-contained DVD extra. What is striking, instead, is the aesthetic battle going on within the theatrical *Game of Death*; for the sake of convenience, let's call its combatants 'Bruce Lee', 'Robert Clouse' and 'Sammo Hung'. Clouse made something of a career out of 'Westernising' Hong Kong stars, later working with Jackie Chan. *Game of Death*, significantly, was filmed in English, and is populated by B-list American stars. Billy Lo may be a stand-in for Bruce Lee, but he is not the populist, 'local' Lee; he is reclusive, troubled by fame, the celebrity who goes everywhere in shades.[16] The soundtrack is by John Barry, and the animated titles, too, make us think of James Bond (and, by extension, the 'Bondian' Lee of *Enter the Dragon*). But it is an incidental Lion Dance that really gives the game away; in the only 'Bruce Lee' film set in Hong Kong, the territory itself is reduced to exotic 'colour'. Its Ed Wood approach to continuity notwithstanding, Clouse's *Game of Death* wants to look like a 'classy', international (read: American) film. But shifts in the fan cults surrounding Hong Kong cinema have brought other elements to the fore, not least Sammo Hung's exuberant choreography, Kim Tai-jung's precision kicking and Yuen Biao's athleticism. Hung and Yuen are a reminder that other action traditions, with different influences and inflections, had developed since Lee. During a rousing locker-room fight between 'Billy' and Bob Wall's karate heavy, Bey Logan discerns "an object lesson in the real Sammo Hung style" (DVD commentary). Hung's mastery of fast-edits, undercranking and 'power powder' to 'sell' the action contrast with the comparative sobriety of Lee's fights, but they re-territorialize a film that had otherwise floated from its time (1972) and threatened to float from its cultural context.

Tower of Death, dazzlingly choreographed by Yuen Wo-ping, confirms this impression. Lee now appears only in outtakes from *Enter the Dragon*, and is never seen in action; he is, once again, doubled by Kim Tai-jung and Yuen Biao. *Tower of Death*'s eagerness *not* to be a 'Bruce Lee' film is confirmed by the death of his character about a third of the way through the film, leaving Kim Tai-jung to take over as his brother. The *Enter the Dragon* footage is disquieting, unfamiliar images from familiar settings; Lee is more ghostly than ever, but no longer a 'spectre of absorbtion'. On *Tower of Death*'s DVD commentary, Bey Logan talks us through who performs what in the film, breaking what is already a fairly precarious 'illusion'. Liberated from the need to unify 'Lee', this starts to feel less like *cinéma discrépant*. Again, this is bound up with technologies of consumption; DVD accomodates both the fetishization of performance in a martial arts film and the kind of cult capital disseminated by Logan's commentary. Far from simply 'spoiling the illusion', Logan resurrects and re-positions the 'aura' supposedly lost to the doubling process, shifting it to Yuen Biao, who seems to perform the film's most dazzling moves.

It makes perfect sense that fans insist that more *Game of Death* footage exists to be unearthed. Part of its enduring appeal is a tantalisingly unfulfillable desire that somehow stands in for Lee himself. *Game of Death* offers us Lee as auteur, martial arts philosopher, 'shadow', fetish and corpse. It offers itself as incomplete 'masterpiece' (the kind that never disappoints or falls short of its reputation), or 'cursed movie' (Brottman 2000: 112). When Billy Lo is killed by 'blanks' on the film set, the scene uses Lee's final leap from *Fist of Fury*, but also looks forward, uncannily, to Brandon Lee's death on the set of *The Crow* (1993).[17] Brandon's 'presence' was synthesised by digital head replacements attached to a double – unlike *Game of Death*, you cannot see the joins – and *The Crow*'s Goth-chic appeal has become inseparable from its star's tragic shooting.

According to Mikita Brottman, "dead celebrities are symptoms of a kind of cultural psychosis because they embody social values (mainly to do with the nature of the human body, and bodily death) that are, in one way or another, in serious crisis" (2000: 106). The rise of the star system parallelled a new sense of the "contemporary public self", a growing conception of selfhood as individualist rather than collective (111). Death, she suggests, held fewer terrors within a collectivist selfhood, because the larger group guaranteed survival and continuity. By contrast, within an individualist ethos, "the self becomes more vulnerable to death, since death in modern societies takes away not only life, but that which gives life its value" (111). Stardom, an extreme manifestation of individualist selfhood, underlines the centrality and attendant vulnerability of the expressive body:

> Part of the horror of the celebrity death ... is the sudden loss of revelatory power suffered by the star's body. That public body, once so expressive and so intensely scrutinized, is abruptly transformed into a limp marionette ... And yet somehow, paradoxically, this detached puppet still purports to be the eminently notable celebrity its strings once so publicly animated. (111)

Given the existence of "cultic myths surrounding celebrity deaths", it seems fair to say that death gives as well as taking away, and Bruce and Brandon are a case in point. At the risk of sounding brutal, and not underestimating his talent, Brandon's death gave him a star persona that he did not previously possess (except as 'celebrity son') and the perfect movie to cement it. *The Crow*'s romantic morbidity has made it a perennial Goth favourite. With Bruce, things are rather more complicated because his death was experienced in very different cultural contexts. This is partly a matter of timing. When Lee died, two of his films had opened in the US, *The Big Boss* in May 1973, *Fist of Fury* in June. In the UK, *Fist of Fury* came first, opening on 19 July, the day before he died. In other words, the Western Lee cult was always founded on the paradox of an impossibly athletic and charismatic star who seemed to have burned out on first contact. In this context, Lee's death was always part of his 'aura'. In Hong Kong, Li Siu-lung was already known for his Cantonese films, but had in any case been breaking box office records in South-East Asia for two years. One only needs to look again at the Hong Kong funeral footage to see that when Lee's 'strings' were cut, the effect was rather more traumatic than the curiosity it provoked in the West. No celebrity corpse has ever been so visible, and perhaps no star seemed quite so 'alive' prior to his death. The first Bruce Lee magazine I ever bought, *Kung Fu Monthly* no. 1 (1974), offered tantalising images of him from his films, but also the (then) shocking picture of him in his coffin, his face barely recognisable. Many are startled by the inclusion of his funeral in *Game of Death*, but given that it also turns up in *Tower of Death* (English version), *The Clones of Bruce Lee, Exit The Dragon, Enter the Tiger, Bruce Lee: The Man, The Myth, Dynamo* and many more, is there perhaps more at stake than 'good' and 'bad' taste? Perhaps there is also the sense of an enigma being replayed, scrutinised, obsessively returned to. Bruce Lee's body 'meant' so much in life, on screen; what did it now mean in its lifeless state?

Kip Fulbeck poses a quite different set of questions in *Critique of Game of Death* – "Why do we want to keep Bruce Lee alive? If the Chinese man needs a hero is this how we get one?" Fulbeck is primarily concerned with Lee's potential (or not) as a hero for Asian-Americans, and wonders whether "the Chinese loved him or maybe ... loved America loving him". There are no easy answers to these questions, and once again they involve the interrogation of ghosts and doubles. Bey Logan suggests that the effect of Lee's films on the Hong Kong industry was "negligible", and that the "big Chinese hits released the year after his death ... look pretty much as they would had Bruce never returned to Hong Kong" (1995: 43). For a 'Legend' and local hero, his legacy is not always easy to pin down, which brings us back to the conundrum of where the King of Kung Fu's Kingdom actually is. Hong Kong? America? The nomadic space of the émigré? Lee's successors – some of them his former 'shadows', or performers *in* his shadow (stuntmen like Jackie Chan, opponents like Sammo Hung) – would shine in very different, and much more 'local', films. If Chan later became a 'legend' of sorts, it was by defying death rather than being 'immortalised' by it. The drunken masters, fat dragons, iron-fisted monks and prodigal sons who populated kung fu comedy provided a line of continuity into 'modern' Hong Kong cinema, whereas Lee marked a road that seemingly led nowhere without his presence. Their acrobatic, vulgar and cynical exploits are the subject of the next chapter.

Chapter Four
Fat Dragons and Drunken Masters
Kung Fu Comedy

Amongst the many pleasures on offer in Michael Hui's satirical comedy *Private Eyes/ Banjin Baliang* (1976) are two knockabout kung fu sequences choreographed by Sammo Hung. The first is the one that often turns up on compilation tapes – Hui and a suspected pickpocket square off in a restaurant kitchen, using woks, pans, a swordfish and a shark's jaw (cue *Jaws* theme) as weapons. As a *pièce de résistance*, Michael wields a string of sausages as a nunchaku, albeit one cut down to size by his opponent's snapping shark jaw. The second scene involves Michael's brother, Cantopop idol Sam, as his put-upon assistant, taking on a pair of shoplifters in a supermarket. One of the thieves, cornered by Sam, breaks into Shaolin Five Animal shapes to the accompaniment of 'Under the General's Orders', the musical theme associated with Wong Fei-hung. But the Tiger and the Crane are no match for Sam's streetsmart fighting – kicked into a frozen food compartment, the shoplifter emerges with a frozen turkey on his head before being unceremoniously deposited amidst a pile of toilet rolls. Comedy was in the frontline of the new Cantonese-dialect cinema that emerged in Hong Kong from the mid-1970s, and here it is giving the Mandarin martial arts film a good-natured going-over. Classical kung fu is parodied and rendered incongruous by supermarkets and frozen food, signifiers of Hong Kong's Westernisation and metropolitanisation (not that the film wholeheartedly embraces those either). Sam Hui, significantly, is not a kung fu master – he knows just enough to get by and is quick-witted enough to outsmart various antagonists in the film. His fighting style anticipates the non-style Jackie Chan will later use to battle through shopping malls, restaurants and other urban spaces. His adaptability and pragmatism are mirrored by the kung fu novices played not only by Chan, but Sammo Hung, Yuen Biao and others.

One might argue that martial arts and comedy are Hong Kong's two most important genres. But if kung fu has enjoyed a certain global mobility, then comedy often finds it more difficult to cross cultural, linguistic and geographical borders, and such is largely the case here. Hong Kong comedy has a rich history comparatively unknown in the West – post-war social comedy, Michael Hui's satires of rapid urbanization, the crowd-pleasing antics of the *Aces Go Places* series, and the 'nonsense' comedy of Stephen Chiau. Some of this critical neglect is bound up with the nature of comedy. Notwithstanding the global reach of Hollywood, comedy is arguably the most culturally specific of genres, dependent on linguistic nuances, shared reference points, and the social boundaries and negotiated inclusions/exclusions that allow 'us' to laugh at 'them' (or, alternatively, 'ourselves'). Stephen Chiau's Cantonese puns, slang and insults are an interesting case in point – his sometimes untranslatable 'nonsense' comedy, Linda Chiu-han Lai argues, "addresses the Cantonese-speaking Hong Kong insider as a privileged viewer who alone can understand the puns, jokes, and generic allusions of the films, thus fulfilling the function of collective identities formation" (2001: 232). More recently, some of Chiau's films have enjoyed video releases in the West, but only those which draw on and parody elements taken to be synonymous with Hong Kong cinema – martial arts, gunplay and other action genres.

Jenny Lau, in her excellent analysis of Michael Hui's comedies, attributes their Western marginalization not only to problems of translation but to a crude polarization of Hong Kong cinema into 'action' and 'art' cinema that excludes the popular genre that has most consistently addressed local concerns and experiences. Lau has little time for those accounts that see Hong Kong cinema only 'discovering' itself after the Sino-British Joint Declaration. Rather, comedy is part of a longer cinematic tradition that reflected the experience of "dislocation and relocation, rejection and identification, and other aspects of an exile/colonised culture" (1998: 23). Where Hong Kong comedy has travelled successfully – most conspicuously in the films of Chan – it has been part of a more hybridised package, and one in which action is compulsory. The kung fu comedy and its offshoots are such an example, but they can still be seen as being governed by some of the same determinants that Lau outlines. Moreover, while Western fans (myself included) primarily enjoy their physical (and, therefore, more 'universal') comedy, they too engage in bouts of verbal jousting such as the following rapid-fire exchange from *Prodigal Son*:

Leung Yi-tai (Lam Ching-ying): Now tell me who you are.

Leung Tzan (Yuen Biao): Your father.

Leung Yi-tai: My father is no ordinary man.

Leung Tzan: Neither am I.

Leung Yi-tai: My father is handsome.

Leung Tzan: So am I!

Leung Yi-tai: My father has syphilis.

Leung Tzan: Me too! (Double-take – realises what he has just said.)

Fig. 7 The rogue master takes charge of the trickster hero: Beggar Su (Yuen Siu-tin) and Wong Fei-hung (Jackie Chan) in *Drunken Master*

Fat Dragons and Drunken Masters

Kung fu comedy is a transitional sub-genre, positioned between the emerging Cantonese cinema of Hui and the 'new wave' directors and the declining Mandarin kung fu film in which its key players (Chan, Hung *et al*) began their careers. Chan Ting-ching observes that while the kung fu comedies were nominally set in period, they were contemporary in atmosphere and outlook, not only in their incongruous reference points (catchphrases from television and advertising), but in their "reflection of a modern competitive society in which only the fittest survive and the younger are generally fitter" (1980: 149). Ng Ho, too, discerns a break from the values of classic kung fu films and an "emphasis on individual achievement and an outdoing of one's own master [which] parallels the ethos of capitalism" (1980a: 43). I would agree that the films map an urban sensibility onto the thinnest of Qing Dynasty settings, and that they mark a shift from the genre's investment in 'China' to the more Hong Kong-centred Cantonese cinema. But there is another way of looking at their survivalism beyond simply seeing them as unequivocally embracing Hong Kong's hyper-capitalist ethos. The directors, choreographers and most of the leading players in these films all came from the same background and had followed similar career trajectories. The films, therefore, also seem to be rooted in the collective experience of former Opera performers 'surviving' as stuntmen until they became stars, directors or choreographers (or, in some cases, all three). This was a dangerous, often poorly paid, and intensely macho environment, which might partly explain (but not excuse) the misogyny that often comes with such a rough-tough homosociality.[1] The 'outdoing' of the Master can be seen as an ambivalent reflection on their own 'masters', such as the notorious Yu Zhanyuan, brutal patriarch of the 'Seven Little Fortunes' troupe that included Chan, Hung, Yuen Biao, Corey Yuen and Yuen Wah. The quintessential kung fu comedy master is played by Yuen Siu-tin, literal father and Opera *shifu* to Yuen Wo-ping and his brothers. In *Drunken Master*, Beggar Su (Yuen Siu-tin) tells Jackie Chan's youthful Wong Fei-hung that he must first learn how to fall properly – odd advice for a fighter, but perfectly sound training for an Opera performer. The training is relentlessly cruel, and has often been mapped biographically onto Chan's brutal experiences at the hands of Yu Zhuanyuan. But, equally importantly, these were performers trained in a dying tradition (Beijing Opera),[2] whose careers began in another declining tradition (Mandarin martial arts films) before developing the more locally flavoured kung fu comedies, which also had a limited lifespan in their original form. Just as the films' heroes invent new styles, the most talented film-makers invented new subgenres and variations – Sammo Hung's kung fu ghost comedies, Jackie Chan's mixture of stuntwork, silent slapstick and action-adventure, and the Taoist magical slapstick of Yuen Wo-ping's *Miracle Fighters/Qimen Dunjia* (1982). The films celebrate survival and resilience in a constantly changing environment, a context mirrored in Hong Kong's film industry and socio-geographic space.

What constitutes a kung fu comedy? Martial arts films have always accomodated comic characters and elements – Wong Fei-hung's pupils Leung Foon and 'Buck Tooth' Soh, the broad fish-out-of-water comedy of *Way of the Dragon*'s first third, Fu Sheng's often mischievous persona, the knockabout episodes in Lau Kar-leung's films. Alternatively, as we have seen in the case of *Private Eyes*, kung fu can feature as one component in urban comedy. Stephen Chiau, in particular, seems especially fond of including martial arts in his films and has paid tribute to Bruce Lee in several films. Sek Kei sees *The Good, the Bad and the Loser/Yi Zhi Guanggun Zou Tianya* (1976) as the start of the trend for comic kung fu (1980: 35–6). Between 1977 and 1979, Sammo Hung, Yuen Wo-ping and Jackie Chan had made their directorial debuts, with *The Iron-Fisted Monk* (1977), *Snake in the Eagle's Shadow/Shexing Diaoshou* (1978) and *The Fearless Hyena/Xiao Quan Guaizhao* (1979) respectively. By 1982 the trend was fizzling out, as indicated by the failure of Chan's *Dragon Lord/Long Shaoye*. Sammo Hung was already exploring further possibilities, producing and/or directing supernatural kung fu comedies like *Encounters of the Spooky Kind* (1980), *The Dead and the Deadly/Ren Xia Ren* (1982) and the *Mr Vampire* series (1985), and developing a variation on the *Aces Go Places* series starting with *Winners and Sinners* (1983). The 'Lucky Stars' films adhered to a standardised structure – periodic martial arts fight scenes involving a guest-starring Jackie Chan and Yuen Biao, but largely given over to what some have seen as the Asian *Carry On* team (Hung, Richard Ng, Eric Tsang, Charlie Chin and Fung Shui-fan). These, in turn, spun off into films simply showcasing Hung, Chan and Yuen Biao, including *Project A* (1983) and *Dragons Forever* (1988).

The kung fu comedies of the 1976–82 period grew out of rather than making a clean break from some of the classic kung fu film's narrative/thematic tropes. Most of them are about Master/Pupil relationships, but with an irreverent or cynical flavour. Their archetypal *shifu* is minor Shaolin legend Beggar Su, a vagabond, drunkard and rogue with a mean streak when training disciples. "The sky is my roof and I sleep where I want", he says in *Drunken Master*, but his long-suffering wife in *Dance of the Drunk Mantis/Nanbei Zui Quan* (1979) puts it rather less romantically – "You shit and I must wipe your ass". Bickering husband-wife teams share *shifu* duties most memorably in *Miracle Fighters*, but also appear in *Drunken Tai Chi/Xiao Taiji* (1984). As for the pupil, he is no longer the diligent, patriotic student of the Shaolin films. Ng Ho characterises him as:

A bright but hopelessly lazy kid, who lacks both the staying power needed for martial arts training and respect for his *shifu* ... Often, after suffering a defeat, he will master the perseverance to train in martial arts more seriously, and will eventually reach the point where he surpasses the skills of his *shifu* ... After his ultimate victory, he has no interest in furthering himself in the martial arts world; he prefers to go on living from day to day, aimlessly. (1980a: 43, 46)

Such protagonists can be found in *Drunken Master* and, particularly, the conmen-heroes of *Knockabout*, who adopt a *shifu* so that he will have to feed them, and learn kung fu so that they will be 'set up for life'. Only when Taipao (Leung Kar-yan) is killed by their unscrupulous master, a wanted criminal (Lau Kar-wing), does Yipao (Yuen Biao) train in earnest under the vagabond detective Beggar Bo (Sammo Hung). But the hero can just as easily be a Fool-Hero, such as the hapless Foggy (Yuen Hsin-yi) in *Dance of the Drunk Mantis* or the aptly-named Mouse (Yuen Biao) in *Dreadnaught/Yongzhe Wuju* (1980). Most importantly, he does not become a 'master', in spite of his training; in fact, he resists it as a form of stasis or death. He is not superior to the powerful villain he defeats – he beats him under specific conditions on a particular day. In *Encounters of the Spooky Kind* and *The Dead and the Deadly* (1992), for example, Hung acquires at least some of his skills via supernatural possession. The hero is pragmatic and adaptable, creative and unpredictable; a figure, Steve Fore suggests, "that much of Hong Kong's younger generation could relate to far more easily" (2001: 126), a younger generation that felt less connected to 'China' than to urban Hong Kong. The majority of kung fu comedies also adhere to the mastering of a special style, such as Hung's two films about *Wing Chun* master Leung Tzan, *Warriors Two* and *Prodigal Son*. More commonly, the special style belongs to kung fu's more outlandish, carnivalesque variations. *Zui Quan* (Drunken Fist), the style based on the Eight Drunken Immortals popularised and modernised in *Drunken Master*,[3] involves reeling and swaying in a simulation of intoxication before unleashing disorienting attacks. Monkey style, the screeching, scratching, gambolling style featured in *Mad Monkey Kung Fu/Feng Hou* (1979) and the climax of *Knockabout*, works on similar principles. In *Knockabout*, Yuen Biao and Sammo Hung intimidate Lau Kar-wing by squatting on tables, rattling them violently while emitting deranged simian chatter. Just as often, the style is a bizarre or comic new invention, an irreverent break from tradition – the Cat's Paw (*Snake in the Eagle's Shadow*), Holy Ghost Claw (*Buddhist Fist*), 'Sick' kung fu (*Dance of the Drunk Mantis*), 'Laundry' kung fu (*Dreadnaught*), and, most paradigmatic of all, 'Garbage Boxing' (*Knockabout*), a style based on the detritus of other styles. Finally, some of the films extend and/or subvert the tradition of hagiographies of 'Great Masters' – Wong Fei-hung, Leung Tzan, Zhuangmi Liu, Beggar Su – a feature usually allied to their cynical take on the *shifu* and Master/Disciple relations.

It is, of course, problematic to reduce a sub-genre to three 'Great Men', yet equally difficult to downplay the importance of its prime movers, Sammo Hung, Jackie Chan and Yuen Wo-ping, whose careers converged in a number of ways.[4] Yuen directed Chan's breakthrough films, while Chan and Hung grew up together and worked together many times in what many regard as a complex love/hate relationship.[5] Yuen and Hung collaborated on *The Magnificent Butcher* and Yuen later made one of his increasingly rare onscreen appearances in Hung's *Eastern Condors* (1986). But director-choreographers never shine without their units or 'clans', and kung fu comedies also showcase the talents of performers like Yuen Biao, Lam Ching-ying, Leung Kar-yan ('Beardy' to his English-speaking fans), Lau Kar-wing and various members of the Yuen family. Each film-maker brought his own specialities to the genre. Hung was the first director-choreographer to experiment with visual style, in contrast with the sober classicism of Lau Kar-leung. In *Prodigal Son*, the extras freeze theatrically (it is not a freeze frame) until the opening narration is over; when Sammo hits Dean Shek in *The Iron-Fisted Monk*, he spins on the spot like a cartoon character; he uses undercranking and 'power powder' to enhance the impact of the fights. Yuen Wo-ping brings a carnivalesque quality to fight scenes – *Miracle Fighters* makes dizzying, exhilarating use of mannequins, puppets, masks and other disguises. As in Bakhtin's carnival aesthetic, the body is "unfinished, outgrows itself, transgresses its own limits" (1965/1984: 26). When the evil Bat Master (Yuen Hsin-yi) fights irascible Taoist Wizard (or *fat-si*) Leung Kar-yan, the latter appears to grow a third leg, which enhances his kicking power. Limbs start to emerge from unexpected places – a fist from the neck of his robes, which then opens to reveal an eye in its palm. It turns out that apprentice hero Yuen Yat-chor is concealed within Leung's robes and providing the extra limbs. In the fights' most hilarious scene, Leung and his pupil position themselves behind a curtain and converge into a midget fighter, using Yuen's upper body, while Leung's hands provide the feet. It was some time before Jackie Chan could compete with Hung and Yuen's inexhaustible inventiveness – I would suggest that he came into his own when he 'transcended' (for want of a better word) the kung fu film. His own unique contribution to cinematic spectacle was his distinctive way of interacting with the ever-changing urban environment of Hong Kong. *Police Story 2/Jingcha Gushi Xuji* (1988) includes one marvellous example. Ka Kui (Chan) is on the first floor of a building – the villains are on the first floor of the building on the opposite side of a busy street. How to get to them in the quickest possible time? He jumps off a ledge onto a bus, then from the bus onto a lorry travelling in the opposite direction (jumping over and ducking under objects overhead), then off the lorry and through the window in the opposite building. This is exactly the sort of stunt that Chan's legion of fans worship him for, but there is more going on than his simply putting his body on the line. As Jenny Lau argues, some of the best modern Hong Kong comedies were about the experience of Hong Kong's mutating cultural, technological and physical space. Chan found a brilliant way of embodying this concern in physical movement – he seems simultaneously to be under constant threat from the environment and yet always able to outmanoeuvre and barely outpace this transmutative space. According to Ramie Tateishi, Chan's aesthetic is founded on "dynamic movement and reconfiguring of space" (1988: 78) – "objects are not only turned active by being incorporated into the action, but they become a natural extension of the very terrain *itself* across which Chan travels" (80). Mark Gallagher (1997: 25) has likened Chan's relationship to objects and environments to Tom Gunning's account of Buster Keaton's interaction with turn-of-the-century technology, in which the star "merges with the central device, becoming a projectile in thrall to the laws of mechanics" (1995a: 99). Gunning locates Keaton's "fascination with the way things work" within an 'operational' aesthetic bridging the late nineteenth and early twentieth centuries, a "romance with the devices of a heroic but already fading age of machines" (100). While 1970s/1980s Hong Kong is not quite the same thing – try throwing in the cultural schizophrenia comcomitant with colonialism and globalisation – one can see a similar dynamic in Michael Hui's Tashlinesque fascination with gadgets,[6] and Chan's conception of modernity as obstacle course.

If Chan reinvents the "mischief machine" of silent American comedy, Aaron Anderson also observes his "uncanny ability to find and use the empty space around him" in a fight from *Rumble in the Bronx* (1995):

> When pinned behind a refrigerator he slides into the space underneath. When pinned behind a shopping cart, he leaps through the space of the cart itself. When his base of support is pushed from behind him, he rolls with the fall, using the moving side of the refrigerator as a space on which to fight. Even when trapped against a wall, he finds new space to attack. (2002)

Again, it might be useful to think of this capacity for finding empty, active space, in relation to overpopulated Hong Kong, where every empty space is built (and rebuilt) on, where maximum bodies and buildings are squeezed into minimal spaces.

'Fight' and 'Chase': Narrative, Gags and Comic Kung Fu

If equating Hong Kong cinema with early American cinema is problematic, Jackie Chan, in particular, has frequently invited such a comparison. "Right now, the video is my instructor", he has said, suggesting a newly mediated *shifu*. "I like to watch Charlie Chaplin, Buster Keaton..." (Logan 1995: 67). The comedy in kung fu comedy is very broad, often crude (fart gags are especially popular), physical, sometimes nonsensical and disruptive of the fictional 'frame'. In *Prodigal Son*, two characters break into a musical number while fighting, as if to acknowledge the comparison of martial arts films with musicals. In *Miracle Fighters*, the late Yuen Siu-tin 'appears' in a painting of the Taoist clan's deceased master – offered a drink, 'his' mouth is animated to accept it and 'his' cheeks flush after the tipple. Such gags, in addition to the often very theatrical fight scenes, seem to ally kung fu with what Gunning calls a 'cinema of attractions' (1990), an early performative cinema whose setpiece structure was rooted in the acts or 'turns' of live performance rather than narrative. The 'cinema of attractions' has been to seen to have survived in modes ranging from gag-based comedy (Crafton 1995; King 2002) to the Hollywood musical to the theme-park spectacle of contemporary Hollywood blockbusters (King 2000). Clearly, martial arts films can be seen in this way, too – Lo (1999: 116) describes Chan's films as "multiple loops of actions and stunts", and the following description of an 'attraction' from *Twinkle Twinkle Lucky Stars/Xiari Fuxing* (1985) points to the role video has played in foregrounding 'turns' over narrative:

> The warehouse fight scene ... contains one of the best kicks in cinematic history. Yuen Biao, coming off the side of a crate in a mid-air cartwheel, landing perfectly, feigning a 180-degree roundhouse kick followed by a perfect side kick. It's a moment that will have you rewinding your video in disbelief! (Baker and Russell 1994: 206).

Kung fu comedy, like American slapstick and gag-based comedy, has its origins in live performance – variety, music hall and burlesque in the former case (King 2002: 24), street acrobatics, northern-style martial arts scenes in Beijing Opera, and the amalgamation of martial arts, dance and drama in China's post-Cultural Revolution "model revolutionary works" (Ng 1980a: 42) in the latter. The concept of 'slapstick' – named after the sound of two joined slats 'slapping' as one clown strikes another (Crafton 1995: 108), and encompassing "various forms of violent comedy" (Kramer 1995: 200) – takes on particular resonance in kung fu comedy. "To transform acts of willful maliciousness and intense pain into comedy", Peter Kramer argues in reference to American slapstick, "performers had to signal clearly that their actions were make believe, and constituted highly accomplished athletic routines" (1995: 200). Signifiers of this 'make-believe' were coded through "excess" and "fantastic exaggeration" (200). Kung fu comedies include such 'make-believe' signs – the contorted faces, winces and reactions of Jackie Chan or

Sammo Hung (both of whom can mug like troopers), comic sound effects and 'wah-wah' musical cues. When bald characters are struck on the head repeatedly (as in *Drunken Master* and *Knockabout*), they immediately break out in golfball-sized lumps which proliferate until they resemble a mass of angry haemorrhoids. But such comic violence can rub shoulders with more graphic, 'realistic' brutality, especially in Sammo Hung's films, which also run to eye-gougings, impalings and other blood-soaked demises. Ng notes such radical shifts in tone in Hung's films "throwing the overall tone into doubt" (1980a: 42).

Early film comedy – and, by extension, gag-based comedy in general – has generated a debate about which 'attraction' takes precedence; as Donald Crafton subdivides it, 'pie' (gag) or 'chase' (narrative) (Crafton 1995). In our case, perhaps the demarcation should be 'fight' and 'chase', except that many of the fights also involve generous slices of 'pie'. Crafton polarises gags and narrative, and sees the former as largely expelling the latter, while Gunning sees their relationship as often anachronistic but ultimately linked – "forces of disruption *are essential* to even the most conventional narrative" (1995b: 120). Certainly, in the case of kung fu comedy, narrative, however formulaic and rudimentary, never quite goes away. In Yuen Wo-ping's films, it tends to be much looser and more episodic, the visual style presentational, narrative impetus almost non-existent. But some of Sammo Hung's films are more carefully constructed – *Prodigal Son* not only parallels two overprotected, spoilt sons, hero Leung Tzan and royally connected villain-by-default Ng (Frankie Chan), but actually develops this idea with comparative sophistication. The film extends its structured pairs to its contrasting *shifu* figures who once shared the same master, the slightly built Leung Yi-tai, who plays female roles in the local Opera, and rotund, rough-and-ready Wong Wa-bo (Hung).

Ng Ho identifies two types of kung fu comedy – one in which the narrative structure and situation are inherently comic, and one in which comic characters are inserted into otherwise 'straight' kung fu films. Yuen Wo-ping has perhaps made more of the former – in *Drunken Master* and *Miracle Fighters*, comic characters vastly outnumber the serious ones (the villain is a kind of 'straight man') and the narratives are geared to the maximum number of comic 'turns'. *Miracle Fighters'* plot is built on both mistaken identity – Yuen Yat-chor mistaken for a missing prince – and a more familiar tale of his apprenticeship as fighter and wizard. But the film seems driven primarily by the antics of Leung Kar-yan's dissolute Taoist, equipped with a huge stomach and a goatee you could cut paper with – his love/hate relationship with dragged-up Yuen Cheung-yan, exaggerated vanity and enjoyably innapropriate behaviour (he drenches a rival with a 'Golden Shower' while he's praying for rain). Assassins try to kill him while he sleeps, dripping poison from a roll of cotton, but his snoring is so violent that he blows the poison back up the string and kills his enemies without even waking. When the villain tries to impersonate him, he gives himself away by not smelling badly enough. Sammo Hung's *Knockabout* follows similar principles – everyone in the film is a trickster of some sort – but several of his films fall into the second category. In many of his films, Hung himself provides most of the comedy, exploiting his physical appearance and 'fool' or 'trickster' personas. When we learn that his character in *Encounters of the Spooky Kind* is known as Courageous Cheung, we are laughing already – we know how skillfully Sammo can play cowardly or lazy characters. Often his best visual joke is the discrepancy between his appearance – supporting characters routinely call him 'Fatty' – and what he can physically do: "I'm built like an elephant, but I move like a monkey", he proudly proclaims in *Prodigal Son*. Sometimes, his bulk works for him – subduing opponents by sitting on them, hitting Dean Shek with his arse in *Warriors Two*. But it can work against him, too, literally bringing him down to earth – in *Encounters of the Spooky Kind*, he flattens several police officers with athletic *élan*, but rather spoils the effect by sitting on a bench that gives way under his weight. Hung's body epitomises the conflicting corporeal messages that kung fu comedy sends out – athletic and grotesque, superhuman and all too flawed by the limitations of flesh. *Warriors Two* plays largely as both straight Master/Pupil and revenge narrative – Hung plays one of Leung Tzan's pupils, Fei Chun. When Leung is killed through treachery, the villains arrive to massacre the school, but Fei Chun survives by pretending to be dead, rubbing his face in a dead comrade's blood, grimacing when someone treads on his hand. The three surviving heroes plan their revenge by matching their skills to the most appropriate opponent, but Fei Chun gets their names mixed up and each has to fight the very person they did not want to. He triumphs anyway, battering his enemy while screaming his master's name hysterically. Exhausted and close to tears, his face suddenly fills with exaggerated bravado – "Don't run into me in the underworld", he warns his dead adversary, "or I'll kill you again." During the climax, he is pitted against the only other comic character in the film, Dean Shek's arthritic weasel Chui, with his lopsided gait and jerky, angular movements, his body periodically stiffening with cramp. Chui conceals a metal bowl in his hat which clangs when Fei Chun makes painful contact. Inevitably, the bowl changes hands and Fei delivers a devastating headbutt to his adversary. Chui crumples, and a puddle spreads beneath him: "You've wet your pants", Fei Chun helpfully points out – "I know", concedes Chui before expiring.

"A Fart for the King of Sticks": Kung Fu Karnival

There is a scene in *Prodigal Son* where Sammo Hung teaches Yuen Biao how to gather his *qi* while maintaining his *Wing Chun* stance. Their faces strain before giving way to looks

Fig. 8 Spoiled brawler Leung Tzan (Yuen Biao) courts the unconventional Leung Yi-tai (Lam Ching-ying) as his master in *Prodigal Son*

of intense relief; the next stage is to "wipe the Buddha's face with gold" (cue mime of tearing off and using a strip of toilet paper); finally, each pulls an imaginary chain to the accompaniment of a 'flushing' sound. The gag is, of course, anachronistic (flushing toilets and toilet paper in the Qing Dynasty), but, more importantly, irreverently scatalogical – *Wing Chun* form reduced to shitting, wiping and flushing. The scene is the very epitome of the "lowering of all that is high, spiritual, ideal, abstract" (Bakhtin 1965/1984: 19–20) – the refined gathering of *qi* gives way to the movement of the bowels that all bodies (even those of kung fu masters) have to make. In *Drunken Master*, the most noble kung fu hero of all, Wong Fei-hung, farts in the face of the 'king of sticks' before pushing his face into shit ("That's called 'Hungry Dog Eats Shit'"). Earlier in the film, he is caught blagging a free meal in an inn – the proprietor's burly henchman Gorilla punches Wong repeatedly in the stomach until he regurgitates the entire meal. *Miracle Fighters* includes the best fart joke ever. The Bat Master transfixes hero Shu Gun (Yuen Yat-chor) by pinning his shadow with his magical powers. Shu strains to free himself, strains so hard, in fact, that he lets loose a gigantic fart (we see his trousers move with the force) that blows out the torch behind him, removing his shadow and freeing him.

This is tame stuff compared to the gross-out traditions of the Farrelly Brothers, or even some of Stephen Chiau's comedies, but it marked a powerfully vulgar turn for the kung fu film. We might see Bruce Lee struggling with Western toilets and negotiating the stomach upsets brought on by foreign menus in *Way of the Dragon*, but the film

Kung Fu Cult Masters

remains discreet about his actual bodily functions. The martial hero's body was largely above such things. There is a tradition within *wu xia* fiction of eccentric protagonists who are "abnormal among men, but akin to nature" (Koo 1981/1986: 27), but their lowly or grotesque appearances belied their internal power and virtue. Beggar Su, the dissolute vagabond of so many kung fu comedies, has inner strength but nothing resembling virtue – he is actually made stronger by intoxication when practicing Drunken Fist. His hair a mop of gray straw, nose permanently red, Su is an abject, but invincible, figure. He has few redeeming features, largely living up to his "cunning, violent and mean" reputation during the notoriously sadistic training sequences. In *Dance of the Drunk Mantis*, he actively dislikes his pupil – Foggy is forced on him by Su's wife. He responds by eliminating the actual pedagogic content from the training scenes, so that they degenerate into undiluted cruelty. Foggy's arms are tied to a huge fan, which he operates as Su lies on his makeshift hammock. He force-feeds him alcohol until he passes out and then hurls obscene insults at him. In *Drunken Master*, he shakes uncontrollably when (horror of horrors) he sobers up, rendered virtually helpless. In *The Magnificent Butcher*, where Beggar Su is played by Fang Mei-sheng,[7] the *Popeye* theme plays on the soundtrack as he drinks mid-fight – foul-smelling (people recoil from his breath) and with a rip in his trousers, wine is his spinach, the 'lower bodily stratum' the source of his power (he, too, makes pugilistic use of anal gasses). In several English-dubbed prints (and some English subtitles), Beggar Su becomes 'Sam the Seed', a suggestive anglicisation. Clearly intended to invoke his intimacy with the grape, it also points to his *seminal* role in the kung fu comedies, as 'father' of the new trickster hero.

It has become almost impossible to discuss vulgar comedy without reference to Mikhail Bakhtin, and this chapter is no exception. As a number of writers have reminded us, there are problems in reconciling the ritualistic and historically specific cultural practices of the Middle Ages with the variety of commodity forms that have been labelled 'carnivalesque' (King 2002: 64). And yet anthropological studies have supported the wider applicability of grotesque subversion – Native American myth, for example, celebrates a 'trickster', "an unruly figure who breaks the rules, is governed by uncontrollable urges for food and sex and who often lacks a sense of unity and control of his own body" (64). Take the sex out of the equation – only villains exhibit such priapism – and this is perfectly serviceable as a description of Beggar Su, Pai Chang-tien (Yuen Siu-tin) in *Snake in the Eagle's Shadow* (first seen attracting flies), Leung Kar-yan in *Miracle Fighters* and Sammo Hung's "uneducated, mindless rogue" Wong Wa-bo in *Prodigal Son*. Sammo Hung is often a consummate trickster figure. In *The Iron-Fisted Monk*, he plays Zhuangmi Liu, ostensibly training for revenge, but using a variety of cons to get the monks to teach him more quickly. Cornered by the villains in a brothel, he avoids fighting to placate Buddhist San-de (Chen Sing). Forced to crawl through their legs, he steals their purses and loosens their trousers so that they fall down just as he is ejected. In fact, San-de slaps him for being *too* submissive (he has not noticed the trouser-loosening trick), so Zhuangmi gets the better of them twice over, re-entering the brothel, flipping and somersaulting as he humiliates his enemies, forcing them to crawl through *his* legs.

With its colonised history and ambivalent relationship with the 'mother country', it is not difficult to see how a carnival aesthetic might operate in Hong Kong. Kung fu comedy carnivalises a genre with strong mythical links to 'China', and does the 'lowering' of legendary masters not serve to localise them, re-situate them within the heterogenous space of Hong Kong and make them more accessible? One can even detect moments (they are not licensed to be more than that) of colonial carnival. In *Drunken Master 2*, Wong Fei-hung (Jackie Chan) unleashes a horde of ducks and geese amongst the first-class (British and Westernised Chinese) train passengers, creating chaos. The white Christian priest in *Snake in the Eagle's Shadow* gets *two* slaps for turning the other cheek, is walloped with a broom by an old Chinese woman who he unwisely calls a sinner, and almost dragged into a brothel. He turns out to be a villain, of course, his crucifix concealing a dagger, like a James Bond villain. Roger Garcia suggests that the comic Wong Fei-hung films are "irreverent, but not subversive", and that they "allow audiences to laugh without feeling that tradition is being threatened" (1980b: 137). This is a valid observation, but films like *Drunken Master* seem to me to exhibit a dynamic not dissimilar to the British *Carry On* films' take on 'history' (Caesar and Cleopatra, Henry VIII, colonial India) – the great figures of legend and myth, these films seem to say, consist of the same grubby desires and bodily functions as the rest of 'us'. Even so, one 'legend' is visibly displacing another in these films. In *The Magnificent Butcher*, we first encounter Beggar Su as he falls off a cart in a drunken stupor. Waking, he catches a chicken by spiking its grain with wine. Soon, he will be teaching Lam Sai-wing (Sammo Hung), Wong Fei-hung's favourite pupil. Significantly, this isn't Jackie Chan's youthful, irresponsible Wong Fei-hung, but the 'real' one (as a Chinese shopkeeper once described him to me), Kwan Tak-hing. Equally significantly, he is departing from Fa Shan (and the film) just as Beggar Su enters.

The Man of Virtue is Obsolete: Rogues, Vagabonds and Wise Guys

[Wong Fei-hung] had always been so serious ... I wondered what he was like before he became this Chinese superhero. Maybe he was just another naughty boy!
– Ng See-yuen, producer of *Drunken Master* (quoted in Logan 1995: 63)

"He's the good monkey, and I'm the bad one!"
— Beggar Bo (Sammo Hung), *Knockabout*

Early in *The Magnificent Butcher*, Wong Fei-hung is challenged by a rival master, Ko, angered by the antics of Lam Sai-wing. Wong is characteristically reluctant to fight, but takes the opportunity to teach a moral lesson even as they engage in a duel of kung fu calligraphy: "Everything must begin with tradition", he insists, "everything you do must be righteous." He inscribes the message 'The Man of Virtue is invincible' and draws the character for 'respect', reversed, on Ko's palm. "Do you know how to spell 'respect'?" he asks, prompting Ko to clasp his hand angrily to his head, leaving the word imprinted there. This scene places Wong (and Kwan Tak-hing) within the intricate choreography of kung fu comedy – Kwan is doubled for some of the stunts – but the 'Man of Virtue' is more or less intact. However, Tony Williams has described this scene as "a marginalized island in a film belonging to an entirely different genre" (1998: 74). Wong soon leaves the film, but not before we (and he) have witnessed Lam Sai-wing impersonating him (as Mouse will also do in *Dreadnaught*); moreover, his students grumble that he never teaches them anything new. Lam will defect to Beggar Su, who *does* teach him new techniques, and, in the burly form of Fang Mei-sheng, reinforces Lam's visible embrace of corporeal gratification. *The Magnificent Butcher* was the second Golden Harvest film to return Kwan Tak-hing to the role of Master Wong. *The Skyhawk/Huang Feihong Shaolin Quan* (1974) was a more serious film, but also featured Sammo Hung as choreographer and in a supporting role. But, as Williams argues, the non-comic *Skyhawk* stands alongside *Butcher* and its follow-up *Dreadnaught* in its visible "tension between tradition and changing values" (1998: 71). In *Dreadnaught*, the timid Mouse, too scared to collect the laundry money owed to him, courts Wong (Kwan Tak-hing, one last time) as his *shifu* gains him, loses him, gains him again. But Wong never actually teaches Mouse. Mouse seems to have developed his own style of fighting, based on his laundry skills – all he needs is the confidence to use it. Wong's *actual* student, Leung Foon (Leung Kar-yan), is killed, but Mouse not only triumphs over the fearsome White Tiger (Yuen Hsin-yi), but actually rescues Wong, injured by concealed weapons. As Williams puts it, "victory now results from spontaneous practices and not from the revered master's special form of martial arts training" (76).

Sammo Hung, Yuen Wo-ping and Jackie Chan were twenty-six, thirty-one and twenty-two, respectively, when the kung fu comedy cycle began in 1976 – young enough to target a more youthful and Hong Kong-centred audience, but just old enough to be connected to cultural traditions from China. Hung and Chan were Hong Kong-born, Yuen a Cantonese émigré. This might partly explain the varying degrees of ambivalence in their films towards 'tradition' and modernity. The sidelining of the 'Man of Virtue' is a feature particularly of Yuen Wo-ping's early films (intriguingly, given that Yuen had been an extra and stuntman in the original Kwan Tak-hing/Wong Fei-hung series). *Drunken Master* essentially returns to the premise of the more canonical *Challenge of the Masters*, whose young Wong is more recognisable as the embryonic legend than Jackie Chan's "naughty boy". In both films, Wong finds an alternative teacher to his father. In *Challenge of the Masters*, Wong Kei-ying simply refuses to teach him, but *Drunken Master*'s Wong senior sends his son to Beggar Su to discipline him. In the former, Lu Acai stands in for Wong Kei-ying and takes over the role that the failed father should have adopted. But while Beggar Su's role is ostensibly a manifestation of paternal authority, he actually inducts Wong into a different set of values. Contrary to Chan Ting-ching's contention that "the younger are generally fitter" (1980: 149), Beggar Su is tough and cynical enough to make it in the new world. In *The Magnificent Butcher*, he soon dispels Lam Sai-wing's belief that he is stuck in the past. Age is not important, he responds (although he also preaches that "like wine, the older the better"); it is outlook that matters. Ng Ho's description of the kung fu comedy hero's basic qualities – lazy, unscrupulous – are manifested by Su above all. But unlike his younger counterparts, he has mastered a style, *Zui Quan*, which allows him to live as he pleases.

Sammo Hung's films are a little more elegiac than Yuen's, perhaps because his film-making career began a little earlier. The traditional *shifu* is presented more sympathetically, but tends to die, falling victim to ruthless treachery and cut-throat values – in *Warriors Two* (1978), the villain is a banker. Consequently, the heroes must either rely on themselves or find an alternative, usually more pragmatic, teacher. In *Prodigal Son*, the androgynous Leung Yi-tai, whose voice can switch from 'masculine' to 'feminine', is in some ways an unconventional master figure. His first fight is with an aggressively insistent would-be suitor who takes him for a woman. In the Macho World According to Sammo, it is hard to escape the impression that Leung is rendered more vulnerable by his fluid gender identity – he is given a physical flaw in the form of asthma. But in other ways, he is the most traditional figure in the film, and *Wing Chun* was, after all, supposed to have been developed by a woman to allow slighter opponents to defeat large ones. In a telling scene, he explains to Leung Tzan why he will not teach him – the 'prodigal son' is too impetuous, he will make enemies and bring about his own death. But as Master Leung sits open-mouthed, his would-be disciple then lectures *him* – everyone must die in time and kung fu itself will die if it is not passed on. This presumptuous reversal of roles works rather well because he actually gets *two* masters. While Leung Yi-tai teaches 'pure' *Wing Chun*, burly Wong Wa-bo teaches a more rough-and-ready version that includes headbutts and

Fig. 9 Carnivalesque kung fu: Yuen Biao and Sammo Hung throw Monkey shapes in *Knockabout*

other dirty tricks. In the film's climactic fight, Leung Tzan fights to avenge Leung Yi-tai – killed by Ng's bodyguards, hired by his overprotective father to ensure he never loses a fight. But his fighting style is based entirely on the (conspicuously modern) streetfighting taught by Wong Wa-bo.

In *Knockabout* and *Odd Couple/Duoming Dandao Duoming Qiang* (1979), the Master/Pupil relationship succumbs entirely to competitive values and mutual exploitation. Taipao and Yipao adopt Lau Kar-wing's "old fox" to "learn his art and then get rid of him", little realising that he is more ruthless than they could ever be. Seeking an alternative master, Yipao first makes contact with Beggar Bo, a self-deprecating tramp with a nervous twitch, by stealing his chicken. Bo recognises the exploitative nature of the relationship, but is enlisted via a further con. But it turns out that he is a detective who needed to replace his departed assistant – he and Yipao have managed to exploit one another. *Knockabout* is stylistically the broadest of comedies, but it is also a film that has no faith in anything – master/pupil or fraternal relationships, revenge or justice. Even language breaks down as Yipao and Bo embrace a kind of regressive incoherence, marked by their high-pitched monkey babble and such sublime non-sequiteurs as "He's the good monkey, and I'm the bad one!" *Odd Couple* is built on the intense rivalry between the King of Spears (Lau Kar-wing) and the King of Swords (Sammo Hung), who engage in a series of inconclusive fights to prove who is best. They agree to recruit students to fight for them (Hung and Lau each play the other's pupils). The students survive their masters, who die still bickering ("You died before me"/"I didn't"), but in spite of their recognition of their *shifus'* exploitation of them, they end the film locked into the same cycle. The film freezes on them still arguing.

Sobering Up: *Drunken Master 2*

> Now everyone is drunk, so I must be sober.
> – Jackie Chan (quoted in Logan 1995: 66)

Most of the 'new wave' martial arts films of the 1990s included elements of comedy, but it was *Drunken Master 2* (1994) that most visibly looked back to the earlier cycle, albeit from a position of 'maturity'. It also marked Jackie Chan's return to the period kung fu film and, of course, to the role of Wong Fei-hung. While its stunning choreography is very different from the wire-fu of its contemporaries, *Drunken Master 2* seems to take some of its inspiration from two Jet Li series. From the *Once Upon a Time in China* series, it takes its colonial villain – British plunderers and their Westernised Chinese lackeys, stealing the Emperor's Jade Seal and other national treasures. From the *Fong Sai-yuk* films, it takes its anarchic mother (Anita Mui), the closest the film has to a Beggar Su figure – she encourages Wong to drink in contravention of his father's admonitions. Wong Kei-ying is now a more substantial presence – he is played by Ti Lung, who brings to the role the authority bestowed by his roles for Zhang Che and John Woo. Wong spends part of the film in conflict with his hard-but-fair father, but in many ways, this is the young Fei-hung of *Challenge of the Masters* rather than the original *Drunken Master*. Drinking is now a more perilous activity – just enough seems to oil him up sufficiently to perform a more fluid *Zui Quan*, but too much renders him helpless, leading to a humilating beating from the villains and a contrite return to his father's authority. Wong even finds a second 'father' in the form of the highly decorated Manchu officer played by director Lau Kar-leung – it is he who gives Wong his anticolonial mission to protect the jade seal. Wong must drink one more time to overcome the superkicking skills of Ken Lo, but the fight pays tribute to the climax of *The Young Master/Shidi Chu Ma* (1980), in which Chan drinks effectively to anaesthetize himself, absorbing punishment in an unnervingly unstoppable fashion.[8] Urban cynicism could still be found in a younger generation of comic film-makers such as Stephen Chiau. But overall, in pre-Handover Hong Kong, the comic kung fu hero had found something to fight for. The 'Man of Virtue' may not have been invincible – he needed a bit of industrial alcohol to toughen him up – but, as in *Once Upon a Time in China*, he once again had a role to play.[9]

Chapter Five

The Lady is the Boss?
Hidden Dragons and 'Deadly China Dolls'

When we Chinese girls listened to the adults talking-story, we learned that we failed if we grew up to be wives or slaves. We could be heroines, swordswomen. Even if she had to rage across all China, a swordswoman got even with anybody who hurt her family. Perhaps women were once so powerful that they had to have their feet bound ... On Sundays, from noon to midnight, we went to the movies at the Confucius Church. We saw swordswomen jump over houses from a standstill; they didn't even need a running start ... After I grew up, I heard the chant of Fa Mu Lan, the girl who took her father's place in battle ... I would have to grow up a warrior woman.

    – Maxine Hong Kingston, *The Woman Warrior: Memoirs of a Girlhood Among Ghosts* (1977: 25)

The whole idea of sexy Chinese girls wearing tight superhero-type costumes, fighting and then having sex, is possibly the finest development in the hundred years of cinema history a man could possibly hope for. There's absolutely nothing in these movies that I find anything but joyful.

    – Jonathan Ross (in Baker and Russell 1996: 7)

For Western viewers and critics whose only exposure (if any) to Chinese martial arts films came courtesy of Bruce Lee or Jackie Chan, *Crouching Tiger, Hidden Dragon* (2000) evidently came as something of a revelation. It was not just the production values or the compelling drama and characterisation that seemed to elevate it above lowbrow 'chop sockeys' but the fact that two out of its three central protagonists were fighting women. But, as Asian audiences and critics were well aware, women warriors are nothing new in

Chinese storytelling and have a much longer history than their Western counterparts.[1] There is the warrior Fa Mulan, who drags up to replace her father in battle, *Wing Chun* legends Ng Mui and Yim Wing Chun (the one prominent female Master/Pupil pairing), White Crane exponent Fang Wing Chun, the wife of Hung Hei-kwun. Their literary and cinematic counterparts include the Maiden of Yueh (*Annals of the Kingdom of Wu and Yueh*, 1 AD), the flying swordswomen of silent Shanghai cinema, Golden Swallow, the Deaf-Mute Heroine and the Bride with White Hair. Nor should Hong Kong cinema's male stars be allowed to obscure the line of charismatic and talented female action stars; Zheng Pei-pei, Xu Feng, Angela Mao Ying, Hui Ying-hung, Cynthia Rothrock, Michelle Yeoh and Brigitte Lin. *Crouching Tiger* is self-consciously rooted in the *wu xia* martial women tradition. Its generic motifs – a stolen sword, deadly poisons, secret Taoist sects, a heroine who dresses as a boy – can all be found in a formulaic, but extremely successful, film like *Dragon Swamp/Du Long Tan* (1969).[2] *Dragon Swamp*'s star was Zheng Pei-pei, crowned 'Queen of Swordswomen' on Hong Kong television in 1969 and later describing her screen persona as "a girl who is beautiful, but who kills people as if they were cattle" (Bren 1998: 81). Zheng's youthful heroines, such as the swordswoman Golden Swallow, anticipate the figure of Jen/Yu Jiaolong (Zhang Ziyi) in *Crouching Tiger*, and, of course, she plays Jen's villainous mentor Jade Fox.[3]

The action heroine, as Yvonne Tasker has argued, is an equivocal figure. On the one hand, she manifests a "symbolically transgressive iconography", disrupting "the conventional notion ... that women are, or should be, represented exclusively through the codes of femininity" (1993: 132). But such active, 'masculine' qualities are usually counterbalanced by signifiers of 'femininity', which can take a number of forms: 'desirability', maternal instincts, or such archetypes as the 'tomboy', "a girl who has not accepted the responsibilities of adult womanhood" (15). Chinese cinema has other 'safety valves', such as filial duty (Mulan, for example) or the heroine 'poisoned' (and thus rendered 'unfeminine') by revenge like Angela Mao Ying in *Lady Whirlwind/Tiezhang Xuanfeng* (1972) or Shih Szu in *The Young Avenger/Xie Fu Men* (1970), in which "Hatred replaces filial piety".[4] Tasker is talking primarily about Western cinema, and yet we can see how some of her ideas apply to a film like *Heroic Trio/Donfang San Xia* (1993). The film offers three glamorous superheroines with extraordinary powers within a *mise-en-scène* clearly modeled on Tim Burton's *Batman* films. 'Wonder Woman' (Anita Mui) seems to be the strongest of the three, but she is also the most maternal. When she fails to save a kidnapped baby, a single tear rolls down her silver mask, and she is careful not to compromise her cop-husband throughout the film. Invisible Woman (Michelle Yeoh) finds her counterparts in the 'beautiful ghosts' of the Chinese Gothic; initially in the service of an evil supernatural figure, she is redeemed by (doomed) heterosexual love and female bonding. Chat the Thief Catcher (Maggie Cheung) is the sexy tomboy, clad in leather jacket, fishnets and suspenders, and Lara Croft shorts. She rides a motorbike and wields a shotgun, but her haphazard approach to combat underlines her immaturity and irresponsibility. The film ends with the irresistible image of our three heroines striding towards the camera in slow motion, capes swirling around them. *Heroic Trio* is one of many genre films from its period to allude to the 1997 Handover; its villain wants to absorb Hong Kong into an implicitly tyrannical Imperial China ("China must have a King"). This is characteristically undeveloped, but taken much further in a dystopian, post-nuclear sequel, *Executioners/Xiandai Haoxia Zhuan* (1993), which includes some of Hong Kong cinema's most blatant references to the Tiananmen Square massacre. Given that the 1997 'crisis' seemed to bring traditional male heroism to the fore – the return of Wong Fei-hung, John Woo's modern-day Knight-Errants – it is no small thing for three powerful women ("We're sisters forever!") to save the island from impending apocalypse. As Tasker suggests, the value and pleasure of such films might lie in the "struggle to become powerful in difficult circumstances" (1993: 30–1).

If the Chinese heroine has a longer history than Hollywood's action women, she has been vulnerable to some shifts in the gendering of Asian cinema. Zheng Pei-pei has observed of the 1970s 'remasculinisation' of Hong Kong cinema, "Chinese films usually had women as leads and men were mostly used ornamentally. All that changed after Bruce Lee" (Bren 1998: 85). This was already starting to happen in Zheng's heyday, and she tells a perfectly plausible anecdote of working with macho trendsetter Zhang Che. On the set of *Golden Swallow*, Silver Roc (Wang Yu), Golden Whip (Lo Lieh) and the film's eponymous heroine (Zheng) make a dramatic departure after a fight scene. Zhang Che wanted the two men to jump out of the window, but Golden Swallow was supposed to leave in a more 'feminine' way by using the door. Zheng Pei-pei was having none of this: "I was a swordswoman after all", she points out, "why is it they could jump out the window and I had to walk through the door?" (Hong Kong Film Archive 1999: 56). She won the battle, but lost the war. In spite of its title – Golden Swallow is more central in the earlier *Come Drink with Me* (although still subordinate to male hero Drunken Cat) – the film is more interested in the brooding, death-seeking Silver Roc. She may jump out of the window, but he *soars* (the technique that gives him his name). The boys were, indeed, back in town.

The Chinese action heroine is even more vulnerable when crossing cultural and geographic boundaries; specifically to what I shall call 'Deadly China Doll' syndrome. If the martial heroine can be an empowering identification figure in one context (as in

Maxine Hong Kingston's novel), she can just as easily be appropriated as exotic fetish in the Western Orientalist imaginary. The Asian woman is a prime object of what Asian-American critics call 'racist love', which in this instance endows her with "an excess of 'womanhood'"; if Asian men are represented as emasculated and asexual, Asian women are "only sexual, imbued with an innate understanding of how to please and serve" (Cheung 1990: 236). In the Western pornographic imaginary, Chinese women have often been configured as "submissive and dainty sex obects" (235).[5] A similar dynamic informs Western fanboys' fetishization of Category III stars like Chingamy Yau, or 'dainty' action stars like Moon Lee. Such stars are celebrated for "kicking ass" but the other attributes of the 'China Doll' are rarely far away. Moon Lee, one admirer tells us, has "kickass moves and kewpie-doll looks"; as his mind wanders to Japanese S/M porn, he announces, "if only Moon would wind up bound and gagged, my column would be complete" (Meyers 1998: 59).[6] Again, I do not want to present Hong Kong fandom as monolithic; Baker and Russell's *Essential Guide to Deadly China Dolls*, for example, is an informative and well-researched history of Hong Kong's action women. But it cannot help but reinforce 'China Doll' syndrome even, tellingly, when it tries to challenge it:

> Before the kung fu craze hit in the early 1970s, the West's preconceived image of the China doll was anything but deadly. A delicate porcelain concubine or a reclining empress were about the limit of the Westerner's understanding of the classical Chinese woman. (Baker and Russell 1996: 15)

But the 'glamour' photos and the references in Jonathan Ross' foreword to "high kicking, gun toting, scantily clad Asian babes" (8) confirm that the 'China Doll' is not powerful instead of being 'delicate'; she is powerful *as well as* being 'delicate'. As another well-meaning celebration puts it, she wields 'Nail-Polished Fists' (Hammond and Wilkins: 1997: 49)

In *Enter the Dragon*, Angela Mao Ying plays Bruce Lee's sister, Su-lin. Sexually harassed by the villain's men, led by white Oharra (Bob Wall), she strikes back, leading to a protracted fight-chase sequence. Cornered and outnumbered, she stabs herself with a piece of broken glass rather than submit to what is clearly signaled as imminent rape. Consigned to a flashback, threatened with sexual violence, introduced simply to motivate Lee, Mao is a more marginal presence than her impressive star turn in *Hapkido* the previous year. Her marginalization is sometimes attributed to the film's Hollywood credentials and a Western antipathy to fighting women. Verina Glaessner, for example, sees Su-lin's death as being "at odds with the whole conception of the fight hero or heroine in Chinese films – everyone knows he or she would have gone down fighting" (1974: 81). This is in some ways a reasonable assertion; the scene offers the quintessential 'Deadly China Doll' scenario, a heroine simultaneously lethal and frail. But I am not sure that the scene is at odds with the rest of Bruce Lee's filmography, or the dominant ethos of early 1970s kung fu films. Mao is, after all, the only woman to have a memorable fight scene in a Bruce Lee film. His most frequent female lead, Nora Miao, was a distinctly passive figure, in spite of being a swordplay queen herself a few years earlier; in *Way of the Dragon*, she is there to gaze admiringly or be rescued from the villains. Angela Mao Ying was one of the few female stars to be allowed to shine in the early 1970s kung fu cycle; she was Golden Harvest's first signing and the first post-Lee star to be sold in the West.[7] But as we shall see later, films like *Lady Whirlwind* and *Hapkido* never quite allow her to dominate the action as Lee and Wang Yu did. The Warrior Woman clearly has a limited license, and one that can be rapidly revoked if it comes into conflict with the masculine heroic ethos. As Bruce Lee, Wang Yu and Zhang Che's macho roster dominated the *wu xia pian*, a roughly contemporaneous 'remasculinisation' was taking place within Asian-American literary criticism. The literary 'reconstruction' of Chinese masculinity drew on *wu xia* literature for empowering 'heroic' archetypes to counter the legacy of Fu Manchu, Charlie Chan and the 'Yellow Man' in *Broken Blossoms* (1919) (Cheung 1990: 236). Maxine Hong Kingston's *The Woman Warrior*, a novel which is critical of patriarchal Chinese values, drew fire from some Chinese-American men for seeming to collude with white racist conceptions of Asian masculinity.[8] For a Chinese-American feminist like King-kok Cheung – sensitive to the racist 'emasculation' of Chinese men, but wary of a phallocentric (and sometimes homophobic) 're-masculinisation' oppressive to Chinese women – there is something of a dilemma embedded in the "confrontation between 'heroism' and 'feminism'" (1990: 238). If, as Maxine Hong Kingston's narrator speculates, "women were once so dangerous that they had to have their feet bound", the martial heroine must tread (or fly) carefully when exercising her power. In the early 1970s, the action heroine did have her wings clipped somewhat, giving way to the *yang gang* of Zhang Che and others. But new contexts can create new possibilities; the flux and mutability of postcolonial Hong Kong, as well as a more visible queer presence in Hong Kong cinema, created a new space for powerful warrior women in the early 1990s.

It is broadly true to say that the action heroine has fared better in the swordplay film than the kung fu film. Usually set further in the past than kung fu, with a frequent emphasis on myth and magic, swordplay accommodates Hong Kingston's prelapsarian fantasy of mythic female power. *The Deaf and Mute Heroine/Longya Jian* (1971) features a particularly memorable protagonist, the nameless, silent bandit played by Helen Ma, who uses mirrored bracelets to give her 360-degree vision. Wounded by the gang she robbed, she is nursed back to health by a well-meaning, but ultimately weak, peasant man, Yang Shun. She falls in love with him, but everything suggests that this is a compromising relationship; a neighbour jokes that a mute wife is ideal. Yang Shun steals the Deaf-Mute Heroine's bracelets to pay off gambling debts and later inadvertently leads her arch-nemesis, the Reflex Swordsman, to her. The hapless Yang is killed ("I've erred" are his dying words) before the heroine dispatches her enemy and re-enters jianghu as a loner. Throughout the film, men try to erode the power of her gaze – Yang Shun takes her bracelets, the Reflex Swordsman flicks sand in her eyes – but she is resourceful enough to transform every lack into a source of power.

The swordplay film offers some alternatives to the patrilineal pedagogic structures of kung fu films.[9] The Maiden of Yueh grew up in a forest and trained herself, not unlike Brigitte Lin's Wolf Girl in *The Bride with White Hair/Jianghu* (1993); "I did not receive it from anyone; I just got it" (Liu 1967: 85). In *Crouching Tiger*, Jen learns *wu dang* swordplay from a stolen manual and from the outlaw Jade Fox, who promises her that "we'll be our own masters, at last". Everything about the Deaf-Mute Heroine's past, including how she acquired her swordplay skills, is a mystery; only her emotions are 'known' by the audience, thanks to Helen Ma's expressive face.

The kung fu film, on the other hand, deals primarily with the male hero interacting with History, a history both patriotic and patrilineal. Only Ng Mui and Yim Wing Chun depart from this patrilineage, and they are under-represented in the kung fu film. *Shaolin Temple* (1976) largely keeps them out of the action, but at least locates Ng Mui within Shaolin pedagogic history. In *Wing Chun* (1993), she turns up to resolve the conflict Wing Chun (Michelle Yeoh) experiences between her martial arts skill and her 'femininity'. "No matter how strong you are", she counsels, rather surprisingly given her own monastic lifestyle, "you still have to settle down ... Go and get married." Wing Chun has learned kung fu to avoid marrying a local villain, but when her childhood sweetheart (Donnie Yen) turns up, her 'masculine' qualities must be set aside. On their wedding night, they replay the leg-parting challenge from *Executioners from Shaolin*, but her husband overcomes her stance simply by tickling her. As in *Crouching Tiger*, Zheng Pei-pei plays the female master, but Ng Mui speaks *for* patriarchy as opposed to Jade Fox's bitter recognition of how *wu dang* underestimated her.

In terms of stardom, it is the kung fu film that has placed the greater emphasis on physical 'authenticity', an emphasis that has reflected some of the gender inequalities in 'real' martial arts. Some female stars, like Angela Mao Ying, performed as *Wu dan* ('martial girls') in Beijing Opera and acquired their physical skills onstage; in the Opera

Kung Fu Cult Masters

Yang Paifent, Mao deflected twelve successive spears with perfectly co-ordinated kicks (Logan 1995: 155). Hui Ying-hung and Michelle Yeoh, two of Hong Kong's most graceful performers, both drew on dancing backgrounds, although it is still difficult to believe that neither were trained martial artists. Hui, in particular, is a match for any martial arts star, male or female, who ever appeared onscreen. The only 'authentic' female martial arts stars were foreign, such as Cynthia Rothrock and Yukari Oshima, but they, in turn, seemed to initiate a trend for female stars to perform more grueling fight scenes and stunts. Rothrock, a North American kung fu champion, was the only white martial artist to make the transition from heavy (in *Shanghai Express/Fugui Lieche* [1986] for example) to leading roles such as *Righting Wrongs/Zhi Fa Xian Feng* (1986) and the crossover *China O'Brien* films. Her career hinges, as Tasker argues, on the "novelty attached to the fact that she is a white woman working in a genre associated with white men in the West and Chinese performers in Hong Kong" (1993: 24–5). She is often an abrasive presence in her Hong Kong films, a marked outsider. In *Yes, Madam/Huang Gu Shi Jie* (1985), Rothrock and Yeoh play initially antagonistic British and Chinese cops. Rothrock comes tainted with colonial power, a Scotland Yard 'expert' brought in to oversee a tricky case, and the film also constructs her as being less 'feminine' than Yeoh, who had first come into the public eye as Miss Malaysia.[10] In the opening scene, Yeoh traps a flasher's genitals in a hardback book, but averts her eyes demurely. Rothrock arrives at Kai Tak airport in a power-dressing suit, can speak Cantonese (and thus understand Chinese cops' sexist comments) and makes short work of a criminal who tries to take her hostage. She later reveals that she knows her nickname is "white bitch", but does not seem unduly concerned. These two 'opposites' bond as rule-bending mavericks and team up to take on the villains, most memorably in the fist-to-fist climax. Yeoh's career was initially facilitated by her looks, but her star persona was based on her growing reputation for bravery. According to the DVD packaging, *Yes, Madam* (under the title *Police Assassins*) contains "one of the best stunts ever for a female lead". During the climax, she hooks her legs over a banister, swings backwards, arching her back and plunging face first through a pane of glass to grab her opponents' legs and send them crashing to the floor below. Yeoh's subsequent career followed the path of corporeal authenticity, matching Jackie Chan stunt-for-stunt in *Police Story 3/Chaoji Jingcha* (1992) and injuring her back on the set of Ann Hui's *Ah Kam/A Jin* (1996), in which she plays a stuntwoman.

In *Irma Vep* (1996) director Jean-Pierre Leaud tells Maggie Cheung that he wanted her as his heroine after seeing *Heroic Trio* in a fleapit in Marrakesh: "You are like a dancer, and also like an acrobat", he tells her, "and this film is very, very beautiful, like floating in the air". Maggie thanks him for the compliment, but points out that most of the stunts were done by doubles. The wirework, special effects, coloured filters and fast editing of 'new wave' martial arts films once again created a space for martial arts stars who, as Xu Feng once described herself, "hardly (knew) the martial arts". Of the *Heroic Trio*, only Michelle Yeoh does the majority of her own stunts but does not by any means upstage her co-stars (could anyone?); Maggie Cheung, Anita Mui and, above all, Brigitte Lin were largely doubled for fight scenes, but they were the most charismatic swordplay queens since the 1960s. It is the consistency of Lin's persona – particularly as a transvestite or transsexual swords(wo)man – that ensures her place amongst the greatest of martial arts stars.

Let us look in more detail at three case studies across three generic phases. Firstly, two 1970s kung fu stars, Angela Mao Ying and Hui Ying-hung, provide some ways of thinking about the position of the martial heroine within the patrilineal kung fu film. Secondly, Brigitte Lin's 1990s vehicles reinvent the swordplay queen by heightening her transgression of polarised gender identity. Finally, we will conclude with a consideration of *Crouching Tiger, Hidden Dragon*, the most globally visible 'heroine' film of recent years.

'Lady Whirlwind' and 'Auntie': Angela Mao Ying and Hui Ying-hung

In her insightful analysis of Angela Mao Ying's films, Verina Glaessner observes the different world the star inhabited in her transition from swordplay to kung fu films:

> Her movements are more circumscribed than her predecessors' because her world is too. It is tighter, more classical, less romantic. If she is still the repository of purity and self-denial it is a purity based less on the freewheeling romanticism of the characters she creates in her other films, and more on the rigorous pursuance of a series of spelt-out rules. The hero or heroine is given a surrogate family, a band of fellow workers, as in *The Big Boss* or, more usually, of fellow classmates at the martial arts school with the revered teacher at their head. Often as not, it is also an environment in which it is easy to mix themes of personal and national destiny. (1974: 54–6)

In the swordplay film, of course, *jianghu* (the 'world of vagrants') by its very nature suggests mobility, if not necessarily freedom from rules and restraints – "In *jianghu*", the saying goes, "a man cannot decide for himself" (Ng 1981/96: 74). But if the swordplay queen enjoys a freedom of movement far from the constraints of the circumscribed, more Confucian, world of the kung fu film, it also renders her power more abstract and fantasmatic. Angela Mao Ying and Hui Ying-hung/Wei Ying-hung offer contrasting responses to the gendered

Kung Fu Cult Masters

Fig. 10 Warrior, 'Western' glamour girl and stern traditionalist: Hui Ying-hung's masquerade in *My Young Auntie*

The Lady is the Boss?

constraints of the kung fu film. Mao was signed to Golden Harvest and initially appeared in swordplay films like *Angry River/Gui Nu Chuan* (1970); she would also play a supporting role in King Hu's *Fate of Lee Khan/Yingchun Ge zhi Fengbo* (1974). But her most widely seen kung fu films belong to the otherwise 'masculine' cycle that wedded nationalism to revenge; she takes on Japanese villains in *Lady Whirlwind, Hapkido* and *When Taekwondo Strikes* (1973). Hui, on the other hand, was signed to Shaw Brothers, and usually cast in supporting roles or as part of ensemble casts. She joined Lau Kar-leung's team, and was both his pupil and partner offscreen. *Dirty Ho/Lantou He* (1979) contains an interesting scene in which Hui plays a concubine entertaining a Manchu Prince (Lau Kar-fai), who is a martial arts master. The Prince is attacked by the thief Ho (Wong Yue) and must defend himself while concealing his fighting skills. He tells Ho that the concubine is his bodyguard and 'works' her like a fighting puppet while pretending to cower behind her. The scene makes full use of Hui's grace and speed, while attributing her character's abilities to a male 'author'; just as, in a sense, Lau becomes the 'author' of his star's martial skills. Hui plays a more substantial fighting role in *Legendary Weapons of China/Shiba Ban Wuyi* (1982) as an assassin dressed as a boy, while Fu Sheng's death during the making of *Eight Diagram Pole Fighter* (1983) gave her a more prominent role than originally intended. It is entirely appropriate that she should join the final fray, given the Yang women's reputation as warriors themselves. But Lau designed two films as star vehicles for Hui Ying-hung, both of them comic in tone, *My Young Auntie/Zhang Bei* (1981) and *The Lady is the Boss/Zhangmen Ren* (1983). If Angela Mao Ying fights in the generic terrain of patriotic stoicism, Hui is located amidst Lau's favourite themes – Master/Pupil relationships, the survival of tradition(s), literal and structural 'families'.

In *Lady Whirlwind*, Angela Mao Ying plays Tien, a taciturn loner who "fights like a man, even better". As she strolls laconically into the gambling den she is about to decimate, the scene, as Verina Glaessner observes, recalls "the western hero's portentous stroll into a bar room in territory that we sense is not his own" (1974: 76). Tien is formidable bordering on invincible; she flattens everyone in her path in her quest for revenge. Nevertheless, the film cannot or will not embrace her unequivocally as the heroine. She seeks revenge on Ling Shih-hua (Chang Yi), who made her sister pregnant before abandoning her and driving her to suicide. Ling, however, is a reformed character and begs a reprieve long enough to free the town from Japanese gangsters. In other words, Tien's vendetta runs counter to patriotic duty and she must be realigned; or rather, Ling becomes the 'real', if more vulnerable, hero. It is he who must learn a special technique (the most inaccurate Tai Chi ever seen on film) to triumph and put things right. To stack the deck further, he is given a more conventionally feminine love interest – how can Tien possibly obstruct

Fig. 11 Taking on the masculine world of the kung fu film: Angela Mao Ying in *Hapkido*

both patriotic justice and true love? She holds back, reluctantly, long enough for Ling to eliminate the villains, then insists that the debt must be paid. As she lays into the battered Ling, his girlfriend tries to intervene and is accidentally struck by Tien. The lovers once again appeal for mercy and Tien simply stalks off sourly; refused any kind of closure, she is the epitome of unconsummated hatred and frustration.

Hapkido's main point of interest, apart from Sammo Hung's scorching fight scenes, is its obvious debt to *Fist of Fury*, with Mao in the Bruce Lee/Chen Zhen role. Except that, as Glaessner rightly argues, the film "stops short" of allowing her an equal position of power (1974: 80). Instead, the patriotic hero is distributed across three characters; Yu Ying (Mao), Kao Chang (Carter Wong) and the headstrong Fan Wei (Sammo Hung), who is "brave, but not too smart". The variation on *Fist of Fury* lies in the Korea factor. The film opens in Japanese-occupied Seoul, where our three heroes are learning Hapkido from their Korean *shifu* (Chi Hon-tsoi) and his senior student (Wong In-sik). Back in China, the Japanese Black Bear School threatens their school, and we know exactly where the narrative is heading. Yu Ying and Kao Chang initially resemble Chen Zhen's seniors in *Fist of Fury* rather than the hot-tempered patriot himself, and try to live up to their teacher's creed of 'Patience'. It is Fan Wei, if anything, who is the Lee figure; although he has

'Patience' stamped on his hand, he is soon provoked by the invaders' bullying and becomes a local hero and outlaw. He does not, however, survive until the end of the film; nor does Kao, in spite of Carter Wong looking like the more conventional leading man. It is left to Yu Ying to re-ignite the spirit of *Fist of Fury*'s 'Sick Man of Asia' scene; in the film's most memorable sequence, she returns another insulting plaque and takes down the Black Bear School with some devastating kicking techniques that actually surpass those of the earlier film. But two factors keep Yu Ying from achieving Chen Zhen's stature. Firstly, although Fan Wei dies, he, like Zhen, is the martyr, prepared to pay the price for what must be done. Secondly, when Yu Ying heads off for her final confrontation with the leading villains, she is accompanied by Wong In-sik's Hapkido senior, who is drafted into the climax as though simply to ensure that a woman does not triumph where male heroes have failed.

In *My Young Auntie* and *The Lady is the Boss*, Hui Ying-hung embodies values (youthfulness, 'femininity', Westernisation, consumerism) that threaten the implicitly Confucian traditions of a benign patriarch, played in both films by Lau Kar-leung. Both of Lau's characters are associated with Wong Fei-hung, whose musical theme accompanies a *Hung Gar* workout in *My Young Auntie* and Lau's defence of his gym in *The Lady is the Boss*. Both films culminate with the 'old guard' coming to the rescue of impulsive youth, but, as Tony Rayns observes, both films are about "testing the integrity and resilience of tradition against the clamour and confusions of the twentieth century" (1984: 55).

In *My Young Auntie*, Hui Ying-hung plays Ching, the young widow of her former Master whom she married in order to protect his inheritance from an unscrupulous younger brother (Wang Lung-wei). She takes the will to Guangdong, where she meets her late husband's more benign brother, Yuen (Lau Kar-leung). Immediately, patrilineage is thrown into (comic) disarray; Ching is 'Auntie' to the older Yuen and takes on the role of his senior. Moreover, she is a superb martial artist; later in the film, she gets the older men back into shape for battle. But the real conflict between tradition and modernity is fought on the terrain of Ching's body. Superficially stern and old-fashioned – she insists that an elder should not wear bright colours – her youth and gender ally her with Yuen's mischievous, Hong Kong-educated son Yu Tai (Xiao Hou). Hui generally plays girls, rather than women – she pouts and sulks when she gets upset – so that 'Auntie' is just one of a series of masquerades. Initially she clashes with Yu Tai, who does not respect tradition and has been conspicuously Westernised in Hong Kong. He embraces Western music, dance and sport and even has an anglicised name, 'Charlie Yu', amongst his friends. In two key sequences, both of them focused on dressing-up, Ching begins her transformation. In the first, Yu Tai takes her into Guangdong, where she is immediately seduced by consumer culture. She sees her first car, gazes rapt at the neon lights and presses her nose against shop windows, captivated by lipstick, pearls, and even a blonde wig. She overhears the fashionable local girls mocking her rather severe outfit, and a white split-to-the-thigh cheongsam proves too much for her to resist. In other words, there is a glamorous, modern Hong Kong girl waiting to get out of this austere country girl, and she is miraculously transformed, effortlessly stealing attention from the girls who derided her moments before. Kicking, however, proves difficult in high heels and revealing dresses, as she discovers when dealing with some unwelcome attention from lecherous onlookers.

The second sequence is a Masquerade Ball arranged by Yu Tai specifically to humiliate 'Auntie'. In European period dress, blonde wig and pearls, she is forced to dance by Yu's friends. But when unwelcome guests working for the villains arrive, this cruelty becomes rather more serious and Ching has her dress slashed by the 'Three Musketeers'. She calls for a sword to fight back, and the prevailing Westernisation of Chinese youth is neatly underlined by Yu Tai's response; "Props department – Chinese sword!" What follows is a dazzling display of Hui's weapons skills, but once again the trappings of Western 'femininity' work against her. Her elaborate dress keeps obstructing her movements and she is left in a distinctly undignified position; upside down, skirt around her head, frilly underwear on display. When she must fight more seriously in the latter part of the film, she opts for a unisex 'stealth' outfit that blurs both gender and age. The climactic shift back to Yuen, who saves the day, is as much about age as gender. As 'Auntie' and Yu Tai team up, they assume their youthful superiority over their elders, but are overpowered by the more experienced villains. But the Westernisation and 'feminisation' of 'Auntie' is reprised in the final scene, which finds Ching back in her Masquerade Ball outfit – "My name is Suzy!" she announces flirtatiously.

The Lady is the Boss is set in modern-day Hong Kong, where urban mutability and the vulnerability of 'tradition' are immediately apparent; Wang Hsieh-yuen's (Lau Kar-leung) kung fu school is threatened by redevelopment. Wang gets a new gym, but also a new boss, the American-born daughter of his ailing *shifu*, Mei-ling (Hui). Mei-ling combines the attributes of 'Auntie' and Yu Tai from the earlier film; she wants to run the school like a business (with advertising and discounts), throws what looks like aerobics into her training regime, and attracts a distinctly non-traditional clientele. Wang is appalled by the "undesirable elements" – hookers, drag queens and gay men – at his school. "She's too modern, but you're outmoded", he is told by another elder, and the film starts looking for a middle ground. As in *My Young Auntie*, youth is impetuous, and once again, Lau's character must save the day when Mei-ling antagonises the pimps at the local clip joint. The finale is a good-natured pastiche of Lau's earlier films; Lau Kar-fai fights as *36th Chamber*'s San-de and Xiao Hou reprises his *Mad Monkey Kung Fu*. But Mei-ling's modernisation of martial arts has some markedly beneficial effects. She empowers the local hookers by training them, thus incurring the wrath of their pimps; they have a newfound power over their clients, who no longer find them "obliging enough". Even the fight choreography embraces modernity; in one of its most memorable sequences, Mei-ling and her students attack the pimps on BMX bikes. The film is broadly comic, thus its license to 'test' martial tradition, but even more so than in *My Young Auntie*, the young heroine is able to revitalise rather than simply threaten the martial world. Wang's Confucian code does not extend to prostitutes, but Mei-ling's is rather more inclusive. The final scene again finds resolution through dressing-up; Mei-ling turns up at Kai Tak airport in traditional Chinese dress, Wang in a Western tuxedo.

Both Mao and Hui find a place in the patriarchal kung fu world through a kind of gender performance. In assuming a role usually associated with heroic masculinity, Mao performs a kind of drag act, carefully policed by narrative constraints and male helpers. Hui's best roles, on the other hand, embrace the fluidity of dress codes more flamboyantly in an ongoing masquerade. The flux of dress codes, more specifically through drag and trans-gender identity, was to be a major motif in the films of a later martial arts star.

Gender-Bending with a Vengeance: Brigitte Lin

"In the end, I couldn't tell Yin from Yang."
  – Ouyang Feng (Leslie Cheung), *Ashes of Time/Dongxie Xida* (1994)

"I come to bury everything!"
  – Invincible Asia (Brigitte Lin), *The East is Red/Dongfang Bubai Fengyung Zaiqi* (1993)

The early 1990s 'new wave' cycle of martial arts films produced the last great swordplay queen, Brigitte Lin Ching-hsia. According to Howard Hampton's breathless rhapsody, she is "just possibly the most uncanny presence in film today ... the late twentieth century's last, strangest movie goddess" (1996: 42). Like Jet Li, Lin's persona was reinvented, 'authored' even, by Tsui Hark. In Stanley Kwan's *Yang + Yin*, Tsui describes Lin as a "carefree, elegant boy, except that she's a girl", and emphasises his own role in her creation: "The more you twist her form, the more interesting she is", he insists, "Take her as she comes and it may be less interesting". But even a master manipulator like Tsui could not author all of the fantasies Lin must have generated.[11] In Lin's own words, "I seem to fulfil some fantasy the audience has about a beautiful girl performing violent acts" (quoted in Hammond and Wilkins 1997: 96). Death can be dispensed by fist, sword, bullwhip, hair or blasts of palm power, but is usually accompanied by the unleashing of what Hampton calls 'The Look':

> Suddenly she will return the camera's mesmerised gaze with a blinding eye-for-eye intensity – a blast of Dreyerian silence before the poetry of doom will be writ in blood and severed limbs. (1996: 42)

Tsui first used Lin in *Zu: Warriors of the Magic Mountain* (as a literally glacial warrior, ensconced in an ice fortress), and *Peking Opera Blues/Dao Ma Dan* (1986). While the latter is not a martial arts film, it is important in establishing her androgynous Warrior Woman persona. Lin plays a revolutionary during the 'Warlord' era (c. 1910–20s) who dresses in men's clothes; as the English title might suggest, there is a lot of cross-dressing in the film. In its most excruciating scene, she is captured and tortured, the wounds inflicted on her being so severe that her captor can insert his finger into one of them. Taken in itself, this seems to be a violent reminder of her biological gender, of her penetrable female body. But the narrative complicates this 'pornographic' assertion of gender norms. Her wounds heal as quickly as only Hong Kong heroes' can, and she seems to grow more powerful as a result of this rite-of-passage. During the climax, she takes flight across rooftops, gunning down the villains like a John Woo hero. Mutilation is an important masculine rite in Woo's and Zhang Che's films, so Lin's suffering does not provide the clearcut gender alignment that it might at first appear to.

The Bride with White Hair (1993) gives us one of Lin's quintessential Warrior Women, "an exterminating angel, a negationist Pandora" (Hampton 1996: 42). Like the Deaf-Mute Heroine, her Wolf-Girl assassin has no real name, perhaps because being named seems to be inextricably linked to being owned. She works for an evil cult led by polymorphous Siamese twins (Francis Ng/Elaine Lui), joined at the back, who have tattooed the name 'Lien' on her shoulder. When she falls in love with *wu dang* swordsman Cho Yi-hang (Leslie Cheung), he names her 'Lien Ni-chang'. But Cho will betray her, and the cult try to destroy her for her own 'betrayal', transforming her into the more primal white-haired figure of the film's English title, who announces that 'Lien Ni-chang' is "dead". *The Bride with White Hair* is set during the final, turbulent years of the Ming Dynasty, and the narrative set-up has some similarities to the earlier *Swordsman II*. The hero and heroine are supposedly on opposite sides, but succumb to forbidden love; consummated, in *The Bride with White Hair*, in an underground spring and waterfall. She is as passionate in love as she is ferociously brutal in combat (we first see her dismembering bandits with a bullwhip); he is compromised by conflicting loyalties. In both films, the hero is alienated from *jianghu*, but cannot break free from the constraints of heroic masculinity. When Cho's comrades are slain, and Lien framed by the Siamese Twins, he turns on her, a betrayal that transforms her into an apocalyptic "witch"; her red dress bursts open to reveal a white one underneath (white is the colour of death). As in *Swordsman II*, Lin's character exits the film in the knowledge that her former lover will never forget her: "I want you to regret it for life", Invincible Asia tells Ling (Jet Li) as she falls to her death, "And you'll remember me forever!" Cho retreats to a snow-covered mountaintop in the film's framing sequence, waiting for a rare flower to bloom that will transform the white-haired witch back into the wolf-girl 'Ni-chang'.

In *The Bride with White Hair*, polymorphous perversity is largely confined to the flamboyant Siamese twins; the sister is jealous of her brother's love for Lien, and writhes in ecstasy as he tries to have sex with the wolf-girl. But Lin is not always such a heterosexual figure as she is in that film. In *New Dragon Gate Inn/Xin Longmen Kezhan* (1992), she strips Maggie Cheung during their swordfight. In *The East is Red*, the third film in the *Swordsman* series, she comes to reclaim her former concubine Snow (Joey Wong), who has impersonated her throughout the film. But Lin's claim to queer iconic status can perhaps be best found in her crossing of gender identities, as transvestite and transsexual.

Several of Lin's films use iconography that one might associate with the horror film, casting her as what Barbara Creed (1993) calls the 'Monstrous Feminine'. Creed draws on Julia Kristeva's notion of the 'abject', that which "disturbs identity, system, order" and "does not respect borders, positions, rules. The in-between, the ambiguous, the composite" (1982: 4). For both Creed and Kristeva, the maternal functions of the female body are those that are most frequently represented as monstrous or abject. Lin is never a literal monster, but is sometimes invested with monstrous attributes. If the notion of the abject polices borders by provoking disgust, Lin's characters are offered more as objects of sexual fascination. In *The Bride with White Hair* and *The East is Red*, she is a Medusa figure, promising death or mutilation to men who gaze at her; "Whoever sees me shall be blinded!" she tells Cho during their first meeting. In *The Bride with White Hair*, her hair becomes lethal tendrils, throttling the *wu dang* warriors; in *The East is Red*, Invincible Asia returns from the grave like a Barbara Steele vampire or witch. She is equated more explicitly with the maternal body in *Swordsman II*, where Invincible Asia of the Sun Moon sect castrates himself in accordance with a Sacred Scroll in order to achieve incredible internal power. In the course of the film, 'he' gradually changes sex, but his/her body remains concealed. Asia may travel from yang to yin, but also evokes the archaic, phallic, mother, "the parthonogenic mother, the mother as primordial abyss, the point of origin

東方不敗

風雲再起

新藝城 ⑪

Fig. 12 Gender-bending Warrior-Woman: Brigitte Lin as 'Invincible Asia' in *Swordsman II*

The Lady is the Boss?

and of end" (Creed 1993: 17).[12] *The East is Red* configures Asia most pointedly as point-of-origin as s/he taunts invading Spanish soldiers:

> Your science is shit ... Your God is useless ... Your bible should be re-written. From now on, the God mentioned in your Western Bible should be re-written as Asia the Invincible.

In *Swordsman II*, Asia emerges from oceans, burns leaves and birds from the trees, sends dust clouds spiraling in her wake. When s/he first meets the besotted Ling, s/he speaks to him from beneath the waters of a lake, disguising his/her masculine voice, but also conjuring the Mother-Child intimacy of the womb. Asia is both 'Father' and 'Mother', although the archaic mother is a phallic figure who "exists prior to the child's knowledge of castration and sexual difference. The boy imagines the mother is like himself" (Creed 1993: 157). But Asia is also at war with the film's more literal 'Father', Wu (Lam Sai-kwun), the overthrown leader of the Sun Moon sect. Their conflict is over possession of the Sacred Scroll, that which empowers Asia by castrating 'him' but phallicizing 'her'.

That Wu is the 'Father' is made explicit by his relationship to Jet Li's Ling, who is ostensibly courting Wu's daughter, Ying (Rosamund Kwan). The Oedipus complex is predicated on a repudiation of the mother – "There is no love between us", Ling insists – but Asia remains an object of desire. Wu becomes the more monstrous figure, with his Energy-Absorbing Stance, literally earth-shaking laugh and wave of tyranny following Asia's defeat. Paranoid and deranged, he puts Ling on his death list and those heroes who survive must flee at the end of the film. Ling is, in any case, ambivalent about *jianghu* and has already sought to withdraw. The attraction of Asia, even if it is founded on gender misrecognition, is that 'she' offers an escape from this world, a blissfully sensual (and implicitly pre-oedipal) union as they soar through the trees together. Ling strikes me as being far from the simple "boozer" and "fool" that Lisa Oldham Stokes and Michael Hoover describe him as (1999: 105). If the film is, as Stephen Teo argues, "a telling attack on the stereotype of the male hero" (1997: 200), then Ling does seem to be groping towards an insight into some of the pitfalls of heroic masculinity. But as subversive as Lin's transsexual anti-heroine already is, the film's auto-critique must also queer the chastest, most sexually reticent, of all martial arts stars, Jet Li.

If Asia is an abject figure then, as Rolanda Chu argues, the border that *Swordsman II* most radically transgresses is that between genders; Lin's character represents an "undifferentiated abject" (1994: 35), but one which is profoundly complicated by the codes of romance. When Ling arrives to consummate his relationship with Asia, s/he substitutes the concubine Cici (the name by which our hero will remember his great love). "I want him to remember me always", Asia explains, a desire bitterly reiterated during the climax. There are two ways of looking at this substitution. In *Yang + Yin*, Stanley Kwan believes that Tsui Hark's films "always end by reaffirming heterosexual norms". Thus, Ling (and Jet Li) does not sleep with a man or a transsexual. But as Chu rightly points out, even when he knows Asia's 'secret', he wants him/her to be 'Cici': "Please tell me that you're Cici", he pleads as she plunges from a clifftop. But the ending also keeps Asia's 'secret' as just that, a secret, still on the border. It is here, Chu argues, that the film offers its "boundary-breaking pleasure":

> The viewer is set up to want the Ling and Fong (Asia) characters to be together. If the utopian prospect is of a vision at least momentarily of the fluidity of gender options, then the most radical dynamic of pleasure put forth in *Swordsman II* is the prospect of loving the monster: the taboo of embracing the abject. (1994: 35)

Lin's gender-bending warrior roles clearly have some connections to Hong Kong's sexual liberalisation. For example, homosexuality was decriminalised in 1989 and legislation on sex discrimination passed in 1995.[13] But, at the same time, gender-bending was nothing new in Chinese performance traditions. Brigitte Lin's gender-bending persona has its roots in the tradition of the martial heroine, who often drags up, while cross-dressing is also an important part of what Marjorie Garber calls "a transvestite theatre that traditionally presents 'woman' as a cultural artefact of male stagecraft" (1992: 244–5), namely Chinese Opera.[14] If the 'abject' marks out an ambiguous "in-between", in Lin's case this also suggests Garber's "third" space of transvestism. The "third" is "that which questions binary thinking and introduces crisis ... a way of describing a space of possibility" (11), that which "deconstructs the binary of self and other" (12). Transvestism is a "third" because of its generation of "category crisis", offering "a space of possibility structuring and confounding culture: the disruptive element that intervenes, not just a category crisis of male and female, but the crisis of category itself" (17).

Not all of Lin's films offer such a "category crisis", and *Swordsman II* makes for an interesting comparison with the more celebrated arthouse film, *Ashes of Time*. As much as I love *Ashes of Time*, the film makes far more conservative use of Lin, reducing gender 'confusion' to schizophrenia and narcissism. Lin plays "the first daughter of the famous Murong Clan", who assumes male and female personas, Murong Yang and 'his' sister, Murong Yin. "Are you a man or a woman?" she is asked during her first scene. Huang (Tony Leung Kar-fai) sees through 'Yang's disguise, flirts, caresses her face and promises to marry 'his' sister. His jilting of Murong Yin propels her into madness, 'brother' and 'sister' now at odds with one another. Murong Yang hires Ouyang Feng (Leslie Cheung) to kill Huang, while Murong Yin counters by putting a contract on her 'brother'. The Yin/Yang episode is framed by Ouyang Feng's narration; Murong is "someone with a wounded soul"; after watching her over the course of a night, "I couldn't tell Yin from Yang". She re-invents herself as an androgynous swordsman, the Defeat-Seeking Loner, who practices on 'his' own reflection, setting off seismic explosions in a lake. *Jianghu* is resolutely masculine and hetero-normative in *Ashes of Time*, albeit a masculinity characterised by Wong Kar-wai's trademark regret and longing as much as action. In some ways, the film seems to be offering the origin of the swordswoman, a figure who stumbles into *jianghu* when scorned in love, her heroism scarred by insanity and self-loathing. This is not the way of Invincible Asia; when s/he announces that "I come to bury everything", fixed gender identity seems to be first in the queue for the graveyard of meaning. Gender is literally skin-deep in *Swordsman II* and *The East is Red*. In the latter film, Snow, passing for Asia, seduces her concubine, passing opium from tongue to tongue, shortly before the 'concubine' peels off her skin to reveal an albino ninja of entirely unknown gender. Brigitte Lin arguably took the figure of the Martial Heroine in more radical directions than might previously have been thought possible. But once again, she could only go so far, not only because the 1990s cycle soon burned out, but also because Lin retired from the cinema after her iconic appearance in *Chungking Express/ Chongqing Senlin* (1994). The Martial Heroine would return in another arthouse vehicle, but one with a distinctly global impact.

Kicking Over *Wu dang* Mountain: *Crouching Tiger, Hidden Dragon*

"I am the Invincible Sword Goddess, armed with the incredible Green Destiny ... I am the desert dragon! I leave no trace! Today I fly over Eu-Mei! Tomorrow I'll kick over *Wu dang* Mountain!"
– Jen/Yu Jiaolong (Zhang Ziyi), *Crouching Tiger, Hidden Dragon*

Not since the heyday of Angela Mao Ying has a martial arts film with such strong female protagonists been so widely seen outside Asia. Jen is the daughter of a wealthy Manchu family, seeking escape from an arranged marriage; escape sought first in *wu xia* fiction and then the real *jianghu* adventures offered by Jade Fox, and also in a desert romance with dashing bandit Luo (Chang Chen). Yu Shu-lien (Michelle Yeoh), a kung fu expert, runs a security firm. She is in love with, but cannot consummate her relationship with *wu dang*

Fig. 13 Jen (Zhang Ziyi) seduced with "a dream of the *jianghu* underworld" by her 'illegitimate' *shifu* Jade Fox (Zheng Pei-pei) in *Crouching Tiger, Hidden Dragon*

Swordsman Li Mu-bai (Chow Yun-fat) because of the *jianghu* code; her fiance, killed by Jade Fox, was Li's 'brother' by oath and they cannot dishonour his memory. The difference between these two heroines, one romantic and impulsive, the other pragmatic and self-denying, is made clear in a discussion of the literary and 'real' *jianghu*:

Jen: It must be exciting to be a fighter, to be totally free.

Yu: Fighters have rules, too: friendship, integrity ... Without rules, we wouldn't survive for long.

Jen: I've read all about people like you. Roaming wild, beating up anyone who gets in your way.

Yu: Writers wouldn't sell many books if they told how it really is.
      [Talk turns to Jen's impending marriage]

Yu: Congratulations. It's the most important step in a woman's life, isn't it?

Jen: You're not married, are you?

Yu: What do you think?

Jen: No! You couldn't roam around freely if you were.

Yu: You're probably right.

It seems no accident that Yu Shu-lien is trained in the 'hard' Shaolin arts, while Jen has acquired 'soft' *wu dang* techniques (and learned them 'illegitimately' from an outlaw and a stolen manual). Yu seems to me to be a heroine from a kung fu film. She is strong, but 'knows her place'; respectful of tradition and (male) heroic codes, she allows Li Mu-bai to define the 'chivalrous' terms of their relationship. Jen's world, on the other hand, is that of the swordplay queen, defined by freedom and mobility, or at least a longing for them. She resists Li's offer of being her *shifu*: "You need a real master", he tells her, "I've always wanted a student worthy of my *wu dang* secrets". But he explains to Yu Shu-lien that this desire is also a matter of 'containing' Jen's restless spirit, to prevent her from becoming a "poisoned dragon".

Jen finds an alternative Master in the form of Jade Fox, a relationship partly expressed in terms of seduction: "You enchanted me with a dream of the *jianghu* underworld", Jen tells her, but she has surpassed her illiterate Master, who was unable to read the manual. Jade Fox may be a symbolic mother (she has nurturing, if manipulative, qualities), but class differences mean that Jen is likely to seek legitimation elsewhere, in the 'good' father, Li Mu-bai.[15] If Jade Fox is the film's villain, with a Rosa Klebb blade in her shoe to prove it, she is also its most tragic figure, underestimated (and, it seems, sexually exploited)[16] by the *wu dang* and betrayed by her adopted 'daughter'. "You know what poison is?" she asks, dying, "An eight-year-old girl full of deceit ... My only family, my only enemy". This failed Master/Pupil relationship is as much the core of the film as Yu and Li's abortive romance. It is hard to resist seeing *jianghu* as a metaphor for the *wu xia pian* and Jade Fox as interchangeable with the former 'Queen of the Swordswomen' who plays her. Just as male heroes and stars sidelined Zheng Pei-pei and others, so, too, is Jade Fox marginalised by the 'heroic' world. She can only find an 'illegitimate' place, and power, in *jianghu*. Jen, on the other hand, is the quintessential postmodern heroine, her loyalties uncertain and unfixed. She learns from, but will not ally herself with, her generic predecessor, and is both attracted by and wary of the masculine ethos of *jianghu*.

The final scene of *Crouching Tiger*, as Jen jumps from *Wu dang* Mountain and 'floats' off into the clouds, has continued to intrigue and tantalise audiences; my students frequently ask me what I think it "means". In narrative terms, it is explicitly set up by the legend told by Luo of a young man who leapt from a mountain in order to have his wish granted: "He floated away, far away, never to return. He knew his wish had come true". But what is Jen's wish? Is it the same as Luo's, "to be back in the desert, together again"? Or is it a heroic sacrifice to restore Li Mu-bai to life? I would like to suggest that the scene is more suggestive in relation to Jen's own future, to the limited options available to even such a powerful swordswoman. She can, indeed, return to the desert with Luo, give up her *jianghu* adventures, and, in a sense, find herself in a more benign version of the arranged marriage planned by her parents. Or she can join *wu dang*, if they will accept her – we are told that they have never accepted women before – and risk the marginalisation that 'poisoned' Jade Fox. But there is a third option – third in the way that Marjorie Garber uses the term – to remain in flight, resist a fixed identity or space, not fitting neatly here or there.[17] Here, perhaps, is both the fate and the romance of the *wu xia* heroine. She can fly, she can even soar, but she can never really afford to land.

Chapter Six

Last Hero in China?
Jet Li and the 'New Wave' Kung Fu Film

If the success of *Enter the Dragon* represented the commercial apotheosis of Western kung fu fever in 1973, Chinese martial arts were to play an equally public role in US-Chinese relations the following year. Richard Nixon, the first American president to visit China as part of the PRC's new 'openness', was entertained at the White House by the Beijing *wu shu* team. The President was reportedly particularly impressed by 11-year-old Li Lianjie, who one year later would be China's national champion for the first of five times. This was not the last time Li would visit the US; he toured the world as part of the Beijing team, lived in San Francisco on a two-year exit visa in the late 1980s and currently resides there as a modestly successful Hollywood star under his anglicised name 'Jet Li'. Li may now be an American citizen, but his film-making remains encouragingly international, with the French-US *Kiss of the Dragon* (2001) and the Pan-Chinese *Hero* (2002). In between, perhaps the most geographically mobile of all kung fu stars became one of Hong Kong cinema's biggest box office draws. As Wong Fei-hung and Fong Sai-yuk, he was a major figure at the South-East Asian box office in the early 1990s. Li is arguably the last significant kung fu star. This elegaic claim is supported by Hong Kong genre cinema's virtual demise, by the transnationalisation of Asian genres and aesthetics, by the encroachment of technology, and by the way his 1991–94 output seemed to replay the martial arts film on fast-forward. His martial arts rivals, Donnie Yen and Zhou Wen-zhou, never achieved his popularity, and there is no one in line to take his place. As his thumbnail biography suggests, Li brings a lot of cultural baggage, and thus resonance, to the genre: 1974/Nixon, the re-opening of the Shaolin Temple and China's reclaiming of its martial 'heritage', US-China, Hong Kong-China, Hong Kong-Hollywood. Tsui Hark has described Li as a "national treasure" (Hong Kong Film Archive 1999: 64), and gave him further resonance, re-igniting a seemingly fading career by casting him as the 1990s Wong Fei-hung. As a Mainlander playing a 'local' hero, he was an iconic figure in Hong Kong cinema's countdown to 1997. While Li's career has stalled several times, he is, as Tony Williams suggests, "a flexible and adaptable actor" who has both negotiated numerous cultural and geographic boundaries and adapted to "changing historical and industrial circumstances" (2000: 8).

At one level, Li has lived his life very publicly, coinciding with some key cultural events almost as fortuitously as Tsui Hark has Wong Fei-hung interact with modern Chinese history. But he is a diffident celebrity, as though 'Jet Li' does not exist outside his films and martial arts. Bruce Lee and Jackie Chan have irresistible biographies, but Robert James Parish (2002) struggles to make Li more than the sum of his achievements, because his subject comes over as a defiantly closed book.[1] Furthermore, in some respects, Li does not seem to have authored his star persona in the way that Lee and Chan did, in spite of running his own production company in Hong Kong. Although he directed a film early in his career, Li has never choreographed his own fight scenes, the distiguishing mark of a kung fu star-auteur; his most frequent collaborator remains Corey Yuen, but he has also worked memorably with Yuen Wo-ping. Jet would have made a magnificent Shaw Brothers contract player, combining Wang Yu's stoicism, David Chiang's unconventional, quiet charisma and Fu Sheng's irrepressible boyishness. Indeed, in the early 1990s, he seemed determined to play every classic martial arts hero, like a one-man kung fu star system. As a star persona, Li always seemed to be Tsui Hark's creation. His two best post-Tsui films display the producer-director's influence; *Fong Sai-yuk* (1993) echoes Tsui's fondness for burlesque and cross-dressing, while *Fist of Legend* (1994) extends the revisionism of the *Once Upon a Time in China* cycle.

Li was considered by many to be too young to play Wong Fei-hung.[2] After all, his is not the callow Wong of *Challenge of the Masters* or *Drunken Master*; rather, he incarnates the mature *shifu* in the body of an athletic young man with matinee-idol looks. In *Once Upon a Time in China 2*, set in 1895, the real Wong Fei-hung would be forty-eight, but Li has not aged from the first installment set some twenty years earlier. His aura hinges on his paradoxical appearance; boyish, while seemingly infused with a calm sagacity that belies his apparent age. When Zhou Wen-zhou, whose physical abilities more than match Li's, took over as Wong Fei-hung in Parts 4 and 5, it was even more apparent how inspired the original casting had been. Zhou excelled in the fight scenes, but he could not pull off the role; he lacked Jet's presence and simply looked too *young*. Li has been described as having "the aspect of a boy and the grace of Gene Kelly" (Dannen and Long 1997: 27). His 'presence' frequently challenges those who seek to define it, while some simply judge it not to exist. For every critic who finds him charismatic or "luminous" (Hammond 2000: 94), there is a dissenter who finds him wooden, inexpressive, all physical ability and no personality.[3] Andrew O'Hehir (2000: n.p.) discerns "a quiet unquantifiable something", but also acknowledges "an almost standoffish Garbo quality, a little mystery", a quality that works in favour of characters who tend to be "shy, lonely, easily wounded". Howard Hampton, while by no means Li's sternest critic, clearly finds the "mystery" more of a barrier:

> Jet Li is an enigma. The camera loves him – he's like a lithe, compact Schwarzenegger – yet he withholds himself so much he might as well be wearing a hairshirt and a cowl. (Quoted in Dannen and Long 1997: 344)

There is a deceptive stillness, even diffidence, about Li, and he *can*, as Hampton seems to suggest, 'disappear' as an actor, deferring to scene-stealing and more experienced performers like Josephine Siao and Eric Tsang. But Li never wastes a close-up, and at his best is a subtle and expressive performer. There's a corny, but affecting scene in *Black Mask/Hak Hap* (1996), where his fellow workers throw a surprise birthday party for him, complete with Mickey Mouse cake. He has already decided that he cannot afford to make friends; his life is too dangerous and he does not want to put them at risk (classic superhero dilemma!). He curtly shuns their display of affection and leaves; a lingering shot shows him glance longingly back at the cake, his face a masterpiece of conflicting emotions. Li's dramatic speciality is the tension between big (even repressed) emotions and the heroic need for reticence and control. It takes three films for Wong Fei-hung and 13th Aunt to kiss; when he sweeps her up in his arms, his students gape at him in bewilderment. His virtually wordless performance in *Lethal Weapon 4* (1998) gives unexpected depth to what is otherwise the most stereotypical of 'inscrutable' Chinese heavies.

The more interesting judgement of Li is the question some have raised (for example Logan 1995: 178) about his suitability for modern-day roles. Granted, in his twenty-four Hong Kong films, only seven and a half had contemporary settings; the 'half' is *Dr Wai in 'The Scripture with No Words'*, with its dual time-frame. Eleven are set during the Qing Dynasty, three during the Ming, one just after World War Two and one-and-a-half (*Dr Wai* again!) around the late 1920s/early 1930s. But what does it mean for an actor in his early thirties to be considered incongruous in modern settings? Some of this is to do with *wu shu*; while many question its authenticity, its appearance is of a very 'traditional' and very *Chinese* fighting style. Bruce Lee and Jackie Chan adopted transnational, hybridised fighting styles that looked ready-made for urban settings. While Li's martial arts knowledge is in some ways the broadest of the three – unlike Lee, he learned 'internal' as well as 'external' styles – it is more rigidly 'Chinese', eschewing, for example, the Korean-derived kicking techniques that someone like Donnie Yen excels at.[4] Certainly Li's fighting style allies him with 'China' rather than 'Hong Kong'; more specifically, the martial arts film's mythical 'China'. But the question of Li's modern-day 'fit' also seems connected to his non-'belonger' status in Hong Kong; how to incorporate this mainlander with very traditional martial arts skills into the cosmopolitan space of modern Hong Kong? In other ways, however, Li cuts a very modern figure, even before *Bodyguard from Beijing/Zhong Nan Hai Bao Biao* (1994) dumped the Qing Dynasty queue and equipped him with designer suits and an immaculately coiffed haircut. His anglicised name suggests a fusion with technological 'speed'; an important theme in the Wong Fei-hung series (where he encounters trains, cameras, guns and clocks) and in the spectacle of Li's fight scenes (no other kung fu star has embraced technology so unreservedly). Li's casting in science fiction roles (*Black Mask, The One,* aborted roles in *The Matrix* sequels) is the most obvious example. Like Tsui Hark's Wong Fei-hung, Li conjoins the past and the future; his Wong is an outdated Confucian patriarch who simultaneously looks like a gleaming digitized fighter from a computer game, who in opposing guns (in Part One) actually *becomes* a gun, firing a bullet to lethal effect with his finger.

Li's early films trade on his reputation as 'national treasure'; he performs stand-alone *wu shu* forms in *Shaolin Temple* and *Dragon Fight/Long Zai Tian Ya* (1989); in the latter, he plays a Mainland *wu shu* performer, adrift in San Francisco (as Li was during the same period). None of his films prior to *Once Upon a Time in China* suggest anything like a star persona, or acting abilities that rise above the monochrome emotional scale of formulaic action movies. Li was initially based in China, paid a standardised state-approved rate to star in films on which Hong Kong stuntmen took home considerably more money than he did. During his sojourn in America, he again looked to Hong Kong cinema in two films about Chinese émigrés. The second of these, *The Master/Huang Feihong 92 zhi Long Xing Tianxia* (1989), his first film with Tsui Hark and one that nods to the Wong Fei-hung legend, ought to be more interesting than it is, but was not even considered releasable until after his 1990s reinvention. Instead, the most interesting of Li's early films is his one excursion into directing, *Born to Defence/Zhong Hua Ying Xiong* (1986), because of its foreshadowing of the nationalism in the later Wong Fei-hung series and its contrast with his 'mature' persona.[5] The film is set in Shandong shortly after World War Two. Li plays a war hero returning home to find his hometown overrun by US marines. The film is crude, but often powerful, contrasting local poverty (children offer themselves for sale) with arrogant Westerners driving recklessly through the crowded village. Li must give blood to make money, the kung fu hero's body literally drained by imperialism. The marines throw some familiar taunts at the locals – "were your balls cut off by the Japanese?" – but their boasts about the atomic bomb ending the war prompt Li's memorable response,

"Fuck your atomic bomb! What about my fists?" As this line suggests, this is not the neo-Confucian Jet Li of the 1990s and after. Li subsequently distanced himself from *Born to Defence*'s *gwailo*phobia:

> I was quite young and quite angry ... I felt so strongly the need to express my sentiments about social conditions – about how outrageous it was that favouritism for foreigners still existed even after so many years. (Parish 2002: 57)

The film condenses its Sino-US conflict into two images; the Chinese bar dominated by a Western boxing ring and the difference between Asian and Western bodies. The conflict first turns physical in the ring, with Li constrained by Western fighting rules; he only wins when he is allowed to use his feet and elbows. An early scene shows marines trying on Chinese shoes that barely fit their toes, and Jet's major antagonist is a huge naval officer. They fight to a virtual standstill as a thunderstorm floods the ring, but Li is brutally beaten during the match. A rematch is scarcely more conclusive; he cannot put the huge American down and only wins by luck, a stray cargo load knocking his opponent out. Like many kung fu films, anti-imperialism descends into racism (it is a black marine who makes the comment about castrated Chinese), but it comes with a masochism that might make even Jackie Chan wince. Li is beaten until his face is unrecognisable, drained of blood, and even urinated on (by Chinese jailers). This was the last time a shirtless Li would appear onscreen until *Hero*, although he is nothing like the muscular presence Bruce Lee once pitted against foreign aggressors. Thereafter, Li's body, usually covered up, is the epitome of corporeal integrity. In *Fist of Legend*, he hooks his fingers into an opponent's mouth to throw him, and then wipes the saliva contemptuously from his fingers. *Born to Defence* is an extraordinarily *defeated* film, but Li was to be reinvented as patriotic 'defender' in the early 1990s, conjoining China's past and Hong Kong's uncertain future as the kung fu film's two most popular heroes.

Heroes Two: Wong Fei-hung and Fong Sai-yuk

> "Only the kind-hearted people will be invincible, but most important of all, we should educate the people. Only wisdom plus strong bodies can make our country strong."
> – Wong Fei-hung, *Once Upon a Time in China 3*

> "I love fighting!"
> – *Fong Sai-yuk*

Two southern heroes; the 'father' of the Hong Kong kung fu film and its eternal 'boy', who either dies romantically young or (in Jet Li's version) remains in the realm of 'mother'. Tony Williams has described the *Once Upon a Time in China* series as one of the major achievements of 1990s Hong Kong cinema (2000:4). He is not wrong, but I would go further; it constitutes one of the high points of 1990s cinema full stop. As breathtaking spectacle alone, it leaves the wealthier Lucases and Spielbergs in the dust kicked up by Wong Fei-hung's slippers. But more than that, and what makes it unique as a franchise, is its object lesson in how to combine visceral thrills, comedy and romance with revisionist history, myth and cultural self-reflection. The critical consensus, from academic analysis to popular biography (Parish 2002) to DVD commentary, is that the series uses China's turbulent past as a mirror to Hong Kong's uncertain future. The Tsui Hark/Jet Li Wong is, in Siu-leung Li's words:

A man in the process of becoming a father, resituated in an extremely unstable moment of China's first modern revolution; a symbolic figure repositioned in a disruptive site of struggle and negotiation intersecting Hong Kong, China and the colonial Other as Hong Kong was coming to terms with the return to the father-land. (2001: 533)

The central premise of the cycle has been summed up by Tsui Hark, to "link Wong [Fei-hung] with every incident in the modern history of China" (quoted in Hwang 1998: 12). Thus, Wong interacts with the aftermath of the Treaty of Nanjing, which first ceded Hong Kong to Britain and opened Chinese 'Treaty Ports' for foreign trade, Sun Yat-sen (alleged model for Kwan Tak-hing's Wong), the Boxer Rebellion, the Empress Dowager, President Li Hong-zhong, even Billy the Kid. The tone is "untimely" or "antihistorical", "a retroactive reduction of everything past to the giddiness and incertitude of the present" (Lo 1993: 89). References, to past, present and future fly thick and fast. The xenophobic White Lotus Cult (in Part Two) are often taken as the Red Guard of the Cultural Revolution. When Sun Yat-sen takes refuge from the Manchus at the British Embassy (again in Part Two), the referent seems to be democracy activist Fang Lizhi, who sought sanctuary at the US Embassy after Tiananmen Square. Part One takes place in "a new age of international cooperation" according to the head of the 'Sino-Pacific Corporation', the global as a convenient cover for neo-colonialism; Western slave traders and other imperialist villains. But in Part Two, the villains are closer to home; the White Lotus cult and the compromised Manchu commander (a superbly nuanced performance by Donnie Yen) who must "do what is best".

In Ackbar Abbas' equation, colonialism is always coded through masculine heroism in the kung fu film, in the representation of "what is felt to be possible" (1997: 29). The Chinese title of Part Two translates as 'Men Should Empower Themselves'. During the title sequence of Part One, we see Wong training the patriotic Black Flag militia on a beach. At the climax of the sequence, we see him stand alone on a sand dune, in silhouette; a similar image of Jet Li under a blood-red sky was the film's original poster. The theme song's lyrics underline this national strengthening of the male Chinese body that flows from the individual to the group:

> With pride I face thousands of waves
> My blood is hot like the sun
> My courage is as strong as iron
> My bones are refined as steel ...
> I strive to strengthen myself
> Be a hero![6]

Jet Li incarnates a radiant, but intangible, masculinity; the first film's most memorable scene is not a fight, but 13th Aunt caressing his shadow (he flinches when she seems about to touch his actual body). It is 13th Aunt, above all, who checks this inviolable patriarchal image.[7] Dressed in Victorian clothes, educated in England, she both introduces a kind of Confucian screwball comedy into the series and mediates Wong's encounter with Western modernity: "There will be railways and a telegraph company soon", she tells him in Part One, "Everything will change. China will change with the world." The films' elegiac English titles invite comparison with Sergio Leone's *Once Upon a Time in the West* (1969), another film about heroic masculinity under siege from technology. But their equation of technology and gender is very different. The railroad in Leone's film (built by émigré Chinese) is implicitly castrating, equated with the crippled businessman Morton (**Gabriel Ferzetti**) and the former prostitute Jill (Claudia Cardinale), who, according to Leone, represents the coming of a "world without balls" (Frayling 1981: 202). Lo observes that technology is split and gendered in the Wong Fei-hung series. On the one hand, there is an "aggressive, masculine" technology associated with imperialism (1993: 83). 'Iron Robe' Yim (Part One) is gunned down and dies observing that "we can't fight guns with kung fu". In Part Three, Russian officer Tomansky tells Wong that whoever controls technology rules the world. On the other hand, 13th Aunt represents the "affable, feminine aspect" of technology; for Lo, she is the "embodiment of a dazzling kind of knowledge", what he calls "*techné*, not exactly equivalent to technology, though it is always translated as such" (83). Above all, she is equated with, and in control of, the photographic and cinematic image. She 'authors' Wong-as-image, framing him as romantic lead and transnational 'progressive' as well as patriarch of a strong nation. Her caressing of his image is revisited in Part Two, where an unwelcome kung fu lesson gives way to a fantasy shadowplay of him leading her in a waltz. In *Once Upon a Time in China and America/Huang Feihong zhi Xigu Hongshi* (1997), she restores Wong's memory by 'directing' a potted version of the first five films, boiled down to their climactic fights; a live band plays his signature theme while Clubfoot (Xiong Xin-xin) plays each antagonist in turn, from 'Iron Robe' Yim to Part Five's Pirate Leader. 13th Aunt is explicitly allied with Sun Yat-sen, forever looking at his watch because "time is important – we Chinese waste a lot of it";[8] at the end of Part Two, they are on the same boat to Hong Kong. But while Wong wonders "what will we turn into", he, too, succumbs to this *techné*, and kung fu becomes, as Lo puts it, "an old technology renewed" (1993: 94), fighting within the terrain of 'special effects'. Sound effects add further to the impression of technological embodiment; in Part Two, Li and Yen's swinging poles sound like helicopter blades, while leaps and spins are accompanied by an uncanny 'roaring tiger' effect.

During an early scene in *Fong Sai-yuk*, our hero has been fighting (again!) and the authorities ask him for his name. "Wong...", he begins, assuming the southern master's trademark pose as his theme starts up, "...Jing!"[9] When he later uses an English phrase, his mother Miao Cuihua (Josephine Siao) asks him where he learned it; "Josephine Siao taught me", he replies.[10] The Fong Sai-yuk films, Li's most successful alongside the Wong Fei-hung series and *Swordsman II*, highlight the other dominant strategy in reinventing martial arts in the early 1990s; pastiche and parody. Where the Tsui Hark films and *Fist of Legend* are about connecting their hero to modern history, the Fong Sai-yuk films show much less interest in the mythology surrounding the younger Cantonese legend. This can be seen as either a willful forgetting or a parodic de-Sinicisation of a local hero. Li had no apparent qualms about sending up his image, including Wong Fei-hung. In *Last Hero in China/Huang Feihong Tieji Du Wu Song* (1993), Wong's famous clinic and school, Po Chi Lam, is placed next door to a brothel; during the climax, he fights dressed as a chicken while practicing 'Chicken Beak' kung fu. *Kung Fu Cult Master/Yitian Tulong Ji zhi Mojiao Jiaozhu* (1993) has fun with his sexually reticent image. He plays a pupil of *wu dang* patriarch Zhang San-feng (Sammo Hung), so enfeebled by a childhood blow from the 'Jinx's Palm' that he cannot achieve an erection. It is not the Shaolin Great Solar Stance that cures him, as the narrative leads us to expect, but a night huddled in the arms of pouting Chingamy Yau. Is that a Butterfly Sword in his pocket or is he just pleased to see her?

In *Fong Sai-yuk*, the antagonist Tiger Lui becomes a former bandit from northern Shandong struggling to fit into Guangdong society. He seeks to ingratiate himself by offering his daughter's hand in marriage via a challenge match with his wife Siu-wan (Sibelle Hu); "One kick subdues Guangdong" the challenge reads, perhaps a little tactlessly. The gauntlet is picked up by "one of the outstanding young men of Guangdong, the Invincible Magic Fist, Fong Sai-yuk". They have the most quintessential of 1990s fights, balanced precariously on the shoulders of a crowd; whoever touches the ground first loses. Fong takes a deliberate dive when he mistakes the unglamorous family maid for the daughter, prompting his outraged mother to drag up as his brother 'Fong Tai-yuk' to restore family honour.[11] Miao not only defeats Siu-wan, but wins her heart, leading to more mistaken identity and cross-dressing; this is one of three films in which Li puts on a dress. But the real focus of the film and its sequel is the relationship between mother and son, partners-in-disobedience who carve out their own anarchic world of fighting, dressing up and postponing responsibility. It is Fong's father, a merchant and scholar, who realigns them with patriotic duty for a while; he has affiliations with the Red Flower Society and finally places Sai-yuk in the care of its leader Chen Jialuo (Adam Cheng). But Miao and Fong are experts in the performance, if not practice, of submissiveness. Both endure beatings from Fong senior even though they know kung fu and he does not; Miao explains to her son that "a man's status is very important". The sprawling sequel, even more episodic than the first film, sets about undoing filial piety. For one thing, it opens with an extraordinary love song between mother and son ("Mother, you are my great love") and builds towards re-uniting them. Fong struggles within the disciplined environment of the Red Flower Society and is told to "go back home to your mother". Rather than chastening and galvanising the hero into 'becoming a man' by severing maternal ties, the narrative allows Fong to do the exact opposite. Torn between rescuing his Master and his mother, it turns out to be no contest: "My mother brought me into this world. I swear by my life to save her." They fight together, performing their speciality, Invisible Fists; a flurry of synchronised blows forces the villain to block furiously before they stand back, arms folded, while he continues to flail wildly at the air. "Why are villains so stupid?" Miao asks, amazed that the same trick works in both films. Where Li's Wong Fei-hung seeks to adapt heroism to unstable times, his Fong regards it with good-natured scepticism and quits the Red Flower Society to go home with his mother and the two wives he has acquired in the course of his adventures. He may be an 'immature' mother's boy, but at least he gets to survive.

From Beijing with Love: To 'Belong' or not to 'Belong'

Unlike Jackie Chan, an 'action' star who had 'transcended' martial arts, Jet Li was, quite unambiguously, a kung fu star. This was one of the reasons why his film career ran aground in the 1980s, when kung fu was out of fashion. When the early 1990s cycle also began to fizzle out, he faced the same problem again. Judging by Li's comments, the tension between 'traditional' and modern-day action films also seems to have been the choice between authenticity and global ambition. On the one hand, period movies allowed him to show off the breadth of his knowledge of classical forms and weaponry:

> In modern movies, there are fighting scenes that a talented actor without a martial arts background can learn to do in three months. But in traditional movies, the audience can tell the difference. (Parish 2002: 94–5)

But, pre-*Crouching Tiger*, costume films had limited export value outside Asia:

> It's difficult to tell older Chinese stories to a foreign audience. They don't know Chinese history, who is the bad guy. In a modern movie, it's very easy to get the meaning ... That's why everybody changed. (108)

Li's modern-day films are shamelessly derivative (as many Hong Kong films are) of Hollywood sources. *Bodyguard from Beijing* is a kung fu/gun fu reworking of *The Bodyguard* (1992); *High Risk/Shu Dan Long Wei* (1995) steals from *Die Hard* (1988); *Dr Wai*, like Jackie Chan's *Armour of God/Longxiong Hudi* (1986), gives us a Chinese Indiana Jones. But they are pointedly 'local', too, from *High Risk*'s film industry bitchiness to what looks like the trickle down of Wong Kar-wai's self-conscious voice-overs and quirky lovelorn characters in *Dr Wai* and *Black Mask*.[12] The febrile *Black Mask* is the most eclectic of all. Li's superhero, neurally modified to feel neither pain or emotion, has his trans-pacific ancestors in *Blade Runner* (1982) and *Universal Soldier* (1992). Kwai-cheung Lo has likened *Blade Runner*'s 'replicants', who not only want to be human but have (artificial) *memories* of being human, to Hong Kong cinema's desire to be 'Hollywood' (2001: 465–6). But just as it strives for 'sameness', "it produces an irresolvable difference" (466). *Black Mask*'s hero Tsui Chik (Li) 'replicates' the desire of *Blade Runner*'s synthetic outsiders, but also dresses like Bruce Lee's Green Hornet sidekick, Kato, the 'Oriental' dogsbody promoted to leading man. The outlawed Super-soldiers, the 701 Squad, seem to be identified as Mainlanders, from "a certain country up north", seeking to dominate 'humanity' as its new masters. But they are actually a multi-racial group, a kind of transnational drug conglomerate with a particularly violent grip on the market. *Black Mask* can be read as the migrant's dream of 'belonging' in Hong Kong, as an apocalyptic countdown to 1997, as Tsui Hark's, Yuen Wo-ping's and Jet Li's calling

Fig. 14 Hong Kong 'replicant': *Black Mask*'s eclectic mix of *Blade Runner, animé* and *The Green Hornet*

card to Hollywood, or simply as a dizzying montage of generic and cultural reference points (Hollywood sci-fi, Japanese *animé* and S/M softcore, Batman, Green Hornet and other comic book heroes).

Wade Major calls Li's modern-day films his "toughies", "tougher, more realistic contemporary films" (2000: 165). The initial ones invest their star with a certain incongruity. As a contemporary Mainlander, he is no longer allowed to represent a community, and the "toughies" are often about the need to Westernise him in some way.[13] His character in *Bodyguard from Beijing*, a saturnine Mainland soldier sent to protect a spoiled Hong Kong socialite (Christy Cheung), is a machine that must be humanised, softened up through a *Ninotchka*-like romance. "Early Handover?" wonders slovenly, horse-racing-obsessed Hong Kong cop Kent Cheng when Li turns up in uniform. Brusque and charmless, Li imposes an inhospitable austerity on Cheung's affluent household (the metaphor is too blatant to miss). In contrast with the flamboyant *wu shu* of his earlier films, Li's Hui Ching-yeung moves with breathtaking, but mechanical efficiency; his kicks are lower, his hands pummel like pistons. But "when love comes, even a great fighter can't stop it", and Cheung makes romantic overtures as he tracks her on mobile surveillance equipment. As kung fu gives way to romance, the film brings on its real bad Mainlander, a former Chinese Liberation Army fighter turned assassin (Ngai Sing). Li defeats him, pointedly, by using the affluent apartment against him; a variety of kitchen appliances and a venetian blind are turned into weapons. The China-Hong Kong romance cannot be resolved, however. Li is sacrificed and then miraculously resurrected, the final shot showing him in front of the Chinese flag. But he has learned how to be a 'Defender', as 'China' must; early scenes show him as being too aggressive, putting those he is meant to protect at risk. *My Father is a Hero/Gei Ba Ba De Shen* (1995) breaks the deadlock through family melodrama. Kung Wei (Li) is a Mainland undercover cop sent across the border because "we want Hong Kong to be peaceful and prosperous". He leaves behind a sick wife and a talented *wu shu* champion son (Xie Miao) to join a vicious Hong Kong gang that is being tracked by Anita Mui's indefatigable cop. When Kung Wei's wife dies, it is only a matter of time before Mui replaces her; the son has already adopted her as 'Auntie'. After a stunning extended setpiece of father and son double-teaming the bad guys, the Hong Kong-China 'family' is reconstructed.

A second theme began to emerge in Li's modern-day films as they became more self-conscious; that of the hero as a fiction or illusion. Major has referred to a "creeping identity crisis" in Li's later Hong Kong films (2000: 165), filled with secret identities and multiple personalities, even amnesia; Black Mask, the 'King of Adventurers', the 'Angel of Death', 'God's assassin' in *Hitman/Sha Shou Zhi Wang* (1998). *High Risk* is concerned with stunt doubles and 'fake' kung fu stars, although its cruellest jokes seem directed at Jackie Chan. In *Dr Wai in 'The Scripture with No Words'*, Li plays two roles, the Indiana Jones-derived 'King of Adventurers' and his creator, a meek, bespectacled serial writer facing an impending divorce and writer's block. His estranged wife Monica (Rosamund Kwan) finds her counterpart in the "hard-hearted" Japanese villainess in the serial (also played by Kwan), who wields a bullwhip and samurai sword and conducts cruel experiments on men. But her misogynist inflection is modified by the input of Li's assistants (Takeshi Kaneshiro and Charlie Yeung), who set about redeeming her as romantic lead; a nice cross-diegetic gag has the King of Adventurers accidentally call her 'Monica'. As several writers have noted, *Dr Wai* does not entirely fulfil the promise of its central conceit; Howard Hampton imagines a "Cantopop Dennis Potter" with Li as "The I-chinging detective" (Dannen and Long 1997: 341). But it is still an interesting comic unravelling of 'heroic' cinema. The casting points to two different cinematic traditions. Li and Kwan inevitably invoke their romances in *Once Upon a Time in China* and *Swordsman II*, now soured and bitter, while the pairing of Takeshi Kaneshiro and Charlie Yeung recalls their pairing in *Fallen Angels* and Wong Kar-wai's fractured city romances. Wong's characters, too, tell stories obsessively, most pointedly in his one martial arts film, *Ashes of Time*; even his swordsmen are, as David Bordwell puts it, "not-quite-grown-up characters brooding on eternally missed chances" (2000a: 281). But action stars rarely survive such postmodern playfulness (witness Schwarzenegger after *The Last Action Hero* [1993]).[14] Even if he did not already have his eye on Hollywood, *Dr Wai*, appropriately the most stunt-doubled and effects-heavy of Li's Hong Kong films, confirmed that his career as a 'local' star was coming to a close.

Jingwu Mun Revisited: *Fist of Legend*

Made during the same period as the 'toughies', but thematically closer to the 'new wave' period films, *Fist of Legend* is, for many fans, Jet Li's definitive cult classic. Here, the two 'Jet Lis' converge; the reflective Wong Fei-hung figure fashioned by Tsui Hark, and the 'authentic' kung fu star sometimes obscured by Tsui's stylistic excesses. Moreover, in remaking the 'classic' *Fist of Fury*, the film both 'sells' Jet Li as inheritor of the Bruce Lee mantle and underlines some of the aesthetic and political shifts embodied by the modern kung fu star. For Li to be equated with Lee, the heightened authenticity and minimal wirework becomes doubly important; Wade Major describes the film as "a virtual clinic on the martial arts, with Jet demonstrating a mastery of nearly every imaginable fighting style in the world" (2000: 171). This is central to its cult reputation, the 1990s kung fu film

Kung Fu Cult Masters

Fig. 15 'Progressive' national hero: Jet Li's Chen defeats Huo Yuanjia's son (Chin Siu-ho) in *Fist of Legend*

(along with *Drunken Master 2*) that even some 'old school' fans like; a film that, as one admirer puts it, "doesn't lose sight of its roots" (Amazon.com 2000) On internet forums like Amazon.com's customer reviews, *Fist of Legend* continues to generate a lively debate, in contrast to its minimal presence in critical accounts of Hong Kong cinema. Topics range from historical and martial authenticity ("you see traces of authentic traditional kung fu, you get some excellent historical fiction"), outrage at changes made in the dubbed DVD,[15] to inevitable comparisons with *Fist of Fury* and of Li with Lee. A few dissenters, in arguing that Jet Li is 'miscast' as Chen Zhen, make an interesting conflation of Bruce Lee with Chen, the fictional pupil of a real-life master (Huo Yuanjia):

> Zhen was an unorthodox fighter who was brutal and hot-tempered ... (Li's) 'Zhen' became too reflective and composed. (Ibid)[16]

For another, Li's Wong Fei-hung coolness "takes the patriotism of chen zhen out". What fans and detractors agree on, however, is *Fist of Legend*'s revisionism.

Like *Fist of Fury*, *Fist of Legend* is set in the British settlement of Shanghai in the late 1920s as Sino-Japanese tensions simmer to boiling point, exacerbated by Huo Yuanjia's mysterious death. To a certain extent, the film supports Ackbar Abbas' contention that in the 1990s kung fu film, "it is no longer possible to appeal with any conviction to some vague notion of Chineseness" (1997: 31). The story no longer plays as a revenge tale – Jet Li's Chen kills one person, the rabid militarist General Fujita (Billy Chow), in contrast with Bruce Lee's high body count. Instead, Li plays a more contradictory national hero. His first fight defends his right to be educated in Japan; he is studying engineering at Kyoto University and even has a Japanese girlfriend, Mitsuko (Shinobu Nakayama).[17] Chen embraces modernity and returns to Shanghai with a more cosmopolitan outlook; as he investigates Huo Yuanjia's death, he displays a knowledge of pathology. Even his martial arts embrace 'foreign' influences. The joint-locking techniques he uses to disable racist bullies in Kyoto seem derived from Japanese Aikido as much as Chinese *Chi na*. A training sequence shows him using skipping, push-ups and chin-ups to condition his body, demonstrating Karate sidekicks, before leading his classmates into a more classically Chinese form that invokes the beach scene from *Once Upon a Time in China*. Later in the film, he is challenged by his friend, Huo Yuanjia's son Huo Ting-en (Chin Siu-ho), for leadership of Jingwu Mun. They begin in the Huo style, but, in a clear nod to *Way of the Dragon*, Chen wins by shifting to Western boxing and footwork as well as northern Chinese kicking techniques. As Siu-leung Li observes, Jet Li's Chen absorbs Bruce Lee not through the xenophobia of the original film, but by co-opting heterogeneity into a new nationalism (2001: 529). If *Fist of Fury* is the most Sinicist of kung fu films, can *Fist of Legend* (like the *Once Upon a Time in China*) be seen as a new, 'progressive' strain of Sinicism, inflected by Hong Kong's modernity and hybridity? *Fist of Legend*'s hero is patriotic but non-racist, culturally inclusive in outlook and influence. In this respect, Li's geographic mobility – a Beijing boy reinvented in Hong Kong – once again adds resonance to his casting.

Fist of Legend alludes not only to the Bruce Lee 'classic', but to a less well-known film about Chen's real-life master, Huo Yuanjia, the northern Wong Fei-hung. *Legend of a Fighter/Huo Yuanjia* (1981) reworks the Wong Fei-hung/Wong Kei-ying/Lu Acai triangle, as the young Huo (Yuen Yat-chor) is unable to persuade his father to teach him kung fu. He finds his 'Lu Acai' in his tutor Chiang Ho-shan (Yasuaki Yurata), who is in fact a Japanese spy sent to learn the Huo fist. Chiang's enduring lesson is that "all styles flow into each other", and that the concept of "style" is "the greatest obstacle to development". The real Huo was a precursor to Bruce Lee's heterogeneity, and Leung Kar-yan plays the mature Yuanjia as a muscular, Lee-like presence, trouncing arrogant *gwailos* and Japanese. But Japan's imperial ambitions force the former friends into a tragic fight; Chiang is ordered to prove Japan's superiority over the "sick man of Asia". The Japanese master reluctantly

Fig. 16 Stepping into Bruce Lee's shoes: Jet Li's Chen takes on the imperialist aggressor Fujita (Billy Chow) in *Fist of Legend*

takes on his former pupil, but will only mobilise such xenophobic rhetoric to push Huo into not holding back. Yasuaki Kurata began to specialise in 'honourable Japanese' roles in Hong Kong movies (in *Shaolin Challenges Ninja*, for example), and plays an iconic role in *Fist of Legend* as Mitsuko's uncle, Master Funakoshi.[18] Funakoshi, a former friend of Sun Yat-sen, represents a more humane martial tradition that is seen, romantically, to precede Japan's imperialism, and the film's more explicit anti-imperial critique is articulated by him and the (enlightened) Japanese Ambassador. When the Ambassador likens Japan to "a strong ant determined to consume a sleeping elephant", Funakoshi explains the economics of war to him:

> For the past decades Japan has benefitted greatly from winning wars. There are too many people who see Japan's future as a great empire.

After the death of the 'father', Huo Yuanjia, it is Funakoshi who replaces him. Ordered to challenge Jingwu to a duel, he instead engages Chen in a more pedagogic fight, teaching him about the need to adapt and the limitations of kung fu as a response to technologically mediated violence:

The best way to beat your opponent is to use a gun. The aim of martial arts is to teach you to maximise your energy. And to achieve that, you must be at one with life and the universe.

Earlier in the film, as Chen and Mitsuko watch Japanese troops massing, destined for China, she asks him if he hates the Japanese. He answers that he does not know; "it's fate, I have no choice in this". In order to 'know', Chen must liberate himself from a hermetic and parochial definition of national belonging, must be able to separate the political (imperialism) from the racial ("the Japanese"), to adopt a Japanese patriarch as substitute for a dead Chinese one. When he fights General Fujita in the climactic scene, he wears the black Japanese student uniform we first saw him wear in Kyoto, fighting for enlightened Japanese as well as his fellow Chinese. This profoundly complicates his heroic trajectory, pushes him into inaction and reflection rather than the patriotic certainties of Bruce Lee's Chen. In this sense, Jet Li's quieter, more reserved, presence is in perfect accord with the revised Chen. At the same time, 'Chen' is effectively split in two in *Fist of Legend*. The real son, Huo Ting-en, is provincial and uneducated, hostile to Mitsuko and ultimately ineffective against the real threat to China. The adopted son, Chen, unwittingly undoes Jingwu Mun in adopting a more transnational, 'enlightened' outlook. When he is forced to fight Huo for leadership of the school, and to defend Mitsuko, he naturally wins but refuses to assume the head teacher role. In doing so, he effectively negates it; defeated Huo degenerates into drunkenness, and Chen is cast into the wilderness, branded a traitor by his fellow Chinese. But he is shrewd, adaptable and sufficiently mobile to survive the film. Unlike the Chen of the 1970s, he is a pragmatist, not a martyr. Rarely has the division of labour between 'director' and 'martial arts director' created such a sense of two 'films' pulling in different directions. Gordon Chan's sober historical drama almost seems to edge towards a kung fu film where the hero realises that fighting cannot solve any of the conundrums about identity, loyalty and belonging that he faces, while Yuen Wo-ping's kung fu "clinic" pulls the film back to spectacle and heroism; only in the Chen/Funakoshi fight (appropriately a stalemate) do the two converge. But this 'flaw' is also one of *Fist of Legend*'s points of interest as it tests out generic heroism within a more fully developed political arena. More sober and 'realist' than the playful *Dr Wai*, *Fist of Legend* nevertheless acknowledges the obsolescence of such narratives even as Yuen Wo-ping's superb fight scenes give the kung fu star one last kinetic showcase.

I have confined myself here to Jet Li's Hong Kong films, but of course his career was to enter a new phase as he joined the Hong Kong movie diaspora and relocated to Hollywood. In the next chapter, I shall look in greater detail at how Chinese martial arts stars and choreographers (Li included) have fared in Western vehicles.

Chapter Seven

Transnational Dragons and 'Asian Weapons'
Kung Fu and the Hong Kong Diaspora

"It's kind of a combination of East meets West", says stunt co-ordinator Gary Hymes of the action scenes in Jet Li's *The One*. This deceptively benign cliché has become a popular way of describing what David Bordwell calls the "Hong-Kongification of American cinema" (2000a: 19).[1] "The fastest hands in the East versus the biggest mouth in the West" was the tagline for *Rush Hour* (1998), marking a clear division of star labour – physical (Jackie Chan) and verbal (Chris Tucker) – which, in turn, reinforces some broader binary oppositions (nature/culture, body/intellect). But the meeting of 'East' and 'West' is not just a matter of combining stars from different industries, but of converging aesthetics and technologies. *The Matrix* arguably established a new template for the 'Asianisation' of Hollywood – Hong Kong choreography combined with what Hymes calls "our technology" (for example, CGI).

Many longstanding fans have been disappointed by Jackie Chan and Jet Li's Hollywood fight scenes and found Yuen Wo-ping's *Matrix* choreography inferior to his earlier work – too short, too slow, lacking the intricate rhythms and dynamic power of their Hong Kong films. Already, the meeting of 'East' and 'West' does not look quite so neat. Then there are other issues inevitable in such a crossover – how have Chinese stars fared in a national cinema that has traditionally marginalised Asians? Is it possible to imagine an embryonic Chinese-American action aesthetic, or has Hong Kong talent simply fallen to the insatiable appetite of the globalising entertainment industry?

What interests me particularly is the 'in-betweenness' of Hong Kong-Hollywood action, and the mutation of this indeterminate aesthetic space. In the 1970s, the 'kung fu craze' allowed a handful of Hong Kong stars to make international films, most notably Bruce Lee, the only one to truly 'crossover'. In several cases, these films used Hong Kong choreographers and even entire crews, but directors and writers were invariably

Westerners. The post-1990s diaspora suggests not the trans-pacific traffic of the 1970s, but the de-territorialisation of global culture, the sense of 'Hong Kong cinema' put into some futuristic matter transporter, materialising here and there, often in fragments. The sense of atoms re-assembling, *Star Trek* fashion, is perhaps most frequently seen in the dialogue between different *action technologies*, the very different spectacular regimes embodied by CGI and wirework.

Hollywood has assimilated three kinds of 'Hong Kong action' – the high-octane gunplay of John Woo and Chow Yun-fat,[2] the stunt-filled action-comedy of Jackie Chan and Sammo Hung, and the 'wire fu' of Tsui Hark, Yuen Wo-ping and Jet Li. Obviously, the second and the third are of particular relevance here, but they also raise implications about the production methods of different national cinemas, the valuing of certain types of cinematic labour (choreography) and for culturally specific constructions of the 'real'.

In some ways, 'Hong Kongified' Hollywood can be seen to be positioned precariously between 'Asiaphilia' and Asiaphobia. Both can be seen in the way *Enter the Dragon* both fetishizes the 'Orient' and replays 'Yellow Peril' archetypes, but this ambivalence is even more blatant in *Lethal Weapon 4*, in which Jet Li made his US debut as a sadistic Triad. Hollywood's 'romance' with the 'Orient' has always been deeply contradictory, and is made no less so by the requirements of 'political correctness'. Gina Marchetti detects a kind of postmodern Orientalism in films like the Chinatown-set *Year of the Dragon* (1985), in which '"yellow peril' clichés coexist with antiracist discourses ... Chinatown functions as pure style with neon dragons, pop songs, lion dances, and displays of martial artistry" (1993: 203). Marchetti could easily be describing *Lethal Weapon 4* (1998), where 'colourful' Chinatown is also a front for money laundering and traffic in illegal immigrants. The film's 'good' Chinese seek assimilation in the great democratic 'melting pot', like the immigrant Hongs, who belong to a history of frail, passive Chinese in Hollywood cinema. Jet Li is offered to us simultaneously as dynamic spectacle – "How the hell did he do that?" marvels Mel Gibson's Riggs after he dismantles a gun at lightning speed – and inscrutable Other, garrotting old men and kicking pregnant women. Such spectacle, as Marchetti argues, pulls in two directions:

It both attracts and repulses, encouraging viewer identification while keeping that involvement at a distance. Moments of spectacle that feature ethnic and racial differences can define and reinforce the boundaries between ethnic and racial groups to keep the dominant culture's own power intact. However, these moments also often include violent eruptions that challenge the dominant culture's ability to define those differences and boundaries. Violence bursts forth against the racial

Kung Fu Cult Masters

and ethnic status quo, and the viewer may identify with this antiestablishment aspect of the spectacle as well as with its ostensible condemnation (207).

The climax of *Lethal Weapon 4* is a case in point, as Riggs and Murtaugh (Danny Glover) face off against Wah Sing Ku (Li). Our two aging heroes have good reason to hesitate before taking on the impossibly agile martial arts master, but ultimately must prove to themselves that they are not "too old for this shit". The fight can also be understood in the light of Riggs's status as Vietnam vet – he has faced the Asian Other before and acquired martial arts skills in the 'Encounter with Asia'. Li has performed some unconscionable acts in the film, speaks only one line of dialogue in English, and is ultimately exterminated as though he was not human. But there is another set of generic determinants that inform the scene – the spectacle (familiar from numerous kung fu films) of a five-foot-six Chinese man taking on two six-foot-plus American men. Earlier in the film, Riggs and Murtaugh throw their weight around in a Chinese restaurant, make references to Green cards and joke about "flied lice" – change the dynamics a little and the scene could be lifted from *Way of the Dragon* or Li's *gwailo*phobic *Born to Defence*. For the Jet Li/Hong Kong/kung fu fan, it is no great leap to see his character as an underdog antihero, his violence partially motivated by legitimate rage (even though he oppresses other Chinese) and a response to the heroes' casual racism. However, I think *Lethal Weapon 4* is smart (or cynical) enough to second-guess all of this, thus exemplifying the kind of postmodern racial politics that Marchetti is talking about. It both plays to a 'dominant' reading of the sadistic, mysterious 'Oriental' and allows some notional (if limited and peripheral) identification with him for the 'cult' audience that Li's casting was clearly meant to attract.[3] Just before his final fight, Li is 'humanised' by a moving scene with his dying brother, the character he has been trying to release from a Chinese prison throughout the film. The romancing of the Other (usually prior to its destruction or co-opting) can be seen as characteristic of what Christopher Sharrett calls the "sacrificial excess" of late capitalism. Such texts are marked by "a sacrificial violence that acknowledges the Other by its obliteration, a strategy that admits both the credulity and the scepticism of the spectator; the 'specialness' of the Other and our sympathies with it are acknowledged as its monstrous aspect is confirmed" (1996: 257). But, perhaps more significantly, this sacrifice also seems to be in the service of renewal of a cinema that (like its protagonists) fears that it may be "too old for this shit". Thus, Hollywood both incorporates and symbolically annihilates its 'younger', more dynamic, counterpart.

To some extent, Hollywood's 'Hong Kongification' can be seen as the latest manifestation of America's 'Encounter with Asia', a conquest rather than the benign meeting implied by 'East' meeting 'West'. After all, one of the factors in the diasporic journey of Hong Kong film-makers was Hollywood's conquest of the South-East Asian market. And yet there are problems, too, with regarding certain cultural forms as off-limits, as the essential property of a particular group – Hong Kong cinema has, after all, had global aspirations for some time. Steve Fore suggests that Jackie Chan's later Hong Kong films were already starting to 'disembed' him from "a core of cultural meanings and experiences characteristic of the Hong Kong ecumene" (2001: 117), his persona restructured for the global marketplace. This was evident in their (often exoticized) use of international locations and Chan's globetrotting persona – Fore likens these films to the James Bond series, even down to their ethnocentric representation of other cultures (116). Kwai-cheung Lo sees Hong Kong identity as being doubly negated in the transnational/ Hollywood films made by Hong Kong film-makers. In the first instance, Hollywood negates Hong Kong diegetically, by characterising its Chinese leads as "Mainland Chinese at the expense of Hong Kong's particularity" (Lo 2001: 466).[4] But Hong Kong's construction of a 'local' identity was already contingent on a "certain negation of Chineseness" – thus, "Hong Kong's transnational crossing to Hollywood initiates another negation that negates the very symbolic realm common to Chineseness" (467). Lo asks whether this 'negation of negation' can be seen as a "strategic move for the becoming of a new postcolonial subject leading up to and after 1997" (478). Ding-Tzann Lii (1998) goes further by suggesting that Hong Kong cinema, at its peak, represented a form of 'marginal imperialism', which both reproduces the dynamics of traditional imperialism and poses a threat to it – the Jackie Chan/James Bond comparison is suggestive in the light of such a hypothesis. On the one hand, Hong Kong's Asian expansionism contributed to the underdevelopment of Taiwanese cinema, just as Hollywood did to Hong Kong itself after 1993. But Lii also argues that there are significant (cultural if not economic) differences between 'core' and 'marginal' imperialism – the latter represents a 'rupture' in global capitalism "where the peripheral 'Other' surfaces as a subject" (1998: 127) – in this case, Hong Kong's 'localised' media imperialism contributed to an 'Asianisation', blending into other Asian countries and "creating a synthesis-form with a higher cognitive order" (128). One might expect the dynamics to be rather different, however, when core imperialism (in this case, Hollywood) aborbs its peripheral counterpart (Hong Kong). Lii distinguishes between *incorporation*, where the 'Other' is transformed by imperialism, and *yielding*, a "synthesis which transcends both the self and the Other" (134). Ackbar Abbas seemingly has something similar in mind for his hypothetical "third space", where "East and West are overcome and discredited as separate notions, and another space or a space of Otherness is introduced"(1996: 300). But is it possible to imagine Hollywood *yielding* to Hong Kong, rather than simply appropriating its talent and aesthetics? Steve Fore was (initially) optimistic, likening the exodus to Hollywood's European émigrés of the 1930s and 1940s – he described them as "transnational design professionals" belonging to "image-projecting and consciousness-transforming industries" (1997a: 133). Lii, like Fore, is hopeful that "Hollywood movies will be changed dramatically" and that "Jackie Chan ... will definitely be of equal importance to Stallone and Schwarzenegger" (1998: 136). Instead, Chan found himself "of equal importance" to Chris Tucker and Owen Wilson – in *Rush Hour 2* (2001), he had even slipped to second billing. It was not until *The One* that a former Hong Kong star, Jet Li, received sole top billing in a Hollywood film – he was, after all, playing both lead roles.

Chinese Encounters – First Kind: Bruce Lee and his Aftermath

Between mid-1972 and the end of 1973 – the peak of the Western 'kung fu craze' – Warner Bros. had distributed *King Boxer* in Europe and North America, broadcast the early episodes of the *Kung Fu* television series, and co-produced *Enter the Dragon*. Hong Kong films were regularly topping box office lists (Desser 2000). This short-lived period also saw a series of Hong Kong co-productions with Britain (*Legend of the Seven Golden Vampires* [1974], *Shatter* [1974]), Italy (*Blood Money* [1974]) and Australia (*The Man From Hong Kong* [1974]), most of them attempts to break Hong Kong action stars in the West.

It seems entirely appropriate, as I have argued elsewhere (Hunt 2000), that *Enter the Dragon* should take place on an island of uncertain ownership – we learn that the villainous Han's island rests partly in 'British' waters. This island, marked as it is by hybrid identity and contested cultural affiliation, can stand in for both 'Hong Kong' and 'Bruce Lee'. If *The Big Boss*, *Fist of Fury* and *Way of the Dragon* can be seen as constituting a more or less coherent 'Lee' – populist, local, nationalist – then *Enter* points to the problems and contradictions inherent in cultural mobility and a star characterised by his "cross-cultural savvy" (Chiao 1981: 32). Lee plays a former Shaolin monk employed by the British government to infiltrate the island fortress of Shaolin renegade Han (Shek Kin), a figure commonly compared to Fu Manchu (decadence, drugs, white slavery) and Dr No (a lethal artificial hand), but who can also be connected to *wu dang* villain Bai Mei (traitor-patriarch marked by 'absence').[5] As David Bordwell suggests, the casting of Shek Kin also points to the Wong Fei-hung series in which he was a regular villain, and casts Lee as the "heir of Kwan (Tak-hing), a 1970s update of a classic hero" (2000a: 52). But the necessity, in Lee's films, of slaying the father, marks them as a departure from, as much as a continuation of, the Wong Fei-hung ethos.

There are only traces of the 'hometown boy' in *Enter the Dragon* (Lee defends Chinese boatworkers from a *gwailo* bully) and, concurrently, a reminder of the way Lee also carried "the aura of the empire's modernity" (Li 2001: 529). For Stephen Teo, the film demonstrates "the West's antipathy towards Lee's nationalism, and it shows a sullen and sulking Lee forced to submit to the West's perception of him as mere action hero" (1997: 117) There is undoubtedly some truth in this – Lee is inserted into an interracial trio, including Afro-American Williams (Jim Kelly) and caucasian adventurer Roper (John Saxon), as the film astutely gauges its market. It is Roper who negotiates the film's emotional curve – will he be seduced by Han's empire or join the virtuous Lee? – while Lee singlemindedly pursues his mission, pausing only to avenge his dead sister. Meanwhile, it is Williams, rather than Lee, who embodies ethnic populism. But if one is considering the case *against Enter the Dragon*, one need look no further than the director's comments about his star:

> My first impression of Bruce's Chinese films was we had to 'kick the strut' out of him. The Chinese, of course, liked his cocky ways and the way he slid his thumb across his nose like they used to do in American gangster movies of the 1930s. It was my belief (and Bruce's too), that he had to play to an international audience and not just to his adoring countrymen. I felt if he was to be an international star, he would have to look as much at home in New York or London as he would in Hong Kong or Los Angeles. He could wear the beautiful silk Chinese suits with their flowing lines and wide cuffs, but he would also have to be carefully fitted in the best Western tailoring ... This type of attention to detail combined to form a mosaic of the new Bruce Lee. (Clouse 1987: 43–4)

It is, of course, easy to react to the arrogance of the cosmopolitan director who helps his semi-provincial star transcend his unsophisticated 'countrymen'. Furthermore, "kicking the strut out of Lee" comes directly into conflict with the star's conscription into the 're-masculinisation' of Chinese cinema. It is not uncommon for the compromises inherent in 'crossing over' to be seen as a form of emasculation – Sue Wise has examined the way that Elvis Presley's mainstream success (and consequent increase in female fans) was perceived as a transition from "macho folk hero" to "teddy bear" (1990: 390–8).[6] Yvonne Tasker, meanwhile, has suggested that David Carradine's casting in *Kung Fu*, rather than Lee, had as much to do with the different versions of masculinity each star embodied as simple network racism (2001: 124). But what I find equally suggestive is Clouse's characterisation of Lee as a "mosaic", even if he reduces this to his culturally polarised wardrobe. If, as Teo contends, the film's "Chineseness ... does not integrate with the Western sense of narrative decorum" (1997: 118), it now seems strangely appropriate, as much a testament to Lee's postcolonial and transnational identity as *Fist of Fury* is to his Sinicist persona. That this 'mosaic' does not always hold together – inscribing Lee simultaneously as both Shaolin Avenger and Colonial Enforcer – adds to rather than detracts from its continuing fascination. More importantly, its 'Yellow Peril' clichés aside, there is rather more of Bruce Lee and Hong Kong cinema in *Enter the Dragon* than tends to be acknowledged.

If Teo sees Lee "at a disadvantage" with Western film-makers, one might also see the film's compromises as a reflection of the problem of Lee's self-representation as much as his simply being *mis*represented. Lee's creative role in *Enter the Dragon* seems to have been substantial, and some of his disparaging comments about Mandarin "Won Ton Kung Fu flicks from HK" (Little 1998: 181) suggest an awareness of his cultural liminality. Lee might have felt more at home in the cosmopolitan 'new wave' cinema that emerged after his death, but looked askance at much of the local cinema, even as he was all too aware of how little Hollywood was prepared to offer. Lee's fight choreography – which departed equally from Mandarin and Hollywood conventions – both inscribes his authorship onto the film ('Fight Scenes Staged by Bruce Lee') and integrates a local production process into a Western film. But Lee's authorship is also evidenced by *Enter the Dragon*'s flirtation with martial arts philosophy. When Warner Bros. reissued the film on video in 1998, they restored a scene originally cut from the English-language version, but left intact in Hong Kong. Lee discusses his approach to fighting with the Abbott of the Temple – "when my opponent expands, I contract; when he contracts, I expand. And when there is an opportunity, *I* do not hit, *it* (holds up his fist) hits all by itself." The reinsertion of this scene can be attributed to the completist fetishism surrounding Lee, and the publishing and video industries selling him as a martial arts philosopher. But it also re-orients the film significantly, given that the Abbott tells Lee that Han has brought dishonour to Shaolin. In the shorter version, Lee fights a 'friendly' duel with Sammo Hung, watched by British emissary Braithwaite, the film's equivalent of James Bond's M; in the next scene, Braithwaite recruits Lee and gives him his mission. The 'Abbott' exchange comes between these two scenes and prioritises Lee's role as avenger for the Shaolin Monastery. His colonial role, while not insignificant, becomes secondary, an impression reinforced by Lee's sardonic response to Braithwaite's comment that "we" would like Lee to attend Han's tournament – "*We*, Mr Braithwaite?"

Enter the Dragon has Vietnam partly on its mind – its two American heroes are vets, the narrative goal is the securing of an unstable territory – and its context is also Nixon's visit to China. *Legend of the Seven Golden Vampires* is more explicitly British-colonial in

Fig. 17 Transnational hero and 'Yellow Peril' villain: Bruce Lee and Shek Kin in *Enter the Dragon*

focus. The film attempts to marry the English Gothic of Hammer films to Shaw Brothers' blood-soaked heroic sacrifice, and also anticipates Hong Kong's later *jiangshi dianying*, with its army of hopping zombies. The opening scene depicts the merging of two genres. Kah, the High Priest of the Seven Golden Vampires, travels from China to Transylvania to enlist Count Dracula in restoring his moribund cult to its former glory. The Count chooses, instead, to 'possess' Kah's body and sets out for China. Stephen Teo has read this scene as an unwitting comment on how "globalization proceeds from the idea of dominance and repression" and wonders whether Hong Kong cinema (Kah) is the bearer of the Western image (Dracula) (2000: 5). But, in cinematic terms, who is 'appropriating' who here? It is not just the 'national' that merges, but two very distinctive studio styles, each carving out distinctive generic worlds.

The film's central conflict is between two white Europeans – the Count and his old nemesis Van Helsing (Peter Cushing) – who, between them, enact a form of mythological colonisation. When we first encounter Van Helsing, he is delivering a lecture on ancient Chinese legends to a frankly sceptical audience at Chungking University. But the Professor knows best, and enlists the aid of Hsi Ching (David Chiang), his brothers and his sister Mai

Kung Fu Cult Masters

Kwei (Shih Szu). As they travel to the cursed village of Ping Kwei, Van Helsing experiences a 'been-here-before feeling', an anticipation of what is around the next corner. In other words, for the coloniser of the 'Orient's' imaginary, China's mysteries are already 'known'. "My brothers would die in your defence", Hsi Ching promises with unwitting prescience. It is nothing new for Chiang to sacrifice himself bloodily – he impales himself on a bamboo stake – but here it is explicitly designed to sever the interracial couple formed with the wealthy Vanessa Buren (Julie Ege). The film is more comfortable with the relationship between Mai Kwei and Van Helsing's son (Robin Stewart). Characterised, China-doll fashion, as both "fighting tigress" and "porcelain kitten", Mai Kwei's formidable fighting skills mysteriously desert her during the climax as the vampires abduct her. She is rescued, but clearly re-positioned as colonial spoils for the white conqueror.

Ian Hunter (2000; 2002) has offered a rather different reading of the film, seeing it as configuring a 'bad' colonialism in the figure of Dracula – "the figure of arch-evil is a Western invader", embodying a threat that is "global and cross-cultural" (2000: 85), while the "the film respects the Otherness of the East" (2002: 86). He offers two ways of seeing Dracula; as "Western colonialist who ... goes East to gratify sadistic sexual and feudal desires" or "the man of power who goes native and like Kurtz in *Heart of Darkness* (1899) blends his identity with that of the Other" (2002: 144). This is an interesting, if sometimes willfully 'positive', reading. Hunter is correct to point out that Hammer's 'colonial' films (*The Mummy* [1959] for example) are more ambivalent than they might first seem, and concludes that *Legend of the Seven Golden Vampires* is "both anti-colonial and patronisingly Orientalist" (2002: 145). Nevertheless, while I share his fondness for the film, I have a couple of reservations about its anti-colonial credentials. Dracula and Van Helsing seem to support not a critique of colonialism but rather the notion that colonialism can take 'bad' and 'good' forms', that it can be rapacious and cruel, but also beneficial and 'civilising'. Moreover, there is a correlation between Van Helsing's recruitment of the Chinese fighters and the English Gothic's co-opting of the Hong Kong kung fu film. If *Enter the Dragon* can encompass the Shaolin Temple and Wong Fei-hung as well as James Bond and Fu Manchu, one looks in vain for any real sense of the *wu xia pian* in *Legend of the Seven Golden Vampires*, even though Teo speculates (mystifyingly) "that there is more of Shaw Brothers in it than of Hammer" (2000: 5). Its all too brief fights (choreographed by Lau Kar-leung and Tang Xia) are explicitly played out for a Western gaze – "It was the most fantastic display", Cushing tells Chiang rather condescendingly after one battle, as though they had just performed a Lion Dance for him. I do not want to over-romanticise the 'sacrifice' in, say, Zhang Che's films – it is, undoubtedly, macho, sentimental and symptomatic of the kind of repressed homeoroticism that can just as easily be manifested as homophobia – but it is still significantly different from a 'sacrifice' that is designed to keep dominant racial and sexual relations securely in place.

The Man from Hong Kong was designed by Golden Harvest to break Wang Yu in the West. His co-star was former James Bond George Lazenby, the closest Hong Kong came to enlisting a major Western star.[7] In the 1970s, Lazenby's career had descended into a world of low-budget international films, but he was apparently set to raise his profile by appearing in *Game of Death*. When Lee's death put the project on pause, Golden Harvest cast Lazenby instead in *Stoner/Tie Jin Gang Da Po Zi Yang Guan* (1974), *The Man from Hong Kong* and *Queen's Ransom/Etan Qunying Hui* (1976), pairing him with Wang Yu and Angela Mao Ying. A crash course in martial arts and Sammo Hung's expert choreography transformed Lazenby into a creditable performer – in *The Man from Hong Kong*, he moves rather better than nominal leading man Wang Yu does.

Inspector Fang Sing-ling (Wang Yu) of Hong Kong Special Branch travels to Australia to extradite a Chinese drugs courier (Sammo Hung) and soon crosses swords with Jack Wilton (Lazenby), a drugs baron with an alligator's smile and a penchant for chinoiserie in his bachelor pad. Fang's modus operandi is to batter, crush and blow up every human obstacle until he gets to Wilton – "This country's got a small population", observes one character, "and he's getting through them very fast". Wang was the only Chinese kung fu star to travel to the West with his libido intact. The neutered Asian hero hinges both on Western representations of the asexual 'Orient' and comcomitant anxieties about "the irresistible, dark, occult forces of the East" which have equated Asian male sexuality with sadism (Fu Manchu), rape (*Broken Blossoms*) or captivity (*The Bitter Tea of General Yen*) (Marchetti 1993: 2, 8). In *Enter the Dragon*, Lee declines female company, in contrast to black Williams (stereotypically insatiable) and white Roper – a response which allegedly prompted audience derision in Hong Kong (Dennis and Atyeo 1974: 63). *The Man from Hong Kong*, by contrast, seems keen to offer a kind of Chinese Superstud – Fang has seduced one Australian woman before he's even left Hong Kong and beds another while recovering from his injuries ('A Man is a Man is a Man', insists the song on the soundtrack, as though auditioning for an aftershave ad). This is not to say that the film's racial politics are any more 'progressive' than its sexual ones. Both love scenes are framed by self-conscious jokes, and the film overall reinforces stereotypes about the brutal 'Far East', attributing Fang's motivation to some inscrutable Eastern code – "To understand ... you would have to be a Chinese", he says. Hong Kong is reduced to its usual tourist guide signifiers – skyscrapers, harbour, Victoria Peak, marching colonial police – and characterised as "beautiful, squalid, exhilarating and frightening; all the traditional contradictions of the East in one city". Yet amidst all this, there are some pointed reminders of Fang's colonised status. Wilton taunts him for his English – "All your officers have to speak English, don't they?" – while spelling out the cultural-colonial implications of his own linguistic skills:

> My business takes me to the East regularly. I find the Chinese make the best servants. I understand your culture, and your language, Inspector, and your martial arts. Especially those.

Lazenby's short-lived fame as James Bond is especially resonant here – the colonial playboy is now the villain, the colonised ethnic underdog the hero. *The Man from Hong Kong* is a less 'accomplished' film than *Enter the Dragon*, but in other ways it's the most interesting of the 1970s crossover films, in its willingness to transgress some of the taboos the other films tread more carefully around – colonialism, Chinese masculinity, interracial sex.

According to choreographer Sammo Hung, "Wang was never a martial artist in the way that Bruce Lee was ... basically it was just street fighting" (quoted in Logan 1995: 87). Hung has a reputation for making the most limited fighters look good onscreen, but he largely works *with* Wang's limitations, locating him within a more 'realistic' milieu (none of his fights are won easily) and suggesting (like Jackie Chan, later) not so much a martial arts *master* as a hero with some martial arts skill who wins through endurance, bravery and determination, an impression reinforced by Wang's stunts (hang-gliding, climbing up or hanging from buildings). The film's mixture of kung fu, stuntwork and action now seems very modern, pointing to some future developments in Hong Kong cinema.

Shatter (1974), another Shaws-Hammer co-production, this time co-starring Peter Cushing and Ti Lung, has little to recommend it. In some ways, *Blood Money* (1974), a co-production between Shaws and Italian producer Carlo Ponti, is not much better – its fight scenes are amongst the poorest I have ever seen. Given the Mandarin martial arts films' aesthetic debt to 'Spaghetti westerns' – huge close-ups and zoom shots, lots of recycled Ennio Morricone – one might have expected the collaboration to be more fruitful. The story of a Chinese martial artist in the old West was already familiar from *Kung Fu*, and has resurfaced again more recently. Secular Shaolin student Wang Ho Kian (Lo Lieh) teams up with bandit Dakota (Lee Van Cleef) to locate a treasure map tattooed on the buttocks of four prostitutes. The film is now most interesting for its anticipation of *Shanghai Noon* (2000) as its two characters gradually bond. The once cynical Dakota refuses to "run out on a friend", and the film ends with him accompanying Wang on a sightseeing trip to China.

Of these five films, only *Enter the Dragon* was a major success, and only Lee (if he had lived) seemed set for further global success. Desser points out that the biggest Hong Kong star of the mid-1970s, Fu Sheng, could not find an overeseas audience (2000: 37), although the 'America' reproduced at Shaw Brothers in *Chinatown Kid/Tangren Jie Xiaozi* (1977) suggests that he was possibly being considered for an English-language vehicle. Fu's mischievous boy-next-door persona paved the way for Jackie Chan, who was the next Hong Kong star to crossover. But this was not the dramatic, myth-making breakthrough of Lee – Chan's transition to Hollywood star was a long, probably dispiriting slog, marked by setbacks and compromises.

Coming to America: The Case of Jackie Chan

Honestly, I don't like *Rush Hour*. I didn't like *Shanghai Noon* ... Why? Because I really don't understand the jokes. Even now, "What's up nigga?" What's so funny about it? I don't know.
　　– Jackie Chan (*Giant Robot* 2002: 25)

The failure of Jackie Chan to crack non-Asian markets prior to the crossover success of *Rumble in the Bronx* has become symbolic of the corporate media's incomprehension in the face of Hong Kong action. Two factors, in particular, seem to have created obstacles to Chan's crossover. The first is his legendary perfectionism, which was already in evidence by the time of *Dragon Lord* in 1982 – one scene is rumoured to have taken between 190 and 2,900 takes (Witterstaetter 1997: 110). He progressed to being Hong Kong's most expensive film-maker, even though Golden Harvest tried to reign him in after *follies de grandeur* like *Miracles/Qi Ji* (1989) and *Operation Condor/Feiying Jihua* (1991). If Golden Harvest found Chan excessive, the issue is exacerbated by the different values and priorities of North American cinema. Costly obsessiveness is generally only licensed to 'serious' film-makers like Stanley Kubrick and Francis Ford Coppola. By Hollywood standards, Chan spends a disproportionate amount of time on his action scenes at the expense of story and characterisation. There is also, of course, the matter of the risks Chan takes on his Hong Kong films – regularly injured and almost killed on the set of *The Armour of God*. Behind-the-scenes material on the *Rush Hour 2* DVD is instructive. We learn that the film embraced Hong Kong's piece-by-piece 'constructive' approach to shooting action, as opposed to Hollywood's use of Master shots and multiple inserts. But Brett Ratner must "sit on" Jackie (as he puts it), taking control of his excessive and unbalanced fastidiousness, and his protracted fight scenes:

Jackie is so inventive and so brilliant that he can do a fight sequence that lasts twenty or thirty minutes ... (I said) "Jackie, let's take the best moments and condense it into a two minute fight sequence instead of a twenty minute fight sequence".

According to producer Jay Stern, Chan complained that Ratner spent too much time on dialogue and not enough on action. Stern, in response, paraphrases Ratner's belief that American audiences' attention span means that "two to three minutes is about as long as you can have as a straight action scene".

The second matter is Chan's mixture of action and comedy. On the one hand, the earlier resistance to Chan seems to have partly been a holdover from Bruce Lee's ambivalent legacy. The martial arts master was expected to be serious and near-invincible, not vulnerable and comic. The breakthough *Rumble in the Bronx* had been modified to downplay the comedy in favour of Chan's combat skills (Fore 1997). Chan was finally 'accepted' as a Hollywood star within the context of interracial buddy movies, paired with fast-talking Chris Tucker or stoner Owen Wilson. The question is whether Chan's acceptance, allied to his disembedding from Hong Kong's comic traditions and the generous altruism of his local persona, recasts him as a kind of Chinese 'Minstrel'. Watching Chan on *The Late Show*, good-naturedly acquiescing to David Letterman's jokes about their respective builds, Kwai-cheung Lo worries that American audiences "see the Hong Kong subject as a muscular, though slight, man who only knows how to use his body to amaze them and make them laugh" (1999: 105–6). The *Rush Hour* films get much of their mileage from 'good-natured' racial insults traded between Inspectors Carter (Tucker) and Lee (Chan). In the first film, most of these are directed at Lee/Chan – as the film's tagline suggests, he is not really there to talk.[8] In the sequel, he 'reworks' and replies to Carter's jibes – "I'll bitch-slap you back to Africa", "Don't you ever touch a Chinese man's CD". The comic point seems to be that Chinese men *do not* say things like that; 'they' do not display the kind of ethnic militancy embedded in the latter remark. At one point, Carter tells Lee that he is "Third World ugly", provoking the following exchange:

Lee: I'm not Third World Ugly. Women like me. They think I'm cute, like Snoopy.
Carter: Lee, Snoopy is six inches taller than you.

The exchange is driven by their mutual interest in sexy Latin special agent Isabella (Roselyn Sanchez), who has a small Snoopy tattoo on her lower back. Lee's equation of himself with Snoopy both accords with Carter's jokes about Chinese men's stature and, of course, renders him sexually unthreatening, a cuddly cartoon figure. Carter, meanwhile, might as well be played by Jim Kelly, defined by his strut, his verbal cockiness and his sexual appetite – at a Chinese massage parlour, he follows Kelly's example by selecting numerous Chinese women. "You don't jump in front of a black man in a buffet line", he complains when Lee tries to hurry him. Everything is grist to the *Rush Hour* films' postmodern mill – in part one alone, we get 'racist' jokes, the Handover of Hong Kong to China ('local' villain Jintao turns out to be a British commander), silky, villainous Chinese (a peroxide bad boy with a scarred lip) and guileless, good-natured ones (guess who).

Prior to the success of *Rush Hour*, Chan made four English-language films – *Battlecreek Brawl* (1980), *The Cannonball Run* (1981), *The Cannonball Run II* (1983) and *The Protector* (1985). The all-star *Cannonball Run* movies feature Chan in a small role, alongside Michael Hui, as a Japanese (!) driver. The consensus on *Battlecreek Brawl* and *The Protector* is that they are "substandard films directed by American hacks" (Fore 1997a: 134), but they still occupy a key place in the Chan myth. Firstly, they have come to symbolise the failure of "American hacks" to recognise Chan's abilities as a film-maker rather than simply a martial arts performer. Secondly, what little value they are grudgingly accorded lies not in their achievements but in indirectly inspiring superior films made by Chan in Hong Kong – *Battlecreek Brawl*'s 1930s gangster milieu becomes *Miracles* and *The Protector*'s rogue cop heroics become *Police Story* (Logan 1995: 66). Chan has helped add fuel to this version of events: "[Glickenhaus] told me I'm just an actor. For me, it's just say my lines and back to the motor home. After *The Protector* I decided it's back to Asia. I told Glickenhaus, 'You do *The Protector* and I'll do *Police Story*, and I'll show you what the action movie is all about'" (quoted in Witterstaetter 1997: 127). Granted, *Battlecreek Brawl* and *The Protector* are less accomplished films than *Rush Hour* and *Shanghai Noon*, yet their 'failure' tells us as much as the later films' 'success'.

If the 'international' version of *Rumble in the Bronx* sold Chan as a physical performer at the expense of other aspects of his star persona (Fore 1997b: 250), *Battlecreek Brawl* does not do a bad job with Chan's persona, which was still in the process of being fully formed even in his Hong Kong films. It incorporates (but does not develop) aspects of the Master/Pupil narratives of the kung fu comedies. His uncle-teacher, played by Mako, recalls the dissolute rogue-masters played by Yuen Siu-tin; part sage, part mischievous roue, part sadistic tutor. Ironically, it is Chan the performer who figuratively goes missing in action. He does backflips and handstands, delivers multiple kicks and punches, and skillfully wields a bench and pole against butterfly swords. But 'Jackie Chan' is arguably the sum of Chan and his stunt team, his mastery of camera placement and editing, the irresistible pace that subtle undercranking bestows on an elaborately composed fight. "American stuntmen are so slow", Chan has complained, "I hit bam-bam-bam, and, by the

Fig. 18 Jackie Chan, looking ambivalent about his arrival in Hollywood, on the set of *Battlecreek Brawl*

third time, he will have blocked the first punch!" (Logan 1995: 66). But slow stuntmen are only part of the problem – barring a brief fight with two Chinese assassins, his opponents are overweight sluggers, and these confrontations are not conducive to the intricate rhythms of Hong Kong choreography.

When Stephen Teo suggests that *The Protector* "looks surprisingly like a made-to-order Hong Kong kung fu action movie" (1997: 130), one assumes that he is talking about the Asian-language version. In an interesting reversal of what later happened to *Rumble in the Bronx*, Chan re-shot, re-edited and re-dubbed the film for its Asian release. Some of the changes are to do with his 'family' image – there is no nudity and no swearing in the Hong Kong version. But Chan also cranked up the action, adding a trademark comic scene in a gym, where he bounces off benches and uses weights machines as weapons, and re-shooting his climactic fight with kickboxing champion Bill Wallace. For all his talk of slow American stuntmen, Chan is as fond of pounding *gwailo* martial arts champs as Bruce Lee was – witness his two 'classic' battles with Benny 'The Jet' Urquidez in *Wheels on Meals* and *Dragons Forever*. In the US cut of *The Protector*, the Chan-Wallace fight follows the 'realist' conventions of North American martial arts films – "a blend of two-or-three-step sparring drills and barroom-brawl tactics" (Reid 1993–94: 32). Interestingly, Wallace's flashy kicking comes out of this version perfectly well, captured in extended master shots, but Chan merely seems to flail ineffectually with unextended kicks and underpowered flurries of defensive blows. Chan's version varies the rhythm of the fight, the editing and the speed of the film – undercranking pumps up the speed of the confrontation, while he slows down some of the moves retained from the original version. More use is made of props and environment – twice Chan is bounced off a wire fence and each time turns it into a different stunt. The Hong Kong version ditches the scrappy 'realism' of the original in favour of Bordwell's 'expressive amplification' (2000a: 232) – after a powerful punch from Chan, Wallace (or, rather, his stunt double) performs a corkscrew spin and then crashes to the ground. But is this a fair and representative comparison, of a straight-to-video hack (Glickenhaus) with an experienced, respected action director (Chan)? Brett Ratner presents himself as more sympathetic to Chan, a mixture of knowledgeable fanboy and expert on what will 'work' in an American film. Not unlike the way the Wachowski Brothers' would use Yuen Wo-ping on *The Matrix*, this was a combination of toning him down and having him 'quote' himself:

> I gave him ideas of things that he's done before in other movies or things that I've seen before ... I felt like I knew what Jackie needed. I knew what to do to take a chopsocky star and put him into an American formula and make it work. (*Rush Hour* DVD commentary)

If Ratner's 'formula' finds a middle ground between *Beverley Hills Cop* and *Police Story*, *The Protector* has more in common with the films of Chuck Norris and other 'White Warriors'. The role of Jackie's 'buddies' in *Rush Hour* and *Shanghai Noon* is to 'Americanize' him, but Vietnam vet Danny Garroni (Danny Aiello) goes further by symbolically enlisting him in the conquest of Asia. Chan's New York cop Billy Wong accompanies Garroni to Hong Kong in a case mixing drug trafficking with kidnapping. Garroni's knowledge of Hong Kong derives from 'R'n'R' during his Vietnam days, a connection which positions Asia as a space for sexual conquest as well as imperialist adventure – "I never go anywhere in South-East Asia without an Uzi", Garroni explains. The promise of "adventure and forbidden pleasures" (Marchetti 1993: 1) is a central trope in Hollywood's 'Orient' – Garroni 'initiates' Billy by taking him to a massage parlour, where the women are both compliant and deadly.[9] Chan cut the scene extensively for the Asian version, removing the nudity and the blow jobs delivered from beneath massage tables, which suggests that there is more at stake here than action aesthetics and star personas. He also introduced a subplot involving actress/Cantopop star Sally Yeh, which goes some way towards locating him within the Chinese population of Hong Kong rather than simply appropriating him as colonialist aggressor.

In both *Battlecreek Brawl* and *The Protector*, Chan plays Asian-Americans – only the latter film specifies how long he has been in New York (ten years). Interestingly, it is a Hong Kong film, *Rumble in the Bronx*, that first dramatises his cultural acclimatisation in North America. As Tony Rayns observes, *Rush Hour* and *Shanghai Noon* tells effectively the same story of Jackie "'becoming American', with a little help and hindrance from a reluctant American sidekick" (2001: 26). Much the same is true of Sammo Hung's television series *Martial Law* (1998–2000). But *Rumble in the Bronx* is part of a series of Hong Kong movies filmed and set in America which, as Julian Stringer suggests, can be seen to "represent Asian-American screen identities that are in the process of formation" (2000: 298). While these action films explore the theme of hybrid identity formation less fully than dramas like *Comrades: Almost a Love Story/Tian Mimi* (1996), their treatment is very different from the 'melting pot' narratives of Hollywood. To borrow Lii's distinction, the Hong Kong films seem to be about *yielding* – "the self goes out of oneself and blends into the 'other' (1998: 133) – while the Hollywood films are about *incorporation*.

Jackie Chan and Jet Li (*Dragon Fight, The Master, Once Upon a Time in China and America*) each made films set in North America prior to their recent Hollywood films. In both *The Master* and *Once Upon a Time in China and America*, Li interacts with other 'peripheral' communities – a young Mexican street gang who idolise him as their *shifu* in the former, Native Americans in the latter, whose loss of 'home' is implicitly linked to Hong Kong's own 'identity crisis'. As most Chan aficionados know, *Once Upon a Time in China and America* was 'stolen' from Chan's cherished project about a Chinese hero who loses his memory in the 'Old West' (Chan and Yang 1998: 348–50). Chan subsequently revamped his kung fu western into *Shanghai Noon*. He plays Chon Wang – a running gag has his name misheard as 'John Wayne' – a Qing Dynasty Imperial Guard sent to America to negotiate the release of kidnapped Princess Pei Pei (Lucy Liu). His 'American Education' is at the hands of Roy O'Bannion (Owen Wilson), a kind of slacker-bandit, who articulates the exotic appeal of Chon's mission – "Forbidden City? I like that. The Forbidden City, Princess, kidnap – it's so mysterious". Chon must learn to lighten up – "You're the most irritable guy I've ever met" – but otherwise he is as much 'Jackie Chan' as one could reasonably expect to see in a Hollywood film. There is rather more reciprocity in this cross-cultural education than in *Rush Hour* – Carter teaches Lee how to sing 'War' properly in the earlier film, while Chon Wang teaches Roy a Chinese drinking song. The knockabout tone and period setting seem to facilitate a more fully extended dose of Chan's trademark action-comedy, supporting the impression of heightened control suggested by the onscreen credit 'In Association with A Jackie Chan Films Production'. In an early scene, he dodges a couple of flying tomahawks, twirls them impressively and tosses them back at their owners, who promptly catch them and continue their pursuit. Yet a comparison with *Once Upon a Time in China and America* reminds us that there is a difference in Chan making his eastern-western *in* the West. Both films initiate their heroes into Native American tribes, both films feature a blonde cowboy who finds himself attracted to Chinese culture and both feature an exploitative Chinese turncoat (played by the same actor, Roger Yuan). When Chon Wang bonds over a 'Peace Pipe', it is only to accommodate some throwaway gags about "powerful shit" and failing to cross language barriers. *Once Upon a Time in China and America* is not the most reflective of the Wong Fei-hung series, but it is able to make something of Wong Fei-hung/Hong Kong's identity crisis – "I envy you guys", he tells the tribe who rename him 'Yellow', "At least you know where your roots are. I don't even know where I come from". The question of retaining one's identity is treated partly as a joke – Wong's audience fall asleep during his lengthy speech, but his sermon includes the salutary reminder that "When they leave home, goods are worth more and people are worth less". The film ends with the building of the first Chinatown, and the optimistic impression that the Chinese diaspora can both "copy the merits of foreigners" and yet still "know who you are". *Shanghai Noon* opts instead for America-as-Melting-Pot, where cultural difference must be partially erased. Roy's earlier lesson – "This isn't the East, this is the West. The sun doesn't rise here, it sets here" – is echoed by Chon as he defies the Imperial Decree and supports the Princess' desire to remain in the West. The villainous Lo Fang cuts off Chon's queue and insists that "he will always be a slave" (like the indistinguishable railroad workers used to conjure images of Chinese servitude). He can only be free by being 'American'.

Kissed by the Dragon: Jet Li in Hollywood

Not unlike Jackie Chan, the repackaging of Jet Li for Western multiplexes was founded on a combination of carefully chosen English-language roles and dubbed versions of his more 'Westernised' Hong Kong films. His scene-stealing debut in *Lethal Weapon 4* was followed by a repackaged *Black Mask*, dubbed and rescored with a hip-hop soundtrack. *Black Mask*'s US soundtrack was a reminder of Hollywood's continuing belief in the symbiotic relationship between kung fu movies and urban black youth. *Romeo Must Die* (2000) was described in advance publicity as a "hip-hop kung fu movie", and Li was cast opposite the late r'n'b Diva Aaliyah – he appeared in the promo video for her hit single 'Try Again'.[10] "I know hip-hop", Li's Han Sing insists at one point, turning his baseball cap around and tugging his trousers down slightly, as the narrative works hard to ally him with Afro-American culture. The film deals with tensions between Afro-American and Chinese-American criminal empires operating on the Oakland waterfront. The conflict comes down to competing patriarchs. Isaak O'Day (Delroy Lindo), father of Aaliyah's Trish, is avuncular, a doting father who wants to go legit but is betrayed by his manipulative enforcer (Isaiah Washington), while Ch'u Sing (Henry O), betrays both of his sons, allowing Hong Kong cop Han to take the fall for him (we first meet Li in a Hong Kong prison) and having his younger son killed when he threatens to rock the boat. Han overthrows his Chinese father, while his 'forbidden' romance with Trish finds him a new father, namely Isaak. But *Romeo Must Die* does not work quite as neatly as this reading might suggest, largely because of its inability to integrate Li successfully into the film. Its nominal star is often a peripheral figure – we are 45 minutes in before his backstory is explained, and his 'romance' with Trish largely has to be taken on trust. While the narrative seeks to displace Han from his Chinese family, Li (the star) works best within the 'Chinese' scenes, delivering his lines in Mandarin and bringing his usual quiet intensity to the scenes with his father. At the opposite extreme, when Trish takes him to a club, cajoles him into dancing and then sings to him – a showcase for Aaliyah's talents, just as the fights are for Li's – his acute embarrassment and discomfort are all too evident. If the film cannot integrate Jet Li into his own film, it stumbles even more over its incorporation of 'Hong Kong action'. *Romeo Must Die* is, visually, a post-*Matrix* film, but it does not have its predecessor's fantasy remit to explain why fighters float weightlessly in mid-air, the air around them looking like a computer simulation. While most of the film follows 'realistic' conventions, the CGI-enhanced wirework looks as though it has strayed in from a very different movie.

If Jackie Chan's unassuming persona once seemed at odds with Hollywood's conception of an action hero, Jet Li's chaste asceticism seems to have posed a similar conundrum; a number of Western critics have commented on his "lack of chemistry" with female leads, as though sexual potency was the ultimate test of a leading man.[11] In the very different context of Hong Kong cinema, Li has worked perfectly well as a romantic lead of sorts, albeit a reserved one who needs women to take the lead. But Li's English-language films sometimes feel the need to 'explain' his sexual reticence. In *Kiss of the Dragon*, Bridget Fonda's hooker-with-a-heart comes right out with it and asks him if he is gay – quizzed about his 'type', he has earlier blurted out that "I don't have (a) type". *Lethal Weapon 4* envelopes the question in a racial jibe – "Enter the Drag Queen", smirks Mel Gibson, trying to provoke Li into making a move. The scene recalls a similar moment from Bruce Lee's original, pre-*Big Boss*, Hollywood career, menacing James Garner's eponymous hero in *Marlowe*: "Say, you're pretty light on your feet", offers Garner, "Perhaps just a little bit gay?" In *The One*, Li's bad guy Yulaw arrives at a prison colony, prompting one inmate to comment on his "pretty mouth". "I'm nobody's bitch!", he roars before beating them all senseless, "*you are mine!*" *Lethal Weapon 4* draws on a sado-polymorphous decadence familar from the 'Yellow Peril' fantasy – he smiles sensuously as he garrottes one of his own gang. *Kiss of the Dragon* seems especially titillated by the enigma of Li's sexuality – making his first contact in Paris, he receives the terse instruction, "Men's toilet – *now!*"

Romeo Must Die was perceived by many to have 'wasted' Li, and *Kiss of the Dragon* was made partly in response to fan's comments on the Jet Li website. As co-star Bridget Fonda says, "he's doing something that's absolutely real ... we're not talking special effects, we're not talking what the camera can make it look like", while Li promised "no cable, no special effects, just hardcore fighting" (DVD commentary). The fights carry some kinetic force, even if they lack the grace of Li's best work. An early fight plays like a more brutal variation on Jackie Chan as Li makes use of steam irons, spin-dryers and a meticulously projected billiard ball. Later, he takes out twenty odd karate experts with fighting sticks, his arms a blur. *Kiss of the Dragon* has its shortcomings – it gets rather too much mileage out of having Fonda slapped around and humiliated by various brutal pimps. But one could never mistake it for anything other than a Jet Li vehicle, and its rapid production seemed to accomodate Hong Kong cinema's guerrilla film-making. The film grew out of what seems to have been a genuine collaboration across national cinemas – a Hong Kong star (Li co-produced and devised the original story) and choreographer (Corey Yuen), a French director (Chris Nahon) and a producer whose career blurs the line between 'French' and 'American' cinema (Luc Besson).

Kiss of the Dragon is described in its pressbook as a combination of Luc Besson's *Leon* (1994) and Li's *Fist of Legend*. The debt to *Leon* is a fairly obvious one – the metallic hues of Thierry Argogast's cinematography, a Mephistophelian cop villain (Tcheky Karyo replacing Gary Oldman), and an immigrant hero whose facility in combat is matched by his naivety with women. Jean Reno's Leon must, of course, contend with underage Natalie Portman, but co-writer Robert Mark Kamen played to a blurring of Li's on and offscreen persona:

> Jet is the most straightforward and upstanding man I've ever met in my life, and we made Liu the same way. Luc and I asked ourselves what's the most uncomfortable position we could put the character in ... And Luc said, "Oh, it's very simple; she's a prostitute". (*Kiss of the Dragon* Pressbook)

The connection to *Fist of Legend* is more tenuous, except as an assurance that *Kiss of the Dragon* would showcase a grittier Li than *Romeo Must Die* had done. Liu Juan, a Beijing special agent, is closer to the character Li played in *Bodyguard from Beijing*, a tough 'professional' whose defences the heroine must break down. Liu has "no wife, no children. His only dedication is to his work." In *Bodyguard from Beijing*, romantic and political union are conflated, but *Kiss of the Dragon* has rather less on its mind. Nevertheless, there is evidence of a yielding to both 'Hong Kong' and 'China'. If the 'Coming to America' narrative stresses the need for the Asian hero to accommodate to the West, *Kiss of the Dragon*'s postcard Paris (Eiffel Tower, Arc de Triomphe, Place de la Concorde) is a moral cesspool to be cleaned up by the upright Chinese cop. At one point, he flattens several policemen with the French Tricolour. Franco-Chinese relations are less than amicable – "What is our miserable history compared to yours?" sneers Tcheky Karyo's psychotic Richard. Liu's expertise is defined by both 'History' and 'Technology' – deprived of his gun, he makes imaginative use of acupuncture needles sellotaped to his wrist. The titular, and fatal, 'kiss' is given to Richard by one of these needles, sending all of his blood on a one-way trip to his head, whereupon it exits via his nose, mouth, ears and eyes.

How to read this apparent European self-loathing, this yielding to the other? The film sends out conflicting messages about racial difference, messages coded through differently proportioned bodies. We are forever reminded of how everyone towers over Li, a device often used to stress his deceptive vulnerability in an unfamiliar locale. But as he assures Fonda's Jessica that she can trust him, a long shot seems designed to underline the fact that she, too, is significantly taller than her Chinese Knight. The shot looks like a visual joke, but at whose expense? Jet Li's? Our assumptions about bodies and their capacity for certain kinds of action? In one scene, Liu trounces the pimp who slaps Jessica once too often – "I would really appreciate it if you don't do that again", he says slowly, but the warning falls on deaf ears. Just when the fight seems to be over, a huge figure fills the doorway – a large, black fighter removes his coat to reveal a mass of muscles. A slow tracking shot sutures us into Liu's reaction – *now* he is going to have his work cut out! But this film backs speed over size every time, and Liu cuts his gigantic opponent down to size. At least one commentator has seen this sequence as exhibiting an "unchallenged, conventional" racism, making stereotypical and dehumanising use of the figure of the black behemoth (White 2001: 13). But how might one read this scene in relation to Li's later fight with the white, blonde-haired brothers, one of whose gigantic build suggests an equally stereotypical Aryan *übermensch*?

The One, like its scenery-chewing villain Yulaw (Jet Li), travels across parallel universes policed by 'Multiverse' agents. Yulaw is himself a former agent, corrupted by the discovery that the death of his parallel 'selves' empowers his remaining incarnations exponentially until there is "only one". One other 'self' remains – L.A. county sheriff Gabe (also Li), who finds himself Yulaw's target. The film was originally designed as a pretext for World Wrestling Entertainment star The Rock to lay the smackdown on himself, and the film was re-written to incorporate Li's 'spiritual' concerns when he took over as lead. *The One*'s most interesting concession to its star is the equipping of his two characters with different fighting styles. Yulaw, who adheres to the principle that "the shortest distance between two points is a straight line", practices the straight-line attack of *xingyi*, an 'internal' style with a 'hard', forward rolling power; a *xingyi* boxer, so the saying goes, "never backs up" (Allen 2001: 37). The gentler Gabe, yin to Yulaw's yang, practices the 'soft', circular *bagua*, which has its basis in Taoist circle-walking meditations derived from the *I Ching*. The specificity of the film's fighting styles, and particularly their use as shorthand characterisation, indicates *The One*'s debt to the Hong Kong martial arts tradition, which frequently makes economical, accessible and instructive use of characters with contrasting fighting styles. Granted, Li's *bagua* 'shapes' are the best thing about the film, even as the sub-*Matrix* effects seem annoyingly determined to upstage them. But the film does not feel the need to explain the protagonists' opposed styles – only martial arts fans and practitioners would be able to name them – so that, in effect, they function largely as both 'exotic' stylisation and a means of telling 'good' Jet Li from 'bad'.[11] The film makes references to "balance", but it seems to derive from conflicting discourses and origins. One version is implicitly indebted to Taoism and the interdependence of yin and yang – both Gabe and Yulaw need to survive at the end of the film to preserve this harmony. But the grey-suited Multiverse bureaucrats invoke a "balance" that seems more suggestive of a moribund status quo in need of shaking up by the anarchic Yulaw, finally seen kicking ass on an intergalactic prison colony as the camera pulls back into an elaborate 'effects' shot. *The One* is interesting, but incoherent, partly because its primary agenda is to be as many things to as many people as possible. Of course, Hong Kong cinema can be overeager to please, too, and in any case, there is some yielding going on in *The One*. *Kung Fu Qigong* magazine used the film's release as a focus for a special *bagua/xingyi* issue which further served to orient a cult audience towards reading *The One* as a 'real' martial arts film (Burr 2001; Allen 2001). But, ultimately, *The One* and, conversely, the isolated success of *Kiss of the Dragon*, suggest that Li's Western vehicles need building from the ground up for his physical and acting talents to shine, and for his quietly heroic persona to make sense. Even more so than Chan, he seems especially vulnerable in his disembedding from Chinese generic traditions. Take away the *bagua* and the FX and *The One* starts to look worryingly like a Jean-Claude Van Damme vehicle, as several unsympathetic critics pointed out.

"All Under Heaven": Breaking Out of *The* (Hollywood) *Matrix*

The choreographer-as-star is the most recent development in Hong Kong's infiltration of Western cinema. Jackie Chan largely choreographs his own fight scenes, as Bruce Lee did, even though he has sometimes had to liaise with American stunt co-ordinators. Jet Li brought Corey Yuen with him to work on his first four English-language vehicles, and Yuen recently directed the Luc Besson-produced *The Transporter* (2002). Meanwhile, Sammo Hung choreographed Tsui Hark's Van Damme vehicles *Double Team* (1997) and *Knock Off* (1999), while Donnie Yen worked on *Highlander: Endgame* (2000) and *Blade 2* (2002) as well as appearing in *Shanghai Knights* (2003). However, it is Yuen Wo-ping who has enjoyed the highest profile, for his contribution to *The Matrix, Crouching Tiger, Hidden Dragon* and Quentin Tarantino's forthcoming *Kill Bill*.[13] Nevertheless, Yuen was conspicuously absent from *Crouching Tiger*'s Academy Award nominations – no such category presently exists (unlike special effects), another indicator of how different kinds of cinematic labour (and spectacle) are valued. Yuen has been in the forefront of every major development in martial arts-based Hong Kong action, from comedy to modern day action, and his career found a new lease of life in the 'new wave' martial arts films of the early 1990s. Ackbar Abbas has argued that the *Once Upon a Time in China* series was distinguished by "its mastery of *special effects*" (1996: 298), but it would be misleading to suggest that performative skill completely disappeared because Hong Kong wirework has largely remained a pro-filmic spectacle. Neverthless, this points to the dialogue between different action technologies in recent Hollywood films. Hong Kong's representation of 'speed' – undercranked action – remains too low-tech for Hollywood, too reminiscent of silent cinema, however exciting it is when done well. Compare Donnie Yen's breakneck-speed 'invisible kicks' in *Iron Monkey* with *The Matrix*'s digital 'bullet-time' for two very different representations of martial arts velocity. But wirework and CGI could profitably converge – in Hong Kong, wires are "lit out" (Orick and Matthews 2000: 58), but *Crouching Tiger* used 300 digital wire-removals as well as effects like sky replacement in scenes like Chow Yun-fat's bamboo-treetop duel with Zhang Ziyi (Lee and Schamus 2000: 122). *Hero*, choreographed by another wire-fu maestro Ching Siu-tung, uses similar technology when Jet Li fights Tony Leung on the surface of a lake or Zhang Ziyi takes to the treetops once more in her fight with Maggie Cheung's Flying Snow.

The Matrix seemed to create a new genre, 'Cyber-fu', in which kung fu skills are downloaded from a computer programme. In one emblematic scene, Trinity (Carrie Anne-Moss) floats into the air and holds the pose as the camera circles her, until this suspended moment is broken by a lethal kick. She dodges bullets by running up and around the walls of the room, but the final *pièce de résistance* is an over-the-shoulder kick to the face of a police officer who unwisely grabs her from behind. *The Matrix* did not only set a new standard for special effects; it also initiated a trend for 'authenticating' Hollywood stars when Yuen had the cast trained so that they could perform their own fight scenes.

"Our sense of reality is different from their sense of reality", explains Richard Donner on the DVD commentary for *Lethal Weapon 4*, explaining his modification of Hong Kong action. Hollywood, Bordwell suggests, is "unusually fastidious about realism of detail, restraint of emotion, and plausibility of plot" (2000a: 19). Hong Kong cinema, too, has its own hierarchies of 'realism' – wirework is much less extravagant in modern-day films than period fantasies. In Hollywood, wirework initially came in through the fantasy door.[14] What *The Matrix* does is to download and authenticate Hong Kong 'reality', to reconstitute it as a virtual action space into which it can insert its protagonists. Morpheus (Lawrence Fishburne) explains to Neo that in the digital world, "rules like gravity ... are no different than the rules of the computer system. Some of them can be bent, others can be broken". As some commentators have noted (King 2000: 191), *The Matrix* is only superficially dystopian and easily seduced by possibilities of the virtual action world. By the end of the film, Neo and Trinity do not just 'do' John Woo – with the sort of limitless ammo usually only enjoyed by Lara Croft – they *outdo* him as they scale walls, performing cartwheels as countless spent shells litter the floor. *Romeo Must Die*'s 'failure' to incorporate wirework seemed to lie precisely in its inability to negotiate a coherent 'reality' for its interfamilial/interracial crime drama and wired-up action – "This isn't *The Matrix*, idiots!!!" commented one disgruntled viewer (Internet Movie Database 2000).

But there is another narrative embedded in *The Matrix*, where the 'utopia' of Hollywood showcasing Hong Kong talent gives way to a 'dystopia' of appropriation and marginalisation – there was some hope of Jet Li appearing in the sequels, but Joel Silver clearly felt the money could be better spent. In any case, the film's downloading of 'Hong Kong' can also be seen as a metaphor for the Wachowski's use of Yuen Wo-ping. In Hong Kong, fight choreographers are like Second Unit directors, sometimes more. Fight scenes are not storyboarded or scripted – action and camera angles are semi-improvised by the stunt director's team, pretty much 'edited' in camera with little coverage and no 'masters' (see Bordwell 2000a: 210–47). Hollywood's authorial discourses, however, favour the deification of the director(s). According to Larry Wachowski:

> Wo(-ping) was the choreographer, but we were the ones who were in complete control at all times ... He positioned the camera where he thought it should be – Hong Kong choreographers always pick out the camera angles – and then Andy and I would look at them. Some of them we liked, some of them we didn't like ... Many times Wo's shots just didn't meet our criteria, so we added moving camera shots, dollies, stuff like that around sections that we wanted. (Quoted in Persons 1999: 21)

Yuen had a slightly different interpretation:

> In American movies, they're all storyboarded and they leave little room for inspiration on the set. It's good that everything's organised, but if I have any inspiration on the set, it's only good if the actors can follow. Jet Li and Jackie Chan can follow, but not these actors. (Quoted in Fischer 1999: 26)

The fight scenes were scripted and storyboarded by the Wachowskis, based on scenes from Yuen's Hong Kong films. They showed the storyboards to Yuen, who shot video footage using his stunt-team; the footage was shown to the Wachowskis, who approved and/or vetoed scenes. The cast were then 'taught' the moves from the videos so that they could perform them in the final film (Orick and Matthews 2000: 58–9). Spontaneity is not the only casualty in the martial arts scenes – postmodern appropriation can erase any sense of context or resonance. When Neo mimics Bruce Lee (cockily thumbing his nose) and Wong Fei-hung's signature stance (arm extended, palm turned upwards in 'invitation'), he points to the limits of 'de-territorialised' images and commodities. *The Matrix* does not need Jet Li precisely because "goods mean more and people mean less" in certain transnational image-flows.

In some ways, *The Matrix* and its many imitators offer worst-case scenarios for the future of diasporic Hong Kong action – Asian expertise absorbed into a cinema that continues to marginalise Asian performers. In 1997, Steve Fore envisioned a "best-case scenario" with "directors, cinematographers, actors, and other personnel oscillating semi-permanently between hemispheres, working on a range of projects with different geolinguistic emphases" (1997a: 135).[15] Until recently, only Jackie Chan displayed anything like this kind of mobility – *Rush Hour* was followed by the more 'local' *Gorgeous/ Bor Lei Jun* (1999), *Shanghai Noon* by *The Accidental Spy/Te Wu Mi Cheng* (2001), *Rush Hour 2* by *Highbinders* (2002). Jet Li, too, seems to be pursuing a degree of international mobility, not only with *Kiss of the Dragon* but Zhang Yimou's *Hero*, a Mandarin-language historical martial arts epic distributed and partly funded by Miramax.

It is difficult to predict the long-term influence and the significance of the crossover success of *Crouching Tiger*, but *Hero*, the most expensive Chinese film to date, suggests that it was not a one-off. There are some complex issues raised by what was seen as *Crouching Tiger*'s comparative 'failure' in parts of Asia (Rose 2001), but in many ways, Ang Lee's film seemed to realise precisely the kind of cinema Fore might have envisioned – an émigré Taiwanese director, a script produced by an ongoing process of translation between Chinese and American writers, two stars and a choreographer from Hong Kong, one Taiwanese and one Mainland star. Most importantly, it suggested that Asian action had a broader range of options than simply being grafted onto variable Hollywood films until another 'fad' came along. Seemingly conceived as a pan-Asian blockbuster, *Crouching Tiger* played in the West as what *Sight and Sound*'s cover copy dubbed 'Martial Arthouse' (December 2000), seemingly bestowing cultural capital on a lowbrow genre (at least for critics whose exposure to the genre was narrow). Ang Lee's film succeeded partly by appealing to audiences who would not normally watch kung fu films, thus the inherent appeal of Jane Austen seemingly let loose in *jianghu*. At its worst, the film's Western success could be construed as "a visually and narratively exoticized representation of China's past that does not challenge white, Western stereotypes of the 'Orient'" (Fore 1997b: 248).[16] Yet its breathtaking action scenes confirm that there was more going on than a particularly sophisticated manifestation of neo-Orientalism – cult Asian-American magazine *Giant Robot* dubbed it "the best kung fu movie ever" (Ko 2001: 20–1). Yuen Wo-ping's choreography blends wirework, CGI and performative skill so artfully that Abbas' "space of otherness" starts to materialise in bamboo forests, crowded taverns and across the rooftops of Qing-era Beijing – it is not just 'East' and 'West' which are overcome, but 'past' and 'future', technology and the performing body.

Taken together, *Crouching Tiger* and *Hero* augur well for a transnational (and 'Asianised') prestige martial arts cinema; sumptuous production values, state-of-the-art choreography, to-die-for Chinese casts and distinguished auteurs not usually associated with 'chop sockies'. In some ways, *Hero* seems packaged to replicate *Crouching Tiger*'s Western success, with a virtually identical score by Tan Dun and similarly CGI-enhanced wirework, although Chris Doyle's photography (as several reviews have noted) also recalls *Ashes of Time* (as does the casting of Cheung and Leung). If its fights surpass its predecessor, some of this is attributable to its cast; many kung fu fans were eager to see Jet Li and Donnie Yen's first on-screen duel since *Once Upon a Time in China 2*. But there are important differences, too. Ang Lee's description of *Crouching Tiger* as "*Sense and Sensibility* with martial arts" underlines its cross-cultural conception, but *Hero* is more Sinicist in outlook. The film is set during the Warring States Era (403–221 BC), during which Qin Shihuang (Chen Daoming), King of Qin, sought to conquer and 'unify' China; the film has been widely read as a metaphor for the PRC's desire to unify China, Hong Kong and Taiwan. But the film's notion of "All Under Heaven", like its tyrant King, is decidedly ambivalent. Qin Shihuang is both a Sinicist visionary (he built the Great Wall and founded China's first Dynasty) and a homogenising dictator who will erase local 'difference'; he tells would-be assassin Nameless (Jet Li) that he will standardise written Chinese. Nameless and Broken Sword (Tony Leung) spare the King and sacrifice themselves in anticipation of a unified China, a 'message' that has not found favour with all of the film's reviewers. *Hero*, interestingly, has outperformed *Crouching Tiger* in South-East Asia, and was nominated for an Academy Award, but it remains to be seen whether it will repeat its predecessor's success in the West. Of course, global mass media, too, threatens to unite "all under heaven" in the most homogenising way. *Crouching Tiger* and *Hero* find *wu xia* hero(in)es, as stealthy, resourceful and irresistible as Nameless, Broken Sword and Flying Snow, still storming the global 'palace'. The 'palace' seems unlikely to surrender, much less fall, to this invasion, but there is evidence that it is starting to *yield*.

CHAPTER EIGHT

"I Know Kung Fu!"
The Martial Arts in the Age of Digital Reproduction

What is a cyberpunk action hero supposed to do when he is dragged out of a "computer-generated dreamworld" and thrust into the "desert of the real", like a gamer rudely separated from their console or PC? The answer, of course, is to download some combat skills and conquer the virtual world with his "digital self".[1] This is the trajectory of Neo (Keanu Reeves) in *The Matrix*. As he downloads martial arts skills from a computer programme, an array of fighting styles flicker across the monitor – Ju Jitsu, Savate, Kempo, Drunken Boxing, Taekwondo. Suddenly, he sits up and, with a mixture of shock and pleasure, utters the line that prefaces this chapter. Neo's implanted 'knowledge' offers a metaphor for two ways in which Asian martial arts have been reconfigured in contemporary culture – console and PC 'beat-em-ups' and the transformation of Hollywood stars into martial arts action heroes. Both offer a quick-fix way of 'learning' and 'knowing' martial arts. I first 'knew' kung fu when I bought a PlayStation specifically to play *Tekken 3* (Namco 1998) because of my love of kung fu films. Keanu Reeves, Tom Cruise (*Mission: Impossible 2* [2000]) and the casts of *X-Men* (2000) and *Charlie's Angels* (2000) came to 'know' kung fu through Hong Kong choreographers like Yuen Wo-ping, 'wirework' and CGI effects. Hollywood action films have frequently appropriated the 'look' of Hong Kong films; Hong Kong films have, in turn, drawn on the stylisations of computer games and vice versa; martial arts films and games have both incorporated aspects of Japanese Manga (comics) and *animé* (animation), again in a mutual exchange.[2] Mary Fuller and Henry Jenkins (1995) have wondered whether Japan's colonisation of digital space through games represented "Asia's absorption of (North America's) national imaginary" or a more "dialogic" relationship marked by an "intermixing of cultural traditions" (71–2). The interface between martial arts games and films seems to be a three-way dialogue and not simply dependent on blurring East/West binaries – Hollywood ('blockbuster'-spectacle, CGI, *The Matrix*), Japan (*animé*, Manga) and Hong Kong (action aesthetics, kung fu films and stars).

The Matrix explicitly evokes the world of computer games when Morpheus (Lawrence Fishburne) describes "a world without rules and controls, without borders or boundaries, a world where anything is possible". But it also references kung fu and *anime* like *Ghost in the Shell/Kokaku Kidota* (1995); producer Joel Silver called *The Matrix* "full-cel animation, only with people" (quoted in Clarke 1999: 24). The sparring program Neo plugs into is essentially a virtual elaboration of the training mode available in most beat-em-ups – the space where you master Ken or Ryu's Fireball technique (*Streetfighter 2*), Lei Wulong's Shaolin Five Animals Style (*Tekken* series) or Kasumi's devastating Heaven Cascading Kick (*Dead or Alive* series). But just as arcade, console and PC games 'download' kung fu stars and films – Bruce Lee and Jackie Chan have made both official and unofficial appearances in games – so, too, does *The Matrix*, as Neo's "digital self" mimics Bruce Lee and Jet Li. Similarly, in *Charlie's Angels*, Dylan (Drew Barrymore) 'samples' moves from *Iron Monkey*, while Natalie (Cameron Diaz) performs a running-on-air flying kick from the same film. *The Matrix* is especially interesting because, in its comic book way, it is concerned with the 'real' and the 'virtual' and their relationship with a spectacle founded on physical performance. These are important issues for the martial arts genre, in both its filmic and gaming forms, given its investment in notions of 'authenticity'. If digital spectacle is supposedly about "surpassing the real" (Hayward and Wollen 1993: 1), the kung fu film has largely retained its investment in the 'real'. At one level, games have sought to refashion this cinematic authenticity through mimetic fidelity. For a gaming aesthete like Steven Poole, motion capture can be "aesthetically impoverishing" because it "limits the achievable virtual movements and gestures to those that are physically possible in real life" (2000: 154), but most polygon-based beat-em-ups use the movements of real martial artists as a signifier of authenticity.[3] Motion capture also guarantees a degree of stylistic authenticity, either by synthesising an existing fighting style or adding 'realistic' touches to more fantastic characters. In *Tekken 3*, the super-kicking Taekwondo moves of Hwoarang are based on world champion Suira Huang, while Space Ninja Yoshimitsu incorporated some of the signature moves of Pancratium Master, Minoru Suzuki (Mortlock 1998: 21), although one assumes that Suzuki did not use his sword as a pogo stick. Like martial arts films, games like *Tekken* and *Virtua Fighter* (Sega 1993) seek to enhance the 'real', to bend its rules rather than escape it altogether. On the other hand, games offer their own hyperreal authenticity, what Jay David Bolter and Richard Grusin call "authenticity of experience" (2000: 71), which has, in turn, impacted on the martial arts film.

The Matrix is at the centre of these paradoxes and sends out mixed messages about technological and 'authentic' spectacle, about the real and the digital. According to Manohla Dargis, it created "a new kind of action hero, one heavily predicated on digital effects" (2000: 23), but if the plot reduces humans to "wet-ware" (23), the same is not necessarily true of its stars. By training its cast in martial arts, *The Matrix* initiated a trend for 'authenticating' Hollywood stars, as though to counter the "oft-repeated threat that [the] digital will eventually render the human actor superfluous" (Dargis 2000: 23). In *Charlie's Angels*, we are meant to be impressed by the fruits of the stars' four months' training as much as all the CGI dazzle – "that *is* Drew, that *is* Cameron and that *is* Lucy", enthuses director McG on the DVD commentary, "They're all doing their own stunts and they're all doing their own thing". But where do *The Matrix* and *Tekken* leave stars like Jackie Chan and Jet Li, the former the star of his own game (*Jackie Chan Stuntmaster*, Radical 2000), the latter interacting with digital effects in *Romeo Must Die* and *The One*. What is the place of the performing body and the 'star' (real or virtual) in new digital technologies?

Bust-a-Move: Martial Arts Films and Games

According to one players' guide, a skilful *Tekken* bout is "like watching a good Kung Fu film" (Mortlock 1998: 18), while, on the other hand, the film adaptation of *Mortal Kombat* (1995) left one underwhelmed critic feeling that its fight scenes were like "watching someone playing the game badly rather than feeling as if you are in the game itself" (Felperin 1995: 48). What this suggests is that fight games refashion kung fu movies while simultaneously distinguishing themselves by their heightened *immersiveness* (being "in the game itself").

In terms of adaptations, the film/game crossover has been almost entirely one-way; from game to film (and television) rather than the other way around. *Street Fighter 2* (Capcom 1991) spawned two feature films, the live-action *Street Fighter: The Movie* (1994) starring Jean-Claude Van Damme, and a more faithful *animé* version (1994) which retained the 'special moves' from the game.[4] Animated *Street Fighters* have also materialised on television and DVD-only releases (*Street Fighter Alpha: The Animation*, 1999). Jackie Chan bought the rights to *Street Fighter 2* and included a brief parody of the game in *City Hunter*, while Wong Jing deployed thinly disguised *Street Fighter* characters like Ryu, Guile and Vega in *Future Cops/Chao Ji Xue Xiao Ba Wang* (1994). The ultraviolent *Mortal Kombat* (Midway 1992) generated two feature films, an animated television series and a live-action television series. While there is presently talk of a series of *Crouching Tiger, Hidden Dragon* games, to date there has been no martial arts equivalent of the *Die Hard* or James Bond games.[5]

It is more useful to think of the kung fu/beat-em-up interface in terms of what Bolter and Grusin call 'remediation', the process whereby a medium "appropriates the

Kung Fu Cult Masters

techniques, forms and social significance of other media and attempts to rival or refashion them in the name of the real" (2000: 65). Fight games remediate varying combinations of four media forms – (live-action) martial arts films, *animé*, Manga and Wrestling.[6] But this is not simply a linear, successive process, because sometimes media *remediate* each other. Kung fu films, in the first instance, remediate forms such as Beijing Opera (graceful, acrobatic performance) and the storylines, heroic codes and extraordinary feats of *wu xia* fiction. But in recent years, martial arts films and console fight games have been engaged in a process of mutual remediation. Kung fu films use wirework and SFX to recreate the digital spectacle of hi-tech games, just as those games use motion capture to simulate real martial arts moves and stunts. In *Dead or Alive 2* and *3* (Tecmo 2000; 2002), Kasumi's 'Heaven Cascading Kick' – a staccato tapdance on her (standing) opponent's head – goes one step further than the wire-enhanced stunts of Hong Kong cinema. On the other hand, Ayane's pirhouetting slaps are harder to imagine in a film, but draw on the spinning/ twisting dynamics of martial arts choreography. Games also remediate the 'presence' of martial arts stars. *Tekken*'s Lei Wulong is widely taken to be Jackie Chan, even down to his Drunken Master style, but his Shaolin animal styles (Snake, Tiger, Leopard, Dragon, Crane) suggest a broader-based remediation of the kung fu star. His endgame film in *Tekken 3*, for example, alludes to the 'Four Seasons' training sequence from Jet Li's *Shaolin Temple*.

Bolter and Grusin also provide some ways of thinking about authenticity in the digital age, although their conclusions are somewhat different from those of Walter Benjamin, for whom it always eludes technological mediation. They suggest, rather, that "remediation does not destroy the aura of the work of art; instead it always refashions that aura in another media form" (2000: 75). New Media have two seemingly opposed, but in fact closely interlinked goals – *transparent immediacy*, which seeks to render mediation invisible, and *hypermediacy*, which foregrounds it (2000: 272). At one level, these goals are poles apart – one is characterised by invisibility, the other by opacity of mediation (70–1). But Bolter and Grusin suggest that each also embodies the same desire "to get past the limits of representation and to achieve the real ... that which would evoke an immediate (and therefore authentic) emotional response" (53). Transparent immediacy facilitates a feeling of 'presence', while in the case of hypermediacy, the "experience of the medium is itself an experience of the real" (71). In other words, authenticity (of experience) does not disappear. Martial arts films have had to respond to this logic, wherein the 'real' has been refashioned by hypermedia. Bruce Lee's films offer a kind of transparent immediacy – 'presence' and 'authenticity' guaranteed by the invisibility of his cinematic mediation. Jackie Chan is a much more mediated performer, but is able to re-inscribe his 'presence' in other ways. Jet Li is the most visibly mediated of the three, precisely because of the contemporary synergy between films and games; wirework is almost an analogue approximation of digital spectacle, computerised effects recreated in pro-filmic space. Computer games are both more and less 'real' than Bruce Lee and Jackie Chan, offering an authenticity and intensity of experience that transparent immediacy might not be able to match. The hypermimesis of computer games has redefined how a kung fu fight 'feels' – Yuen Wo-ping wants to make the audience "feel the blow" (Bordwell 2000a: 244), but the PlayStation's vibrating Dual Shock Controller ensures that you can't *not* feel it. Similarly, digital regimes have transformed our perception of speed – games like the *Dead or Alive* series move at a dizzying velocity.

Martial arts pervade a number of gaming genres, including third-person stealth/ action games like the X-Box's *Buffy the Vampire Slayer* game (EA/Fox Interactive 2002), where fight combos are part of Buffy's combat repertoire. But the purest distillation of the genre is the beat-em-up, where narrative is largely relegated to extra-textual backstory (endgame films, the often tortuous plots in the games' booklets).[7] *Shaolin* is an interesting, if flawed, attempt to remediate the narrative as well as spectacle of kung fu films. A mix of adventure/Role-Playing Game and beat-em-up, *Shaolin* is marred either by undeveloped gameplay (its RPG elements are flat and uninvolving) or, equally likely, ambitions bigger than the PlayStation's capabilities. Each 'level' consists of a town or province in nineteenth-century China (Guangzhou, Fuzhou, Shanghai) or a more specific location (the Black Lotus Temple), as the game's selected character pursues a quest from childhood to 'mastery'. Equipped with one of six fighting styles, s/he acquires skills and techniques progressively, maturing at intervals after overcoming challenges. The details of Shaolin mythology – the Wooden Men, vague allusions to Manchu tyranny – are mixed with characters who resemble Jackie Chan and Sammo Hung, and anachronisms like Bruce Lee's Jeet Kune Do appearing a century before its originator. What is particularly interesting is the apparent attempt to remediate the pedagogic structure of classic Shaolin movies, even though the learning process itself is elided; techniques are 'unlocked' by defeating the master of each temple. In most beat-em-ups, pedagogy is not narrativised, but rather built into the learning curve of the game, a learning curve specific to the player and not their digital counterpart. Whatever else *Shaolin* offers, it is not a digital equivalent of *The 36th Chamber of Shaolin*.

The most popular beat-em-ups generally comprise a series of fights within a tournament structure, culminating in a battle with the Main Boss, usually a malignant patriarch like Bison (*Street Fighter*) or Heihachi Mishima (*Tekken*). Beat-em-ups first appeared in arcades between 1984 and 1985 – *Karate Champ* (Data East 1984) kicked off in the arcades, while *Kung Fu* (Bug Byte 1984) brought the genre to the PC. Fondly remembered games like *Way of the Exploding Fist* (Melbourne House 1985) and *Yie Ar Kung Fu* (Konami 1985) had a limited range of moves, but introduced some of the basics of the genre (the best-of-three fight structure). But Steven Poole is not alone in proclaiming *Street Fighter 2* (Capcom 1991) – a hugely popular refinement of the more modestly successful *Street Fighter* (1987) – the first modern fight game (2000: 45). *SF 2* offered more sophisticated gameplay through the innovation of 'combos' (continuous animations produced by elaborate button sequences). It offered selectable characters, organised along lines of cultural, ethnic and stylistic difference – Shotokan Karate Masters (Ken and Ryu), Grapplers (Zangief), Chinese Martial Artists (Chun-Li), Thai Boxers (Sagat), an Indian Yoga Master (Dhalsim). It was a more notably cinematic game in its global *mise-en-scène* – "a Brazilian dock, an Indian temple, a Chinese street market, a Soviet factory, a Las Vegas show palace" (Fuller and Jenkins 1995: 62) – and the visual excesses of its 'special moves', with "enormous blue light trails from swishing limbs and fireball attacks" (Poole 2000: 45).

Street Fighter 2's International Martial Arts Tournament to find the "strongest street fighter in the world" and its global cast of characters suggest that the cinematic model for the beat-em-up was *Enter the Dragon*. This film too, revolves around a tournament organised by an Evil Mastermind – 'Final Boss' Han is the predecessor of Heihachi and Bison, supported by formidable sub-bosses (Oharra and Bolo). The tournament structure allows narrative to progress *through* a series of fights – the climactic Hall of Mirrors would make an effective game level. *Enter the Dragon*'s three heroes anticipate the racial-cultural inclusivity of fighting games, while the cast represent as many different fighting styles as possible. Like beat-em-up characters, Lee, Roper and Williams are all backstory – each gets a flashback to motivate their entry into the tournament (revenge/honour, gambling debts, problems with racist cops). The *Mortal Kombat* film pretty much turns the beat-em-up back into *Enter the Dragon*, albeit with Ray Harryhausen-style fantasy trappings – the central characters' arrival on the island, welcoming feast, and the Han-like speech of 'Main Boss' Tsang Sung consciously invite such a comparison.

But *Street Fighter 2* has other cinematic referents for its visual (and aural) spectacle, which conspicuously avoids the B-movie ambience of *Enter the Dragon*. Fireball attacks and other special moves derive equally from the 'Palm Power' and Flying Swords of *wu xia pian* and the extravagant death moves of Kenshiro, the post-apocalyptic hero of manga and animé, *Fist of the North Star/Hokuto No Ken*. The *wu xia*'s *fantastique* tradition has always been dependent on special effects – wires, reverse footage, even animation. 'Palm Power' could propel flying daggers and thunderbolts from the hands of Taoist masters. The Flying

Sword used *qi* to "drive a sword flying like a rainbow and behead enemies hundreds of miles away", a technique "as accurate as any modern day missile system" (Hong Kong Film Archive 1999: 40). As this description suggests, *shen gong* (mystical powers) evokes technology as much as physical and spiritual refinement. Digital technology first infiltrated the martial arts film in *Zu Warriors of the Magic Mountain*, which employed Western special effects experts for its mythical tale of wizards, blood demons, flying swordsmen and white-haired masters with improbably long, but usefully combat-ready, eyebrows. *Zu Warriors* now looks like an interesting hybrid of technologies – 'Western' optical effects, wirework and 'magical' animation. It led indirectly to Hong Kong's first special effects unit, the Cinefex Workshop, established in 1987. But digital effects were not fully integrated into Hong Kong martial arts films until recent movies like *Storm Riders/Feng Yun Xiong Ba Tian Xia* (1998) which included 550 shots (approximately forty minutes) using CGI (Hong Kong Film Archive 1999: 50). In *The Avenging Fist/Kuen Sun* (2001), Hong Kong action films had progressed to virtual sets and environments. Significantly, *Storm Riders*, like *The Matrix* and *Charlie's Angels,* had no need for real martial arts performers in its lead roles – the latter gives Cantopop stars Stephen Fung and Wang Lee-hom precedence over Sammo Hung and Yuen Biao.

In *Fist of the North Star*, a Manga-derived *animé* television serial (1984–98), Kenshiro's 'Sacred Martial Art of the Great Bear' attacks pressure points, causing exploding heads and bodies (gory 'fatalities' that anticipate the head, heart and spine-removals of *Mortal Kombat*). Woe betides anyone on the receiving end of 'The Gate of Life with a Thousand Fists of Destruction' or 'North Star's Flowing Dance of Ultimate Emptiness'. Not only do these moves sound as though they should be accompanied by joypad button combinations, but they appear as onscreen captions as Kenshiro administers them. As one writer notes, the narrative follows an "arcade game-style progression" (Swallow 1999: 30), as Kenshiro tackles bigger and more lethal opponents. Like the *fantastique* swordplay films of Hong Kong or science fiction *animé*, fight game combos may be 'special effects' pyrotechnics as much as recognisable fighting techniques. In *Street Fighter EX 3* (Capcom 2000), Zangief's 'Corkscrew Slam' lifts his opponent out of the Earth's orbit before descending with a bone-shattering powerslam. *Bloody Roar 2* (Hudson 1999) already encompasses werewolf-style transformations, but Bakuryu's 'Double Inferno Hell' is especially apocalyptic, surrounding his opponent within a circle of flames which incinerates them at the point of two intersecting fiery lines.

The remediation of martial arts stars is the closest that fight games have come to film adaptations. Bruce Lee, Jackie Chan and (strictly unofficially) Sammo Hung have appeared in several games, and a Jet Li game is currently in development. *Bruce Lee* (US

Gold 1985) was one of the earliest fighting games, a platform game which has Lee fighting his way through a maze to defeat a wizard. But prior to the X-Box's *Bruce Lee: Quest of the Dragon* (Vivendi-Universal 2002) Lee was more vividly represented when his presence was 'unofficial' – Fei Long (*Super Street Fighter 2*, Capcom 1993), Jann Lee (the *Dead or Alive* series) and, above all, Marshall (*Tekken, Tekken 2, Tekken 4*) and Forest Law (*Tekken 3, Tekken Tag Tournament*). The younger Law, Forest, has Lee's hairstyle and features, his cocky strut, a similar vocal repertoire of shrieks and squawks. He also seems to have inherited his onscreen wardrobe – the yellow and black one-piece tracksuit from *Game of Death*, flowing white shirt from *Enter the Dragon*, and the pectoral-enhancing white vest from *Way of the Dragon*. In addition, he performs several moves recognisable from *Enter the Dragon* – a headlock kick, a backflip somersault kick (although, interestingly, the latter move was performed by Lee's acrobatic double, Yuen Wah).[8]

Chan has appeared officially in *Jackie Chan's Action Kung Fu* (1988) on the PC, and *Jackie Chan: Kung Fu Master* (1993), an arcade game in Asia only (Beale and Simons 2000: 19). *Jackie Chan Stuntmaster* is more ambitious, an attempt to transform an all-purpose (if distinctly Westernised) 'Jackie Chan film' into a third-person adventure game. Chan was motion-captured for the game and also provides his own voice – "Don't leave me!" he wails when the game is paused, or, when admonishing villains during a fight, "I am *very* angry with you." Most pleasingly, the game features 'outtakes' of the digitized Chan getting his FMV stunts wrong – alas, awkward controls mean that the gameplay often resembles these outtakes. In Chan's films, the end-credit outtakes serve both to authenticate Chan – by showing his on-set injuries – and undercut the invincibility of the action hero. In *Stuntmaster*, the in-joke both distances Chan from the digital – virtual stunts do not hurt – and further synthesizes his vulnerable 'presence'. The game's blocky visual style seems to make few concessions to mimetic realism in its character design, yet motion-capture is evident in the inimitable dynamics of Chan's perpetual motion. He can reach ledges by bouncing off the opposite wall and is literally never still (he fidgets, practices kung fu or sings if the player is a bit slow in operating him). *Stuntmaster* captures a good deal of the good-natured ethos of Chan's films. He will often try to talk henchmen out of fighting him, and the fights are given a comic edge. Like his cinematic counterpart, Jackie uses objects as makeshift weapons – brooms, tables, frying pans and, best of all, a very large fish.

Like Lee, Chan has also had unofficial game incarnations and spin-offs. Sometimes this takes the form of references to *Zui Quan* and *Drunken Master*; *Virtua Fighter 2*'s Shun De (Sega 1995) is a digital variation on Beggar Su, and *Dead or Alive 3*'s Brad Wong is also a Drunken Boxer. *Tekken*'s Lei Wulong performs Drunken Fist as part of his repertoire, while his FMVs connect him to both Chan's *Police Story* series – he is a Hong Kong cop known as 'Supercop' – and more 'classical' kung fu films (Buddhist temples, flowing silk robes). By adding comic elements to his endfilm, *Tekken 4* (Namco 2002) cements the Lei-Chan connection.

Perhaps the most important relationship between the Hong Kong martial arts film and games is in their *affectivity* – their capacity to act directly on the body. In *The Cinematic Body*, Steven Shaviro's "mimetic, tactile, and corporeal" cinema (1993: 55) leaves out Hong Kong action, yet could easily be describing a great kung fu film or, indeed, any immersive game – an "ecstasy of expenditure ... and self-abandonment ... the blinding intoxication of contact with the Real" (54), wherein the body is defined by its "capacity for being affected" (59). Most games vary their pace and pleasures – puzzle-solving, shooting, searching, climbing, jumping – but the beat-em-up offers relentless excitation, non-stop "sensory overload" (59), constant gratification or its opposite, abject defeat – in *Tekken Tag Tournament*, one's fallen "digital selves" sink to their knees in humiliation.

For David Bordwell, Hong Kong cinema is the ultimate tactile cinema. Not only does it have the largest performative repertoire of any popular cinema, finding "ever more inventive ways of displaying the human body's efforts to burst its earthly bonds" (2000a: 220), but its cinematic arsenal carries a multitide of ways of generating a kinesthenic response – "the films seem to ask our bodies to recall elemental and universal events like striking, swinging, twisting, leaping, rolling" (244). Bordwell makes these films sound even more like games in the way they "offer us the illusion of mastering the action ... the kinetics have stamped the action's rhythm onto our senses" (244). To make the connection between kung fu films, fighting games and cyber-action like *The Matrix*, it is useful here to refer to Alison Landsberg's notion of 'prosthetic memory', "memories which do not come from a person's lived experience" (1995: 175) – memories such as the Jackie Chan fan's, the *Tekken* player's or Neo's of being able to 'master' powerful, graceful fighting skills? Landsberg cites 1930s empirical/effects research into the sensorial/emotional effects of movies. Phrases such as 'imaginative identification' and 'emotional possession' suggest ways in which media images affect spectators so powerfully that they become "part of their personal archive of experience" (179). When Landsberg suggests that mass media "might be an undertheorised force in the production of identities" (1995: 177), she anticipates Bolter and Grusin's notion of the 'remediated self', the way that "new media offer new opportunities for self-definition, for now we can identify with the vivid graphics and digitized videos of computer games" (2000: 231). Her arguments also suggest that identification in games might blur 'real' and 'virtual' memories more than films do. After playing for a lengthy period, I sometimes find myself dreaming in 'Game Vision', as though digital afterimages of action/adventure remain imprinted on the retina. In what ways does this reinforce the memories of my *Tekken*-self, who has won and lost fights in Chinese temples, Aztec ruins and Japanese schoolyards?

'Expressive amplification' is omnipresent in fighting games. Powerful blows send opponents into corkscrew spins. After delivering a decisive blow, Lei Wulong is fond of rising into *bai he du li* (White Crane Stands on One Leg) stance and holding the pose in a 'frozen' moment so common in Hong Kong action. Hong Kong choreography's rhythmic principles partially determine the role of combos in the more 'realist' fight games, those which downplay the fantasy effects of the more *animé*-derived games. Several game guides construct a category of player known as the 'Cheesy' Player, who "picks the easiest character ... and learns only the most basic moves to gain them an easy victory ... [they] will launch repeated attacks on you with a wearying absence of skill or variation" (Parkinson 2000: 23). The dedicated player learns the combos, which takes time and patience. However, the guides are forced to concede that combos can offer diminishing returns on the harder levels when playing against the computer or against defensive players, while on the other hand, 'cheesy play' and random 'button-mashing' can, in some cases, get results – some even recommend a bit of 'cheese' on stubborn levels. Steven Poole argues that combos are the "Achilles' heel" of the genre because of their preset status – once an animation has started, it must finish and there is no chance of either changing tactics or designing one's own combos (2000: 47). In terms of identification, combos allow us to 'be' Jet Li, but never Yuen Wo-ping – they constitute the most 'choreographed' element in the game. They are, however, aesthetically pleasing, because, in a game like *Tekken*, they construct intricate, rhythmic compositions out of punches, kicks and throws, high, mid and low range attacks. Some moves have even less combat value than combos, but add stylised flourishes to a fight – in his 'Drunken' stance, Lei Wulong can sip from an imaginary cup while swaying in mock intoxication. This is an authentic move from *Zui Quan*, but in a computer game, the 'Tiger sip' does not even have a defensive capacity but adds a graceful, 'choreographed' quality which momentarily re-situates the gamer as spectator rather than full participant.

Downloading Authenticity: The *Tekken* Series

While it made little impact on its release, *Shaolin* was promoted as "the most authentic 3D martial-arts based game" on the PlayStation. Players could choose from (Northern) Shaolin, *Hung Gar*, Jeet Kune Do, Drunken Boxing, Tai Chi and Eight Extremities Fist, with the added guarantee that motion capture "accurately represents the different fighting disciplines". This claim for authenticity, albeit only partially true, has roots in the martial arts film's documentary/archive tradition, with its interest in accurately rendered 'real' fighting styles. Authenticity in fight games can take a number of forms – mimetic realism (motion-capture), immersion/transparency ('feeling' the game), 'cinematic' qualities (Hong Kong-style aerodynamics), recognisable moves and fighting styles, satisfying gameplay and 'learning curve'. Poole suggests that there is a tension in the genre's aesthetic development between a visual excess facilitated by increasingly powerful consoles, on the one hand, and some nominal realism on the other (2000: 45). Nevertheless, I would suggest that some notion of authenticity remains central to the best-known games.

Three franchises have been especially prominent in the aesthetic evolution of the beat-em-up. *Street Fighter* offered increasingly intricate gameplay, and a growing range of fighting styles and moves, but it arguably remediated *animé* more than live-action martial arts and has less of an investment in 3D mimesis than some other games. This has accommodated some conspicuously hypermediated effects – in *Ex* 3, Vega can drag his opponent into the extreme foreground and smack their head into the 'television screen'. *Mortal Kombat* used digitized actors to give greater realism to its fighters, but was even more *fantastique* both in its multi-armed villains and over-the-top carnage. *Virtua Fighter*, was the first fighting game to use polygons to create a 3D look – textured clothing, multilevel environments and sidestepping abilities gave greater 'depth' to the game. If each of these games innovated, *Tekken* has arguably consolidated their innovations rather than add new ones, yet it is one of the most popular and aesthetically evolved fight game series.

The original *Tekken* was one of the first games to appear on the Sony PlayStation and the first PS game to sell over a million copies (Hill 1998: 152). Namco, the game's publisher, had developed the first polygon-based system board and signed exclusively to design games for Sony (Parkinson 2000: 11). *Tekken* appeared in arcades in 1994 and moved to the fledgling console in 1995, shortly after the PlayStation's launch. The game's aesthetic development has been driven by technological advances. *Tekken 2* (arcade 1995; PS 1996) added more characters and modes, 60 frames-per-second animation, and improved light sourcing, which added texture and shadow. The original PlayStation could barely accommodate the technical advances of *Tekken 3* (arcade 1997; PS 1998). Namco had developed a more powerful arcade board (the System 12) and only a combination of compression and background reduction could fit the game on the more modest System 11 board (Parkinson 2000: 13). The game made more extensive use of motion capture and 3D body movement (including sidestepping).

Tekken Tag Tournament (2000) was one of the first games to test out the engine of the more powerful PS2 (or not, as some critics suggested). As its name suggests, the game deployed tag team battles, but otherwise used the PS2 to make the game more aesthetically pleasing, with moving backgrounds and enhanced detail (we can see Ling Xiaoyu blink as she fights and get the full benefit of Law's Lee-derived facial expressions). Its rival *Dead or Alive 2* also used tag fighting (and did it rather better), but emphasised three-dimensional, interactive space rather than the detail and sparkle of *Tekken Tag*'s backgrounds. *Dead or Alive 2* and its X-Box follow-up bring their *mise-en-scène* into the action, with exploding walls, multi-level sets, waterfalls to be kicked *off* and walls to be kicked *through*. In the Dragon Hills set, combatants can be sent hurtling over the side (with the other fighter floating 'weightlessly' down to continue the assault) or sent through a wall into an elaborate temple setting below. For some gaming magazines, *Dead or Alive 2* was the more innovative game, not least for its extensive countering system – carefully timed use of the counter button could follow blocks with elaborate reversals making the game more tactical than the all-out attack of other fighters. But later reviews found it lacking the depth of the more cautious *Tekken Tag* – the latter had a greater range of moves and techniques distributed amongst its 34-plus characters and required one to *learn* these moves as opposed to the instant button-mashing thrills of *Dead or Alive 2*.[9] More recently, *Tekken 4* seems to have re-established the franchise's state-of-the-art reputation, albeit again through incorporation; namely the interactive environments of *Virtua Fighter* and *Dead or Alive*. One of the arenas even allows fighters to punch members of the surrounding crowd.

Like most fighting games, the 'narrative' of the *Tekken* series focuses on a tournament, the King of the Iron Fist Tournament organised by Heihachi, head of the Mishima Corporation. Like many kung fu films, *Tekken* focuses on conflicting families, both literal and figurative – the interlinked Mishima and Kazama families, and a network of Master/Pupil relationships and families of martial arts styles. In terms of game design, this also economises on fighting moves and explains why Jin Kazama's repertoire includes techniques from his mother (Jun Kazama), father (Kazuya Mishima) and grandfather (Heihachi). In a nice touch, Jin changes his fighting style in *Tekken 4* to straight Karate to signify his opposition to the Heihachis. Master/Pupil relationships include the masked wrestlers King/Armor King, Wang Jinrey and his pupils Lee Chaolan and Ling Xiaoyu, and the Taekwondo kicks passed from Baek to Hwoarang. *Tekken* has a range of fantasy characters – cyborgs Gun-Jack and Combot, the demonic Ogre and boxing kangaroo/dinosaur duo, Roger and Alex, the animate wooden training dummy Mokujin. But its main focus is on Japanese (karate, ninjutsu, Sumo), Chinese

(Shaolin, *wu shu*, Jeet Kune Do), Thai (Muay Thai) and Korean (Taekwondo) martial arts, as well as Mexican *lucha libre* wrestling. The literal authenticity of martial arts in fighting games is, by necessity, limited. In the *Dead or Alive* series, Lei Fang's nominal style is Tai Chi, but she really only performs Tai Chi moves in FMV sequences. Rather, her fighting style evokes the 'soft', flowing *idea* of an 'internal' style like Tai Chi. Similarly, Lei Wulong's Five Animal Shaolin style is less 'authentic' than the moves documented in 1970s martial arts films, and draws similarly on the *idea* of Tiger- or Snake-based attacks. That said, 'real' moves are added to more dynamically fabricated ones – his 'Snake Bite' remediates *qing she chu dong* (snake comes out of his hole), a sequence of coiled fingertip strikes. The Five Animals system distributes 128 moves across five animal impersonations (Wong and Hallander 1988: 5) designed to balance hard/external with soft/internal power – Dragon, Snake and Crane are comparatively soft and fluid, with sudden explosive attacks mimicking a cobra's head or crane's beak, while Tiger and Leopard are aggressive, powerful forces. Such principles – fundamental to Chinese martial arts and philosophy – mean little in digital space except as aesthetic surface. They also play a role in *Tekken*, however, in distiguishing Lei's fluidity from the more aggressive styles of Jin Kazama, Hwoarang and Paul Phoenix. Ling Xiaoyu's style draws extensively on *wu shu*, with graceful, balletic sweeps and wide, extravagant stances – like Lei, she is a 'shapes'-based fighter and harder to learn than the Japanese or Korean boxers.

Some of Lei's and Ling's multi-part moves are thrilling in their complexity and precision, but I always wonder what I am thrilled *by* – am I seeing *through* the technology to the (diminished) aura of the motion-captured martial artist? The mutual dynamic of remediation means that the cinematic is the most constant authenticating referent. Where games surpass films, at least in this genre, is in their mastery of space and their technologically enhanced tactility. Many traditional kung fu films suffer from an impoverished *mise-en-scène*, and even the most lavish cannot match *Tekken*'s arenas – Gothic chambers with fire-breathing gargoyles, helicopter launch pads which double as steel-mesh wrestling rings as guards patrol below, Shaolin monks performing 'stamping' exercises in a courtyard of Golden Buddhas.[10] The shock-dispensing joypads, fast-cut action replays and inevitable kinesthetic identification may have set new challenges for film choreography – Yuen Wo-ping commented that "it's developing into magnifying the movements like you think you can do it, the audience think they can do it, but you can't do it as powerfully as it appears on the screen" (quoted in Smith 1995: 67) – but the kinetic pleasures of fighting games remain rooted in remediated martial arts action and a cinematic construction of the authentic.

From Wire-fu to Cyber-fu: Did Video(games) Kill the Kung Fu Star?

> If characters in *The Matrix* can have information instantaneously downloaded into their heads, they should, for example, be able to be as good a kung fu master as Jackie Chan.
>
> – The Wachowski Brothers (quoted in Clarke 1999: 23)

> The fighting just plain sucks. It sucks because it's all made up, with computers and wire-assisted jumps. Jet Li doesn't need that stuff to show his abilities. In fact, it just worsens the show, because it looks like anyone could do that, hanging from all those wires.
>
> – User comments on *Romeo Must Die* (Internet Movie Database 2000)

In the final scene of *Jackie Chan: My Stunts*, our hero is joined by his CGI self, who solidifies next to him like the liquid metal T1000 from *Terminator 2: Judgement Day* (1991). The 'real' Jackie addresses the camera as his virtual counterpart throws playful punches like the overexcited upstart it is clearly meant to be. "Digital effects may be fun", Jackie begins, as though delivering a public service warning on the dangers of special effects, "One day I might use [them], but now you have to see the real thing" – he punches the CGI Jackie, who shatters into pixellated shards. Once again, Chan presents himself as the champion of the 'real', but there is also a sense of the digital breathing down his neck – we all know how the T1000 kept reconstituting itself. There is something almost elegaic about this moment, both because we know Chan is not getting any younger – real bodies do not get upgraded – and because we have seen him working on *Rush Hour* in the previous scene and perhaps wonder how 'real' he can remain in Hollywood. In *The Tuxedo* (2002), CGI finally caught up with him, downplaying his physical abilities in deference to the fantastic powers of his eponymous outfit. Paradoxically, Hollywood welcomed some of Hong Kong's most physically gifted stars at a time when its technology seemed to be trying to prove that real bodies and real performances were no longer necessary.

Motion capture techniques have recently created 'digital' characters and performances in films like *Star Wars Episode 1: The Phantom Menace*, *The Mummy* (1999) and, particularly, *Final Fantasy: The Spirits Within*, an animated film that sets out to 'pass' for live-action. Japanese popular culture has developed virtual stars like computer-generated Yuki Terai, who mimics Jackie Chan in the short film *Comet the Thief* (2000). Games already have their own hyperreal star system. Walter Benjamin once argued that the "cult of the movie star" was symptomatic of the "shrivelling of the aura with an artificial build-up of the 'personality'" (1935/1979: 860) – how could he have foreseen the reign of Lara Croft, a star "built completely from the ground up" (Poole 2000: 151)? By Benjamin's logic, the shrivelling of 'aura' into 'personality' further diminishes into 'design', except for the role of fans (and fan fiction) in giving 'life' to Lara, to the cast of the *Final Fantasy* games, to *Tekken*'s most widely circulated star, Jin Kazama. Ackbar Abbas' suggestion that the 'real' was now 'co-produced' by special effects in modern martial arts films (1997: 32) needs to be revisited in the light of these developments. The question is: are performance and technology equal partners in this 'co-production' now that special effects are at least partly digital?

If Jackie Chan only submitted to digital technology after a struggle, Jet Li seems to have embraced it more enthusiastically. Nevertheless, to a certain extent, Li must 'keep it real', too, sandwiching the grounded action of *Kiss of the Dragon* between the SFX-aided spectacle of *Romeo Must Die* and *The One*. *Romeo Must Die* reflects the game/movie interface through two types of visual excess. The first was referred to as 'Ultra Pain Mode', computer-animated 'X-ray' shots used to represent internal injuries inflicted by Jet Li – during the climactic fight, the camera follows the flow of *qi* through someone's shattering spine. In both name and effect, this 'Mode' suggests the hypermediated violence of beat-em-ups, especially those, like *Mortal Kombat*, that fetishize physical damage. But in fact the device was first used, in cruder form, in Sonny Chiba's Japanese *The Street Fighter/Gekitotsu! Satsujin Ken* (1974, no relation to the game). Secondly, CGI was used not only to remove wires from shots, but in at least one case, to digitally combine shots. In the film's most notorious scene, Li jumps, rotates horizontally in mid-air to kick a group of henchmen, 'reverses' onto a ledge and then jumps down to deliver a couple more kicks. This 'continuous' take – technologically complex and yet breathtakingly silly – was in fact three 'morphed' shots, which already relied on digitally removed wirework. Li had long been the most wired-up of kung fu stars, but the fan response on the internet suggests that this was a step too far. If wirework is a bone of contention for some fans, it does at least require performative skill. I suspect that what fans objected to, above all, was the impression that Li had been motion-captured and reduced to an animated combo, not so much Jet Li as Nintendo Li. His spine-shattering kick to Russell Wong's skull follows a single shot of both performers taking flight – an initial kick 'repositions' Wong in mid-air for the *coup de grace*. Such a scene would once only have been possible through constructive editing, as in the mid-air kicks exchanged between Lee and Han in *Enter the Dragon*. But such a single-take f(l)ight scene simply looked like a computer game – technology exposed 'Wicked Lies' more than editing ever had. However, *Romeo Must Die*'s most overmediated moment is quickly followed by the blinding return of the real – Li's virtuoso use of a firehose as a rope dart, circling and spinning in a way that only a highly trained physical performer can. It would take more than four months' training to get Keanu or Cameron to do *that*, and, as yet, technology might 'capture' it but never surpass it.[11]

As we have seen, *Romeo Must Die* alienated some viewers not only by 'wasting' Li's physical talents, but by failing to locate its fantastic spectacle within a coherent diegetic world. When *The Matrix* and *Charlie's Angels* 'downloaded' Hong Kong dynamics, they generated self-contained worlds to motivate their hypermediated fight scenes – one cyber-digital, one retro-camp – but *Romeo Must Die* had no such narrative frame. *The One*, on the other hand, is a science fiction fantasy, in which it makes 'sense' for Li to float weightlessly, move at hyperspeed, and crush a motorcycle cop between two Harley Davidsons, one in each hand. Nevertheless, other questions persist – where do Li's kung fu skills fit into this spectacle? With all this technological wizardry, can "anyone do it"? *The One* also raises some more specific issues in its doubling of its star.

More than its parallel universes and 'wormholes', *The One*'s ultimate 'high concept' is: Jet Li versus Jet Li. In the course of the film, he wields CGI motorbikes as weapons and fights CGI opponents, but what we really want to see is Jet Li fighting himself, and therein also lies the problem. For the film's climactic fight, Jet Li fights his stunt double(s) – in some ways, *The One* brings to a head the ongoing doubling of Li and the issues it raises about authenticity. For much of the fight, the double's face is concealed by careful camera placement and editing, but the film also makes use of digital head replacements to generate its two Jets. Problem number one is that for the scene to work, the double(s) must be able to do pretty much everything that Li can. Secondly, if a star's head can be digitally added either to a stuntman or something even more virtual, how can we trust the veracity of the star's performance? This is really only an issue for a star partly defined by physical skill – digital head replacements were used in *The Phantom Menace* to allow Ewan McGregor and Liam Neeson to perform Hong Kong-style stunts in their martial arts duel with Darth Maul. *The One*, on the other hand, must re-authenticate Li, which happens in two ways. Firstly, *xingyi* and *bagua* serve not only to distinguish between 'good' and 'bad' Jet, but to offer something that only a trained martial artist can do. These are very specialised martial arts that require many years' training – do not expect the *Matrix* cast to do *bagua* any time soon. It is unlikely that Li's double – a Hong Kong-trained stuntman taught to fight in a more all-purpose style – would have the same in-depth knowledge as the star. A good Hong Kong stuntman can usually *mimic* such forms, but we largely see Li himself throwing the more intricate shapes. But, given *The One*'s use of digital imaging, how can we know that it really is Jet Li performing these moves even when it appears to be? The answer is that, of course, we cannot (short of visiting the set). In this respect, Li can only be authenticated extra-textually – behind-the-scenes DVD extras and Home Box Office featurettes provide 'evidence' of who did what. Films like *The One* put endless effort into blurring the real and the virtual, but to make capital out of Jet Li's participation, they must then put almost as much effort into separating out the one from the other. According to Tanya Krzywinska, writing about another authenticity-based genre (porn), new technologies offer a version of authenticity by promising to circumvent mediation. Their 'newness' acts as a fetish that "functions as a means for covering over representation's inability to capture the real event" (1998: 168), but technology also carries the promise to "reveal what has previously not been shown" (169). In the case of the kung fu star, one populist discourse sees technology as having precisely the opposite effect, of obscuring or visibly fabricating the 'real event'. But at present, a digital technology of consumption (DVD) is working in the way that Krzywinska suggests, with its obsessive documenting of the 'real'; more 'complete' versions of the text, outtakes, behind-the-scenes evidence of what happened on set.

One must beware of mobilising anecdotes as 'evidence' of anything, and yet *The One*'s director James Wong tells an irresistible story on his DVD commentary for the film. During a preview screening, sections of the audience allegedly mistook the 'real' for the technologically enhanced – Jet Li moved so fast while throwing *bagua* shapes that they thought he had been speeded up. The scene was cut because some audience members laughed and others commented negatively on preview cards. I say the story is 'irresistible' – it is irresistible in the same way that the 'real' Jackie Chan punching out the 'virtual' Jackie Chan is. It reminds us of the extraordinary capacity of human bodies even in the age of digital reproduction, or maybe it just reminds us of a desire to see the real surpass the virtual. But ultimately, in the case of martial arts, at least, it is not just films and games that remediate one another, but, by necessity, technology and the body, too. The martial artist's body may be extensively (re)mediated, but technology has yet to make it disappear.

Kung Fu Reloaded and Upgraded

The focus of this book has been on kung fu (in the broadest sense) as a *performing art* as much as, if not more than, a *martial art*. The 'martial' component of the 'art' has been severely compromised in an age of technological weaponry and, some would say, by its dilution by a Westernised pedagogic industry offering quick-fix self-defence classes; these two phenomena are not entirely unconnected. Kung fu as performance art has, as we have seen, had its own (mediatised) encounter with technology; from early *wu xia pian* to advanced analogue film-making FX to CGI and motion-capture. And yet, as I hope is apparent in this study, Chinese martial arts have always been characterised by their resilience, their ability to mutate and adapt. For a genre whose historical-cultural moment(s) seem to have passed – or, at least, with *Crouching Tiger* and *Hero*, moved into a kind of post-phase – it was striking how much last-minute updating I needed to do in the final stages of completing the manuscript. With Jet Li, Jackie Chan, Michelle Yeoh, Yuen Wo-ping, the *Matrix* sequels and game, *Hero* still awaiting release in a number of Western markets (but already circulating on disc), kung fu seems to be *everywhere*. So how does its 'future' look?

One 'future' for Chinese martial arts media still lies in archiving its past. One of the most exciting developments of the last year has been Shaw Brothers opening their vaults (the Fort Knox of *wu xia pian*) to allow remastered DVDs of 760 of their films by Celestial Pictures in Hong Kong. Many of these are kung fu and swordplay classics long unavailable in anything but multi-generation video form on the 'grey' market.[1] When I wrote about *Heroes Two* in chapter two, for example, I worked from a second-generation (at least!) dubbed, panned-and-scanned video; I had seen it once in 'Shaw-Scope' (again, dubbed) in the late 1970s on a double-bill with *The Men from the Monastery*. Now it is restored in widescreen, in Mandarin with optional English subtitles, albeit missing *Three Styles of the Hung School's Kung Fu* (which *is*, ironically, on my old video). These releases have already made one thing apparent to me; the omission in this book of detailed discussion of Chor Yuen's adaptations of Gu Long's *jianghu* novels, which look like more than the equal of the Shaolin cycle, with characteristically luminous performances by Ti Lung, David

Chiang and the late Lo Lieh (who really should have been in Tarantino's *Kill Bill*). But then, Chor's martial arts films are a conspicuous absence from most writing about Hong Kong cinema, a possible consequence of their comparative unavailability. In other words, not only is there more work to be done, now it *can* be done.[2]

As I write this, we are about to get the full effect of what the Hollywood hype machine is calling 'The Year of *The Matrix*'. Over the next few weeks (thus my cautiously speculative tone) we will see the release of the first sequel *The Matrix Reloaded* (the second, *The Matrix Revolutions*, arrives in November), a multi-platform game *Enter the Matrix* (Atari) and a collection of animated shorts *The Animatrix*, drawing largely on *animé* film-makers like Shinichiro Watanabe and Koji Morimoto. It will be apparent from chapter seven that I had some misgivings about the original film (although it speaks volumes that I am as excited by the sequels as everyone else seems to be). Yet the expansion (and heightened 'Asianisation') of the franchise suggests that there may be more to its Asiaphilia than superficial magpie borrowing. It has given a high visibility to Asian film-making talent, even if it still needs a Chinese star to clinch the kung fu connection. Jet Li may have been out of their price range, but it is not hard to imagine what Yuen Wo-ping's former protegé Donnie Yen could have brought to it. *Reloaded* promises more virtual action than ever before – some of its FX took over two years to produce after initial 'capture' of the actors – and new challenges for Yuen Wo-ping. I suspect that it will have significant implications for many of the issues raised in chapter eight. Trailers suggest that the Yuen clan have taught the cast a lot more since the first film; Keanu Reeves really does look as though he "knows kung fu". While other post-*Matrix* films have equipped their stars with sufficient kung fu skills for one film (and a lot of doubling), the longer preparation time afforded the trilogy has allowed Yuen to reproduce something like Shaw Brothers' Performing Arts Training Course for a Hollywood blockbuster.

The kung fu-gaming interface looks set to reach a new level with *Enter the Matrix*, which has enjoyed the biggest advance orders of any game to date. It is not just the Wachowski Brothers who had creative input into the game, writing and directing footage to complement the films; Yuen Wo-ping choreographed the motion-captured fighting scenes simultaneously with his work on the movie sequels. In some ways, it is Yuen, more than anyone else, who is the linking, and most paradigmatic, figure in this book. His remarkable career trajectory marks out the territory I have sought to examine; from Chinese Opera to the X-Box, from Wong Fei-hung to Neo, from the 'authentic' kung fu cult master to the virtual action hero.

Notes

Introduction

1 One product of this interchange was the meeting of Japanese and Chinese swordplay heroes in *Zatoichi and the One-Armed Swordsman*/*Dubi Dao Dazhan Mang Xia* (1973).

2 Japan was a major market for Lee's films, and remains the biggest producer of Lee merchandise. There's an interesting study to be made of how Japanese fans negotiated the "Jap bastards" of films like *Fist of Fury*. On *Fist of Fury*'s DVD commentary, Bey Logan offers anecdotal evidence of such negotiation amongst fans who distanced themselves from the villains in the film; Lee's rage was not directed at 'them', but a 'historical' militarism that they hated, too.

3 To the *wu xia*, *gung fu* and *wu da pian*, Craig Reid adds a fourth, the *guo shu pian* (neohero film), which mixes kung fu, comedy and aspects of the *wu xia pian* like heroism and chivalry (1994: 21). I am less convinced that this is a fourth category rather than evidence of some very blurred boundaries between these different trends and cycles.

4 The 'Knight Errant' embodies values like *yi*; righteousness or altruism, "doing more than what is required by common standards, or in other words behaving in a 'supermoral' way" (Liu 1967: 4). He is also a dispenser of justice in a world where institutions of power cannot be trusted.

5 *Wu xia* fiction has a long literary history – Liu Dama (1981/96: 47) traces it back to the essay 'On the Sword'/ *Shuo Jian Pian* from the Warring States era (403–221 BC). Post-1960s *wu xia pian* were indebted to the 'new wave' novels of Gu Long and Jin Yong/Louis Cha. Gu Long's novels were adapted by Chor Yuen at Shaw Brothers in the 1970s, but he has been seen as a less direct influence on Zhang Che's *yang* cinema, with his focus on "the solitary martial arts hero" with a "strong, macho image" (58). James Liu (1967) provides the most detailed English-language account of literary *wu xia*. According to him, the literary equivalent of what we might think of as the kung fu narrative emerges after the Qing Dynasty, in tales emphasising nationalism, great physical feats, different styles and schools (134–5).

6 Literally, rivers (*jiang*) and lakes (*hu*). It has also been translated as 'perilous waters' (Ng 1981/96: 85).

7 During the 1970s, martial arts also became a staple part of Hong Kong television.

8 Under its US title *Fists of Fury*.

9 See Ralph C. Crozier (1972) for an interesting comparison of the émigré escapism of the Chinese swordplay film with the frontier myth of the American western.

10 Bordwell, too, notes (but does not attempt to historicize) "ongoing reappraisals of what counts as heroism" (2000a: 42). In the 1970s alone, there is a marked shift from revenge with a nationalist flavour (*The Chinese Boxer* etc.) to the neo-Confucian humanism of Lau Kar-leung's films or those films solipsistically focused on specific fighting styles.

11 Another ambiguous manifestation of the genre's relationship with colonialism lies in the fact that Hong Kong kung fu films distributed in Britain in the 1970s could be registered as British. This entitled them to money from the Eady levy, the 'tax' on cinema admissions that was fed back into production.

Chapter One

1 Hong Kong film-makers often shoot fight scenes at 22 fps or less – 24 fps is the 'normal' camera speed (Bordwell 2000a: 209). This speeds up the fight without making it look as comical as the Wong Fei-hung film-within-a-film and can give intricate sequences an uncanny precision and velocity.

2 Chan's notion of the 'real' was clearly different from Lau Kar-leung's – they clashed over the 'authenticity' of the Drunken form used in *Drunken Master 2*.

3 Wang was more successful as a swordplay star than in kung fu films. *The One-Armed Swordsman* and *Golden Swallow* established his stoic masochism, and he subsequently directed and starred in what many consider to be the first modern kung fu film, *The Chinese Boxer*, and the first of his own many one-armed variants, *The One-Armed Boxer* (1971). *The Chinese Boxer* was the most successful Chinese-language film at the Hong Kong box office in 1970–71, and second only to *Tora! Tora! Tora!* (1970) overall (Jarvie 1977: 134), but his popularity declined when Bruce Lee returned to Hong Kong. For more on Wang, see *Oriental Cinema* 19 (2000), 'The

Jimmy Wang Yu Issue', or my own 'One-Armed and Extremely Dangerous: Wang Yu's Mutilated Masters' (2002).

4   Tsui Hark has spelled out the influence of Lion Dances on his martial arts setpieces: "I'm a great fan of people doing things on top on tables, on top of posts, because when we were kids we could see these lion dances on top of a post or somebody's shoulder" (quoted in Hwang 1998: 19).

5   Hu's 'glimpses' of preternatural abilities contrasts intriguingly with the digital 'reality' of *Crouching Tiger, Hidden Dragon* where tree-top skirmishes or dashes across a lake or waterfall can be shown in single takes.

6   Two notable Monkey-showcases were made in 1979 – Lau Kar-leung's *Mad Monkey Kung Fu* and Sammo Hung's *Knockabout/Zaijia Xiaozi*.

7   The trigram consists of three broken or unbroken lines – arranged in a hexagram, the eight trigrams represent Heaven, Wind/Wood, Thunder, Water, Mountain, Earth, Fire, Lake. *Bagua* forms follow the positions of the different trigrams – "A young man whirls around in a small circle, but suddenly he dives downward, cuts across his circle and continues circling in the opposite direction, until another swoop, twist, and lightning flash of arms legs and torso sends the performer off into another round of eternally evolving circles" (Reid and Croucher 1995: 98–101).

8   Zhang's 'First Generation' consisted of Wang Yu; his second David Chiang, Ti Lung and Chen Guantai; his third Fu Sheng and Chi Kwan-chun (Tian 1984: 46). The 'Venoms' are named after the cult favourite *The Five Venoms/Wu du* (1978), the film that gave Zhang's career a new lease of life and moved it in a more Gothic direction than the bloodshed and homoerotic bonding of his more celebrated *wu xia* films.

9   The 'secret rivalry' between John Liu and Wong Tao is reminiscent of that between the Man With No Name (Clint Eastwood) and Colonel Mortimer (Lee Van Cleef) in *For a Few Dollars More* (1965) – each has their own reasons for hunting Silver Fox. Given that the soundtrack is lifted from Ennio Morricone's score for *The Big Gundown*, the Spaghetti western link could not be more explicit. My dismissal of the plot is not simply facetious – this is true cut-and-paste formula.

Chapter Two

1   Chan's affection for Carradine is even more interesting given that the latter is something of a *bête noir* for many Western purists. When Carradine won the role of Kwai Chang Caine over Bruce Lee, he was doubly inauthentic – as a martial artist and in the ignoble tradition of white actors playing 'ethnic' roles.

2   Key roles are often played by the same actors. Chen Guantai played Hung Hei-kwun in three Shaws films, Fu Sheng played Fong Sai-yuk in four, Qi Guanjun played Wu Wei-kin in four, including one (*Showdown at Cotton Mill/Hu Hui Gan Xie Zhan Xi Chan Si* [1978]) for a rival studio.

3   In *Yang + Yin: Gender in Chinese Cinema*, Zhang Che scoffs at Freudian theory, while Kwan juxtaposes a scene from one of his films of the hero being lowered onto, and anally penetrated by, a huge spike.

4   Li traces these bloody death scenes back to the *panchang dazhan* of Chinese Opera, "depicting the hero with a wounded torso bandaged up to prevent his bowels from spilling out while he slaughters the bad guys in his last moments" (2001: 525).

5   Strictly speaking, Zhi Shan is the true 'Father' of Southern Shaolin, but Hung cuts a more dashing figure.

6   Wu Wei-kin's attack on the textile mill is also recounted in *Shaolin Avengers* and *Showdown at Cotton Mill*, with Qi Guanjun again playing the role. Wu seems to lend himself to reinvention less than other Shaolin heroes, although *Showdown at Cotton Mill* gives him a new death scene.

7   The 'real' San-de is thought to have possessed a massive physique – he was also known as 'Iron Arms' – but the film makes great capital out of Lau Kar-fai's deceptive 'seven stone weakling' appearance.

8   Shaven-headed Ng Mui/Wu Mei is allowed *shifu* status, transmitting her 'woman's style' *Wing Chun* to Cai Dezhong (Ti Lung). But she is also training Cai to stand in as Yim Wing Chun's (Shih Szu) master. Filmed throughout with her back to the camera, Ng is an ambiguous presence in the film and simply disappears without explanation before the climax.

9   It is during the same period that a politicised Asian-American consciousness began to emerge.

10   Significantly, it is his *father* who is American, conjuring images of other kinds of 'conquests' in the East and casting the 'Orient' as feminine.

11   A sobriquet earned during an exchange in the pilot episode:

       Master Po: Do you hear the grasshopper at your feet?

       Caine: Old man, how is it that you hear these things?

       Master Po: Young man, how is it that you do not?

12   In the later *Kung Fu: The Legend Continues* (1993), set in the modern-day with Carradine as Caine's descendent, an American-based 'Shaolin Temple' is burned by that generic archetype, the renegade monk.

13   The BBC documentary *Under the Sun: Kung Fu Business* (1999) provides a particularly interesting account of the Temple's new economic role, and I have drawn from it in this section.

Chapter Three

1   Dennis and Atyeo 1974 and Thomas 1994 are excellent biographies. Miller 2000 is a contentious but compelling read. Block 1974 is worryingly ethnocentric, even more so than Miller – it is a bad sign when a Lee biography refers to the "inscrutable East" (132) and is so patronisingly dismissive of *Way of the Dragon*. A biography by Lee's widow (Lee 1975) errs on the side of hagiography, as one might expect, but is not without interest. The most useful discussions of Lee's films can be found in: Glaessner 1974: 83–96; Chiao 1981; Rayns 1980 and 1984; Cheng 1984; Logan 1995: 22–43; Teo 1997, 110–21; Bordwell 2001: 49–55.

2   Abbas is looking particularly at two films by Stanley Kwan, the ghost story *Rouge/Yanzhi Kou* (1989) and the biopic of the 'Chinese Garbo' Ruan Lingyu, *Centre Stage/Ruan Lingyu* (1991). In *Centre Stage*, the ghostly star returns via footage from her films, recreations of her lost films (with Maggie Cheung standing in for Ruan) and a dramatic reconstruction of her life, again with Cheung as Ruan. *Centre Stage* announces itself as 'art cinema', consciously using distancing devices (Cheung as herself discusssing the role with Stanley Kwan) marked by authorial intent. Yet the use of heterogenous footage, stars and their stand-ins, to resurrect the dead star is not so far removed from what occurs in the lowbrow but disorienting *Game of Death*.

3   Although the following description of Kim Tai-jung limbering up to double Lee for *Game of Death* makes him sound exactly like an Elvis impersonator: "He loves to imitate Bruce's actions, gestures and expression; almost every day he practices them" (Hui 1978b: 42).

4   Many English-speaking fans pronounced his name 'Bruce Lie'. This was, I suspect, partly a genuine mispronunciation, but also a nod to the deceit embedded in the name. According to Alex Ben Block, Bruce Lee was furious with those sections of the Hong Kong press who spelled his name 'Li' – he favoured the Americanised spelling (1974: 100).

5   See, for example, Carl Jones' internet fanzine 'Exit the Dragon, Enter the Tiger: The Exploitation Cinema of Bruce Li', http://www.geocities.com/many-bruces/brucelizine/. Accessed 06/03/02.

6   I am not suggesting, though, that Davidson is simply being contrary – he never argues for the superiority of 'Li' to Lee. His priorities are, however, embedded in the nostalgic premise of the fanzine – that 1970s Hong Kong cinema is superior to everything that came later.

7   Critical accounts of the film rarely agree on when it is supposed to be set. Huo's death would place it in the final years of the Qing Dynasty, but the film's *mise-en-scène* points to something like the 1920s. Jet Li's remake *Fist of Legend* seems clearer about its historical premise – the Japanese are preparing for the invasion of China – but has to have Huo die later than 1909 in order to do so. Huo Yuenjia seems to have died either from jaundice (Logan 2000d: 46) or a blood disease (Hui 1977: 16). The speculation about foul play derives from the Japanese doctor who gave Huo medicine for his ailment, but the 'Yellow-Faced Tiger' seems to have enjoyed an amicable relationship with Japanese martial artists in Shanghai.

8   These are the two best known names, but what of 'Li Jun-fan' ('Gaining Fame Overseas')?

9   Teo is especially hostile to Rayns' discernment of an implicitly homoerotic 'narcissism' in Lee's persona. He sets out to put Rayns 'straight' in more ways than one – elsewhere, he refers to narcissism as a "code word for homosexual imagery" (quoted in Li 2001: 523). The implication is that only Westerners want to 'queer' Lee's image, but Rayns' reading finds its Chinese counterpart in Stanley Kwan's *Yang + Yin: Gender in Chinese Cinema*.

10   This 'acceptance' was further underlined by the addition of a Bruce Lee Star to the Hollywood Walk of Fame, an event tied in to *Enter the Dragon*'s release.

11   There is a nice joke later in the film, when Bruce is perhaps unwisely confident that he will get the lead in *Kung Fu* – "Who else they gonna get, Mickey Rooney?" he asks. No, David Carradine, as the follow-up scene reveals. Once again, Bruce and Linda cannot quite believe what they are seeing onscreen.

12   Lee's fight with Wong Jack Man (the basis for this scene) is the clearest example of how the 'Legend' inflates rather less heroic episodes. More recent accounts (Thomas 1994; Miller 2000; Little and Wong 2000) relate that Lee's short-range *Wing Chun* dominated but could not finish off Wong's long-range *Choy li-fut*. The fight allegedly degenerated into more of a chase, with Lee punching Wong in the back of the head and finally subduing him by sitting on him. Lee 'won', but was exhausted and his knuckles were painfully swollen. 'Bruce Li' never wins such ignominious victories, while in *Enter the Dragon*, the Wong Jack Man fight takes place on a set seemingly borrowed from *Mortal Kombat* and the fight itself heavily indebted to Lee's movie fights. Yet even the 'real' version sounds like a kung fu movie, the sobering experience that enables our hero to 'learn the hard way'. This was apparently the moment when Lee decided to no longer rely on *Wing Chun* alone and also

to train Western-style (as Miller would put it) for stamina and endurance.

13 "People ask me how Bruce died. I prefer to remember how he lived", 'Linda' narrates at the end of *Enter the Dragon*. Well, she *would* say that. Betty Ting-pei was known to be Bruce's lover, and the fact that he died in her bed fuelled something of a scandal after his death (the 'official' line was that they were discussing *Game of Death*). In the Asian biopics, she is arguably a more important figure than Linda. In 1976, she played herself in Shaw Brothers' *Bruce Lee and I/Bruce Lee: His Last Days, His Last Nights* (Lo Mar, 1976). It is not difficult to see why she was regarded as the more fascinating of the two women in Bruce's life – as Cheng Yu puts it, "There is nothing more ironic than the death of a 'celibate' kung-fu master found in the boudoir of a sex starlet" (1984: 25).

14 These are the three fights Lee actually shot. Two lower floors would probably have contained a Karate expert (Wong In-sik) and a Praying Mantis practitioner (Taky Kimura).

15 I am grateful to Julian Stringer for drawing my attention to *Critique of Game of Death*.

16 Admittedly, this is probably to hide the 'shadow's' face, but it has other effects.

17 *Dragon – The Bruce Lee Story* shows the infant Brandon being menaced by Bruce's Chinese Demon. By the time of the film's release, he had indeed joined his father, and *Enter the Dragon* was dedicated to him. Given that Fu Sheng died while living at Lee's former Kowloon Tong home, many have talked of a 'curse'.

Chapter Four

1 *Encounters of the Spooky Kind*'s final slapstick freeze-frame features Sammo Hung beating his unfaithful wife, while *Dreadnaught* undermines Mouse's laundry-woman sister (Lily Li) by throwing mud at her washing. In *Knockabout* and *The Magnificent Butcher*, women only feature in crowd scenes – there are no female characters as such. Women are only allowed a more substantial presence as harridans or grotesques, like the nagging wives of *Dance of the Drunk Mantis*, *Miracles Fighters* and *Drunken Tai Chi*, but they are, at least, granted the physical and verbal skills to spar with their ne'er-do-well spouses.

2 Significantly, they were the *last* generation of Opera performers to make the transition to film. The next generation of kung fu stars (Jet Li, Zhou Wen-zhou, Donnie Yen) were Mainland-trained *wu shu* practitioners.

3 Ng Ho likens it to "contemporary pop dance styles" (1980a: 45).

4 I should probably also add Karl Maka to this kung fu comedy pantheon – he would work with Sammo Hung a number of times, including their jointly-owned production company Gar Bo Films. But Maka's background is very different from the Opera-trained Hung *et al* – like Michael Hui, a comedian-actor, like the 'new wave', educated in the US, including film courses at New York University. He would later co-produce and star in the *Aces Go Places* series for the successful company Cinema City, co-owned with Dean Shek and Raymond Wong. Like Tsui Hark (who made several films for Cinema City), he can be seen as a prime mover in the 'Westernisation' of Hong Kong cinema.

5 Chan's autogiography is largely blandly ghost-written, but a notable exception is its unflattering portrait of Hung as a relentless bully from childhood to directorial tyrant (Chan and Yang 1998). Other accounts suggest that Hung was both incredulous and resentful of Chan's greater success (Logan 1995: 94) – Chan *has* often been celebrated at Hung's expense. By way of 'revenge', Sammo seems fond of casting Jackie in comparatively unsympathetic roles – he is a humourless presence in the 'Lucky Stars' films, a stunt-machine excluded from the 'gang', and plays an oleaginous yuppie lawyer in *Dragons Forever*.

6 In films like *Will Success Spoil Rock Hunter?* (1957) and his collaborations with Jerry Lewis, director Frank Tashlin satirised the American postwar consumer culture of washing machines, television, advertising and pop music. Within the rather different context of Hong Kong's economic boom, some of Hui's concerns are similar.

7 The film began shooting with Yuen Siu-tin in the role he had virtually made his own, but he died early in the production and his scenes had to be re-shot.

8 In *Last Hero in China* Jet Li's Wong performs *Zui Quan* while drunk to anaesthetize his injured feet.

9 In his reading of the film, Steve Fore implies that the kung fu film had come full circle and shifted its cultural identification back to China – "what (Wong Fei-hung) represents is the implicit support for the notion of a cultural China, a plea for the patriotic unity of Chinese people everywhere", a perspective at odds with the earlier films' addressing "the needs and desires of a younger, faster-moving, and more polyglot society" (2001: 136–7). The film even rehabilitates the Manchus in the form of Lau Kar-leung's decorated veteran.

Chapter Five

1 Nor, for the record, are 'classy' martial arts films anything new, as King Hu and Tsui Hark prove, although their budgets do not come near Ang Lee's.

2 *Dragon Swamp* was the second most successful Chinese-language film at the Hong Kong box office in 1969–70

and the fourth most successful overall (Jarvie 1977: 133).

3 I have fallen into line with calling Zhang Ziyi's character 'Jen' even though that name seems to be the invention of the film's subtitlers. She is audibly named Yu Jiaolong in the film's dialogue, which, as Stephen Teo explains, includes the characters for 'Jade Dragon' (2001). Jade Dragon is also the name of the Sword in *Dragon Swamp*, one of the many precursors of *Crouching Tiger*'s Green Destiny.

4 An extreme literary antecedent would be the Tang Dynasty tale of Tsui Shen-ssu's wife, who becomes a concubine and bears a son as a cover for taking revenge on a prefect who killed her father. When she achieves her goal, she leaves Tsui and the child, but returns briefly, ostensibly to feed her son. In fact, she murders him "to sever all ties with the past" (Liu 1967: 96–7).

5 Or her decadent opposite, the dominatrix, like Fu Manchu's perverse daughter Fah Lo Suee.

6 It sounds like his 'column' is as complete as it is ever going to be.

7 In terms of her promotion, Mao was the first 'Deadly China Doll' (the English title of one of her films). Alex Ben Block calls her "the frail girl who gets her kicks out of the martial arts" (1974: 150). But the American title of *Lady Whirlwind* is most telling of all; as Desser, amongst others, has observed, *Deep Thrust* was clearly meant to sound like *Deep Throat* (2000: 40).

8 The response to *The Woman Warrior* is not dissimilar to the debates generated by Alice Walker's *The Colour Purple*; both books generated tensions between genders within specific ethnic groups (Chinese-American and African-American, respectively). I am not aware of any empirical work on the South-East Asian reception of female-centred swordplay and kung fu films, although such insights would be extremely valuable.

9 Of the three philosophical systems that inform the *wu xia pian*, two are antithetical to the empowerment of women. The Confucian conception of the independent woman, "whether she be promiscuous or public-spirited, is of a 'danger'" (Koo 1981/1996: 32), while Buddhism is egalitarian in principle, but patriarchal in practice. Taoism is more sympathetic, both because of the need to balance yang with yin and because of its championing of the marginalised, often expressed in terms of a "mask hiding some unusual, strong qualities" (31). One might argue that it is the 'soft', Taoist-derived, arts that genuinely allow smaller, less powerfully built fighters to overcome larger opponents.

10 Some of Hong Kong cinema's best contemporary female stars began as Beauty Pageant Queens (or runners-up), including Maggie Cheung and Brigitte Lin.

11 She was further 'legitimated' by another auteur, Wong Kar-wai, who cast her in *Ashes of Time* and *Chungking Express*.

12 In some ways, pure yin itself seems to be conceptualised as a "primordial abyss", dark, cold and empty if not balanced by yang.

13 The examination of gender roles pervaded a range of Hong Kong genres, in particular romantic comedy; see Stokes and Hoover 1999, 228–37.

14 Cross-dressing in Chinese theatre does not just account for 'femininity' as 'male stagecraft'. It has also produced intriguing movie double acts like Pak Suet-sin and Yam Kim-fai who played heterosexual couples in Cantonese Opera films, but were themselves a (known) lesbian couple offscreen. In the 1950s and 1960s, Yam generally played male scholars, with Pak playing the kind of 'feminine' roles often assumed by men onstage. See Teo 1997: 40–2, and also Stanley Kwan's *Yang + Yin*, which rather complicates some Western assumptions about Chinese sexual 'norms'.

15 Strictly speaking, she is also of a higher social class than Li and Yu (both of them Hans), but, by entering *jianghu*, she submits to a different social hierarchy.

16 She tells Li Mu-bai, "Your master underestimated us women. He wouldn't teach me even after he'd slept with me."

17 The transnational packaging of *Crouching Tiger* provides another way of thinking about this 'floating' outside of a fixed space or meaning.

Chapter Six

1 There *is* a more interesting Li biography waiting to be told, some of it touched on by Parish; his clashes with Tsui Hark and Golden Harvest, the Triad-related shooting of his manager Jim Choi (who also had Triad connections), the fact that the currently practicing Buddhist was once regarded as virtually impossible to work with.

2 There were further caveats about a Mandarin-speaking northerner with northern *wu shu* moves playing the Cantonese legend who practiced southern *Hung Gar*. Li's awkward Cantonese was a subject of some mockery in the Hong Kong press; he is dubbed in all of his Hong Kong films (not an unusual practice), except for the last one, *Hitman*.

3   This is especially true of *Western* critics of Li, who often adhere to a polarisation of *physical* and *dramatic* performance. Stars like Arnold Schwarzenegger and Jean-Claude Van Damme, leaving aside their actual abilities, must contend with prejudices about their non-thespian backgrounds. In Hong Kong, and of course in an institution like Beijing Opera, such divisions are less important (I hesitate to say that they do not exist). Some of Hong Kong's most accomplished actors have been pop stars (Leslie Cheung, Anita Mui) and Beauty Queens (Maggie Cheung).

4   Comparing Li with Chan (whose performative range derives from the multi-skilled Opera), Yuen Wo-ping comments, "Jet Li comes from the martial arts. When he fights, it's clear fist and kick" (Hong Kong Film Archive 1999: 64).

5   Li received sole credit, but it is perhaps more accurate to say that he co-directed it. After the star was injured, the film was completed by Tsui Siu-ming, and Li has avoided directing ever since (Logan 1995: 178; Parish 2002: 55–7).

6   The 'Wong Fei-hung theme' is the traditional Cantonese tune *jiangjunling* ('Under the General's Orders'). For an interesting discussion of its different uses, including its adaptation by the Chinese Democrary movement, see Li (2001: 533–4).

7   The umbrella that Wong uses to fight the Shaho protection racket and the White Lotus Cult turns out to be the patriarchal phallus in the spin-off *Iron Monkey*. We learn that it originally belonged to Wong Kei-ying, and we see the child Fei-hung gazing longingly at it.

8   When Wong replies that he cannot read romanised numerals and will "never keep good time", he is temporarily implicated in the reactionary isolationism of the White Lotus, who burn a clock in the pre-credits scene.

9   The name of Hong Kong's most prolific and ruthlessly commercial film-maker, who collaborated with Li several times in the mid-1990s.

10 Siao once taught English on television in Hong Kong.

11 The cross-dressing seems to be a nod to Fong Sai-yuk's transvestite origins in Hong Kong cinema, played by a girl long before Fu Sheng made him one of Zhang Che's martyred pin-ups.

12 Karen Mok's hyper performance in *Black Mask* recalls her role as 'Baby' in *Fallen Angels/Duolo Tianshi* (1995). See also my comments on *Dr Wai*.

13 In *Hitman*, he plays another Mainlander type, the 'Ah Can' stereotype; the bumpkin or buffoon "lacking taste and style without the knowledge to know better" (Stokes and Hoover 1999: 222). As Eric Tsang grooms Li to be a professional assassin, they shop for clothes and Jet models different heroic looks; Chow Yun-fat (long coat and toothpick), Jean Reno's Leon (complete with plant), effete Leslie Cheung.

14 The English-language version of *Dr Wai*, supervised by Tsui Hark, eliminates the modern-day scenes and pads out the 1930s adventure (in spite of the fluctuations in Rosamund Kwan's character). But one extra scene has the King of Adventurers conceal his identity by telling Kwan that he's "the actor Jet Li".

15 Most notably, instead of joining the patriotic struggle, in the English-language version Chen is re-united (a freeze-frame and narration tells us) with his Japanese lover, Mitsuko.

16 When Donnie Yen played Chen in the Hong Kong television version of *Fist of Fury*, he played the same volatile 'Jap-hating' avenger that Bruce Lee did, even adopting some of his mannerisms. According to Yen, in *Fist of Legend*, "Jet Li basically played Wong Fei-hung with a different suit"; of his own performance, he says, "You can't make Beethoven without having Beethoven's essence. You can't change it. That became a legend" (quoted in Stokes and Hoover 2000: 55).

17 The film's liberalism about race (and interracial couples) is less evident in its gender politics, which do not depart significantly from *Fist of Fury*. Mitsuko exists simply to demonstrate Chen's open-mindedness; she is not the equal of Rosamund Kwan's 13th Aunt. But this is a more overtly masculinist world than the *Once Upon a Time in China* series, not only in its obsession with fathers but its masculinising of technology.

18 As Siu-leung Li reminds us, another Funakoshi was the 'Father' of Karate and a contemporary of Huo Yuanjia (2000: 538).

Chapter Seven

1   It is also, of course, a familiar cliché in the characterisation of Hong Kong. In the production featurette *Location: Hong Kong with Enter the Dragon* (1973), the "jewel of South-East Asia" is described as "a curious mixture of modern metropolis and ancient Chinese culture".

2   Interestingly, Chow is the only Hong Kong star to crossover *without* martial arts skills, even though he later acquired some for *Crouching Tiger*. *Bullet Proof Monk* (2003) was quick to capitalize on them.

3   The 'flied lice' jokes suggest that this cult audience was probably not imagined as Chinese. "I was condemned in Hong Kong and Shanghai", says director Richard Donner, "but that was about it" (DVD commentary). In

fact, *Lethal Weapon 4* was heavily criticised by Chinese-Americans for its racist depictions.

4   By contrast, Hong Kong did exist in the realm of the real – the media coverage of the Handover.

5   For another interesting mixture of kung fu, James Bond and (literally) Fu Manchu, see Marvel Comics' *Master of Kung Fu* (1973–), whose hero, Shang Chi, is the rebel-son of Sax Rohmer's 'Yellow Peril'. See Hunt (2000: 81–2), for a discussion of the comic and Fu Manchu's connection to *Enter the Dragon*.

6   I know of no work on Bruce Lee's female fans, who might have had very different investments in him. The British poster magazine *Kung Fu Monthly* – which promoted Lee as pin-up as well as action hero – had a 38 per cent female readership (Robins and Cohen 1982: 488).

7   By the time Lazenby went to Hong Kong in 1972, *On Her Majesty's Secret Service* (1969) had only recently been released there. As the 'current' James Bond, he *was* effectively a star.

8   The end-credit outtakes, primarily a vehicle for authenticating Chan's stunts in his Hong Kong films, now suggest a very specific role for him in generating 'verbal' comedy. Many of them emphasise his problems with the English language, just as interviews love to reproduce his fractured grammar as a signifier of his 'cuteness'.

9   The massage parlour scene in *Rush Hour 2* makes for a interesting comparison, still playing on the sexual conquest of Asia.

10   His most recent Hollywood film, *Cradle 2 the Grave* (2003), teams him with hip-hop star DMX, who plays a cameo role in *Romeo Must Die*. Li's weakest film to date finds him even more peripheral than in *Romeo Must Die*.

11   For an interesting account of Asian-American perceptions of Li's sexuality, see Stringer 2003.

12   At least, this is true of a *theatrical* viewing of the film. Once again, DVD allows a slightly different experience of the film by having Corey Yuen explain its martial arts foundations in one of the 'Extra Features'.

13   Tarantino's eclectic cast includes David Carradine, Lau Kar-fai and Sonny Chiba, while star Una Thurman is clad in a variation on *Game of Death*'s famous jumpsuit. Lau's character in named 'Bai Mei', but whether this is more than fantasy name-dropping remains to be seen.

14   I am thinking especially of fantasy television shows like *Xena – Warrior Princess* (1995–2000) and *Buffy the Vampire Slayer* (1996–). In *Xena*, particularly, the campy tone seemed to licence over-the-top wire-aided stunts. For a discussion of *Buffy*'s debt to East Asian action cinema see West 2001.

15   A pan-Asian cinema that fits this description has existed for a while, but had not until recently extended beyond South-East Asia.

16   In British cinemas, at least, the wire-and-CGI-aided scenes of flight seemed to inspire giggles as well as gasps, another way in which the film could be both enjoyed and marginalised. The 'exoticising' of *Crouching Tiger* can be partly attributed to what Fore calls "semiotic rupture" (1997a: 134), one of the casualties of cultural translation. According to Ang Lee, "the film is a kind of dream of China, a China that probably never existed, except in my boyhood fantasies in Taiwan" (Lee and Schamus 2000: 7).

Chapter Eight

1   Steven Poole suggests that fighting computer games update the medieval sublimation of combat into play-form – "fighting is performed on the player's behalf by a digital 'substitute'" (2000: 175–6).

2   The *animé* look has been evident in the *Street Fighter Alpha* series (Capcom 1995–), which has retained a 'flat' 2D look – only *Street Fighter*'s *Ex* series (1996–) has used the 3D polygon-based look of *Virtua Fighter* (Sega) and *Tekken*. The *Dead or Alive* series reproduces the sexual politics of certain forms of *animé*, with its school uniforms, knicker-flashing female fighters and an inbuilt 'breast engine' to regulate pneumatic bouncing. The American PlayStation 2 version of *Dead or Alive 2* pointedly raised the ages of Kasumi, Ayane and Lei Fang in the game's accompanying booklet.

3   Motion-capture refers to the technique of placing computerised sensors on the bodies of human performers, whose movements can be incorporated into digital characters. Poole's suspicion of the purely mimetic recalls an earlier debate surrounding animation.

4   One of the *Street Fighter* games 'adapted' the live-action film. The *animé* look of the Alpha series of games came *after* the first animated film.

5   For more on the game-film interface, see King and Krzywinska 2002.

6   Most beat-em-ups have at least one wrestler – the masked *luchador* Kings in *Tekken*, father-daughter Bass and Tina in the *Dead or Alive* series. Wrestling moves defy, or reinvent, gravity almost as much as kung fu films do, albeit within 'real' space. Fighting arenas are sometimes based on rings or octagons, while *Dead or Alive*'s exploding walls recall the C4-charged ring posts of Japanese 'garbage' wrestling. Wrestling has, of course, generated its own games, remediating stars like The Rock, Triple H and The Undertaker.

7   Fighting games' backstories largely establish characters' motivations. While it is true, at one level, that "characters play a minimal role, displaying traits that are largely capacities for action" (Fuller and Jenkins 1993: 61), that is not to say that narrative and character are unimportant, as indicated by games-related fan fiction. *Street Fighter*, *Mortal Kombat* and *Tekken* have all generated fan fiction, filling in the 'unrecorded existence' of favourite characters (Ryu, Jin Kazama) and narrative gaps left in between games. When *Tekken 3* announces that Jin Kazama is the son of Jun Kazama and Kazuya Mishima (mortal enemies in *Tekken 2*), it seems to positively invite fans to 'write' the story (see, for, example, 'The Ultimate Tekken Fanfiction Archive').

8   Something very interesting is going on around 'aura' and 'presence' when stills of that backflip are reproduced (as they often are) as images of 'Bruce Lee'.

9   The *Tekken* series has stayed with the evolving PlayStation consoles, while *Dead or Alive* has moved across platforms, seemingly in search of the most powerful (or successful) one; *Dead or Alive 2* was ported from Sega's Dreamcast to the PS2. *Dead or Alive 3* (2002) appeared on Microsoft's X-Box; while visually stunning, it is not a significantly different game. But given that *Dead or Alive*'s next incarnation is to be a bikini-clad volleyball game, the game's developers clearly have no qualms about its eye-candy allure.

10 Fuller and Jenkins note the intriguing paradox of spatial spectacle in a gaming genre that does not, strictly speaking, need more than "the most rudimentary spaces" (1993: 62). However, in a gaming genre which ostensibly offers little variation, elaborate *mise-en-scène* is an important form of product differentiation.

11 In *The Phantom Menace*, too, the 'real' *wu shu* skills of Ray Park (as Darth Maul) overshadowed much of the film's digital wizardry.

Postscript

1   The 'grey' market refers to the semi-legal status of re-copied videos of deleted titles or tapes not officially released in the territory they circulate in. Fuzzy videos, re-copied more times than the cursed tape in *Ring/Ringu* (1998), have been *the* prevalent format for cult cinema in contemporary film culture, as kung fu, horror, *animé* and porn fans will attest. DVD is slowly changing that.

2   I do not want to underestimate the role here of the Hong Kong Film Archive in preserving prints of films and making them available for screening, but research trips to Hong Kong (especially for multiple screenings) are more prohibitively expensive than access to Region 3 DVDs.

Filmography

The Accidental Spy/Te Wu Mi Cheng (Benny Chan, HK 2001)
Ah Kam/A Jin (Ann Hui, HK 1996)
Angry River/Gun Nu Chuan (Huang Feng, HK 1970)
Armour of God/Longxiong Hudi (Jackie Chan, HK 1986)
Ashes of Time/Dongxie Xida (Wong Kar-wai, HK 1994)
The Avenging Fist/Kuen Sun (Andrew Lau and Corey Yuen, HK 2001)
Battlecreek Brawl (Robert Clouse, HK/US 1980)
The Big Boss/Tang Shan Daxiong (Lo Wei, HK 1971)
Billy Jack (Tom Laughlin, US 1971)
The Black Dragon Revenges the Death of Bruce Lee (Tommy Loo-chung, HK 1975)
Black Mask/Hak Hap (Daniel Lee, HK 1996)
Blade (Stephen Norrington, US 1998)
The Blade/Dao (Tsui Hark, HK 1995)
Blade 2 (Guillermo del Toro, US 2002)
Blade Runner (Ridley Scott, US 1982)
Blood Brothers/Ci Ma (Zhang Che, HK 1972)
Blood Money/The Stranger and the Gunfighter (Antonio Margheriti, aka 'Anthony M. Dawson', Italy/Spain/HK 1974)
Bloodsport (Mark DiSalle, US 1987)
Bodyguard From Beijing/Zhong Nan Hai Ba Biao (Corey Yuen, HK 1994)
Born to Defence/Zhong Hua Ying Xiong (Jet Li and Tsui Siu-ming, HK/China 1986)
Boxer From Shantung/Ma Yongzhen (Zhang Che and Bao Xueli, HK 1971)
Breakfast at Tiffany's (Blake Edwards, US 1961)
The Bride with White Hair/Jianghu (Ronny Yu, HK 1993)
Broken Blossoms (D.W. Griffith, US 1919)
Brotherhood of the Wolf/Le Pacte des Loups (Christophe Gans, France 2001)
Bruce Lee: A Warrior's Journey (John Little, US 2001)
Bruce Lee: The Man, The Myth/Li Xiaolong Chuanqi (Ng See-yuen, HK 1976)
Bruce Lee Against Supermen (Chia Chun, HK 1975)
Bruce Lee and I/Bruce Lee: His Last Days, His Last Nights (Lo Mar, HK 1976)
Bruce's Fingers (Joseph Kong, HK 1976)
The Buddhist Fist/Fozhang Luohan Quan (Yuen Wo-ping and Tsui Siu-ming, HK 1980)
Buffy the Vampire Slayer (TV series, US, Warner Brothers/UPN 1996–)
Bullet Proof Monk (Paul Hunter, US 2003)
Burning Paradise/Huoshao Honglian Si (Ringo Lam, HK 1993)
The Butterfly Murders/Die Bian (Tsui Hark, HK 1979)
The Cannonball Run (Hal Needham, US/HK 1981)
The Cannonvall Run II (Hal Needham, US/HK 1983)
Centre Stage/Ruan Lingyu (Stanley Kwan, HK 1991)
Challenge of the Masters/Lu Acai yu Huang Feihong (Lau Kar-leung, HK 1976)
Charlie's Angels (McG, US/Germany 2000)
Chinatown Kid/Tangren Jie Xiaozi (Zhang Che, HK 1977)
The Chinese Boxer/Longhu Dou (Wang Yu, HK 1970)
Chinese Ghost Story/Qiannu Youhun (Ching Siu-tung, HK 1987)
The Chinese Stuntman/Long De Ying Zi (Ho Chung-tao, HK 1980)
Chungking Express/Chongqing Senlin (Wong Kar-Wai, HK 1994)
Cinema of Vengeance: Martial Arts and the Movies (Toby Russell, UK/US 1993)
City Hunter/Chengshi Liren (Wong Jing, HK 1993)
The Clones of Bruce Lee/Shen-wei San Meng-lung (Joseph Kong, HK 1977)
Come Drink With Me/Da Zui Xia (King Hu, HK 1966)
Comrades: Almost a Love Story/Tian Mimi (Peter Chan, HK 1996)
Cradle 2 the Grave (Andrzej Bartkowiak, US 2003)

Crippled Avengers/Can Que (Zhang Che, HK 1978)
Critique of Game of Death (Kip Fulbeck, US 1991)
Crouching Tiger, Hidden Dragon/Wo Hu Zang Long (Ang Lee, China/Taiwan/US/HK 2000)
The Crow (Alex Proyas, US 1993)
Dance of the Drunk Mantis/Nanbei Zui Quan (Yuen Wo-ping, HK 1979)
The Dead and the Deadly/Ren Xia Ren (Wu Ma, HK 1982)
The Deaf and Mute Heroine/Longya Jian (Wu Ma, HK 1971)
Death By Misadventure (Toby Russell, UK/US 1995)
Dirty Ho/Lantou He (Lau Kar-leung, HK 1979)
Disciples of Shaolin/Hongquan Xiaozi (Zhang Che, HK 1975)
Double Team (Tsui Hark, US 1997)
Dr Wai in 'The Scripture with No Words'/Maoxian Wang (Ching Siu-tung, HK 1996)
Dragon: The Bruce Lee Story (Rob Cohen, US 1993)
The Dragon Dies Hard/Chin Se Tai Yang (Lee Koon-cheung, HK 1974)
Dragon Fight/Long Zai Tian Ya (Billy Tang, HK 1989)
Dragon Gate Inn/Long Men Kezhan (King Hu, HK 1967)
The Dragon Lives/Yang Chun Da Xiong (Wang Hsing-lei, HK 1976)
Dragon Lord/Long Shaoye (Jackie Chan, HK 1982)
Dragon Swamp/Du Long Tan (Lo Wei, HK 1969)
Dragons Forever/Feilong Mengjiang (Sammo Hung, HK 1988)
Dreadnaught/Yongzhe Wuju (Yuen Wo-ping, HK 1980)
Drunken Master/Zui Quan (Yuen Wo-ping, HK 1978)
Drunken Master 2/Zui Quan 2 (Lau Kar-leung, HK 1994)
Drunken Tai Chi/Xiao Taiji (Yuen Wo-ping, HK 1984)
Duel of Fists/Quan Ji (Zhang Che, HK 1971)
Dynamo/Bu Ze Shou Duan (Hwa Yi-hung, HK 1979)
The East is Red/Dongfang Bubai Fengyun Zaiqi (Ching Siu-tung and Raymond Lee, HK 1993)
Eastern Condors/Dongfang Tuying (Sammo Hung, HK 1986)
Eight Diagram Pole Fighter/Invincible Pole Fighters/Wulang Bagua Gun (Lau Kar-leung, HK 1983)
Eighteen Bronze Men (Joseph Kuo, HK 1976)
Encounters of the Spooky Kind/Gui Da Gui (Sammo Hung, HK 1980)
Enter the Dragon (Robert Clouse, HK/US 1973)
Enter the Fat Dragon/Feilong Guojiang (Sammo Hung, HK 1978)
Executioners/Heroic Trio II/Xiandai Haoxia Zhuan (Johnny To and Ching Siu-tung, HK 1993)
Executioners From Shaolin/Hong Xiguan (Lau Kar-leung, HK 1976)
Exit the Dragon, Enter the Tiger (Lee Tse Nam, HK 1976)
Fallen Angels/Duoluo Tianshi (Wong Kar-wai, HK 1995)
The Fate of Lee Khan/Yingchun Ge zhi Fengbo (King Hu, HK 1974)
The Fearless Hyena/Xiao Quan Guaizhao (Jackie Chan, HK 1979)
Final Fantasy: The Spirits Within (Hironobu Sakaguchi, US/Japan 2001)
Fist of Fury/Jingwu Mun (Lo Wei, HK 1972)
Fist of Fury 2/Jie Quan Zhao Gong (Jimmy Shaw, HK 1976)
Fist of Legend/Jingwu Yingxiong (Gordon Chan, HK 1994)
Fist of the North Star/Hokuto No Ken (TV series Japan, Toei Animation 1984-8)
Fist of the White Lotus/Hong Wending Sanpo Bailian Jiao (Lo Lieh, HK 1980)
Five Shaolin Masters/Shaolin Wuzu (Zhang Che, HK 1974)
Fong Sai-yuk/Fang Shiyu (Corey Yuen, HK 1993)
Fong Sai-yuk II/Fang Shiyu II (Corey Yuen, HK 1993)
Fong Sai-yuk's Battle in the Boxing Ring (Hong Zhao-hao, HK 1938)
For a Few Dollars More (Sergio Leone, Italy/Spain/West Germany 1965)
Future Cops/Chao Ji Xue Xiao Ba Wang (Wong Jing, HK 1994)
Game of Death/Siwang Youzi (Bruce Lee, HK 1972, incomplete; Robert Clouse, HK 1978)
Games Gamblers Play/Guima Shuangxing (Michael Hui, HK 1974)
Ghost in the Shell/Kokaku Kidato (Mamoru Oshii, Japan 1995)
Golden Swallow/Girl With the Thunderbolt Fist/Jin Yanzi (Zhang Che, HK 1969)
The Good, the Bad and the Loser/Yi Zhi Guanggun Zou Tianyia (Karl Maka, HK 1976)
Goodbye Bruce Lee: His Last Game of Death/The Legend of Bruce Lee/New Game of Death (Lin Pang, HK 1974)

Gorgeous/Bor Lei Jun (Vincent Kok, HK 1999)
The Green Hornet (TV series, US, ABC/20th Century Fox 1966)
Hapkido/He Qi Dao (Huang Feng, HK 1972)
Have Sword, Will Travel/Baobiao (Zhang Che, HK 1969)
Hero/Ying Xiong (Zhang Yimou, China/US/HK 2002)
Heroes Two/Fang Shiyu yu Hong Xiguan (Zhang Che, HK 1974)
Heroic Trio/Donfang San Xia (Johnny To and Ching Siu-tung, HK 1993)
High Risk/Shu Dan Long Wei (Wong Jing, HK 1995)
Highbinders (Gordon Chan, HK 2002)
Highlander: Endgame (Douglas Aarniokoski, US 2000)
Hitman/Sha Shou Zhi Wang (Tung Wai, HK 1998)
House of 72 Tenants/Qishi'er Jia Fangke (Chor Yuen, HK 1973)
I Love Kung Fu (TV, UK, BBC 2001)
Invincible Armour/Ying Zhao Tie Bushan (Ng See-yuen, HK 1977)
Invincible Shaolin/Shaolin yu Wudang (Zhang Che, HK 1980)
The Iron-Fisted Monk/Sande Heshang yu Zhuangmi Liu (Sammo Hung, HK 1977)
Iron Monkey/Shaonian Huang Feihong zhi Tie Houzi (Yuen Wo-ping, HK 1993)
Jackie Chan: My Stunts (Jackie Chan, HK 1999)
Irma Vep (Olivier Assayas, France 1996)
Kickboxer (Mark DiSalle, US 1989)
Kids from Shaolin/Shaolin Xiao Zi (Zhang Xinyun, HK/China 1984)
The Killer/Da Sha Shiu (Corey Yuen, HK 1971)
King Boxer/Five Fingers of Death/Tianxia Diyi Quan (Cheng Chang-ho, HK 1972)
Kiss of the Dragon/Le Baiser Mortel de Dragon (Chris Nahon, France/US 2001)
Kung Fu (TV series, US, Warner Brothers 1972-5)
Kung Fu Cult Master/The Evil Cult/Yitian Tulong Ji zhi Mojiao Jiaozhi (Wong Jing, HK 1993)
Knock Off (Tsui Hark, US/HK 1999)
Knockabout/Zaijia Xiaozi (Sammo Hung, HK 1979)
The Lady is the Boss/Zhangmen Ren (Lau Kar-leung, HK 1983)
Lady Whirlwind/Tiezhang Xuanfeng (Huang Feng, HK 1972)
The Last Action Hero (John McTiernan, US 1993)
The Last Hero in China/Huang Feihong Tieji Dou Wu Song (Wong Jing, HK 1993)
Legend of a Fighter/Huo Yuanjia (Yuen Wo-ping, HK 1981)
The Legend of the Seven Golden Vampires (Roy Ward Baker, UK/HK 1974)
Legendary Weapons of China/Shiba Ban Wuyi (Lau Kar-leung, HK 1982)
Leon (Luc Besson, France/US 1994)
Lethal Weapon 4 (Richard Donner, US 1998)
Longstreet (TV series, US, ABC/Paramount 1972)
Mad Monkey Kung Fu/Feng Hou (Lau Kar-leung, HK 1979)
The Magnificent Butcher/Lin Shirong (Yuen Wo-ping, HK 1980)
The Magnificent Trio/Biancheng Sanxia (Zhang Che, HK 1966)
The Man From Hong Kong (Brian Trenchard-Smith, HK/Australia 1975)
The Man Who Shot Liberty Valance (John Ford, US 1962)
Marlowe (Paul Bogart, US 1969)
Martial Arts of Shaolin/Nan Bei Shaolin (Lau Kar-leung, HK/China 1986)
The Martial Club/Wu Guan (Lau Kar-leung, HK 1981)
Martial Law (TV series, US, CBS 1998-2000)
The Master/Huang Feihong 92 zhi Long Xing Tianxia (Tsui Hark, HK 1989)
The Matrix (Wachowski Brothers, US 1999)
The Matrix Reloaded (Wachowski Brothers, US 2003)
The Matrix Revolutions (Wachowski Brothers, US 2003)
A Meditation on Violence (Maya Deren, US 1948)
The Men From the Monastery/Shaolin Zidi (Zhang Che, HK 1974)
Miracle Fighters/Qimen Dunjia (Yuen Wo-ping, HK 1982)
Miracles/Mr Canton and Lady Rose/Qi Ji (Jackie Chan, HK 1989)
Mission: Impossible 2 (John Woo, US 2000)
Mr Vampire/Jiangshi Xiansheng (Ricky Lau, HK 1985)
Mortal Kombat (Paul Anderson, US 1995)
The Mummy (Stephen Sommers, US 1999)

My Father is a Hero/Gei Ba Ba De Shen (Corey Yuen, HK 1995)
My Young Auntie/Zhang Bei (Lau Kar-leung, HK 1981)
New Dragon Gate Inn/Xin Longmen Kezhan (Raymond Lee, HK 1992)
New Fist of Fury/Xin Jingwu Mun (Lo Wei, HK 1976)
New Legend of Shaolin/Hong Xiguan (Wong Jing, HK 1994)
New One-Armed Swordsman/Xin Dubi Dao (Zhang Che, HK 1970)
No Retreat, No Surrender (Corey Yuen, US/HK 1986)
Odd Couple/Duoming Dandao Duoming Qiang (Lau Kar-wing, HK 1979)
On Her Majesty's Secret Service (Peter Hunt, UK 1969)
Once Upon a Time in China/Huang Feihong (Tsui Hark, HK 1991)
Once Upon a Time in China 2/Huang Feihong II zhi Nan'er Dang Ziqiang (Tsui Hark, HK 1992)
Once Upon a Time in China 3/Huang Feihong III zhi San: Shiwang Zheng Ba (Tsui Hark, HK 1993)
Once Upon a Time in China and America/Huang Feihong zhi Xigu Hongshi (Sammo Hung, HK 1997)
Once Upon a Time in the West (Sergio Leone, Italy/US 1969)
The One (James Wong, US 2001)
The One-Armed Boxer/Dubi Quanwang (Wang Yu, HK 1971).
The One-Armed Swordsman/Dubi Dao (Zhang Che, HK 1967)
Operation Condor/Feiying Jihua (Jackie Chan, HK 1991)
Pedicab Driver/Qunlong Xifeng (Sammo Hung, HK 1990)
Peking Opera Blues/Dao Ma Dan (Tsui Hark, HK 1986)
Planet of the Apes (Franklin Schaffner, US 1968)
Police Story/Jingcha Gushi (Jackie Chan, HK 1985)
Police Story 2/Jingcha Gushi Xuji (Jackie Chan, HK 1988)
Police Story 3/Supercop/Chaoji Jingcha (Stanley Tong, KK 1992)
Private Eyes/Babjin Baliang (Michael Hui, HK 1976)
Prodigal Son/Baijia Zai (Sammo Hung, HK 1981)
Project A/A Jihua (Jackie Chan, HK 1983)
The Protector (James Glickenhaus, US/HK 1985)
Queen's Ransom/Etan Qinying Hui (Huang Feng, HK 1976)
Righting Wrongs/Zhi Fa Xian Feng (Corey Yuen, HK 1986)
Romeo Must Die (Andrzej Bartkowiak, US 2000)
Rouge/Yanzhi Kou (Stanley Kwan, HK 1991)
Rumble in the Bronx/Hongfan Qu (Stanley Tong, HK 1995)
Rush Hour (Brett Ratner, US 1998)
Rush Hour 2 (Brett Ratner, US 2001)
The Searchers (John Ford, US 1956)
The Secret of Bruce Lee/Zhong Yuan Biao Ju (Wu Chun-man, HK 1976)
Secret Rivals/Nan Quan Bei Tui (Ng See-yuen, HK 1976)
Shanghai Express/Fugui Lieche (Sammo Hung, HK 1986)
Shanghai Knights (David Dobkin, US 2003)
Shanghai Noon (Tom Dey, US 2000)
Shaolin Art of War (Video Documentary, 1998)
Shaolin Avengers/Invincible Kung Fu Brothers/Fang Shiyu yu Hu Huiqian (Zhang Che, HK 1976)
Shaolin Challenges Ninja/Zhonghua Zhangfu (Lau Kar-leung, HK 1978)
Shaolin Martial Arts/Hong Quan yu Yong Chun (Zhang Che, HK 1974)
Shaolin Temple/Shaolin Si (Zhang Che, HK 1976)
Shaolin Temple/Siu Lam Si (Zhang Xinyan, HK/China 1982)
Shaolin Wooden Men/Shaolin Muren Xiang (Chen Chi-hwa, HK 1976)
Shatter (Michael Carreras, UK/HK 1974)
Showdown at Cotton Mill/Hu Hui Gan Xie Zhan Xi Chan Si (Wu Ma, HK 1978)
The Skyhawk/Huang Feihong Shaolin Quan (Cheng Chang-ho, HK 1974)
Snake in the Eagle's Shadow/Shexing Diaoshou (Yuen Wo-ping, HK 1978)
Snuff Bottle Connection/Shen Tui Tie Shan Gong (Lui Le-le and Tung Kan-wu, HK 1977)
Star Wars Episode 1: The Phantom Menace (George Lucas, US 1999)
Stoner/Tie Jin Gang Da Po Zi Yang Guan (Huang Feng, HK 1974)
The Street Fighter/Gekitotsu! Satsujin Ken (Sakae Ozawa, Japan 1974)
Street Fighter: The Movie (Steven E. De Souza, US 1994)
Street Fighter Alpha: The Animation (Shigeyasu Yamauchi, Japan 1999)

Street Fighter 2 (Gisaburo Sugii, Japan 1994)

Swordsman II/Xiao'ao Jianghu II Dongfai Bubai (Ching Siu-tung, HK 1991)

Tai Chi Master/Taiji Zhang Sanfeng (Yuen Wo-ping, HK 1993)

Terminator 2: Judgement Day (James Cameron, US 1991)

The 36ʰ Chamber of Shaolin/Shaolin Sanshiliu Fang (Lau Kar-leung, HK 1978)

Three Styles of Hung School's Kung Fu (A Demonstration Film of the Chinese Kung Fu (Zhang Che and Lau Kar-leung, HK 1974)

Thunderbolt/Pili Huo (Gordon Chan, HK 1995)

A Touch of Zen/Xia Nu (King Hu, HK/Taiwan 1971)

Tower of Death/Game of Death 2/Siwang Ta (Ng See-yuen, HK 1979)

The Transporter (Corey Yuen, US/Fr 2002)

The True Story of Wong Fei-hung: Whiplash Snuffs the Candle Flame/Huang Feihong Zhuan: Bianfeng Mie Zhu (Hu Peng, HK 1949)

The Tuxedo (Kevin Donovan, US 2002)

Twinkle Twinkle Lucky Stars/Xiari Fuxing (Sammo Hung, HK 1985)

2001: A Space Odyssey (Stanley Kubrick, UK 1968)

Under the Sun: Kung Fu Business (TV Documentary, UK, BBC 1999)

Universal Soldier (Roland Emmerich, US 1992)

Warriors Two/Zan Xiansheng yu Zhaoqian Hua (Sammo Hung, HK 1978)

Way of the Dragon/Meng Long Guo Jiang (Bruce Lee, HK 1972)

Wheels on Meals/Kuaican Che (Sammo Hung, HK 1984)

When Taekwondo Strikes/Taiquan Zhen Jiu Zhou (Huang Feng, HK 1973)

Wing Chin/Yong Chun (Yuen Wo-ping, HK 1993)

Winners and Sinners/Qimou Miaoji Wu Fuxing (Sammo Hung, HK 1983)

X-Men (Bryan Singer, US 2000)

Xena – Warrior Princess (TV series, US, Renaissance/Universal 1995-2000)

Yang + Yin: Gender in Chinese Cinema (Stanley Kwan, HK/UK 1996)

Year of the Dragon (Michael Cimino, US 1985)

Yes, Madam/Police Assassins/Huang Gu Shi Jie (Corey Yuen, HK 1985)

The Young Avenger/Xie Fu Men (Yueh Fung, HK 1970)

The Young Master/Shidi Chu Ma (Jackie Chan, HK 1980)

Zatoichi and the One-Armed Swordsman/Dubi Dao Dazhan Mang Xia (Kimiyoshi Yasuda, HK/Japan 1973).

Zu: Warriors of the Magic Mountain/Xin Shu Shan Jianxia (Tsui Hark, HK 1983)

Bibliography

Abbas, Ackbar (1994) 'The New Hong Kong Cinema and the *Deja Disparu*', *Discourse*, 16, 3: 65–77.
_____ (1996) 'Cultural Studies in a Postculture', in Cary Nelson and Dilip Parameshwar Gaonkar (eds) *Disciplinarity and Dissent in Cultural Studies*. London and New York: Routledge.
_____ (1997) *Hong Kong: Culture and the Politics of Disappearance*. Minneapolis: University of Minnesota Press.
Allen, Frank (2001) 'The Line and the Circle: Comparing the Fighting Arts of Hsing-i vs. Bagua', *Kung Fu/Qigong*, December: 36–8.
Altman, Rick (ed.) (1981) *Genre: The Musical*. London and Boston: BFI/Routledge.
Amazon.com (2000) 'Customer Reviews: *Fist of Legend*', http://www.amazon.com/exec/obidos/ts/dvd...8NS/ref=pm_dp_ln_v_6/1-2-3499426-3434568.
Anderson, Aaron (1998) 'Kinesthesia in Martial Arts Films: Action in Motion', *Jump Cut*, 42: 1–11, 83.
_____ (2002) 'Violent Dances in Martial Arts Films', *Jump Cut* (online version) http://ejumpcut.org/aarona/andersontextonly.html.
Anon. (1973) 'Chinese Chequers', *Films and Filming*, 20, 1: 26–9.
Anon. (1980) *Jacky Chan: The Martial Artist*. Hong Kong: Kung Fu Supplies Company.
Anon. (1980) *Bruce Lee and Jacky Chan – Great Dragons from Hong Kong*. Hong Kong: Great Dragon.
Anon. (1980) *Bruce Lee and Jacky Chan – Kung Fu Superstars*. Hong Kong: Great Dragon.
Anon. (1982) *The Shaolin Temple – The Origin of Chinese Kung-fu*. Hong Kong: Lee Yuen Subscription Agencies.
Ashcroft, Bill, Gareth Griffiths and Helen Tiffin (eds) (1995) *The Post-Colonial Studies Reader*. London and New York: Routledge.
Baker, Rick (1994) 'A Prodigal Son and a Warrior Too', *Eastern Heroes Special Edition*, 3: 8–12.
_____ (1996) 'The Kung Fu Film is Back', *Eastern Heroes Special Edition* 5: 20-3.
Baker, Rick and Toby Russell (1994) *The Essential Guide to Hong Kong Movies*. London: Eastern Heroes.
_____ (1995) *The Essential Guide to The Best of Eastern Heroes*. London: Eastern Heroes.
_____ (1996) *The Essential Guide to Deadly China Dolls*. London: Eastern Heroes.
Bakhtin, Mikhail (1965/1984) *Rabelais and his World*. Bloomington: Indiana University Press.
Balsamo, Anne (1995) 'Forms of Technological Embodiment: Reading the Body in Contemporary Culture', in Mike Featherstone and Roger Burrows (eds) *Cyberspace/Cyberbodies/Cyberpunk*. London: Sage, 215–37.
Bataille, Georges (1989) *Visions of Excess: Selected Writings 1927–1939*. Minneapolis: University of Minnesota Press.
Beale, Chris and Ben Simons (2000) 'Retroflex Column: It's Only a Game Son!', *Screen Power*, 3, 1: 18–20.
Benjamin, Walter (1935/1979) 'The Work of Art in the Age of Mechanical Reproduction', in Gerald Mast and Marshall Cohen (eds) *Film Theory and Criticism*. New York and Oxford: Oxford University Press, 848–70.
_____ (1979) *One-Way Street*. London: NLB.
Bernstein, Matthew and Gaylyn Studlarn (eds) (1997) *Visions of the East: Orientalism in Film*, London and New York: I.B. Taurus.
'Black Tauna' (2000) 'Zhang Che/Chang Cheh', http://www.shawstudios.com/changcheh/html.
Block, Alex Ben (1974) *The Legend of Bruce Lee*. Frogmore: Mayflower Books.
Bolter, Jay David and Richard Grusin (2000) *Remediation: Understanding New Media*. Cambridge Massachusetts and London: MIT Press.
Bordwell, David (1997) 'Aesthetics in Action: Kung-Fu, Gunplay and Cinematic Expressivity', in Law Kar (ed.) *Fifty Years of Electric Shadows*. Hong Kong: Hong Kong International Film Festival/Urban Council, 81–9.
_____ (2000a) *Planet Hong Kong: Popular Cinema and the Art of Entertainment*. Cambridge, Massachusetts and London: Harvard University Press.
_____ (2000b) 'Richness Through Imperfection: King Hu and the Glimpse', in David Desser and Poshek Fu (eds) *The Cinema of Hong Kong: History, Arts, Identity*. Cambridge, New York and Oakleigh, Melbourne: Cambridge University Press, 113–6.
Bren, Frank (1998) 'Fighting Woman: Cheng Pei-pei and King Hu Legacy', *Metro*, 113/114: 81–5.
Brennan, John (1994) 'The Man from Hong Kong', *Eastern Heroes Special Edition*, 1: 8–11.
_____ (1996) 'From *A Better Tomorrow* to *Zu: Warriors*: Tsui Hark, Hong Kong Movie Maker', *Eastern Heroes Special Edition*, 5: 50–9.
Brottman, Mikita (2000) 'Star Cults/Cult Stars: Cinema, Psychosis, Celebrity, Death', in Xavier Mendik and Graeme Harper (eds) *Unruly Pleasures: The Cult Film and its Critics*. Guildford: FAB Press, 103–19.
Burr, Martha (2000) 'Jet Li is Still the Hero', *Kung Fu Qigong*, 4: 30–7, 40–1, 121–2.

____ (2001) 'The Big Jet Li Interview', *Kung Fu Qigong*, December: 16–29.

Chan, Jackie and Jeff Yang (1998) *I am Jackie Chan: My Life in Action*. New York: Ballantine Books.

Chan Ting-ching (1980) 'The "Knockabout" Comic Kung-fu Films of Samo Hung', in Lau Shing-hon (ed.) *A Study of the Hong Kong Martial Arts Film*. Hong Kong: HKIFF/Urban Council, 149–50.

Chateau, Rene (1976) *Bruce Lee: La Legende du Petit Dragon*. Paris: Editions René Chateau.

Cheng Yu (1984) 'Anatomy of a Legend', in Li Cheuk-to (ed.) *A Study of Hong Kong Cinema in the Seventies*. Hong Kong: Hong Kong International Film Festival/Urban Council, 23-5.

Cheung, King-kok (1990) 'The Woman Warrior versus The Chinaman Pacific', in Marianne Hirsch and Evelyn Fox Keller (eds) *Conflicts in Feminism*. London and New York: Routledge, 234–51.

Chiao Hsiung-ping (1981) 'Bruce Lee: His Influence on the Evolution of the Kung Fu Genre', *Journal of Popular Film and Television*, 9, 1: 30–42.

Chow, David and Richard Spangler (1982) *Kung Fu: History, Philosophy and Technique*. Burbank: Unique Publications.

Chu, Rolanda (1994) '*Swordsman II* and *The East is Red*: The 'Hong Kong Film', Entertainment and Gender', *Bright Lights*, 13: 30–5, 46.

Chu, Rolanda, Grant Foerster and Sek Kei (1994) 'A Brief Historical Tour of the HK Martial Arts Film', *Bright Lights*, 13: 26–9, 50.

Clarke, Jeremy (1999) 'Schismatrix', *Manga Max*, 8: 22–4.

Clouse, Robert (1987) *The Making of Enter the Dragon*. Burbank: Unique Publications.

Cornelius, Sheila with Ian Haydn Smith (2002) *New Chinese Cinema: Challenging Representation*. London: Wallflower Press.

Crafton, Donald (1995) 'Pie and Chase: Gag, Spectacle and Narrative in Slapstick Comedy', in Kristine Brunovska Karnick and Henry Jenkins (eds) *Classical Hollywood Comedy*. New York and London: Routledge, 106–19.

Creed, Barbara (1993) *The Monstrous-Feminine: Film, Feminism, Psychoanalysis*. London and New York: Routledge.

Croizier, Ralph C. (1972) 'Beyond East and West: The American Western and the Rise of the Chinese Swordplay Movie', *Journal of Popular Film*, 1, 3: 229–43.

Dancer, Greg (1998) 'Film Style and Performance: Comedy and Kung Fu from Hong Kong', *Asian Cinema*, 10, 1: 78–84.

Dannen, Fredric and Barry Long (1997) *Hong Kong Babylon: An Insider's Guide to the Hollywood of the East*. London: Faber and Faber.

Dargis, Manohla (2000) 'Ghost in the Machine', *Sight and Sound*, 10, 7: 20–3.

Davidson, Nick (1997a) '"The Real Game Begins ..." The Story Behind Bruce Lee's *Game of Death*', *Fists of Fury*, 1: 7–23.

____ (1997b) 'Dirty Ho?', *Fists of Fury*, 1: 32–9.

De Cordova, Richard (1995) 'Genre and Performance: An Overview', in Barry Keith Grant (ed.) *Film Genre Reader II*. Austin: University of Texas Press: 129–39.

Dennis, Felix and Don Atyeo (1974) *Bruce Lee: King of Kung Fu*. London: Wildwood House.

Desser, David (2000) 'The Kung Fu Craze: Hong Kong Cinema's First American Reception', in David Desser and Poshek Fu (eds) *The Cinema of Hong Kong: History, Arts, Identity*. Cambridge, New York and Oakleigh, Melbourne: Cambridge University Press, 19–43.

Desser, David and Poshek Fu (eds) (2000) *The Cinema of Hong Kong: History, Arts, Identity*. Cambridge, New York and Oakleigh, Melbourne: Cambridge University Press.

Dome, Malcolm (1994) 'Chang-Shaw Massacre', *Eastern Heroes Special Edition*, 2: 17–21.

Ducker, Chris and Stuart Cutler (2000) *The HKS Guide to Jet Li*. London: Hong Kong Superstars.

Editors of *Kung Fu Monthly*, Maydole, Chester (1976) *The Secret Art of Bruce Lee*. London: H. Bunch Associates.

Featherstone, Mike and Roger Burrows (eds) (1995) *Cyberspace/Cyberbodies/Cyberpunk*. London: Sage.

Felperin, Leslie (1995) 'Mortal Kombat', *Sight and Sound*, 5, 11: 47–8.

Feuer, Jane (1982) *The Hollywood Musical*. London: BFI/Macmillan.

Fischer, Dennis (1999) 'Matrix Martial Arts', *Cinéfantastique*, 31, 5: 26.

Fore, Steve (1994) 'Golden Harvest Films and the Hong Kong Movie Industry in the Realm of Globalization', *Velvet Light Trap*, 34: 40–58.

____ (1997a) 'Home, Migration, Identity: Hong Kong Workers Join the Chinese Diaspora', in Law Kar (ed.) *Fifty Years of Electric Shadows*. Hong Kong: Hong Kong International Film Festival/Urban Council, 130–5.

____ (1997b) 'Jackie Chan and the Cultural Dynamics of Global Entertainment', in Sheldon Hsiao-peng Lu (ed.) (1997) *Transnational Chinese Cinemas: Identity, Nationhood, Gender*. Honolulu: University of Hawaii Press, 239–62.

____ (2001) 'Life Imitates Entertainment: Home and Dislocation in the Films of Jackie Chan' in Esther Yau (ed.) *At Full Speed: Hong Kong Cinema in a Borderless World*. Minneapolis and London: University of Minnesota Press, 115–41.

Foster, Damon (1998) 'Shaolin Temple', *Oriental Cinema*, 14: 4–17.

____ (1999a) 'Jet Li', *Oriental Cinema*, 16: 2–25.

____ (1999b) 'Sammo Hung', *Oriental Cinema*, 17: 2–24.

____ (2000) 'Wang Yu', *Oriental Cinema*, 19, 5–25.

Freud, Sigmund (1919/1985) 'The Uncanny' in *Art and Literature*. Harmondworth: Penguin, 339–76.

Fuller, Mary and Henry Jenkins (1995) 'Nintendo and New World Travel Writing: A Dialogue', in Steven G. Jones (ed.) *Cybersociety: Computer-Mediated Communication and Community*. London: Sage, 57–72.

Frayling, Christopher (1981) *Spaghetti Westerns*. London: Routledge and Kegan Paul.

Friedman, Ted (1995) 'Making Sense of Software: Computer Games and Interactive Textuality', in Jones, Steven G. (ed.) *Cybersociety: Computer-Mediated Communication and Community*. London: Sage, 73–89.

Gallagher, Mark (1997) 'Masculinity in Translation: Jackie Chan's Transcultural Star Text', *Velvet Light Trap*, 39: 23–41.

Garber, Marjorie (1992) *Vested Interests: Cross-Dressing and Cultural Anxiety*. London: Penguin.

Garcia, Roger (1980a) 'The Autarkic World of Liu Chia-liang', in Lau shing-hon (ed.) *A Study of the Hong Kong Martial Arts Film*. Hong Kong: HKIFF/Urban Council, 121–34.

____ (1980b) 'The Doxology of Yuen Woo-ping', in Lau Shing-hon (ed.) *A Study of the Hong Kong Martial Arts Film*. Hong Kong: HKIFF/Urban Council, 137–40.

____ (1994) 'Alive and Kicking: The Kung Fu Film is a Legend', *Bright Lights*, 13: 6–7, 48.

Gaul, Lou (1997) *The Fist That Shook the World: The Cinema of Bruce Lee*. Baltimore, Maryland: Midnight Marquee Press.

Giant Robot Staff (2002) 'Robot Reader', *Giant Robot*, 25: 22–5.

Glaessner, Verina (1974) *Kung Fu: Cinema of Vengeance*. London: Lorrimer.

Gunning, Tom (1990) 'The Cinema of Attractions: Early Film, its Spectator and the Avant Garde', in Thomas Elsaesser and Adam Barker (eds) *Early Film: Space, Frame, Narrative*. London: BFI, 56–62.

____ (1995a) 'Crazy Machines in the Garden of Forking Paths: Mischief Gags and The Origins of American Film Comedy', in Kristine Brunovska Karnick and Henry Jenkins (eds) *Classical Hollywood Comedy*. New York and London: Routledge, 87–105.

____ (1995b) 'Response to "Pie and Chase"' in Kristine Brunovska Karnick and Henry Jenkins (eds) *Classical Hollywood Comedy*. New York and London: Routledge, 120–2.

Haddon, Leslie (1993) 'Interactive Games', in Philip Hayward and Tana Wollen (eds) *Future Visions: New Technologies on the Screen*. London: BFI, 123–47.

Hall, Stuart (1991) 'The Local and the Global: Globalization and Ethnicity', in Anthony King (ed.) *Culture, Globalization and the World System*. London: Macmillan, 19–39.

Hamamoto, Darrell Y. (2000) 'Introduction: On Asian American Film and Criticism' in Darrell Y. Hamamoto and Sandra Liu (eds) *Countervisions: Asian American Film Criticism*. Philadelphia: Temple University Press, 1–19.

Hammond, Stefan (2000) *Hollywood East: Hong Kong Movies and the People Who Make Them*. Lincolnwood (Chicago), Illinois: Contemporary Books.

Hammond, Stefan and Mike Wilkins (1997) *Sex and Zen and a Bullet in the Head: The Essential Guide to Hong Kong's Mind-Bending Movies*. London: Titan.

Hampton, Howard (1996) 'Venus, Armed: Brigitte Lin's Shanghai Gesture', *Film Comment*, 32, 5: 42–8.

____ (1997) 'Once Upon a Time in Hong Kong: Tsui Hark and Ching Siu-tung', *Film Comment* 33, 4: 16–19, 24–7.

Harrison-Pepper, Sally (1993) 'The Martial Arts: Rites of Passage, Dramas of Persuasion' in Philip B. Zarrilli (ed.) *Asian Martial Arts in Actor Training*. Madison, Wisconsin: University of Wisconsin, 38–47.

Hayward, Philip and Tana Wollen (eds) *Future Visions: New Technologies on the Screen*. London: BFI.

Hill, Simon (1998) *Tekken 3 – Prima's Official Strategy Guide*. Rocklin, California: Prima.

Hong Kingston, Maxine (1977) *The Woman Warrior*. London: Picador.

Hong Kong Film Archive (1999) *The Making of Martial Arts Films – As Told by Film-makers and Stars*. Hong Kong: Provisional Urban Council.

Hucker, Charles O. (1978) *China to 1850: A Short History*. Stanford, California: Stanford University Press.

Hui Fai (ed.) (1976) *Bruce Lee: His Privacy and Anecdotes*. Hong Kong: Bruce Lee Jeet Kune Do Club.

____ (ed.) (1977) *Bruce Lee: Revenges ...* Hong Kong: Bruce Lee Jeet Kune Do Club.

____ (ed.) (1978a) *Bruce Lee: Combats ...* Hong Kong: Bruce Lee Jeet Kune Do Club.

____ (ed.) (1978b) *Bruce Lee in 'The Game of Death'*. Hong Kong: Bruce Lee Jeet Kune Do Club,

____ (ed.) (1978c) *Bruce Lee: The Fighting Spirit*. Hong Kong: Bruce Lee Jeet Kune Do Club.

____ (ed.) (1978d) *Bruce Lee: The Immortal Dragon*. Hong Kong: Bruce Lee Jeet Kune Do Club.

____ (ed.) (1978e) *Bruce Lee's Game of Death*. Hong Kong: Bruce Lee Jeet Kune Do Club.

____ (ed.) (1980) *Bruce Lee in 'The Big Boss'*. Hong Kong: Bruce Lee Jeet Kune Do Club.

____ (ed.) (1980) *Bruce Lee: Warrior From Shaolin*. Hong Kong: Bruce Lee Jeet Kune Do Club.

Hunt, Leon (1999), 'Once Upon a Time in China: Kung Fu from Bruce Lee to Jet Li', *Framework*, 40: 85–100.

____ (2000) 'Han's Island Revisited: *Enter the Dragon* as Transnational Cult Film', in Xavier Mendik and Graeme

Harper (eds) *Unruly Pleasures: The Cult Film and its Critics*. London: Fab Press: 73–85.

____ (2002) 'One-Armed and Extremely Dangerous: Wang Yu's Mutilated Masters', in Xavier Mendik (ed.) *Shocking Cinema of the Seventies*. London: Noir Publishing, 91–105.

____ (2002) 'Jackie Chan' in Yvonne Tasker (ed.) *Fifty Contemporary Film-makers*. London and New York: Routledge, 99–108.

Hunter, I.Q. (2000) '*The Legend of the 7 Golden Vampires*', *Postcolonial Studies*, 3, 1: 81–7.

____ (2002) 'Hammer Goes East: A Second Glance at *The Legend of the 7 Golden Vampires*', in Xavier Mendik (ed.) *Shocking Cinema of the 1970s*. London: Noir Publishing, 138–46.

Hwang, Ange (1998) 'The Irresistible: Hong Kong Movie *Once Upon a Time in China* Series – An Extensive Interview with Director/Producer Tsui Hark', *Asian Cinema*, 10, 1: 10–23.

Internet Movie Database (2000) 'User Comments: *Romeo Must Die*', http://us.imdb.com/commentsShow?165929.

Jameson, Fredric and Masao Miyoshi (eds) (1998) *The Cultures of Globalization*. Durham, N.C.: Duke University Press.

Jarvie, I. C. (1977) *Windows on Hong Kong: A Sociological Survey of the Hong Kong Film Industry and its Audience*. Hong Kong: University of Hong Kong.

Johnston, Will and Andrew Staton (1998) *Bruce Lee: The Man and the Legend*. Huddersfield: M.A.I.

Jones, Steven G. (1995) *Cybersociety: Computer-Mediated Communication and Community*. London: Sage.

Joyce, John (2000) 'Alas, Poor Romeo: Will the Real Jet Li Please Take Flight', *Impact*, 102: 44–5.

Kael, Pauline (1984) *5001 Nights at the Movies*. London: Zenith.

Kaminsky, Stuart M. (1974) 'Kung Fu Film as Ghetto Myth', *Journal of Popular Film*, 3, 2: 129–138.

Karnick, Kristine Brunovska and Henry Jenkins (eds) (1995) *Classical Hollywood Comedy*, New York and London: Routledge.

Kemp, Philip (2000) 'Stealth and Duty', *Sight and Sound*, 10, 12: 12–15.

Kemp, Sandra (1996) 'Reading Difficulties', in Patrick Campbell (ed.) *Analysing Performance: A Critical Reader*. Manchester and New York: Manchester University Press, 153–74.

Kenny, Simon B. (2001) *The Pocket Essential Bruce Lee*. Harpenden: Pocket Essentials.

Khan, Nadeem (2000) 'Bruce Gets Animated', *Impact*, 97: 30–1.

Kinder, Marsha (1991) *Playing With Power in Movies, Television and Video Games: From Muppet Babies to Teenage Mutant Ninja Turtles*. Berkely, Los Angeles and Oxford: University of California Press.

King, Geoff (2000) *Spectacular Narratives: Hollywood in the Age of the Blockbuster*. London and New York: I.B. Taurus.

____ (2002) *Film Comedy*. London: Wallflower Press.

King, Geoff and Tanya Krzywinska (eds) (2002) *Screenplay: Cinema/Videogames/Interfaces*. London and New York: Wallflower Press.

King, Lucien (ed.) (2002) *Game On: The History and Culture of Videogames*. London: Laurence King.

Ko, Claudine (2001) '*Crouching Tiger*: Its the Best Kung Fu Movie Ever', *Giant Robot*, 20: 20–1.

Ko, S. N. (1988) 'Under Western Eyes', in Li Cheuk-to (ed.) *Changes in Hong Kong Society Through Cinema*. Hong Kong: Hong Kong International Film Festival/Urban Council, 64–7.

Koo Siu-fung (1981/1996) 'Philosophy and Tradition in the Swordplay Film', in Lau Shing-hon (ed.) *A Study of The Hong Kong Swordplay Film (1945–1980)*. Hong Kong: Hong Kong International Film Festival/Urban Council, 25–32.

Kramer, Peter (1995) 'The Making of a Comic Star: Buster Keaton and *The Saphead*', in Kristine Brunovska Karnick and Henry Jenkins (eds) *Classical Hollywood Comedy*. New York and London: Routledge, 190–210.

Kristeva, Julia (1982) *Powers of Horror: An Essay on Abjection*. New York: Columbia University Press.

Krzywinska, Tanya (1998) 'Dissidence and Authenticity in Dyke Porn and Actuality TV', in Mike Wayne (ed.) *Dissident Voices: The Politics of Television and Cultural Change*. London: Pluto Press, 159–75.

La Valley, Albert J. (1985) 'Traditions of Trickery: The Role of Special Effects in the Science Fiction Film', in George Slusser and Eric Rabkin (eds) *Shadows in the Magic Lamp: Fantasy and the Science Fiction Film*. Carbondale: Southern Illinois University Press, 141–58.

Lai, Linda Chiu-han (2001) 'Film and Enigmatization: Nostalgia, Nonsense, and Remembering', in Esther Yau (ed.) *At Full Speed: Hong Kong Cinema in a Borderless World*. Minneapolis and London: University of Minnesota Press, 231–50.

Landon, Brooks (1992) *The Aesthetics of Ambivalence: Rethinking Science Fiction in the Age of Electronic (Re)Production*. Westport, Connecticut and London: Greenwood Press.

Landsberg, Alison (1995) 'Prosthetic Memory: *Total Recall* and *Blade Runner*', in Mike Featherstone and Roger Burrows (eds) *Cyberspace/Cyberbodies/Cyberpunk*. London: Sage, 175–89.

Lau, Jenny (1998) 'Besides Fists and Blood: Hong Kong Comedy and its Master of the 1980s', *Cinema Journal*, 37, 2: 18–34.

Lau Shing-hon (ed.) (1980a) *A Study of the Hong Kong Martial Arts Film*. Hong Kong: Hong Kong International Film Festival/Urban Council.

Lau Shing-hon (1980b) 'The Tragic Romantic Trilogy of Chang Cheh', in Lau Shing-hon (ed.) *A Study of the Hong Kong Martial Arts Film*. Hong Kong: Hong Kong International Film Festival/Urban Council, 91–6.

____ (ed.) (1981/1996) *A Study of The Hong Kong Swordplay Film (1945–1980)*. Hong Kong: Hong Kong International Film Festival/Urban Council.

Lau Tai-muk (1999) 'Conflict and Desire – Dialogues Between the Hong Kong Martial Arts Genre and Social Issues in the Past 40 Years', in Hong Kong Film Archive, *The Making of Martial Arts Films – As Told by Filmmakers and Stars*. Hong Kong: Provisional Urban Council, 30–4.

Law Kar (ed.) (1997) *Fifty Years of Electric Shadows*. Hong Kong: Hong Kong International Film Festival/Urban Council.

Lee, Ang and Schamus, James (2000) *Crouching Tiger, Hidden Dragon: A Portrait of the Ang Lee Film*. London: Faber.

Lee, Bruce (1963) *Chinese Gung Fu: The Philosophical Art of Self-Defence*. California: Oriental Book Sales.

____ (1975) *Tao of Jeet Kune Do*. Burbank, California: Ohara Publications.

Lee, Leo Ou-Fan (1994) 'Two Films From Hong Kong: Parody and Allegory', in Nick Browne, Paul G. Pickowicz, Vivian Sobchack and Esther Yau (eds) *New Chinese Cinemas: Forms, Identities, Politics*. Cambridge, New York and Oakleigh, Melbourne: Cambridge University Press, 202–15.

Lee, Linda (1975) *The Life and Tragic Death of Bruce Lee*. London: Star Books.

Leeder, Mike (1995) 'Jackie Chan Pulling No Punches', *Eastern Heroes Special Edition*, 4: 10–14.

____ (1999) 'Out of the Vaults: Jackie Chan Pulling No Punches – Revisited', *Screen Power*, 2, 3: 23–9.

Leung, Grace L. K. and Joseph M. Chan (1997) 'The Hong Kong Cinema and its Overseas Market: A Historical Review 1950–1995', in Law Kar (ed.) *Fifty Years of Electric Shadows*. Hong Kong: Hong Kong International Film Festival/Urban Council, 143–9.

Li Cheuk-to (ed.) (1984) *A Study of Hong Kong Cinema in the Seventies*. Hong Kong: Hong Kong International Film Festival/Urban Council.

Li Siu-leung, 'Kung Fu: Negotiating Nationalism and Modernity', *Cultural Studies*, 15, 3/4: 515–42.

Li Tianji and Du Xilian (1998) *A Guide to Chinese Martial Arts*. London: McLaren.

Lii, Ding-Tzann (1998) 'A Colonised Empire: Reflections on the Expansion of Hong Kong Films in Asian Countries' in Kuan-Hsing Chen (ed.) *Trajectories: Inter-Asia Cultural Studies*. London and New York: Routledge, 122–41.

Lim, Ron (1999) 'The Martial Artist's Guide to Hong Kong Films', http://ronlim.com/martial1.html#anchor98800.

Lin Nien-ting (1981/1996) 'The Martial Arts Hero' in Lau Shing-hon (ed.) *A Study of The Hong Kong Swordplay Film (1945–1980)*. Hong Kong: Hong Kong International Film Festival/Urban Council, 11–16.

Little, John (ed.) (1998) *Bruce Lee: Letters of the Dragon*. Boston, Rutland, Vermont, and Tokyo: Charles E. Tuttle.

____ (2001) *Bruce Lee: A Warrior's Journey*. Chicago: Contemporary Books.

Little, John R. and Curtis Wong (2000) *Ultimate Martia Arts Encypedia: The Best of Inside Kung Fu*. Lincolnwood (Chicago), Illinois: Contemporary Books.

Liu Damu (1981/1996) 'From Chivalric Fiction to Martial Arts Film', in Lau Shing-hon (ed.) *A Study of The Hong Kong Swordplay Film (1945–1980)*. Hong Kong: Hong Kong International Film Festival/Urban Council, 47–62.

Liu, James J. Y. (1967) *The Chinese Knight Errant*. London: Routledge and Kegan Paul.

Liu, Jerry (1981/1996) 'Chang Cheh: Aesthetics = Ideology?', in Lau Shing-hon (ed.) *A Study of The Hong Kong Swordplay Film (1945–1980)*. Hong Kong: Hong Kong International Film Festival/Urban Council, 159-64.

Lo, Kwai-cheung (1993) '*Once Upon a Time*: Technology Comes to Presence in China', *Modern Chinese Literature*, 7: 79-96.

____ (1999) 'Muscles and Subjectivity: A Short History of the Masculine Body in Hong Kong Popular Culture', *Camera Obscura*, 39: 105–25.

____ (2001) 'Transnationalism of the Local in Hong Kong Cinema of the 1990s', in Esther Yau (ed.) (2001) *At Full Speed: Hong Kong Cinema in a Borderless World*. Minneapolis and London: University of Minnesota Press, 261–76.

Logan, Bey (1995) *Hong Kong Action Cinema*. London: Titan.

____ (1997) 'Aporkalypse Now: Samo Hung is *The Magnificent Butcher*', *Impact*, August: 32–4.

____ (1998a) 'Shaolin Temple of Doom: Ringo Lam Ignites ... *Burning Paradise*', *Impact*, July: 32–3.

____ (1998b) '*Enter the Dragon*: What Really Happened Begind the Scenes' and 'Bruce Lee: Kung Fu's Traditional Fighting Man', *Martial Arts Legends: Enter the Dragon 25th Anniversary Special Issue*: 18–32, 78–83.

____ (1998c) 'Casting Electric Shadows', *Impact*, 78: 22.

____ (1998d) 'Cut and Print', *Impact*, 84: 30–3.

____ (1999a) 'When *Hapkido* Strikes', *Impact*, 85: 26–9.

____ (1999b)) *Wong Fei Hung*, Hong Kong: Media Asia.

____ (1999c) 'Climbing the Tower: *Tower of Death* Part 1' *Impact*, 94: 34–5.

____ (1999d) 'Climbing the Tower: *Tower of Death* Part 2' *Impact*, 95: 34–5 (Pt 2).

____ (1999d) 'Fong Sai Yuk: Hong Kong's First Action Hero', *Impact*, 95: 30–2.
____ (2000a) 'George Lazenby's Far Eastern Odyssey Part 1', *Impact*, 97: 46–8.
____ (2000b) 'George Lazenby's Far Eastern Odyssey Part 2', *Impact*, 99: 36–7.
____ (2000c) 'Snake in the Mind's Eye', *Impact*, 98: 26–9.
____ (2000d) 'The Legend Behind *The Legend of a Fighter*', *Impact*, 101: 46–7.
____ (2000e) 'Once Were Warriors: The Power and Glory of *Crouching Tiger, Hidden Dragon*', *Impact*, 103: 42–5.
Lopez, Roberto (1998) 'Once Upon a Time in Texas', *Manga Max*, 1: 66–7.
Lu, Sheldon Hsiao-peng (ed.) (1997) *Transnational Chinese Cinemas: Identity, Nationhood, Gender*. Honolulu: University of Hawaii Press.
Lupton, Deborah (1995) 'The Embodied Computer/User' in Mike Featherstone and Roger Burrows (eds) *Cyberspace/Cyberbodies/Cyberpunk*. London: Sage, 97–112.
Mackerras, Colin (1975) *The Chinese Theatre in Modern Times: From 1840 to the Present Day*. London: Thames and Hudson.
____ (1997) *Peking Opera*. Oxford, New York and Hong Kong: Oxford University Press.
Major, Wade (2000) 'The Afterburner' in Stefan Hammond (ed.) *Hollywood East: Hong Kong Movies and the People Who Make Them*. Lincolnwood (Chicago), Illinois: Contemporary Books, 148–175.
Marchetti, Gina (1993) *Romance and the 'Yellow Peril': Race, Sex and Discursive Strategies in Hollywood Fiction*. Berkely, Los Angeles and London: University of California Press.
____ (1998) 'Chinese and Chinese Diaspora Cinema Introduction: Plural and Transnational', *Jump Cut*, 42: 68–72.
Marcus, Greil (1989) *Lipstick Traces: A Secret History of the Twentieth Century*. London: Secker and Warburg.
____ (1991) *Dead Elvis: A Chronicle of a Cultural Obsession*. Cambridge, Massachusetts and London: Harvard University Press.
Masinelli, Todd (2000) 'Jackie Chan Stuntmaster', *Screen Power*, 3, 1: 15–17.
Mercer, Chris (1996) 'Top of the 'Pops' Liu Chia Liang', *Eastern Heroes Special Edition*, 6: 54–9.
Meyers, Ric (1998) 'Ric and Infamous', *Asian Cult Cinema*, 20: 57–9.
____ (2000) 'It's *Shanghai Noon* for Jackie Chan', *Martial Arts Superstars: Special Issue*: 14–19, 85.
____ (2001) *Great Martial Arts Movies: From Bruce Lee to Jackie Chan and More*. New York: Citadel Press.
Miller, Davis (2000) *The Tao of Bruce Lee*. London: Vintage.
Mintz, Marilyn D. (1978) *The Martial Arts Film*. South Brunswick and New York: A.S. Barnes.
Morris, Meaghan (1998) 'Learning From Bruce Lee: Pedagogy and Political Correctness in Martial Arts Cinema', *Metro*, 117: 6–15.
Morrison, Alan and Ron Wells (2001) 'Year of the Dragon', *Total Film*, 49: 60–6.
Mortlock, Dean (ed.) (1998) *Playstation Game Strategies Number One – Tekken 3*. Bath: Future Publishing.
Morton, Lisa (2001) *The Cinema of Tsui Hark*. Jefferson, North Carolina, and London: McFarland.
Newman, Kim (1999) 'Rubber Bullets', *Sight and Sound*, 9, 6: 8–9.
Ng Ho (1980a) 'Kung Fu Comedies: Tradition, Structure, Character' in Lau Shing-hon (ed.) *A Study of The Hong Kong Swordplay Film (1945–1980)*. Hong Kong: Hong Kong International Film Festival/Urban Council, 42–46.
____ (1980b) 'When the Legends Die – A Survey of the Tradition of the Southern Shaolin Monastery' in Lau Shing-hon (ed.) *A Study of the Hong Kong Martial Arts Film*. Hong Kong: Hong Kong International Film Festival/Urban Council, 56–70.
____ (1981/1996) '*Jiang Hu* Revisited: Towards a Reconstruction of the Martial Arts World', in Lau Shing-hon (ed.) *A Study of The Hong Kong Swordplay Film (1945–1980)*. Hong Kong: Hong Kong International Film Festival/Urban Council, 73–86.
Nicholls, Richard (1993) 'Asian Martial Arts as a 'Way' for Actors', in Zarrilli (ed.) *Asian Martial Arts in Actor Training*. Madison, Wisconsin: University of Wisconsin. 19–30.
Nieves, Ervin (1999) '37th Chamber of Commerce of Shaolin', *Asian Cult Cinema*, 24: 45–8.
O'Hehir, Andrew (2000) '*Romeo Must Die*', http://www.salon.com/ent/movies/review/2000/03/24/romeo_must_die/index.html.
Orick, Josh and Eric Matthies (1999) 'Wired Style: Wire Work Special', *Giant Robot*, 16: 57–62.
O'Shaughnessy, Wan Chang (1974) 'Raising Caine on Thursday Night: What's Right with *Kung Fu*', *Deadly Hands of Kung Fu*, 1: n.p.
Parish, James Robert (2002) *Jet Li: A Biography*. New York: Thunder's Mouth Press.
Parkinson, Emma (ed.) (2000) *Tekken Tag Tournament: The Official Guide*. Bath: Future Publishing.
Persons, Mitch (1999) 'Matrix: The Wachowski Brothers', *Cinéfantastique*, 31, 5: 20–1.
Pestilence, Darryl (1998) 'Bruce Li: An Appreciation', *Asian Cult Cinema*, 18: 43–6.
Pilato, Herbie J. (1993) *The Kung Fu Book of Caine*. Boston, Rutland, Vermont, and Tokyo: Charles E. Tuttle.
Poole, Steven (2000) *Trigger Happy: The Inner Life of Videogames*. London: Fourth Estate.
Poyer, Jude (2000) 'AIYAH! That Had to Hurt', in Stefan Hammond (ed.) *Hollywood East: Hong Kong Movies and the People Who Make Them*. Lincolnwood (Chicago), Illinois: Contemporary Books, 203–31.

Rayns, Tony (1974) 'Threads Through the Labyrinth: Hong Kong Movies', *Sight and Sound*, 43, 3: 138–41.
___ (1980) 'Bruce Lee: Narcissism and Nationalism', in Lau Shing-hon (ed.) *A Study of the Hong Kong Martial Arts Film*. Hong Kong: Hong Kong International Film Festival/Urban Council, 110–12.
___ (1981/1996) 'The Sword as Obstacle' in Lau Shing-hon (ed.) *A Study of The Hong Kong Swordplay Film (1945–1980)*. Hong Kong: Hong Kong International Film Festival/Urban Council, 155–8.
___ (1984a) 'Bruce Lee and Other Stories' in Li Cheuk-to (ed.) *A Study of Hong Kong Cinema in the Seventies*. Hong Kong: Hong Kong International Film Festival/Urban Council, 26–9.
___ (1984b) 'Resilience: The Cinema of Liu Jialiang' in Li Cheuk-to (ed.) *A Study of Hong Kong Cinema in the Seventies*. Hong Kong: Hong Kong International Film Festival/Urban Council, 51–6.
___ (1992) 'Hard Boiled', *Sight and Sound* 2, 4: 20–3.
Reid, Craig R. (1993–4) 'Fighting Without Fighting – Film Action Choreography', *Film Quarterly*, 47, 2: 30–5.
___ (1994) 'An Evening with Jackie Chan', *Bright Lights*, 13: 18–25.
___ (2000) 'Flying High with Jet', *Martial Arts Superstars: Special Issue*: 36–41, 85.
Reid, Howard and Michael Croucher (1983/1995) *The Way of the Warrior: The Paradox of the Martial Arts*. Woodstock, New York: Overlook Press.
Riley, Jo (1997) *Chinese Theatre and the Actor in Performance*. Cambridge: Cambridge University Press.
Robins, David and Philp Cohen (1982) 'Enter the Dragon', in Stanley Cohen and Jock Young (eds) *The Manufacture of News: Deviance, Serial Problems and the Mass Media*. London: Constable, 480–8.
Robinson, David (1974) 'Life and Death of the Little Dragon', *The Times*, January 18.
Robinson, Richard (1974) *Kung Fu: The Peaceful Way*. Manchester: Ensign Books.
Rodriguez, Hector (1997) 'Hong Kong Popular Culture as an Interpretive Arena: The Huang Feihong Film Series', *Screen*, 38, 1: 1–24.
Rodriguez, Hector (1998) 'Questions of Chinese Aesthetics: Film Form and Narrative Space in the Cinema of King Hu', *Cinema Journal*, 38, 1: 73–97.
Rose, Steve (2001) 'The Film is so slow – it's like grandma telling stories', *The Guardian: G2*, February 13: 14–15.
Said, Edward (1978) *Orientalism*. London: Penguin.
Sardar, Ziauddin (1999) 'Playing the Game', *New Statesman*, April 26: 35–6.
Sarkar, Bhaskar (2001) 'Hong Kong Hysteria: Martial Arts Tales from a Mutating World', in Esther Yau (ed.) *At Full Speed: Hong Kong Cinema in a Borderless World*. Minneapolis and London: University of Minnesota Press, 143–58.
Schveinhardt, Helmut (1998a) 'This Fist Revisited: Once Upon a Time in Shanghai', *Impact*, 74: 36–7.
___ (1998b) 'Every Dragon Has His Day', *Impact*, 81: 32–5.
Sconce, Jeffrey (1995) '"Trashing" the Academy: Taste, Excess, and an Emerging Politics of Cinematic Style', *Screen*, 36, 4: 371–93.
Scott, A. C. (1983) 'The Performance of Classical Theater', in Colin Mackerras (ed.) *Chinese Theatre: From its Origins to the Present Day*. Honolulu: University of Hawaii Press.
Sek Kei (1980) 'The Development of 'Martial Arts' in Hong Kong Cinema', in Lau Shing-hon (ed.) *A Study of the Hong Kong Martial Arts Film*. Hong Kong: Hong Kong International Film Festival/Urban Council, 27–38.
___ (1997) 'Hong Kong Cinema from June 4 to 1997', in Law Kar (ed.) *Fifty Years of Electric Shadows*. Hong Kong: Hong Kong International Film Festival/Urban Council, 120–5.
Sharrett, Christopher (1996) 'The Horror Film in Neoconservative Culture', in Barry Keith Grant (ed.) *The Dread of Difference: Gender and the Horror Film*. Austin: University of Texas Press, 253–76.
Shaviro, Steven (1993) *The Cinematic Body*. Minneapolis and London: University of Minnesota Press.
Smith, Peter (1995) 'Yuen Woo Ping – A Tiger Uncaged' in Rick Baker and Toby Russell (eds) *The Essential Guide to The Best of Eastern Heroes*. London: Eastern Heroes, 64–7.
Stern, Michael (1990) 'Making Culture Into Nature', in Annette Kuhn (ed.) *Alien Zone: Cultural Theory and Contemporary Science Fiction Cinema*. London and New York: Verso, 66–72.
Stokes, Lisa and Michael Hoover (1999) *City on Fire: Hong Kong Cinema*. London: Verso.
___ (2000) 'An Interview with Donnie Yen', *Asian Cult Cinema*, 29: 48–62.
Stringer, Julian (1996/7) 'Problems with the Treatment of Hong Kong Cinema as Camp', *Asian Cinema*, 8, 2: 44–63.
___ (2000) 'Cultural Identity and Diaspora in Contemporary Hong Kong Cinema', in Darrell Y. Hamamoto and Sandra Liu (eds) *Countervisions: Asian-American Film Criticism*. Philadelphia: Temple University Press, 298–312.
Stringer, Julian (2002) 'Tsui Hark', in Yvonne Tasker (ed.) *Fifty Contemporary Film-makers*. London and New York: Routledge, 346–53.
___ (forthcoming) 'Talking About Jet Li: Transnational Chinese Movie Stardom and Asian-American Internet Reception', in Gary Rawnsley and Ming-yeh Rawnsley (eds) *Political Communication in Greater China: The Construction and Reflection of Identity*. London and New York: Routledge-Curzon.
Swallow, Jim (1999) 'Way of the Fist', *Manga Max* 4: 28–31.
Tan, See Kam (2001) 'Chinese Diasporic Imaginations in Hong Kong Films: Sinicist Belligerance and Melancholia',

Screen, 42, 1: 1–20.

Tasker, Yvonne (1993) *Spectacular Bodies: Gender, Genre and the Action Cinema*. London and New York: Routledge.

____ (1997) 'Fists of Fury: Discourses of Race and Masculinity in the Martial Arts Cinema', in Harry Stecopoulos and Michael Uebel (eds) *Race and the Study of Masculinities*. Durham and London: Duke University Press, 315–36.

____ (2001) 'Re-orienting the Television Western: *Kung Fu*' in Anna Gough-Yates and Bill Osgerby (eds) *Action TV: Smooth Operators, Tough Guys and Foxy Chicks*. London and New York: Routledge, 115–26.

Tateishi, Ramie (1998) 'Jackie Chan and the Re-invention of Tradition', *Asian Cinema*, 10, 1: 78–84.

Teo, Stephen (1984) 'The *Dao* of King Hu', in Li Cheuk-to (ed.) *A Study of Hong Kong Cinema in the Seventies*. Hong Kong: Hong Kong International Film Festival/Urban Council, 34–40.

____ (1997) *Hong Kong Cinema: The Extra Dimension*. London: BFI.

____ (2000) 'Local and Global Identity: Whither Hong Kong Cinema?', *Senses of Cinema*, http://www.sensesofcinema.com/contents/00/7/hongkong.html.

____ (2000/2001) 'Love and Swords: The Dialectics of Martial Arts Romance', *Senses of Cinema*, http://www.sensesofcinema.com/contents/00/11/crouching.html.

____ (2001) 'Tsui Hark: National Style and Polemic' in Esther Yau (ed.) *At Full Speed: Hong Kong Cinema in a Borderless World*. Minneapolis and London: University of Minnesota Press, 143–58.

Thomas, Bruce (1994) *Bruce Lee: Fighting Spirit*. Berkeley, California: Frog Limited.

Thomson, David (1980) *A Biographical Dictionary of Film*. London: Secker and Warburg.

Tian Yan (1984) 'The Fallen Idol – Zhang Che in Retrospect', in Li Cheuk-to (ed.) *A Study of Hong Kong Cinema in the Seventies*. Hong Kong: Hong Kong International Film Festival/Urban Council, 44–6.

Ting, Natasha (2000) 'Jet Set', *HK Magazine*, April 28: 34.

Tombs, Pete (1997) *Mondo Macabro: Weird and Wonderful Cinema Around the World*. London: Titan.

'Ultimate *Tekken* Fanfiction Archive', http://www.geocities.com/TimesSquare/Realm/3017.

Video.Gamespot.com, 'Guide to *Street Fighter*', http://www.videogames.com/features/universal/sfhistory/games_01_01.html.

Warner, John David (1974) 'Catching a Killer Red-Handed', *Deadly Hands of Kung Fu*, 1: 34–8.

Watson, Paul and Wong, Amos (1999) 'Streetfighting Man', *Manga Max*, 5: 18–22.

Weisser, Thomas (2000) 'Crouching Tiger, Hidden Dragon', *Asian Cult Cinema*, 28: 4–9.

West, Dave (2001) 'Concentrate on the Kicking Movie: Buffy and East Asian Cinema' in Roz Kaveney (ed.) *Reading the Vampire Slayer: An Unofficial Critical Companion to Buffy and Angel*. London: I.B. Taurus, 166–86.

Wheatley, Sarah (2000) 'Shaw Brothers Movies', http://www.heroic-cinema.com/articles/shaws/html.

White, Armand (2001) 'Reality Bites', *Sight and Sound*, 11, 8: 12–13.

Williams, Linda (1990) *Hardcore: Power, Pleasure, and the "Frenzy of the Visible"*. London: Pandora.

____ (1995) 'Film Bodies: Gender, Genre and Excess' in Barry Keith Grant (ed.) *Film Genre Reader II*. Austin: University of Texas Press: 140–57.

Williams, Tony (1998) 'Kwan Tak-hing and the New Generation', *Asian Cinema*, 10, 1: 71–7.

____ (1999a) 'A Tribute to Jimmy Wang Yu', *Asian Cult Cinema*, 24: 18–20.

____ (1999b) 'Honor and Endurance: A Tribute to Ti Lung', *Asian Cult Cinema*, 25: 17–20.

____ (2000) 'Under "Western Eyes": The Personal Odyssey of Huang Fei-hong in *Once Upon a Time in China*', *Cinema Journal*, 40, 1: 3–24.

Wise, Sue (1990) 'Sexing Elvis' in Simon Frith and Andrew Goodwin (eds) *On Record: Rock, Pop and the Written Word*. London and New York: Routledge, 390–8.

Witterstaetter, Rene (1997) *Dying for Action: The Life and Films of Jackie Chan*. London: Ebury Press.

Wolfman, Marv (1974) 'Fu on You: Sort of an Editorial', *Deadly Hands of Kung Fu*, 1: 51.

Wong, Doc-Fai and Jane Hallander (1988) *Shaolin Five Animals Kung-Fu*. Burbank: Unique Publications.

Wong Kiew Kit (1996/2001) *The Art of Shaolin Kung Fu*. London: Vermilion.

Yau, Esther C. M. (ed.) (2001) *At Full Speed: Hong Kong Cinema in a Borderless World*. Minneapolis and London: University of Minnesota Press.

Yu Mo-wan (1980) 'The Prodigious Cinema of Huang Fei-hong', in Lau Shing-hon (ed.) *A Study of the Hong Kong Martial Arts Film*. Hong Kong: Hong Kong International Film Festival/Urban Council, 79–85.

Zhang Che (1999) 'Creating the Martial Arts Film and the Hong Kong Cinema Style', in Hong Kong Film Archive *The Making of Martial Arts Films – As Told by Film-makers and Stars*. Hong Kong: Provisional Urban Council, 16–24.

Zarrilli, Philip B. (ed.) (1993) *Asian Martial Arts in Actor Training*. Madison, Wisconsin: University of Wisconsin.

____ (1995) '"On the Edge of a Breath, Looking": Disciplining the Actor's Bodymind Through the Martial Arts in the Asian/Experimental Theatre Program', in Philip B. Zarrilli (ed.) *Acting (Re)Considered: Theories and Practices*. London and New York: Routledge: 177–96.

Zhang, Yingjin and Zhiwei Xiao (eds) (1998) *Encyclopedia of Chinese Film*. London and New York: Routledge.

Index

Aaliyah 175
Abbas, Ackbar 2, 10–11, 15–18, 22–3, 42, 46, 71, 76, 146, 154, 160, 179
Anderson, Aaron 2, 25, 28
animé 184, 187, 189, 194, 207
Armour of God 149, 168
Ashes of Time 130, 135–6, 183
'Asianisation' 157, 160, 182–3
'Asiaphilia' 13, 19, 158
Astaire, Fred 27, 42
'aura' (and stardom) 42–6
'authenticity' 4, 8–9, 17–9, 21–4, 27–9, 122–3, 149; archival 24–5; cinematic 29, 35–9; corporeal 29, 39–41, 43; and technology 18, 45–6, 185–6, 193–6

bagua 4, 32, 178–9, 199
Baker, Rick 27, 37, 42, 83, 107
Bakhtin, Mikhail 105, 110–11
Barrymore, Drew 185–6
Bataille, Georges 55
Battlecreek Brawl 39, 170–1, 173
Benjamin, Walter 42, 197–8
Berkely, Busby 26
Besson, Luc 176–7, 179
The Big Boss 13, 15, 36, 67, 86, 88, 97, 124, 161
Billy Jack 68
Black Mask 142–3, 149–51, 175
The Blade 60
Blade Runner 149
Blood Brothers 51, 56
Blood Money 161, 167
Bloody Roar 2 (game) 190
Bodhidharma 1, 49
body 177; 'body genres' 2–3, 22–3, 192; site of authenticity 22, 39–41, 43; 'disappearing' body 17–18, 197–200; muscles 53–4, 87, 144, 169; grotesque body 105, 109–11
Bodyguard from Beijing 143, 149, 151, 177
Bolter, Jay David 186–7, 192
Bordwell, David 2–3, 8–9, 12, 14, 18, 25–6, 28, 36, 39, 55, 64, 80, 152, 157, 161, 180–1, 192, 201
Born to Defense 143–4, 159,
Breakfast at Tiffany's 89–90
The Bride with White Hair 122, 131–2
Brottman, Mikita 196–7
Bruce Lee (game) 191
Bruce Lee: A Warrior's Journey 93
Bruce Lee: Quest of the Dragon (game) 191
Bruce Lee: The Man, The Myth 86, 88–92, 97
Buddhism 32, 34, 49, 64, 69, 71–4
The Buddhist Fist 28, 104
Buffy the Vampire Slayer 188, 207
Burning Paradise 70–3

The Butterfly Murders 11

The Cannonball Run 170
Cantopop 5, 24, 99, 190
Carradine, David 48–9, 68–9, 162, 202
Challenge of the Masters 33, 114, 116, 141
Chan, Gordon 156
Chan, Jackie 2, 5–7, 10, 14, 17, 19–20, 23, 25, 33, 36, 44, 49, 61, 69, 76, 78, 83, 98–106, 112–16, 141–2, 148, 152, 167, 176, 179, 181, 187–8, 204; and 'corporeal authenticity' 5, 17–18, 22–3, 27, 39–41, 197–8, 200; in Hollywood 157–8, 160, 168–75, 182, 207; in games 185–192
Chan Ting-ching 102, 114
Charlie's Angels 184–6
Chen Guantai 5, 23, 32–3, 39, 52, 56–7, 65
Cheng Yu 29, 36–7
Cheung, King-kok 120–1
Cheung, Maggie 24, 119, 123–4, 132, 180, 203
Chiau, Stephen 100, 103, 110, 116
Chi Hon-tsoi 30, 92, 127
Chi Kwan-chun (see Qi Guanjun)
China 16–17; and *wu shu* 31; mythical 'home' in kung fu films 4, 10, 15, 142–3; involvement in martial arts films 2, 6, 51
Chiao Hsiung-ping 84, 86, 161
Chiang, David 5, 55–6, 58, 141, 164–5
Chiba, Sonny 198
The Chinese Boxer 9, 32, 51
Chinese Ghost Story series 5
The Chinese Stuntman 81–3
Ching Siu-tung 5, 24, 26–7
Chow, David 29–30, 33–4, 51, 69, 91
Chow, Raymond 5, 91
Chow Yun-fat 137, 158, 180, 206
Chu, Rolanda 7, 134
City Hunter 78, 186
The Clones of Bruce Lee 76, 78–80, 97
Clouse, Robert 95, 162
colonialism 15–17, 19, 48–9, 68, 163–5, 167, 201
Come Drink with Me 8, 119
Comet the Thief 197
Confucianism 8, 33, 49, 130
Crafton, Donald 107–8
Creed, Barbara 132–3
Crippled Avengers 38–9
Critique of Game of Death 92–4, 97
Croft, Lara 198
Croucher, Michael 29, 48–9, 52, 74
Crouching Tiger, Hidden Dragon 7, 13, 20, 45, 117–8, 122, 136–9, 149, 179–8, 182–3, 186, 202, 205, 207
The Crow 96–7

Dance of the Drunk Mantis 103–4, 111
Dancer, Greg 26, 40, 45
Dargis, Manohla 185–6
Davidson, Nick 35, 83–4
The Dead and the Deadly 103–4
The Deaf and Mute Heroine 121–2
Dead or Alive game series 18, 185, 187, 191, 195–6, 207, 208
Death By Misadventure 81
Deren, Maya 31–2
Desser, David 12, 67, 161, 168
Diaz, Cameron 185, 186
Dirty Ho 126
Disciples of Shaolin 53, 56–8
Dr Wai in 'The Scripture with No Words' 46, 142, 149, 152, 156, 206
Donner, Richard 180, 206–7
Double Team 179
doubles 24, 45–6, 94, 199
Dragon Fight 143, 173
Dragon Swamp 118, 205
Dragon: The Bruce Lee Story 78, 87–92
The Dragon Lives 80, 88–9
Dragon Lord 103, 168
Dragons Forever 40–1, 103
Dreadnaught 104, 113, 204
Drunken Boxing (see *Zui Quan*)
Drunken Master 31, 101–4, 108, 110–12, 114, 116, 141, 191
Drunken Master 2 27, 41, 112, 116, 153
Drunken Tai Chi 103
Dynamo 81, 83–84, 97

Eastern Condors 40, 105
editing 2, 39, 42; 'constructive editing' 26, 36–38, 40; long takes 9, 27, 35–6
Eight Diagram Pole Fighter 33–34, 60, 64, 126
Eighteen Bronze Men 60
Encounters of the Spooky Kind 4–5, 103–4, 109, 204
Enter the Dragon 1, 14–15, 30, 43, 67, 77, 78, 79, 80, 85–9, 91, 94–6, 120–1, 140, 158, 161–3, 164–8, 189, 191, 198
Enter the Fat Dragon 77, 83
Executioners 119
Executioners from Shaolin 30, 36, 52, 60, 65–6, 122
Exit the Dragon, Enter the Tiger 77, 85–6, 97

fandom 4; western 'Hong Kong cinema' cult 13–14, 17–18, 21, 27–8, 83–4; fight choreographers 27, 105; growing importance in kung fu film 6, 10, 18; shifts in style 23–4, 26; transition to directing 10, 23 (see also Lau Kar-leung, Hung, Sammo, Yuen Wo-ping)
Final Fantasy: The Spirits Within 18, 197
Fist of Fury 3, 9, 15, 27, 36, 51, 67, 76–7, 84–5, 91, 94, 96–7, 127–8, 152, 154, 161, 201
Fist of Fury 2 84–5
Fist of Legend 16, 27–8, 141, 144, 147, 152–6, 176–7, 205, 206
Fist of the North Star 189–190
Fist of the White Lotus 52, 65–7

Five Shaolin Masters 52–3, 58–9, 60, 64
Fonda, Bridget 176–7
Fong Sai-yuk (character) 7, 8, 32, 50, 52–5, 57, 59, 65, 70, 72, 76; (film) 36, 45, 57, 141, 144
Fong Sai-yuk 2 148
Fore, Steve 15, 104, 160, 169–70, 182, 204
Foster, Damon 9, 27–8
Freud, Sigmund 71
Fu Sheng 5, 7–8, 17, 32, 34, 52–3, 56–8, 61, 103, 126, 141, 168
Fulbeck, Kip 93–4, 97
Fuller, Mary 184, 189, 208

Gallagher, Mark 106
Game of Death 4, 37, 77–8, 81, 92–7, 116
games: computer, console and arcade 2, 18, 184, 193–6; interface with kung fu films 184, 186–93 (see also *Tekken* series, *Dead or Alive* series)
Garber, Marjorie 135, 139
Garcia, Roger 15, 18, 61, 63, 35–6, 112
'gender-bending' : figure of Bai Mei 64–7, 161; and Brigitte Lin 132, 134–6
Ghost in the Shell 185
Gibson, Mel 158, 176
Glaessner, Verina 52, 120–1, 124, 126–7
globalisation 1, 3, 7, 13, 19, 49, 158, 164, 183
Golden Harvest 5–6, 8, 10, 16, 90, 94, 113, 121, 166, 168
Golden Swallow 7, 9, 55, 119
Goodbye Bruce Lee: His Last Game of Death 81, 82
The Green Hornet 86, 88, 91, 149–51
Grusin, Richard 186–7, 192
Gunning, Tom 106–8

Hall, Stuart 13
Hamamoto, Darrell 13
Hammer films 14, 164–5
Hammond, Stefan 12, 14, 28, 120, 130
Hampton, Howard 130–1, 142
Hapkido 30, 51, 120, 121, 126, 127–8
Harrison-Pepper, Sally 60, 63–4
Have Sword, Will Travel 55
Hero 20, 140, 180, 182–3
Heroes Two 29, 32, 49, 52, 56–7, 60
Heroic Trio 118–9, 123–4
High Risk 149, 151–2
Hitman 151, 206
Hollywood cinema: incorporation of Hong Kong cinema 2, 20, 157–61, 168–79
Ho Chung-tao ('Bruce Li') 19, 78, 80–5, 87–9, 91, 94, 203
Hong Kingston, Maxine 117, 121
Hong Kong: cultural context for kung fu films 2, 7, 15–16, 71–2, 87, 102, 106; impact of Sino-British Joint Declaration 10–11, 16–18, 22, 100, 145, 151; emergence of 'local' sensibility 4, 6, 10–11, 16, 49, 75, 99–100, 102, 104, 112–13
Hong Kong cinema; Cantonese and Mandarin dialects 8–10, 16; studio system 5–6; and the global market 1–3, 9, 12–13, 20, 149, 160–8, 179–83; as 'camp' 11–12

Hoover, Michael 134
Huang Jang-li 6, 23, 30, 37–9, 83
Hui, Michael 5, 99–100, 102, 106
Hui, Sam 99
Hui Ying-hung 19, 23, 66, 118, 123–6, 128–30
Hung Gar 6, 30, 32–3, 35, 63, 65
Hung, Sammo 2, 6, 10, 16, 19, 23, 26–7, 33–5, 40,
    77–8, 94–5, 98–99, 102–105, 108–9, 111–15,
    127, 147, 163, 166–7, 173, 179, 188, 190, 204
Hunter, Ian 165
Huo Yuanjia 84–5, 153–5, 203

incorporation 19, 160, 173
Inosanto, Dan 92–3
Invincible Armour 37–8
Iron Fisted Monk 16, 103, 105, 111
Irma Vep 123
Iron Monkey 35, 45, 206
Isou, Isidore 94

Jabbar, Kareem Abdul 86, 92
Jackie Chan: Kung Fu Master (game) 191
Jackie Chan: My Stunts 5, 41, 43, 45, 197
Jackie Chan Stuntmaster (game) 186, 191
Jackie Chan's Action Kung Fu (game) 191
Japan; as villains in kung fu films 11, 15, 17, 30, 51,
    153–6; martial arts 1, 9, 12, 154
Japanese cinema 2–4, 8, 70, 184
Jeet Kune Do 4, 17, 77, 88, 92, 188
Jenkins, Henry 184, 189, 208
jianghu 7, 26, 55, 124, 132, 134, 136–8, 201
jingju (see Opera, Chinese)

Kamen, Robert Mark 177
Kehr, Dave 41
Kelly, Jim 151, 162, 170
Kids from Shaolin 74
Kim Tai-jung 77, 94–96
King Boxer 3, 9, 11–12, 67, 161
King, Geoff 107, 111
King Hu 7, 9, 26
Kiss of the Dragon 20, *140*, *176*–9, 182, 198
'Knight Errant' 6, 201
Knockabout 104, 108–9, 113, 115
Korean Martial Arts 30, 127, 142; and the
    'Superkickers' 6, 30, 37–8
Kramer, Peter107
Kristeva, Julia 132
Krzywinska, Tanya 200
Kung Fu (TV series) 49, 67–70, 161
Kung Fu Cult Master 147
kung fu film 5; as distinct from *wu xia pian 4*,
    6–7; as emigre cinema 15, 31, 71, 201; kung fu
    comedy2, 6, 10, 35, 98–116; 'New Wave' style
    11, 24, 45, 144–8
Kurata, Yasuaki 27, 154–5
Kwan, Rosamund 21, 134, 152
Kwan, Stanley 54, 30, 135, 203
Kwan Tak-hing 7–9, 11, 17, 112–3, 161

The Lady is the Boss 126, 128–30

Lady Whirlwind 118, 121, 126–7
Lai, Linda Chiu-han 100
Lam Ching-ying 23, 25, 100, 105, 110
Lam, Ringo 72, 192
Landsberg, Alison 192
Last Hero in China 147, 204
Lau, Jenny 100, 106
Lau Kar-fai 23, 32–3, 35, 61–2, 64, 66, 126, 129
Lau Kar-leung 4–6, 10, 15, 17, 23–4, 27, 29, 32–4,
    36, 43, 48, 50, 53, 55, 61, 74, 93, 105, 116, 126,
    128–9, 165, 201
Lau Kar-wing 23, 104–5, 115
Lazenby, George 86, 166–7, 207
Lee, Ang 1, 182–3
Lee, Brandon 96–7, 203
Lee, Bruce 1–7, 9–10, 14, 18, 23–5, 27–9, 36–7,
    39–40, 42–4, 55, 57, 67–8, 103, 110, 119–21,
    127, 141–2, 144, 152, 156, 179, 181, 203; as
    myth legend 76–8, 97–8, 172, 187; nationalist
    readings of 15, 53, 78, 86–7, 91, 93, 162–3;
    death of 78, 86, 96–7(see also *Game of Death)*;
    'biopics' 78, 86–92; transnational positioning 9,
    15, 17, 86–7, 89–90, 93, 97–8, 157, 161–3, 168;
    impersonators and 'Clones' 19, 75, 77–86, 94; in
    games 185, 190–1
Lee, Dragon 79–80
Lee Cadwell, Linda 78, 89–91, 204
Lee, Jason Scott 88
Lee, Moon 120
Legend of a Fighter 154
The Legend of the Seven Golden Vampires 14, 161,
    163–6
Legendary Weapons of China 126
Leon 176–7
Leone, Sergio 146
Lethal Weapon 4 142, 158–9, 175–6, 180
Leung Kar-yan 34–5, 61, 65, 104–5, 108, 111, 113,
    154
Li, Bruce (see Ho Chung-tao)
Li, Jet 2–4, 7, 14, 17–20, 24–5, 30–1, 50, 70, 74, 83,
    130, 132, 134–6, 140–4, 173, 181, 183, 185, 187,
    190, 205–6; and 'authenticity' 26–8, 36, 42–6,
    176, 186, 188, 198–9; as Wong Fei-hung 11, 17,
    21, 116, 141–8, 152–3; as Fong Sai-yuk 8, 36,
    57, 116, 147–52; modern-day films 143, 148–52;
in Hollywood 157–9, 161, 175–9, 182, 207 (see also
    Fist of Legend)
Li, Siu-leung 4, 5, 7–8, 16, 87, 145, 162
Lii, Ding-Tzann 19, 160–1
Lim, Ron 27, 31
liminality 60, 63–5
Lin, Brigitte 19, 24, 47, 118, 122, 124, 130–6
Liu, Jerry 55
Liu, John 23, 30, 36, 37–9, 43
Liu, Lucy 174, 186
Lo, Ken 38, 41, 116
Lo, Kwai-cheung 17–18, 54, 77, 107, 145–7, 160,
    169
Lo Lieh 11, 65, 85, 119, 167
Lo Wei 6, 37, 85, 88
Logan, Bey 39, 43, 49, 55, 71, 93, 95–7, 107, 112,

142, 167, 170
Longstreet (TV series) 4, 86

Ma, Helen 121
Mad Monkey Kung Fu 104, 129
The Magnificent Butcher 10, 105, 111–14
Major, Wade 151–2
Maka, Karl 204
The Man from Hong Kong 15, 161, 166–7
Manga 184, 187, 189
The Martial Club 33
Mao Ying, Angela 19, 118, 120–8, 130, 136, 166, 204
Mao Zedong 31
Marchetti, Gina 13, 158–9, 166, 173
Marcus, Greil 80, 92, 94
Marlowe 86, 176
Martial Arts films: defintions 4–11
Martial Arts of Shaolin 74
masculinity 69, 166, 175–6; male body 15, 53–4, 87; 're-masculinisation' of Chinese cinema 53–4, 119, 121, 162; male bonding in Shaw Brothers films 52, 55, 57–8; homoerotic spectacle 54–5; sacrificial violence 9, 55, 59; images of penetration 54–5, 65
The Master 143, 173
Master-Pupil theme 6, 32–3, 68–9, 195; in Shaolin films 60–7; in kung fu comedy 102–4, 113–16; beggar Su figure 102, 103, 111, 113, 114.
The Matrix 4, 18–19, 143, 157, 179–82, 184–6, 192, 197, 199
Meditation on Violence 31–2
The Men from the Monastery 52, 54, 56, 57, 58, 60, 63
Miao, Nora 121
Miller, Davis 29, 76–7, 80, 87, 89
Mintz, Marilyn 4, 5
Miracle Fighters 102–3, 105, 107–11
Mr Vampire series 5, 103
Morris, Meaghan 58, 77, 90
Mortal Kombat game series 186, 190, 194; film 186, 189
Mui, Anita 24, 116, 118, 124, 151
the Musical (comparison with Martial Arts film) 22, 25–7
My Father is a Hero 151
My Young Auntie 125, 126, 128–30

Namco 194
nationalism 3, 15–17, 143–4, 154–6, 183 (see also Lee, Bruce)
Ng Ho 50, 51, 58, 72, 102–4, 108, 114, 124
Ng See-yuen 5, 112
New Dragon Gate Inn 132
New Fist of Fury 78
New Legend of Shaolin 70
New One-Armed Swordsman 55
Nieves, Ervin 73
Nixon, Richard 12, 140
No Retreat, No Surrender 77, 78
Norris, Chuck 3, 10, 30, 37, 40, 77, 172

Nureyev, Rudolf 42

Odd Couple 115–6
O'Hehir, Andrew 141–2
Once Upon a Time in China series 3, 6, 11, 16, 24, 27, 34, 70, 116, 141, 143, 145–7, 152, 179; Part 1 42–3, 45, 145–6, 154; Part 2 44, 141, 145–6, 154; Part 3 21–3, 43, 142, 144, 146
Once Upon a Time in China and America 147, 173–4
Once Upon a Time in the West 146
The One 4, 18, 143, 157, 161, 176, 178–9, 186, 198–200
The One-Armed Boxer 9
The One-Armed Swordsman 9, 16, 55
Opera, Chinese 2, 31, 60; importance to Martial Arts film 5, 10, 17, 23–5, 102, 107, 122–3; as 'transvestite theatre' 135, 205; *liangxiang* 44
Orientalism 13, 120, 158–9, 165–6, 173, 182

Pedicab Driver 40
Peking Opera Blues 131
PlayStation 188, 194–5
Police Story 4, 5, 41, 170
Police Story 2 105
Poole, Steven 185, 189, 193–4, 198
pornography 2, 22, 25, 200
postcolonialism 3, 14, 16, 19–20, 22, 163
Presley, Elvis 80, 94, 162
Private Eyes 99, 103
The Prodigal Son 6, 30, 100, 104–5, 107–9, 114
Project A 4, 5, 33, 41, 103
The Protector 170–3

qi 12, 49, 65, 190; and 'presence' 43–4
Qi Guanjun 30, 32, 56–8, 61
Qing Dynasty: as setting in kung fu film 7–8, 11, 16, 32, 50–1, 69–70, 74

Ratner, Brett 168–9, 172
Rayns, Tony 3, 23, 33, 35, 55, 60–62, 66, 76, 78, 80, 84, 86, 203
Reid, Craig 4, 22, 44, 49, 175, 203
Reid, Howard 29, 48, 52, 74
'remediation' 186–7, 192, 196
Robinson, Richard 67–68
Rodriguez, Hector 25–6, 31
Romeo Must Die 19, 175–7, 180, 186, 197–9
Ross, Jonathan 117, 120
Rothrock, Cynthia 118, 123
Rumble in the Bronx 41, 106, 108, 169–70, 172–3
Rush Hour 157, 168–9, 172, 174, 182, 197
Rush Hour 2 161, 168–70, 182
Russell, Toby 27, 37, 42, 81, 83, 107, 120

Said, Edward 13,
Sarkar, Bhaskar 72
Seasonal Films 51, 6, 37
The Secret of Bruce Lee 83, 85, 90
Secret Rivals 37–8
Sek Kei 3, 7–8, 10, 16, 103
Shanghai Noon 167–8, 170, 172, 174, 182

Shaolin 1, 11, 19, 31–2; temples 48–51, 53; northern/southern 3, 4, 29–30, 32–3, 99, 196; heroes of 7, 48, 50–1, 76; in Shaw Brothers cycle 5–7, 10, 15–16, 32–3, 48, 52–67, 67; and pedagogic theme 48, 58–9, 60–7, 71, 188; in *Kung Fu* TV series 67–70; in recent Hong Kong films 70–3; Temple as heritage industry 48, 73–5 (see also Fong Sai-yuk, Hung Hei-kwun, Wu Wei-kin)
Shaolin (game) 48, 188, 193–4
Shaolin Avengers 53–5, 65
Shaolin Challenges Ninja 31, 155
Shaolin Martial Arts 30, 52, 27, 60–1, 65
The Shaolin Temple (1976) 48, 58–60, 63, 122
The Shaolin Temple (1982) 31, 50, 73–4, 143, 187
Shaolin Wheel of Life (Live Show) 73–4
Shaolin Wooden Men 60–1
Sharrett, Christopher 159
Shatter 161, 167
Shaviro, Steven 2, 192
Shaw Brothers 5–8, 10, 14, 16–17, 23, 31–2, 37, 51–9, 70, 126, 164
Shek Kin 161
Shih Szu 118, 164
Showdown at Cotton Mill 202
Siao, Josephine 46, 57, 142, 147
Silver, Joel 180, 185
'Sinicism' (see nationalism)
The Skyhawk 113
Snake in the Eagle's Shadow 103–4, 111–12
Snuff Bottle Connection 37–8
'Spaghetti westerns' 167, 202
Spangler, Richard 29–30, 33–4, 51
Star Wars Episode 1: The Phantom Menace 31, 197, 199
Stokes, Lisa Odham 134
Storm Riders 190
Street Fighter game series 19, 185, 188–90, 194; spin-off films 186
The Street Fighter 198
Stringer, Julian 13–14, 173
Sun Yat-sen 8, 145, 147, 155
Swordsman series 11; *Swordsman II* 26–7, 131–5, 136, 147, 152; *The East is Red* 130, 132, 134, 136 (see also Lin, Brigitte)
swordplay film 4, 6–7, 9, 11, 53

Tai Chi 25, 32, 46, 51, 126, 196
Tai Chi Master 60, 70
Tang Xia 5, 53, 165
Tan, See Kam 87
Taoism 7, 34, 49, 64, 178
Tarantino, Quentin 13, 179
Tarapata, Karen 54
Tasker, Yvonne 23, 69, 118–19, 123
Tateishi, Ramie 22, 39, 106
technology 2, 8, 16, 24, 143, 146–7; impact on fight choreography 2, 17–18; special effects 11, 18, 21–2, 28, 45, 157–8, 176, 179–80; digitisation 19, 21, 33, 175, 180, 183, 185, 187, 190, 197–200; 'remediation' 19

Tekken game series 18–19, 184–8, 192–6
Teo, Stephen 3, 6, 65, 77–8, 86–7, 134, 162–5, 171, 203
Terai, Yuki 197
The 36th Chamber of Shaolin 35, 60–4, 69, 74, 129, 188
Thomas, Bruce 28, 88–9
Thomson, David 42
Three Styles of Hung School's Kung Fu 32, 55
Ti Lung 5, 55–6, 116, 167
Ting-pei, Betty 86, 91, 204
A Touch of Zen 7, 26
Tower of Death 77, 94–6
transnational 1–2, 4, 14, 16, 19–20, 22, 46, 140, 158–61, 163, 176
Tsui Hark 5, 11, 16, 22, 24, 26, 33, 130–1, 135, 140–1, 143, 145, 152, 179, 202
Tucker, Chris 157, 161, 169
The Tuxedo 197
Twinkle Twinkle Lucky Stars 107

Under the Sun: The Kung Fu Business (TV documentary) 75, 203
Urquidez, Benny 'The Jet' 40, 172

Van Damme, Jean-Claude 10, 179
'Venoms' team 5, 36, 38–9, 43
Virtua Fighter game series 185, 191, 194

Wachowski Brothers 172, 181, 197
Wallace, Bill 172
Wang Yu 7, 9, 23, 39, 55–6, 119, 121, 141, 166–7, 201
Warner Bros. 67, 87, 161, 163
Warriors Two 30, 31, 34–5, 104, 109
The Water Margin 50
Way of the Dragon 1, 3, 14, 24, 30, 36–7, 67, 76–8, 84–6, 88, 90, 92, 103, 110–11, 121, 154, 159, 161
Wheels on Meals 40
Williams, Linda 2, 22–3
Williams, Tony 94, 113, 140–1, 145
Wilson, Owen 161, 169, 174
Wing Chun (kung fu style) 30, 86–7, 118, 203; in films 6, 30–1, 34–5, 59, 61, 63, 65, 104, 109–10, 114, 122
Wing Chun (film) 30, 122
Winners and Sinners 4–5, 103
wirework 21, 24, 39, 42, 45, 183, 183, 188, 198
women 46–7, 117–24, 205; in swordplay film 6, 118–19, 121–2, 124, 135–6; in kung fu film 121, 122–30; 'Deadly China Doll' fetish 19, 119–21;
Wong, Casanova 30, 55, 95
Wong Fei-hung 29–30, 72, 76, 99, 119, 128, 181, 204; original film series 7, 8, 31, 49, 114, 161; in *Challenge of the Masters* and *The Martial Club* 33–4; in kung fu comedy 10, 102–3, 110, 112–14 (see also *Once Upon a Time in China* series)
Wong In-sik 24, 30, 37, 127–8
Wong Kar-wai 136
Wong Yue 56, 65, 126

Woo, John 116, 119, 131, 158, 180
wrestling 46, 178, 187, 196
wu dang 3, 74; and 'soft' martial arts 31–2, 51–2, 207; villains in Shaolin films 50, 52, 58, 61, 64–5, 161; in *Crouching Tiger, Hidden Dragon* 122, 138
wu shu 1, 17, 21, 31, 75, 140, 142–3, 196
Wu Tang Clan 4, 74
Wu Wei-Kin 32, 50, 52–4, 58–9, 63, 70, 202
wu xia pian 6–10, 16, 24, 26, 33, 36, 39, 49–50, 118, 165, 189–90, 201

X-Box 188, 195, 208
Xiao Hou 23, 128–9
xingyi 4, 32, 178–9, 199
Xiong Xin-xin 42, 147
Xu Feng 26, 46–7, 118, 124

Yang + Yin: Gender in Chinese Cinema 54, 130, 135, 202
Yau, Esther 1, 3
Yen, Donnie 35–6, 122, 140, 142, 145, 179, 183, 206
Yeoh, Michelle 2, 118, 122–4, 136
Yes, Madam 123

'yielding' 19, 160, 173, 177
The Young Avenger 118
The Young Master 116
Yuen Biao 23, 40, 94–6, 99, 102–5, 109–10, 115, 190
Yuen Cheung-yan 23, 108
Yuen, Corey 25, 102, 141, 176, 179
Yuen Hsin-yi 23, 104–5, 113
Yuen Kwai (see Yuen, Corey)
Yuen Siu-tin 23, 61, 101–2, 106, 111, 170
Yuen Wah 23, 25, 191
Yuen Wo-ping 6, 10–11, 19, 23, 26, 33, 95, 102–3, 105, 108, 113–4, 141, 149, 156–7, 179–82, 184
Yuen Yat-chor 23, 105, 108, 110, 154

Zarrilli, Phillip B. 25
Zhang Che 3, 5–6, 9–10, 15–16, 29, 36, 39, 50–59, 65, 74, 116–19, 121, 131, 165–6, 201–2
Zhang Ziyi 47, 118, 136–7, 180
Zheng Pei-pei 46, 118–19, 122, 137–8
Zhou Wen-zhou 140–1
Zu: Warriors of the Magic Mountain 33, 131, 190
Zui Quan (Drunken Boxing) 30–1, 104, 114, 116, 191, 204